EXPLORING THE DYNAMICS OF PERSONAL, PROFESSIONAL AND INTERPROFESSIONAL ETHICS

Edited by Divya Jindal-Snape and
Elizabeth F.S. Hannah

First published in Great Britain in 2014 by

Policy Press
University of Bristol
6th Floor
Howard House
Queen's Avenue
Clifton
Bristol BS8 1SD
UK
Tel +44 (0)117 331 5020
Fax +44 (0)117 331 5367
e-mail pp-info@bristol.ac.uk
www.policypress.co.uk

North American office:
Policy Press
c/o The University of Chicago Press
1427 East 60th Street
Chicago, IL 60637, USA
t: +1 773 702 7700
f: +1 773-702-9756
e:sales@press.uchicago.edu
www.press.uchicago.edu

© Policy Press 2014

British Library Cataloguing in Publication Data
A catalogue record for this book is available from the British Library

Library of Congress Cataloging-in-Publication Data
A catalog record for this book has been requested

ISBN 978 1 44730 899 7 hardcover

The right of Divya Jindal-Snape and Elizabeth F.S. Hannah to be identified as editors of this
work has been asserted by them in accordance with the 1988 Copyright, Designs and Patents
Act.

Cover design by Policy Press
Front cover: Christopher Bruno
Printed and bound in Great Britain by CPI Group (UK) Ltd,
Croydon, CR0 4YY
The Policy Press uses environmentally responsible print partners

Contents

List of figures, tables and boxes

Figures

Tables

Boxes

Notes on contributors

Dr Ghassan Abdullah is the Director for the Centre for Applied Research in Education, Ramallah, Palestine. Dr Abdullah has received numerous global awards for his peace-making through education in Israel/Palestine and has published and translated widely for Palestinian education. Dr Abdullah sits on numerous global peace-making groups.

Dr Rola Ajjawi is Senior Lecturer at the Centre for Medical Education, the University of Dundee, UK. Her research interests incorporate workplace learning in healthcare with a particular interest in health professional judgement and clinical reasoning. She is also involved in research exploring how technology may be used in education to promote dialogic feedback, self-regulation of learning and social learning networks. Her most recently published edited books include *Communicating in the Health Sciences*, 3rd edition (Oxford University Press, 2012) and *Researching Practice: A Discourse on Qualitative Methodologies* (Sense Publishers, 2010).

Dr Ian Barron is a Chartered Senior Educational Psychologist and Reader in the School of Education, Social Work and Community Education, University of Dundee, Scotland. Dr Barron, an accredited EMDR (Eye Movement Desensitization and Reprocessing) practitioner, has researched in the areas of violence/abuse prevention in the UK and trauma recovery in Palestine.

Dr Roger Barrow is Principal Educational Psychologist at Scottish Borders Council, UK, where he manages the Educational Psychology Service and a 16+ Transitions Team that provides through and aftercare services for young people who have been in local authority care. He is immediate past chair of the Association of Scottish Principal Educational Psychologists. He is interested in the development of values-based approaches to service delivery.

Dr Wilma Barrow is an Educational Psychologist at Scottish Borders Council and Academic and Professional Tutor on the Doctorate in Applied Educational Psychology programme at Newcastle University, UK. She is interested in the role of dialogue within all aspects of educational psychology practice and particularly in its transformative potential in teaching and learning and participative practices. Relevant publications include: 'Dialogic, Participation and the Potential for

Philosophy for Children', *Thinking Skills and Creativity*, vol 5, 2010; and Barrow, W. and Todd, L. (2010). 'Beyond Therapy: Supporting a Culture of Relational Democracy', in H. Kennedy, M. Landor and L. Todd (eds) *Video Interaction Guidance: A Relationship-Based Intervention to Promote Attunement, Empathy and Wellbeing*, London: Jessica Kingsley.

Dr Amanda Berry is an Associate Professor at ICLON Graduate School of Teaching, Leiden University, Netherlands. Her main research interests focus on the development of science teachers' pedagogical content knowledge and the professional learning of teachers and teacher educators. She is co-editor of the journal *Studying Teacher Education* and associate editor of *Research in Science Education*. Recent publications include an edited book on a whole-school approach to developing scientific literacy in a primary school and a review study of science teacher educators' pedagogy of practice.

Per Boge graduated as a teacher in 1978 and worked as a primary and post-primary school teacher until 1993. He also worked as a freelance illustrator and writer. He has illustrated several books, posters and magazines and has also written and edited 40 books and educational resources. Since 1993 he has been working as an educational adviser and project manager for the Danish Cancer Society. Since 1995 most of his work has been dedicated to the project OmSorg – Dealing with Bereavement.

Chris Boyle, PhD, is a Senior Lecturer in Educational Psychology in the School of Education at the University of New England, Australia. Chris's most recent position was as a Senior Lecturer in Psychology at Monash University. He has previously worked as a secondary school teacher and as a school psychologist. His main research interests are in the area of teacher perceptions of inclusion and students' attributions for success and failure in learning. He is currently editor of *The Australian Educational and Developmental Psychologist* and he has published widely in psychology and education with over 20 peer-reviewed publications and books. His latest books are *What Works in Inclusion* (Open University Press, 2012) and *Ethical Practice in Applied Psychology* (Oxford University Press, 2014).

Dr Eleanor Brewster is a Consultant in the Psychiatry of Learning Disabilities, and the Lead Clinician for Psychiatry of Learning Disabilities within NHS Tayside in the UK. She has an interest in the interface between psychiatry and the law, forensic governance and the provision of high-quality health services to people with learning disabilities.

Professor Laura R. Bronstein is currently Associate Dean, College of Community and Public Affairs, Professor and Chair, Department of Social Work and Director, Institute for Intergenerational Studies, Binghamton University, State University of New York. She has over 50 publications, most of which are in peer-reviewed journals. She created the *Index of Interdisciplinary Collaboration*, which has been utilised and adapted for a wide array of professionals and settings across the world. The article that she published detailing the model on which the Index is based has been cited as the eighth most influential social work article of the last decade.

Dr Allie Clemans is a Senior Lecturer in the Faculty of Education, Monash University, Australia. Her research spans diverse learning contexts – workplaces, vocational education and training, adult community education and tertiary education. The focus of her research work is the professional learning of educational workers who inspire teaching and learning practices that transform adult learners. Her research interests also include lifelong learning and notions of employability. Recent publications include a Report for the United Nations Educational, Scientific and Cultural Organisation on *Lifelong Learning and Employment Prospects: The Australian Case* (Bangkok: UNESCO, 2013).

Professor Ruth Deery is Professor of Maternal Health. She holds a joint appointment with the University of West of Scotland (UWS) and NHS Ayrshire and Arran. Her research applies sociological and political theory to the organisational culture and context of midwifery in the National Health Service in the UK. She leads and chairs the Maternity Quality Improvement Group at Ayrshire Maternity Unit and leads and chairs the Maternal, Child and Family Health Subject Development Group at UWS. She is co-author of *Emotions in Midwifery and Reproduction* (Palgrave) and lead author of *Tensions and Barriers to Maternity Services: The Story of a Struggling Birth Centre* (Radcliffe).

Jane Fenton is Programme Director of the BA (Hons) in Social Work at the University of Dundee, UK. Her area of research interest is criminal justice social work (CJSW) in Scotland and she has published work on the ethical stress experienced by social workers when they cannot base their practice on social work values. She completed a large scale research project investigating ethical stress within four Scottish CJSW agencies and is in the process of publishing the results.

Tim Glockling is an educational psychologist at Scottish Borders Council. He leads the Scottish Borders Educational Psychology Service's working group on children and young people who are looked after by the local authority. Before practising as a psychologist, Tim worked for a substantial period of time in the residential childcare sector. Tim has an interest in collaborative and participative practices.

Lesley Greenaway is an independent researcher, facilitator and trainer. She is a professional doctorate student at the University of Dundee, UK, where her studies focus on evaluation methodologies that empower and build capacity for individual and organisation voices. Her work is published through commissioned evaluation reports such as: *A Good Fit: A Study of the CashBack for Communities Small Grants Scheme in Scotland* (2012).

Bridget Hanna is a Chartered Occupational Psychologist, a Chartered Scientist and a Fellow of the Higher Education Academy. Following her recent post as a Lecturer in Occupational Psychology, she is now working on staff development initiatives at Edinburgh Napier University in Scotland. Bridget's role focuses on the formulation and development of academic leadership across the University. She has worked extensively in industry and in the public sector, with a particular focus on assessment, and has researched and published reports for the National Health Service, police and government. Bridget's research interests focus on the effects of regulation and assessment on professional identity.

Dr Elizabeth F.S. Hannah is a Senior Lecturer in Educational Psychology in the School of Education, Social Work and Community Education, University of Dundee, UK. She is Programme Director of the MSc in Educational Psychology and the Doctorate in Educational Psychology. Previously, she worked as an educational psychologist in a number of local authorities in Scotland and her last position was Deputy Principal Educational Psychologist in East Dunbartonshire Council. Her main research interests are in the areas of educational transitions and consulting with children and young people. Details of her publications and research are available at: http://www.dundee.ac.uk/eswce/people/ehannah.htm

Dr Ann Hodson is Lecturer in Social Work at the University of Dundee. Her teaching interests are reflective practice, ethical and moral social work, child protection and practice learning. Before moving to Dundee she was a social work practitioner in England and has considerable experience as both a practitioner and a manager. She was vice-chair of a fostering panel and involved in multi-agency training and development and this, along with her first-hand experience, is what prompted her particular interest in pre-birth assessment. More recently she has been involved in research into multi-agency approaches to child protection, early intervention services and pre-birth assessment approaches and practice in Scotland.

Professor Divya Jindal-Snape is Professor of Education, Inclusion and Life Transitions in the School of Education, Social Work and Community Education at the University of Dundee, UK. Having worked in three countries (India, Japan and Scotland) across a range of disciplines, she has been fascinated by the ethical dialogue in these diverse contexts. She has collaborated on research projects and publications with academics internationally, especially in the US, Nigeria, New Zealand, Australia, Finland, Netherlands, Poland, India, China and Japan. She is Director of Transformative Change: Educational and Life Transitions Research Centre. For details, see http://www.dundee.ac.uk/eswce/people/djindalsnape.htm

Lynn Kelly is a lecturer in the School of Education, Social Work and Community Education at the University of Dundee, UK. She joined the University after more than 25 years of practice as a child protection social worker and manager in a range of settings in both the UK and Australia. Her teaching and research focuses mainly on the area of child protection, with a special focus on interprofessional child protection practice and child protection education. Among her publications is: L. Kelly and S. Jackson (2011) 'Fit for Purpose? Post Qualifying Social Work Education in Child Protection in Scotland', *Journal of Social Work Education*, vol 30, no 5, pp 480–96.

Professor Timothy B. Kelly is Chair of Social Work and Acting Dean in the School of Education, Social Work and Community Education at the University of Dundee, UK. His research interests are in the areas of group work, care of older people in health and social care settings, supporting carers and social work education. He has numerous journal articles, book chapters and other publications including the book *Groupwork A to Z*, with Mark Doel. Professor Kelly's academic experience includes senior academic positions in the United States and Scotland.

Dr Suresh Kumar is the Director of the Institute of Palliative Medicine, which is also the World Health Organization Collaborating Centre for Community Participation in Palliative Care and Long Term Care. He has been part of the team that established Neighbourhood Network in Palliative Care, a large community-based palliative care network in Kerala. Dr Kumar is also a Visiting Research Fellow at the University of Bath. He is also an Ashoka Global Fellow. Among his most recent publications is *Public Health and Palliative Care: A Practice Handbook*, edited with Libby Sallnow and Alan Kellehear (Abingdon: Routledge, 2011).

Professor John Loughran is the Foundation Chair in Curriculum and Pedagogy and Dean of the Faculty of Education, Monash University, Australia. His research has spanned science education and the related fields of professional knowledge, reflective practice and teacher research. He was the co-founding editor of Studying Teacher Education and is an executive editor for *Teachers and Teaching: Theory and Practice*. His significant publications include his book *What Expert Teachers Do: Teachers' Professional Knowledge of Classroom Practice* (Sydney and London: Allen & Unwin/Routledge, 2010).

Dr Dawn MacEachern studied biology at Stirling University, graduating as a biology teacher in 1987. She taught in a number of schools across the former Strathclyde region before joining the police in Scotland in 1989. She has over 24 years of police service, with both a uniform and a child protection background. In 2011, she graduated with a Doctor of Philosophy from the University of Dundee, her thesis examining the phenomenon of secondary traumatic stress in detective officers investigating child protection cases. She continues to work to introduce the Scottish Government's GIRFEC approach within a policing context.

Dr Debra McPhee is the Dean of the Graduate School of Social Services, Fordham University, NY. Prior to that she was Chief Operating Officer of Planet Hope/Liiv.com, a health education and technology company located in Palo Alto, CA. She has more than 20 years of international leadership, academic and professional practice experience and has worked throughout North America and Europe. Former Dean of Barry University School of Social Work in Miami,

Florida, she has made academic and research contributions in the areas of international healthcare policy, interprofessional practice and collaboration, child welfare, women, social policy analysis, social problem construction and educational curriculum development.

Edward Miles is a retired police inspector. As an Emergencies Procedures Advisor he provided advice and assistance to Police Incident Officers at major incidents. He studied law and tutored in business/private law for over 10 years. As an investigator with Levy & McRae Solicitors in Glasgow, he was responsible for precognosing/tracing witnesses, locus examinations and developing lines of defence. He is now a Deputy Senior Investigating Officer with the Police Investigation and Review Commission responsible for investigating critical incidents as they affect the Police Service of Scotland.

Dr. Lynn V. Monrouxe is Director of Medical Education Research at the School of Medicine, Cardiff University, UK. Her research interests are around healthcare students' patient-centred professional identities, including narrative identities and how identities are learned and expressed through workplace learning interactions. She is deputy editor for *Medical Education* and has published over 50 articles across a range of journals and books.

Dr Patricia Murray is a senior educational psychologist with Glasgow City Council Psychological Service and a part-time associate tutor on the MSc in Educational Psychology at the University of Dundee, UK. She has worked in the education field for 35 years in a number of capacities such as teacher, lecturer and educational psychologist. Her areas of research interest include school non-attendance, consultation with young people and ethics in professional practice.

Professor Janne Pietarinen is a Professor of Teacher Education in the School of Educational Sciences and Psychology, University of Eastern Finland and Adjunct Professor in the University of Tampere. He is a Co-PI (Co-Principal Investigator) in the Learning and Development in School research group, together with Tiina Soini and Kirsi Pyhältö. His research interests are in educational transitions, pupils' and teachers' learning and well-being in the context of sustainable school development. Among his recent publications is: J. Pietarinen, K. Pyhältö, and T. Soini, 'A Horizontal Approach to School Transitions: A Lesson Learned from the Finnish 15-year-olds', *Cambridge Journal of Education*, vol 40, no 3 (2010), pp 229–45.

Professor Kirsi Pyhältö is Senior Lecturer in Higher Education in the Research and Development Centre for University Pedagogy, University of Helsinki and Adjunct Professor of Educational Psychology. She is a Co-PI in the Learning and Development in School research group together with Tiina Soini and Janne Pietarinen. Her research interests include learning, well-being and professional agency of in-service teachers. Among her recent publications is K. Pyhältö, J. Pietarinen and K. Salmela-Aro, 'Teacher–Working Environment Fit as a Framework for Burnout Experienced by Finnish Teachers', *Teaching and Teacher Education*, vol 27, no 7 (2011), pp 1101–10.

Dr Andrea Raiker is Senior Lecturer in the Department of Education Studies, University of Bedfordshire, UK. Her research is in the field of international and comparative education, with particular focus on the role of technology as a methodology for research. She has published work on theoretic perspectives on learning in higher education and on the epistemologies of e-learning. In 2010, she established the *Journal of Pedagogic Development* and continues to be co-editor.

Dr Matti Rautiainen is Senior Lecturer in Pedagogy and Vice Head in the Department of Teacher Education at the University of Jyväskylä, Finland. His main research interests are education for democracy and teacher education.

Professor Charlotte E. Rees is Professor of Education Research and Director of the Centre for Medical Education, at the University of Dundee, UK. Her research focuses on healthcare students' professionalism development and student–patient–doctor interaction within the healthcare workplace. She is deputy editor for one of the highest-ranked education journals (scientific disciplines), *Medical Education*, and has published over 70 peer-reviewed articles across a broad range of medical education and social sciences journals. She has recently had her first edited book published: *First Do No Self-harm: Understanding and Promoting Physician Stress Resilience*, edited with Charles Figley and Peter Huggard (New York: Oxford University Press, 2013).

Bridget Roberts is a Senior Consultant with Clear Horizon. She has been a practising evaluator for the last 13 years and Research Fellow with Turning Point Alcohol and Drug Centre, Melbourne, and a PhD student and associate researcher with Monash University, Victoria, Australia. Her current study explores policy and practice discourse and health service implications in the field of coexisting alcohol and drug and mental health difficulties. Her publications include several on dual diagnosis and two on evaluation.

Ros Scott is a researcher and independent consultant working in the field of hospice and palliative care. She is Co-Chair of the European Association for Palliative Care (EAPC) Task Force on Volunteering in Hospice and Palliative Care in Europe. She was formerly Director of Organisational Development with the Children's Hospice Association Scotland and was a trustee of Help the Hospices. Her research interests include: volunteers in palliative care, volunteering ethics, transition and life-limited young adults, volunteering and organisational sustainability. Among her recent publications are: 'Transition and Caring for Young Adults: Are You Part of the Solution?', *Progress in Palliative Care*, vol 19, no 6 (2011), pp 299-303 and *Volunteers in Hospice and Palliative Care,* 2nd edition, edited with Steven Howlett and Derek Doyle (Oxford: Oxford University Press, 2009).

Professor Tiina Soini is a Professor of Research on Learning and Teacher Education in the School of Education, University of Tampere and Adjunct Professor in the University of Eastern Finland. She is a Co-PI in the Learning and Development in School research group together with Kirsi Pyhältö and Janne Pietarinen. Her research interests are in the learning and well-being of educational communities, with special focus on teacher communities in comprehensive schools. Among her recent publications is: T. Soini, K. Pyhältö and J. Pietarinen, 'Pedagogical Well-being: The Experience of Finnish Comprehensive School Teachers', *Teachers and Teaching: Theory and Practice*, vol 16, no 6 (2010), pp 735–51.

Lorna Strachan is a Specialist Occupational Therapist in Scotland within NHS Tayside community care team for adults with a learning disability. Her specialist interests include vocational rehabilitation, social enterprise, the adult support and protection agenda, practice education and creative arts with a particular focus on the use of community drama as a media for improved health and well being. She is a director with an emerging social enterprise, Tayberry Enterprise Ltd, which supports empowerment through employment, and she has undertaken research and written for publication in the fields of social inclusion, community drama and interprofessional ethics.

Steve Sweeney is Director of Bereavement Support Sector – Scotland for Child Bereavement UK. He was previously Children's Service Manager for the Barnardo's Scotland Rollercoaster Service, which supports children and young people affected by trauma, bereavement and loss. His practice research promotes the needs and rights of all children and young people to access bereavement support and the influencing of changes required in culture, systems, policy and practice to make this possible. He has devised and is currently coordinating the use of a multi-agency partnership model of trauma, bereavement and loss support that is being evaluated by the University of Dundee.

Professor Kirsi Tirri is a Professor of Education and Research Director at the Department of Teacher Education at the University of Helsinki, Finland. She is also a visiting scholar with the Stanford Center on Adolescence. She was President of ECHA (European Council for High Ability) for the years 2008–12. She is President of the special interest group International Studies at AERA (American Educational Research Association). Her research interests include moral and religious education, gifted education, teacher education and cross-cultural studies. She has published 12 monographs and numerous journal articles related to these fields. She has led the Finnish team in many national and international research projects.

Dr John Young worked in criminal justice social work for 23 years and for 14 years as Team Manager in Scotland. Following his retirement, since 2006 he has worked as Associate Lecturer in the School of Education, Social Work and Community Education at the University of Dundee, UK, where he teaches ethics in the MSc Social Work programme. At present he is writing an introduction to ethics for social work students, focusing on the intertwined themes of 'role', 'resistance' and 'restriction'. He has an interest in the implications of the developing field of neuroethics for social work practice and ethics.

Acknowledgements

We wish to acknowledge our sincere gratitude to the chapter authors who have generously given their time, and shared their insightful personal and professional experiences.

We are also indebted to our colleagues from the Transformative Change: Educational and Life Transitions (TCELT) Research Centre. Without our dialogues within the Centre about personal, professional and interprofessional ethics, this book would not have been possible.

Finally, we would like to express our love and thanks to our families for their support and patience.

Understanding personal, professional and interprofessional ethics within different contexts

ONE

Setting the scene: personal, professional and interprofessional ethics

Elizabeth F.S. Hannah and Divya Jindal-Snape

Introduction

This chapter sets out the background and rationale for the book; conceptual understanding of the term 'ethics'; consideration of some of the major ethical theories; conceptual understanding of the terms 'personal ethics', 'professional ethics' and 'interprofessional ethics'; aims and approach of the book; conceptual framework for the book with a mapping to book parts; and a brief introduction to each of the parts and chapters. The remaining chapters in the book provide further insights into these concepts and understandings, drawing on the 'lived experiences' of the authors and/or other professionals working in person-centred professions. The final chapter pulls together the main themes of Chapters Two to Nineteen, and proposes a revised conceptual framework for understanding the dynamics of personal, professional and interprofessional ethics and a possible way forward in relation to research and practice.

Interprofessional working

A stimulus for writing this book was the chapter authors' experiences of working in interprofessional contexts and the importance of ethical considerations. There appear to be a number of drivers towards greater interprofessional collaboration (IPC) in the caring professions. Internationally, there has been a move towards the promotion and implementation of approaches to improve interagency and interprofessional working practices with children and adults. For example, in the UK, the integration of public services has been advocated as a way of addressing system failings, achieving better outcomes for service users and, potentially, cost savings (Brown and White, 2006).

Models of 'shared care', a term which appears to encapsulate a range of collaborative and integrated approaches to healthcare and treatment, have developed in a number of countries, including the US, UK, Australia and Canada (see for example Kelly et al, 2011; Moore et al, 2012). Furthermore, management structures may result in individuals being managed by professionals from a different discipline. This can create the potential for lack of role clarity, uncertainty and disagreement due to differences in aims, priorities, working style, values, legislative frameworks and so on. For example, Zwarenstein et al (2009), after a review of the literature of interventions designed to improve IPC, suggested that although IPC was promising in terms of the healthcare of service users, very few organisations were effectively implementing it. Some factors that have been suggested as leading to the failure of IPC include poor communication systems (Zwarenstein et al, 2009); difficult power dynamics (Zwarenstein et al, 2009); cultural differences between different professionals (Brown and White, 2006); and the organisational ethos (Brown and White, 2006). These findings highlight the importance of professionals not only giving careful and on-going consideration to the ethical aspects of their practice, but also having an appreciation and understanding of the perspectives and practices of other professionals.

Ethics and ethical theories

There are five branches of philosophy, namely, epistemology, metaphysics, ethics, aesthetics and logic. Ethics, a term derived from the Greek word *ēthikos* (ethical), refers to the study of 'morality', from the Latin word *moralis*, meaning customs or manner. As a branch of philosophy, ethics is concerned with the study of human conduct and human values. In contrast to scientific approaches to ethics, which tend to be descriptive in nature and offer no value judgements as to what is 'right' or 'wrong' behaviour, the philosophical approach to ethics tends to be normative or prescriptive, advocating what an individual ought/ ought not to do in a particular situation (Cranston et al, 2003; Thiroux and Krasemann, 2009). There are different theories of morality, some of which will now be considered briefly and will be further developed by other chapter authors in the context of their 'lived experiences'.

Consequentialist (or teleological) theories of morality take account of the outcomes of an individual's actions (Healy, 2007). The two major consequentialist theories are ethical egoism and utilitarianism, which agree that human beings should act in ways that produce good outcomes but disagree as to who should benefit. Whereas ethical egoism is based on the belief that individuals act in their own self-interest regardless of the interests of others, utilitarianism focuses on actions that result in the greatest good for all concerned. There are two forms of utilitarianism: act and rule utilitarianism. The former focuses on the individual's actions, with each situation being viewed as different and context dependent, and therefore could be considered a form of relativism. In contrast, rule utilitarianism proposes that rules should be developed and followed. Utilitarianism raises a number of questions. For example, do the ends always justify the means? How do you predict the consequences? How do you know how the outcomes will be perceived by others?

In contrast to consequentialist theories of morality, non-consequentialist (deontological) theories focus on the rightness or wrongness of actions, with no consideration of the outcomes or context. These ethical theories, often referred to as duty-based theories, emphasise fixed, universal moral rules which hold true regardless of the context (Healy, 2007). As for consequentialist theories, there are two forms, namely act and rule. In the former, individuals act in an intuitive fashion as to what seems morally right or wrong in each unique situation. Rule non-consequentialist theories propose that there are universal rules which guide moral behaviour, but differ in the way in which these rules are established. For example, Kant's duty ethics places a strong emphasis on the role of reason and the use of logic to establish 'moral absolutes' (Thiroux and Krasemann, 2009). In contrast, Divine Command Theory advocates that individuals should act in accordance with moral commands from a supernatural being.

Virtue ethics theories focus on individuals' character traits which guide their moral thinking and actions. Virtues and virtuous behaviour form the basis for a number of ethical theories. Aristotle (*Nichomachean Ethics*) considered the place of virtues in human lives, proposing the idea of the 'good life' in terms of someone leading a virtuous life (Armstrong, 2006). He conceptualised the soul as possessing three elements, namely passions, faculties and states of character, with virtues viewed as the latter. Possession of moral virtues, for example honesty, reflects habitual behaviour on the part of the individual so that it becomes part of their character (Armstrong, 2006). Ancient Chinese theories incorporated the concept of *de*, meaning 'virtue' or 'power' and the idea that it was possible for an individual to cultivate his/her inherent *de* to lead a morally excellent lifestyle. Confucius (551–479 BC) placed a strong emphasis on the social aspect of human beings and of relationships, termed cardinal relationships, that we have one to another. In contemporary versions of virtue ethics, there is an emphasis on feelings as well as acts. Thus, the virtuous human being intuitively feels that an act is the right thing to do in that situation (Thiroux and Krasemann, 2009). There are a number of criticisms of virtue ethics, such as a lack of agreement over what constitutes virtues; conflicts between virtues; accusations of moral relativism; and the circular nature of the argument related to being a virtuous person and being morally good (Armstrong, 2006).

A principle-based approach to ethics, which has been particularly influential in the fields of medicine and nursing, is grounded on four moral principles derived from common morality, namely respect for autonomy, beneficence, nonmaleficence and justice. It is beyond the scope of this chapter to explore these concepts in any depth and interested readers are directed to the work of Beauchamp and Childress (2013). However, in brief, respect for autonomy refers to the importance of acknowledging and respecting the rights of others to make choices in their lives; beneficence refers to acting in ways which benefit others; nonmaleficence obligates the professional to act in ways which do not cause harm; and justice refers to obligations to treat others in a fair and equitable fashion. Edwards (2009) argues that these four moral principles are fundamental to moral decision making, as they provide the basis for the development of specific rules, which in turn influence professional judgements. He proposes that this approach circumvents some of the difficulties encountered when viewing situations exclusively from a Kantian duty-based moral perspective or a utilitarian perspective. However, he acknowledges one of the perceived challenges of principle-based ethics, namely, attributing relative weight to each of the four principles to assist in situations where the principles may conflict.

Care-based ethics emerged around 1980. Carol Gilligan, an influential figure in this movement, contended that there are two modes of moral thinking, namely an 'ethic of care' and a 'justice approach' (Gilligan, 1982). The former emphasises the uniqueness of situations, relationships, needs, sense of responsibility, emotions and intuition in reaching moral decisions (Bookman and Aboulafia, 2000). In contrast, a 'justice approach' (subsequently referred to as an 'ethics of justice') focuses on rational decision making based on moral rules and principles (Botes, 2000). Though different, these perspectives have been considered to be equally valid, complementary and helpful to moral reasoning and decision making (Thiroux and Krasemann, 2009).

Ethical theories have been subject to considerable debate over the centuries and, as a result, there is no universal consensus. Current writers in the field argue for a synthesis of moral philosophical positions, resulting in the development of new models or theories (for example Miner and Petocz, 2003; Thiroux and Krasemann, 2009), with models that combine two or three different ethical approaches (see Miner and Petocz, 2003 for examples and critique of some models).

Personal ethics

Human beings hold values, morals and principles that guide their thinking and behaviour. Morality is about relationships and how we should act towards one another in human society. In philosophy, there are two opposing views regarding the genesis of morality. The objective view is that moral laws exist in the world, either being revealed to human beings from a higher or supernatural being or as 'natural laws'. The subjective view is that morality emanates from conscious human beings and, as such, there would be no moral values if human beings did not exist. Criticisms have been levied against both of these positions. As a possible way forward, Thiroux and Krasemann (2009) propose a synthesis of these opposing stances so that moral values are viewed as involving conscious human beings (subjective), elements in nature (objective) and an interactive component which takes account of the specific context.

This synthesis appears to be a helpful one in that it allows one to take account of the way in which morality has developed over time in different societies and cultures in response to human needs. It also allows one to account for individual differences, as it appears to be widely accepted that personal values, beliefs and ethics are influenced by a number of factors in an individual's life, including culture, ethnicity, gender, religion, socialisation and conscience (Cranston et al, 2003; Doyle et al, 2009; Ehrich et al, 2011).

Thinking about the main ethical theories considered earlier, to what extent do these have a bearing on how individuals act in different situations? To what extent do individuals focus on the consequences of their actions? To what extent do individuals refer to absolute rules or standards of behaviour? Do they hold strongly to the importance of personal character and virtues? Ehrich et al (2011) developed a model which incorporates the idea of decision makers bringing their values, beliefs and attributes to the decision making process. They refer to 'personal ethics' in relation to both the identification of moral issues and the tackling of the dilemma. Similarly, Reynolds (2006) describes individual differences in 'ethical predispositions', a term used to describe the cognitive frameworks employed by individuals in ethical decision making. Formalism is used to describe an ethical approach which is deontological in nature; whereas utilitarianism is used to describe an approach which focuses on the consequences of actions. Reynolds (2006) reports two empirical studies – the first employing a between-subjects design and the second a within-subjects experimental design – which investigated the influence of business managers' personal ethical predispositions on their ethical decision making. The author concluded that the way in which individuals responded to a moral issue was influenced by their ethical predispositions. Those adopting a formalistic framework appeared to have a greater capacity than those with a utilitarian framework to be sensitive to the characteristics of the moral issue, whether causing harm (teleological perspective) or whether contravening a social norm (deontological perspective).

Professional ethics

The term 'professional ethics' refers to a set of professional values and moral principles governing the behaviour of professional groups, such as doctors, police officers and psychologists (Strahlendorf, 2011). As applied to professional behaviour, ethics has been metaphorically construed as a compass which guides the professional through a complex terrain (Webster and Lunt, 2002). Many professional bodies have established codes of conduct and ethics for their members, in the main designed to protect the public interest; and professionals can be debarred from practising if they contravene these codes. Such codes are intended to provide guidance for members of that profession. Similar to the British Psychological Society (BPS) Code of Ethics and Conduct statement that 'no code can replace the need for psychologists to use their professional and ethical judgement' (BPS, 2009, p 4), the chapter authors believe that codes of ethics and conduct, whilst useful, are not sufficient and cannot replace the role of professional judgement.

This raises a number of questions. What does it mean to use one's professional judgement? To what extent does a professional draw on his/her personal and professional ethics in making ethical decisions? How is this reflected in professional codes of ethics and conduct? Therefore, it is interesting to examine the philosophical basis of professional codes of ethics and other professional ethics guidance and to gauge the perceived utility of that guidance. For example, Healy (2007) describes the International Federation of Social Workers (IFSW) ethical document as adopting a middle ground on the universalist–cultural relativist continuum and questions the utility of this code for social workers operating in increasingly diverse cultural contexts. Miner and Petocz (2003) view the guidance offered by the

Canadian Psychological Association Committee on Ethics as leaning towards a deontological position, given its focus on rights, duties and responsibilities. Although there is some consideration of consequences in the guidance, insufficient detail is offered. In the UK, the British Psychological Society (BPS) Code of Ethics and Conduct states that the 'underlying philosophical approach in this code is best described as the "British eclectic tradition"' (BPS, 2009, p 4). This approach seems to be based on deontological theories of morality, given the reference to Kant's theory and the role of rational thinking in establishing moral absolutes (Thiroux and Krasemann, 2009). However, the Code also states that these moral principles only provide some guidance and that individual professionals need to take account of the context – such as culture and legal requirements – and consequences of their actions. This suggests that the Code is also drawing from the teleological school of ethics (Healy, 2007; Thiroux and Krasemann, 2009). Thus, there appear to be a range of ethical theories and syntheses of theories underpinning these professional codes of ethics, leaving room for professional judgement.

In conclusion, codes of professional ethics appear to offer guiding principles of practice which are open to interpretation in their application. This raises a number of questions. For example, what informs and supports professionals as they go about their day-to-day practice? How do practitioners develop a knowledge and understanding of the principles, morals and values which underpin their chosen profession? What tools, frameworks and ethical theories do professionals employ in their ethical decision making? To address such questions, a number of writers and researchers have developed and tested models of ethical decision making (EDM) (for example Cranston et al, 2003; Miner and Petocz, 2003; Ehrich et al, 2011); have considered ethics in the context of the impact of interactions and consequences of actions over time (for example Green's (2001) IFS model); and have articulated the importance of professional development programmes which instil a sound knowledge and understanding of moral philosophy (Ehrich et al, 2011).

Interprofessional ethics

As discussed earlier, interprofessional working can create the potential for tensions and conflicts, due to different personal and professional values, morals and principles. For example, Doyle et al (2009), from a US context, highlight the increased likelihood of ethical dilemmas being encountered by social workers working in interdisciplinary teams.

Currently, there appears to be limited literature and research investigating the role of ethics in interprofessional working (Parrot, 2010). The role of codes of ethics in interprofessional working appears to have been subject to less scrutiny than other factors. There is even less literature looking at the interplay between personal, professional and interprofessional ethics, whether in a geographically and culturally homogenous interprofessional team or in a more diverse one. Given the discussion earlier of how personal ethics are shaped, as well as the impact of ethical predisposition on moral awareness and ethical decision making, it is imperative that professionals consider this interplay carefully in the context of interprofessional working. These considerations have influenced the aim and conceptual framework for the book.

Aim and approach of the book

The aim of this book is to engage in an informed debate about ethics in practice. It goes beyond looking at professional codes of conduct and ethics, and focuses on the dynamics of an individual professional's interaction with the ethical code of his/her profession and further interaction between this and others' professional ethics. This book presents the 'lived experiences' of professionals from person-centred professions; and includes perspectives from different disciplines as well as the different perspectives of professionals within the same discipline. This illuminates the dynamics of interaction at the internal and external level for individuals. It also highlights how professionals within the same profession interact differently with their code of practice.

The editors of this book, coming from different professional backgrounds to some of the authors, were also aware of these dynamics during the process of editing. Therefore, the editorial approach was to respect colleagues' terminology and stance so that their voices could come through in their preferred language and style, rather than to attempt to enforce unnecessary restrictions of consistency across writing styles that might not be in line with their personal and professional ethics. So, some authors have written in a reflexive manner about their lived experience, others have chosen to be reflexive and reflective within a wider dialogue of their professional ethics and insights into others' lived experiences. What is important here is to hear the lived experiences of professionals rather than the focus being on particular individuals or style. The writing styles vary from a more narrative approach to a more academic style. The extent to which authors have reflected on these experiences varies.

However, there are some common features in each chapter in line with the aims of the book. All the authors have included reference to relevant scholarly literature to provide a background and/or discuss these 'lived experiences'. References to specific professional experiences are used in an illustrative fashion to highlight theoretical perspectives. Each chapter uses case studies or vignettes to provide such examples. Some of these case studies are of individuals, others of professions, organisations and countries. For example, Chapter Ten focuses on the case study of a service user, Chapter Seven on professionals working on a particular programme, Chapter Two on a profession, and Chapter Seventeen on systems in two countries. Thus, the chapter authors have used case studies to illustrate the context in which their reflections are taking place and their contributions provide the reader with a theoretical understanding of personal, professional and interprofessional ethics in those contexts. It was important for these chapters to be written in this way, as the focus is on the authors' lived experience which interacts with their particular context.

Authors were commissioned to work with collaborators from different countries and professions to ensure that the chapters were not parochial and that they had a chance to reflect on the issues from multiple perspectives. Therefore, the aim of the book is not only realised in the final output, that is, providing a springboard for readers to consider and debate the dynamics of personal, professional and interprofessional ethics; it is also embedded in the process of writing the book, and authors have modelled this for the reader.

Contributing authors, from the four continents of Europe, North America, Asia and Australia, bring an international dimension to ensure that the book addresses personal, professional and interprofessional ethics around the world. The authors, representing a wide range of professions and disciplines, both academic and practice based, draw on their expertise in these diverse fields and contexts. This provides insights into how changes in context can have an impact at personal, professional and interprofessional levels. As mentioned earlier, the contexts are multifaceted and include the organisation, professional discipline, culture, country and policy. The chapters that follow contribute to our understanding of the complex picture of professionals working in a dynamic environment. They provide new insights and a lens to take things forward.

A Glossary is supplied at the end of the book, and terms appearing within it appear in bold text on first mention in a chapter.

Conceptual framework for the book

The conceptual framework for the book and chapters (Figure 1.1) is based on the chapter authors' vision of the dynamics of personal, professional and interprofessional ethics, drawing on their prior knowledge, understanding, experience and discourse with colleagues. The framework places the individual professional at the centre with his/her personal values, morals and principles; the influences of culture, religion, ethnicity, gender, family values and community on his/her personal ethics; the dynamics between the individual professional and his/her personal ethics; the dynamics between the individual professional and his/her professional ethics taking account of the influences of peers, organisational code and professional code; and (in the outer circle) the multi-organisational context, including working with professionals from other disciplines with different professional codes of ethics. Understanding the dynamics between personal, professional and interprofessional ethics is key to understanding the process of ethical decision making (EDM) and, as such, EDM is represented in the figure as encircling the overlapping circles. These elements and their interactions formed the basis for the book, enabling further exploration and illumination, as can be seen by the mapping of the parts against the figure.

Figure 1.1: Conceptual representation of the dynamic interaction between personal, professional and interprofessional ethics

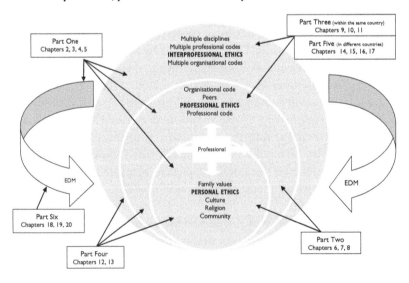

Introduction to the chapters

The book is structured into six parts and comprises 20 chapters. The chapter authors invite the readers to go on a personal journey of exploration and illumination as they consider and reflect on the issues raised in the chapters in relation to their own experiences. It is anticipated that this will result in new insights into the dynamics of ethics in practice and will stimulate further research leading to innovative practices.

Part One: Understanding personal, professional and interprofessional ethics within different contexts

The aim of this part is to set the scene for the reader by highlighting the dynamics of personal, professional and interprofessional ethics in different social, cultural, organisational and political contexts, from the perspectives of different professions. Each chapter has been written by authors from the same discipline, but the part itself covers multiple disciplines.

Chapters Two, Three, Four and Five provide conceptual and theoretical perspectives on the dynamics of personal, professional and interprofessional ethics. The authors, coming from different professions and disciplines, and working in diverse geographical areas, consider the impact of social, cultural, organisational and political contexts. These chapters also offer a rationale as to why it is important for professionals to be mindful of the 'burden' of tensions between personal, professional and interprofessional ethics. In Chapter Two, Barrow and colleagues, all practising educational psychologists, consider the tensions and complexity of their practice in one local authority in Scotland. They illustrate this complexity through illustrative examples, focusing on assessment and research. They conclude with a discussion of the role of organisational culture in professional ethical practice. In Chapter Three, Hanna, an occupational psychologist working in higher education, also considers the importance of the organisational context of interprofessional working and interprofessional ethics. Hanna provides an interesting account of whistleblowing and its function. Greenaway and Roberts, in Chapter Four, consider the concept and enactment of community involvement from their differing professional, cultural and policy contexts. They discuss questions relating to the nature of community involvement and participation, resultant ethical tensions and dilemmas, and forms of professional guidance. They provide illustrative examples from their professional practice and conclude with guiding principles which take account of, and address, the dynamics of personal, professional and interprofessional ethics in relation to community involvement. In Chapter Five, Soini and colleagues explore the relationship between teachers' occupational well-being and their professional ethics in the context of teacher–student interaction. They consider situations which may give rise to tensions, namely differing perspectives with colleagues about achieving ethically sustainable pedagogical practices. Furthermore, they discuss strategies which may be employed in these circumstances and how these can be embedded in initial training and continuing professional development.

Part Two: Personal and professional ethics

The aim of this part is to highlight the dilemmas that a professional might face when there is a difference in their personal and professional ethics. They focus on the dilemma and tensions between personal and professional ethics in the context of criminal justice, education and social work. In Chapter Six, Fenton considers personal and professional ethical tensions for practitioners in criminal justice social work, reflecting on the changing policy context and discourses in the UK and other western societies. The author draws on her research to highlight disjuncture experienced by criminal justice social workers. In Chapter Seven, Clemans and colleagues describe and reflect on ethical tensions experienced in their role as leaders of a government-funded professional learning programme for teachers who are 'professional learning leaders' in schools in Australia. In Chapter Eight, Kelly and Young consider moral challenges facing social workers, specifically those engaging in child protection work, using a case scenario based on the lead author's experiences.

Part Three: Professional and interprofessional ethics

The aim of this part is to reflect on the dynamics of professional and interprofessional ethics experienced by professionals when working within the same national context. Chapters Nine, Ten and Eleven focus on the tensions and dilemmas between professional and interprofessional ethics in the disciplinary contexts of occupational therapy, psychiatry, social work, midwifery and educational psychology. In Chapter Nine, Brewster and Strachan bring together their differing perspectives as clinical psychiatrist and occupational therapist, to discuss some of the conflicts and tensions which may occur in interagency teams, and focus on specific issues relating to working with individuals with an intellectual learning disability. Ethical challenges are illustrated through two 'real life' case studies. In Chapter Ten, Hodson and Deery bring their interprofessional view to discuss some of the ethical issues faced by child protection social workers and midwives in pre-birth assessment. In Chapter Eleven, Boyle, writing from an Australian context, considers some of the ethical issues facing practising psychologists, including issues of consent and confidentiality when working with other professionals, for example teachers, who do not have a written code in Australia.

Part Four: Personal, professional and interprofessional ethics

The aim of this part is to look at multiple dynamics, that is, that between personal and professional, professional and interprofessional, and personal and interprofessional within the same chapter. Chapters Twelve and Thirteen present two distinct examples of disjuncture in personal, professional and interprofessional ethics by looking at the experiences of police officers, lawyers, social workers and professionals from voluntary organisations. In Chapter Twelve, MacEachern and colleagues bring together their interprofessional perspectives as police officer, legal investigative officer and educationist to discuss some of the ethical conflicts experienced by police officers working in the field of child protection. Specifically, the authors discuss the ethical tensions of balancing the rights of the 'accused' and the 'victim', taking account of legislative and interprofessional contexts. In Chapter Thirteen, Sweeney and Boge, working in the voluntary sector in Scotland and Denmark respectively, whilst not focusing on multinational dimensions, discuss some of the ethical issues involved in supporting children and young people who have experienced bereavement, highlighting personal, professional and interprofessional dimensions when working with others, including parents/carers.

Part Five: Professional and interprofessional ethics in multicultural and multinational contexts

The aim of this part is to reflect on the dynamics of professional and interprofessional ethics experienced by professionals when working in collaboration with others across national boundaries. Each chapter has been written by authors co-writing with collaborators from other countries, thereby reflecting the dynamics of multinational interprofessional working in the writing process. There are perspectives from the disciplines of education, healthcare, social work and educational psychology within the UK, the US, Finland, Germany, India and Palestine. In Chapter Fourteen, Raiker and Rautiainen, working as teacher educators in England and Finland respectively, discuss the development of a 'moral self' in teachers in training. They consider the impact of different policy and political contexts and compare and contrast ethical dimensions of teacher education in these two countries. In Chapter Fifteen, Barron and Abdullah describe the first phase of a project in Palestine that involved the training of mental health practitioners in an evidence-based trauma-recovery programme with children living in that region. They discuss the utilisation of an ethical framework designed to address interprofessional and cross-cultural dimensions of project implementation and evaluation. In Chapter Sixteen, Kelly and colleagues compare and contrast the values of different professional groups within the context of the UK, the US and Germany and consider some of the structural barriers to interprofessional collaboration. They present an interesting case study which highlights cultural, geographical, professional and ideological factors. They conclude with recommendations for improving interprofessional working practices. In Chapter Seventeen, Scott and Kumar discuss ethical issues pertaining to the involvement of volunteers in palliative care in the context of the UK and India through a comparison of the two different models of palliative care that operate in these countries.

Part Six: A possible way forward

The aim of this part is to consider how ethical mindfulness can be embedded into the practice of professionals and those in training. Chapters Eighteen and Nineteen consider ways of preparing students to become professionals who can practise in an ethical fashion, including operating well in interprofessional contexts. In Chapter Eighteen, Hannah and Murray focus on the professional training of educational psychologists. They report on a systematic review of teaching and learning approaches on one professional training programme in Scotland. This review incorporated documentary analysis and a qualitative investigation into the ethical perspectives of student educational psychologists at the beginning of their professional training. This led to a re-evaluation of ways to promote the ethical development of students on the programme. In a similar vein, Rees and colleagues, in Chapter Nineteen, consider ways of helping to prepare healthcare students to work with other professionals. They draw on an exemplar narrative from a wider research study to highlight and discuss how healthcare students develop a professional identity through experiences of interprofessional working.

This part also incorporates the concluding Chapter Twenty (Jindal-Snape and Hannah), which capitalises on the learning from the previous chapters and presents a revised framework for conceptualising the dynamics of personal, professional and interprofessional ethics in diverse contexts to inform future research and practice.

References

Armstrong, A.E. (2006) 'Towards a strong virtue ethics for nursing practice', *Nursing Philosophy*, vol 7, pp 110–24.

Beauchamp, T.L. and Childress, J.F. (2013) *Principles of biomedical ethics* (7th edn), New York: Oxford University Press.

Bookman, M. and Aboulafia, M. (2000) 'Ethics of care revisited', *Philosophy Today*, vol 44, pp 169–74.

Botes, A. (2000) 'A comparison between the ethics of justice and the ethics of care', *Journal of Advanced Nursing*, vol 32, pp 1071–5.

BPS (British Psychological Society) (2009) *Code of ethics and conduct*, Leicester: British Psychological Society.

Brown, K. and White, K. (2006) *Exploring the evidence base for integrated children's services*, www.scotland.gov.uk/Publications/Recent.

Cranston, N., Ehrich, L. and Kimber, M. (2003) 'The "right" decision? Towards an understanding of ethical dilemmas for school leaders', *Westminster Studies in Education*, vol 26, no 2, pp 135–47.

Doyle, O.Z., Miller, S.E. and Mirza, F.Y. (2009) 'Ethical decision-making in social work: exploring personal and professional values', *Journal of Social Work Values and Ethics*, vol 7, no 1, www.socialworker.com/jswve/content/view/113/67/.

Edwards, S.D. (2009) *Nursing ethics: A principle-based approach* (2nd edn), Basingstoke: Palgrave Macmillan.

Ehrich, L.C., Kimber, M., Millwater, J. and Cranstone, N. (2011) 'Ethical dilemmas: a model to understand teacher practice', *Teachers and Teaching*, vol 17, no 2, pp 173–85.

Gilligan, C. (1982) *In a different voice: Psychological theory and women's development*. Cambridge, MA: Harvard University Press.

Green, B. (2001) *Medical Ethics*, www.priory.com/ethics.htm#IFS.

Healy, L.M. (2007) 'Universalism and cultural relativism in social work ethics', *International Social Work*, vol 50, no 1, pp 11–26.

Kelly, B.J., Perkins, D.A., Fuller, J.D. and Parker, S.M. (2011) 'Shared care in mental illness: a rapid review to inform implementations', *International Journal of Mental Health Systems*, vol 5, no 31, pp 1–10.

Miner, M. and Petocz, A. (2003) 'Moral theory in ethical decision making: problems, clarifications and recommendations from a psychological perspective', *Journal of Business Ethics*, vol 42, pp 11–25.

Moore, A., Patterson, C., White, J., House, S.T., Riva, J.J., Nair, K., Brown, A., Kadhim-Saleh, A. and McCann, D. (2012) 'Interprofessional and integrated care of the elderly in a family health team', *Canadian Family Physician*, vol 58, pp 436–41.

Parrot, L. (2010) *Values and ethics in social work practice (transforming social work practice)* (2nd edn), Exeter: Learning Matters Ltd.

Reynolds, S.J. (2006) 'Moral awareness and ethical predispositions: investigating the role of individual differences in the recognition of moral issues', *Journal of Applied Psychology*, vol 91, no 1 pp 233–43.

Strahlendorf, P. (2011) *Professional ethics*, Session No 714, www.bcsp.org/pdf/PresentationsArticles/714_1.pdf.

Thiroux, J.P. and Krasemann, K.W. (2009) *Ethics theory and practice* (10th edn), New Jersey: Prentice Hall.

Webster, A. and Lunt, I. (2002) 'Ethics, professionalization and the future landscape of educational psychology', *Educational and Child Psychology*, vol 19, no 1, pp 97–107.

Zwarenstein, M., Goldman, J. and Reeves, S. (2009). 'Interprofessional collaboration: Effects of practice-based interventions on professional practice and healthcare outcomes' (Review), http://www.thecochranelibrary.com/view/0/index.html.

TWO

Beyond procedures: a case study from educational psychology

Wilma Barrow, Roger Barrow and Tim Glockling

The real point of ethics is to offer some tools for thinking about difficult matters, recognising from the start – as the very rationale for ethics, in fact – that the world is seldom simple or clear cut. Struggle and uncertainty are part of ethics, as they are part of life. (Weston, cited by Mockler, 2007, p 93)

Introduction

Educational psychologists (EPs) in the UK are governed by the Health and Care Professionals Council Standards of Conduct, Performance and Ethics (HCPC, 2012) and guided by the British Psychological Society's Code of Ethics and Conduct (BPS, 2009). While professional codes of ethics offer principles for guidance, **ethical practice** requires EPs and other professionals to constantly engage with tension and complexity. Despite the complex nature of the work, the literature on ethics in EP practice is limited. Lindsay notes that, until recently, EP training in ethics offered little by way of 'specific and targeted discussion' (Lindsay, 2008, p 52). The BPS recognises the need for 'opportunities for discourse on these issues' (BPS, 2009, p 2). This chapter reflects on ethical complexity in EP practice and considers the importance of safeguarding space for on-going reflexivity and dialogue (and see also Chapters Eleven and Eighteen for insights from Australia and Scotland, respectively).

In line with the aims of Part One, this chapter highlights the dynamics of personal, professional and **interprofessional** ethics within the context of a discipline (see Figure 1.1), and uses the case study of educational psychology to illustrate these dynamics. The authors identify with the relational underpinnings of the care ethics approach. They do not, however, view care ethics alone as a sufficient basis for ethical practice. They identify the risk that over-identification with others' perspectives may compromise the professional's capacity for principled individual moral judgement. They draw upon dialogic self-theories as a basis for professional action which can be both socially engaged and principled. They discuss examples of ethical tension in assessment practice and practitioner research. Finally, they focus on the place of **organisational culture** in supporting ethical practice. Before addressing these issues, some background will be provided on educational psychology in Scotland, where the authors practise.

Educational psychology in Scotland

Educational psychology is mainly delivered by local authority Educational Psychology Services (EPSs). Five EP functions of consultation, assessment, intervention, training and research are delivered across a range of levels, including the young person and family, the school and the local authority (Scottish Executive, 2002). EPs work with other agencies to meet shared, policy-driven targets focused on achieving positive outcomes for children and young people (Scottish Government, 2008). **Interagency** collaborative working can introduce new tensions but also provides new learning opportunities for professionals working together (Warmington et al, 2004).

A theoretical reflection on tensions in EP practice

EP practice takes place in a dynamic and relational context. As part of this context, EPs experience its tensions and contradictions. These cannot be easily resolved through the application of **ethical codes**, or the principles upon which these rest. The relationship between codes and moral theory is not always clear. The BPS *Code of Ethics and Conduct* (2009) identifies its theoretical roots as British eclectic. Ethical codes, such as those provided by the BPS and the HCPC, offer a broad set of principles to guide professionals. Ultimately, their purpose is to prevent wrongdoing to recipients of a professional service.

There are difficulties in applying broad ethical principles within the fluid contexts in which EPs work. These contexts are often characterised by different, and at times conflicting, interests (Lindsay, 2008). This will be illustrated in more detail in the next section. Pring (2002) argues that reliance on abstract ethical principles in practice is problematic, due to the 'irreconcilable tensions' that exist between deontological and consequentialist principles. These tensions become all too apparent in the complexity of the professional context within which EPs work, where frequently there is a dynamic process of transactions; for example, between the child, the family and the school. This makes it difficult to fully predict the consequences of any particular course of action. Judgement about the ethical status of an action may shift according to newly emerging information about its consequences.

Cameron (2006) comments that one source of tension for EPs arises from conflicting expectations regarding their role. They can be variously expected to rescue, fix, label, empower and facilitate, among other things. The resulting tensions form the landscapes in which EPs work. These tensions are on-going and multidimensional, external and internal.

The complexity of human social interaction influences our thinking. Internal thoughts are often dialogues or debates which have taken place, or are taking place, within communities (Gillespie et al, 2008). The individual's relationships with their various communities (such as professional groups, local authority services, families, and religious or political organisations) are displayed in the many voices used in their speech and addressed by that speech (Markova et al, 2007). The individual, therefore, does not engage with others from a uniform position. Through talk with others, they confront their own thoughts, and those of the others with whom they communicate, in dynamic and at times contradictory ways. Individual professionals are therefore multi-voiced. This suggests that attempting to tease out, for example, a professional from a personal voice is not straightforward. Behind the judgement of an individual EP about how to articulate their professional voice, lie a continuous ethical dialogue, reflection and judgement that cannot be resolved through adherence to ethical procedure alone.

Recognition of the complexity involved in making professional decisions based on broad ethical principles has led to the development of ethical decision making (EDM) models within the organisational literature (Whittier et al, 2006). Whittier et al note that there has been limited empirical testing of the practical applicability of these models. They argue, however, that where there is uncertainty about any action, 'systematic analysis of decisions leads to higher decision quality' (p 245). This entails steps such as problem definition, identification of criteria for decision making and evaluation of outcomes. It is the chapter authors' stance that it would be important to critically evaluate the adequacy of these criteria and to consider from whose perspective they make judgements about 'quality'.

Concern has been raised about over-emphasising EDM in the development of ethical practice (Gray and Gibbons, 2007). Guillemin and Gillam (2004) argue that there is a need to ensure that ethical oversight is not limited to those aspects of practice prompting ethical dilemmas. They consider that there is a need to broaden the focus of attention to the 'ethically important moments' which pervade human interaction. Given the complexity involved, there is a need for continuous reflexivity on the micro-ethical processes involved in encounters with others. This approach rests on the assumption that the professional and the 'other/s' will generally be involved in an on-going negotiation about what is taking place within the professional encounter.

This emphasis on relationship is highlighted by those who argue that the traditional focus on the individual moral agent's rational application of ethical principles provides an insufficient ethical basis for those working within caring professions (see for example, Petterson, 2011). Advocates of care ethics contend that the application of general moral principles (whether deontological or consequentialist) over-emphasise justice over care, and reason over emotion (Rudnick, 2001). Care ethics assumes a relational ontology and does not view the professional to be an impartial and distanced ethical decision maker (Petterson, 2011).

The chapter authors identify with the relational ontology on which care ethics rests and consider this to have implications for the ways in which ethicality is understood in their practice.

Shotter (1993) refers to the 'joint zone of action' (p 122), within which individual activity must be attuned to that of others, and suggests that the consequences of social exchanges are unpredictable. He views such exchanges as 'moral settings' (p 122). This emphasis on co-construction in social exchange, and our moral obligations to others in the process of exchange, helps to provide an alternative ethical emphasis to that of the individual moral agent relying on reason alone in the application of ethical principles to dilemmas in practice. Instead, a relational approach provides a basis for the position that deliberation over ethical action is mediated and negotiated through relationship with others and with context. It is the contention of the chapter authors that evaluations of the moral integrity of a course of action can change as we encounter others' communications about the experienced or predicted impact upon them. Ethicality from this perspective involves more than the rational application of principle. It also requires professionals who are empathetic and emotionally engaged as they deliberate over the most appropriate course of action.

What this means for EPs needs to be examined. It opens up to ethical scrutiny issues that might otherwise be considered ethically neutral, such as ways of knowing about others. Gameson et al (2003) describe how an individual's approach to assessment, report writing or the application of research to practical intervention, for example, is influenced by epistemological assumption, even when this is implicit. The HCPC and BPS codes require psychologists to be mindful of power differentials between themselves and **service users**. Given the role which EPs play in the construction of narratives about service users, it is important that EPs' ethical reflexivity is applied to epistemology.

Critics have raised concerns about the implications of the rejection of principlism in care ethics (see for example Crigger, 1997; Rudnick, 2001). The subjectivist basis of care ethics is problematic, as it involves partiality and risks lack of justice in the delivery of professional care. It is the contention of the chapter authors that in adopting a relational ontology EPs need not be trapped within the subjectivity of the other/s with whom they are engaged. For this reason the authors, while accepting the need for a relational emphasis, do not view care ethics as providing a sufficient basis for their practice.

Psychological theories of the dialogical self (Hermans, 2001; Markova, 2003) adopt a relational model of self which retains space for individual agency (Salgado and Clegg, 2011). From this perspective, the self is not dissolved in social context (Salgado and Clegg, 2011) but is positioned as insider-outsider (Sherif, 2001). Individuals are embedded in but not bound by context, thus they can offer evaluation and challenge (Wegerif, 2011). The ability to challenge and evaluate enables critical reflexivity. This allows space between the EP and the other/s with whom she is engaged. As insider-outsider, EPs can be socially and emotionally engaged practitioners who attend and respond to and interact with others, yet can refer back to principle as a point of reference in dialogues with others. Ethical principles are thus held in dialogic tension with the particulars of the relational context.

Literature on ethics across a range of contexts emphasises the importance of critical dialogue with others in supporting ethical practice (see for example, Hawes, 1998; Verhezen, 2010; Nijhof et al, 2012). Such dialogue needs to provide more than affirmation and mutuality (Markova, 2003). Criticality requires 'productive difference' in the dialogic process (Gergen et al, 2004). In confronting the otherness of those engaged in dialogue, the individual can reach a distanciated perspective (van der Riet, 2008). Kennedy (2004) helpfully refers to this as 'thinking for oneself and with others' (p 747). In this view, dialogue with others can be viewed as a vital and on-going component of ethical practice. The importance of safeguarding space for dialogue within the organisations within which EPs work will be considered in the final section of this chapter.

Illustrating ethical tensions: examples from EP practice

As argued above, **ethical judgements** pervade all EP practice and arise even where ethical guidelines have been followed. It is beyond the scope of this chapter to represent the range of ethical judgements that the practising EP may require to make. The examples discussed below are merely illustrative. They draw upon the authors' practice experience of two distinct areas of activity, both of which represent core EP functions. The first relates to direct assessment with individual young people, and the second to practitioner research where the participants are young people.

A request for educational psychology assessment may be attended by the expectations of multiple parties; young person, parent, teachers and others. On occasion, different parties' beliefs about the purpose and appropriate nature of the assessment may be in tension. For example, an important purpose for the authors, when reporting assessments, has often been to identify previously unrecognised abilities that the young person has shown. Sometimes, this has been in tension with the expectations of parents or teachers who have hoped that the assessments will confirm their beliefs that the young person has significant difficulties which require intensive additional support.

EPs' decisions about whether to become involved in assessment, for what purpose and by what means, all entail ethical judgement. The chapter authors' reflection on practice suggests that assessments may contribute significantly to various parties' narratives about the young person, and to the young person's narrative about him/herself. Given the arguments developed earlier, ethical responsibilities require EPs to think about how the reporting of their findings might influence the beliefs and the attitudes of others towards the young person, and how, as a result, they may act towards that young person in the future. EPs' assessment practice may have implications not only for the young person, but for others with whom they are endeavouring to sustain effective professional relationships: for example, parents, teachers and education authority colleagues. However, the precise consequences of assessments have often been difficult to predict. Basing action on the moral value of expected outcomes may be problematic. For example, the difficulty of judging how EPs' assessments may be received by different parties needs to be recognised. There may be no straightforward causal relationship between EPs' actions, how others make sense of or respond to those actions, and future impact upon the young person. It is possible that even the EPs' best efforts at ethically engaged assessment practice may, on occasions, have unwelcome implications for others. For example, the chapter authors recall occasions when their assessments, insofar as they have recognised abilities and developmental progress, have been received by the parent as a powerful personal challenge to their firmly held beliefs about the young person's **incapacity**.

In such situations, reference to ethical codes or frameworks has not been sufficient to resolve experiences of moral tension or uncertainty. Codes offer clarity in prohibiting activities that would be regarded as unprofessional; and it is important to recognise that many protocols also offer positively framed statements of principle which may helpfully guide practice. However, those principles may license many alternative courses of morally defensible action in complex, dynamic and relational practice situations. They do not relieve EPs from individual responsibility for exercising ethical judgement.

When an EP decides, for example, to observe a young person in class as part of an assessment, there is a need to reflect on the risk that his/her presence may influence how that young person is viewed by his peers. Despite taking measures to ensure that the young person is not identified, subtle cues provided by the teacher may signal to the class the purpose of the observation. Examples such as these highlight the need for EPs to be aware of ethical implications throughout any assessment process.

Ethical complexity encountered in practice will now be further exemplified by drawing upon experiences of research activity with young people. When considering, for example, young people's **consent** to participate, their giving, or withholding, of consent cannot be considered as a straightforward matter. In project work undertaken, practice guidance has required the involvement of those **adult gatekeepers** who are able to give or withhold consent for the young person's involvement; specifically, parents, and representatives of the Education Department, as well as the young people themselves. When doing this, active consideration has to be given to how to manage conflicts of opinion. When, for example, parents and teachers actively wish a young person to participate in a research project, there is a need to consider carefully how to support the young person's right to self-determination, while also taking account of the adult gatekeeper's views of what is in the young person's best interests. This requires critical reflection by the EP on his/her values and motives and the recognition of conflicts of interest. These might include, for example, professional self-interest involved in enrolling participants in the research. Similarly, when a parent does not consent to a young person's involvement in an EP-led class project, but also argues that it would be discriminatory to remove the young person from the whole-class activity, there is a requirement to consider how to balance the interests of the parent, the young person and the other pupils within that particular class. In these examples, the ethical tensions might involve managing several conflicting personal and professional internal voices.

Recognition should be given to the importance of considering the means by which consent is sought, and of the power relations involved in those negotiations. There may be a fine line between establishing trust with prospective participants in order to support them to understand what they are consenting to; and tacit coercion, salesmanship or 'faking friendship' (Duncombe and Jessop, 2002). At times, establishing trust with participants has required some persistence; and it has been necessary to judge carefully how far persistence was justified. Licence could have been found within professional codes for a range of actions, and ethical practice has therefore required the exercise of individual skill and judgement.

Further ethical dimensions may emerge during the course of research activity. For example, participants can offer very different levels of engagement, despite having apparently freely consented to involvement. In an interview-based project, some participants gave minimal responses, while others offered very elaborate personal accounts. Both outcomes raised issues concerning the right to use those participants' data. This led to questions regarding whether it could be reliably concluded that the former group had really wanted to participate; and whether the latter had said more than they intended. An ethical imperative to re-negotiate the terms of their consent was recognised, in order to enable the participants to clarify how much of what they said should be included as data.

Some participants may have misconstrued the **rapport** that was established at interview as signifying an informal social interaction. Consequently, careful thought was given to how to manage further dialogue so as not to reduce the likelihood that they would be willing to reconsider their consent. Procedural guidance may not be able to offer straightforward direction on what is an ethical course of action in such nuanced social situations. Ethical practice needs to be flexible, relational, self-reflexive and grounded in reflection along with others.

When reporting research findings, there has also been a need to reflect carefully about the ethical responsibilities associated with constructing 'knowledge about' service users. For example, when disseminating interview research with young people who are **Looked After**, the requirement to provide accessible research summaries exercised a pressure to extract and highlight participants' most memorable observations. However, there was also a moral duty to avoid objectifying participants by giving these de-contextualised fragments of data undue prominence; as if they could reveal unambiguous, unchanging truths about the participants and their perspectives.

The chapter authors consider that there is an ethical dimension to questions of how power over interpretation and authorship transfers from participants to researchers. There is an equivalent ethical dimension to the reification in formal reports of the knowledge of young people derived from assessment. This knowledge is necessarily limited, not least because time pressures may place a constraint on opportunities to engage in cyclical, cumulative assessment and iterative analysis. When reporting findings, it is important to attempt to explain transparently the contextual nature of any assessments and the conditional nature of the knowledge they offer about the young person. In this way, the risk that EPs' assessments will be over-interpreted, or misinterpreted, by others may be managed.

The question of how young people may exercise control over research or assessment information that may be used to explain them, or to construct stories about them, is not easily addressed by procedural approaches. In practice, this has required continual review of the adequacy of attempts to maintain dialogue with participants about the analysis, interpretation and dissemination of information about them. Further development of approaches which embed consent meaningfully as an on-going process remains an important goal.

It has been argued that attempts to negotiate ethical tensions in practice have required on-going exercise of individual judgement. Practitioners may require continuing support to develop their individual practice in ethical decision making; through engagement with theoretical perspectives, opportunities for reflection and developmental dialogue with fellow professionals. The next section will consider possibilities for creating and sustaining organisational cultures that may support the development of ethical practice.

Creating organisational cultures that support ethical reflexivity

It has been argued above that the complexities of practice demand that EPs maintain continuous ethical reflexivity in all aspects of their work. This final section considers how to foster an organisational culture that supports this through an emphasis on critical dialogue.

The wider literature identifies some organisational risks to ethical practice. First, is the risk of dilution of professional ethics when organisational culture does not reflect the principles of the professional's code of ethics. While the guidance offered by professional ethical codes is limited, these remain an important basis of trust between professions and the public (BPS, 2009; Nijhof et al, 2012). Nijhof et al (2012) highlight the potential for friction between the ethics of the professional and those of their employing organisation. Somers (2001) provides evidence from research with accountants indicating that professional codes have less influence than corporate codes because they are not necessarily part of the organisational environment within which individual professionals work. While there may be limits in what can be generalised from the business context to EP practice, it is apparent that EPs need to be alert to complexity associated with, for example, budgetary pressures.

Weaver, writing from the perspective of social cognitive identity theory, argues that 'depth and frequency of a person's interaction with others is a key influence' (Weaver, 2006, p 356). He contends that when moral differences between a professional and others within the workplace are too great, dissonance will be experienced. This can lead to adjustments in individual practice to reflect organisational culture. Moral muteness in organisations (Bird and Waters, 1989) refers to lack of explicit talk about ethics. Mockler (2007), citing Longstaff (2001), suggests that some organisations resist values talk for fear of conflict within the organisation or inefficient use of time. The key practice implication for organisations is commitment to explicit ethical talk. Organisational cultures promoting shared values and fostering dialogue are most likely to foster professional ethicality (Nijhof et al, 2012). EPs work with others from different agencies, and the sociocultural differences resulting from their respective training and professional roles can lead to interprofessional ethical tensions. One example might be difference in emphases between organisations regarding protection and self-determination agendas.

So far the focus has been on protecting the ethical stance of professionals in the face of ethical disinterest or difference. Earlier, it was suggested that where difference persists, there is value in explicit dialogue about ethics as a means of supporting critical reflexivity. Tensions between professionals can be sites of 'expansive learning' (Engeström, 2001) where 'professionals may begin to respond in enriched ways, thus producing new patterns of activity, which expand understanding and change practice' (Warmington et al, 2004, p 7). Although, as argued earlier, such dialogue must move beyond the comfort of mutuality, a level of interpersonal safety and trust is required in order to tolerate dissonance. Management approaches which legitimise a culture of dialogue and openness are required. Verkerk et al (2001) argue that democratic management styles support approaches to ethics which extend beyond the procedural and thus enable the contextualised understanding advocated in this chapter. Leadership culture within organisations, therefore, has an ethical impact and this has relevance for the ways in which EPSs and the organisations within which they are nested are managed. Some examples of attempts to apply these ideas systemically are now provided.

Supporting ethical practice within multi-agency organisations

The current emphasis on developing integrated working practices in **children's services** provides opportunities to engage in dialogue about shared ethical values and principles for practice. These opportunities operate at a range of levels, from the individual EP in a **casework** context to the development of values, procedures and frameworks to operate at local authority and national level. It is important for EPs to engage with these. The authors have found that in new service configurations, EPs can become involved with a range of professionals in the development, for example, of shared consent protocols. The relevance of this activity is not just the emerging protocol, but also the opportunity provided for explicit talk about the principles underpinning the use of these. Akkerman and Bakker (2011) argue that transformative learning in practice involves continuous joint work and negotiation while maintaining sociocultural difference. Such processes have the potential to foreground a mutually negotiated ethical understanding. They require all involved to nurture reflexivity, recognising that no set of procedures will adequately address the ethical complexities encountered in practice. Space for reflection, and professional and service user dialogue, need to be privileged in organisations in order to avoid reliance on procedures.

Emphasising a values-based approach to EP practice

When a contextualised understanding of practice is emphasised, values and psychological knowledge cannot be mechanistically applied. Context includes the perspectives of service users, including children and young people. Context is dynamic and priorities therefore shift. Services need to support reflection and dialogue about *how* EPs apply their knowledge and skills in different and changing practice contexts. This can be nurtured within a democratic EPS culture that supports dialogue about values and ethicality which can feed into whole-service engagement in activities such as the development of EPS guidelines for practice and principles for contextually sensitive self-evaluation. The chapter authors consider that the application of psychology is not value free and is therefore open to re-construction (Hick et al, 2009). The implication for an EPS is that the service requires to explicitly engage with values in order to support EPs as they draw from, and apply, psychology in their practice. This requires an ethos within the EPS that encourages and supports a willingness to challenge and negotiate.

EPS commitments to space for dialogue

Space for dialogue is needed to enable EPs to open up about their experiences of ethical tension in practice. Useful tools to support individual reflection and dialogue in **supervision** on these issues are provided by the authors of the Constructionist Model of Informed and Reasoned Action (COMOIRA) framework for EP practice (Rydderch and Gameson, 2010). Tools are not enough. The climate of supervision (including peer and group supervision) must foster openness and safety, yet also sustain the 'productive difference' required to support critical reflexivity. In this way ethical voice can be reflected on, supported and amplified.

The publication of this book coincides with a wider concern about ethics in organisations and the problems that can arise where such issues do not receive adequate attention (see also Chapter Three). EP work presents on-going tension and ethical challenge. This chapter has offered a theoretical perspective that emphasises making space for dialogue as a means of supporting critical reflexivity on ethical practice. This has implications for individual EPs, for service managers and for the culture of the organisations within which they work.

References

Akkerman, S. F. and Bakker, A. (2011) 'Boundary crossing and boundary objects', *Review of Educational Research*, vol 81, no 2, pp 132–64.

Bird, F.B. and Waters, J.A. (1989) 'The moral muteness of managers', *California Management Review*, vol 32, no 1, pp 73–88.

BPS (British Psychological Society) (2009) *Code of ethics and conduct*, Leicester: British Psychological Society.

Cameron, R.J. (2006) 'Educational psychology: the distinctive contribution', *Educational Psychology in Practice*, vol 22, no 4, pp 289–304.

Crigger, N.J. (1997) 'The trouble with caring: a review of eight arguments against an ethic of care', *Journal of Professional Nursing*, vol 13, no 4, pp 217–21.

Duncombe, J. and Jessop, J. (2002) '"Doing rapport" and the ethics of "faking friendship"', in M. Mauthner, M. Birch, J. Jessop and T. Miller (eds) *Ethics in qualitative research*, London: Sage, pp 107–22.

Engeström, Y. (2001) 'Expansive learning at work: toward an activity theoretical reconceptualisation', *Journal of Education and Work*, vol 14, no 1, pp 133–56.

Gameson, J., Rydderch, G., Ellis, D., and Carroll, T. (2003) 'Constructing a flexible model of interactive practice. Part I, Conceptual and theoretical issues', *Educational Psychology in Practice*, vol 20, no 1, pp 96–115.

Gergen, K.J., Gergen, M.M. and Barrett, F.J. (2004) 'Dialogue: life and death of the organisation', in D. Grant, C. Hardy, C. Oswick and L. Putnam (eds) *The Sage handbook of organisational discourse*, London: Sage, pp 39–60.

Gillespie, A., Cornish, F., Aveling, E.L. and Zittoun, T. (2008) 'Conflicting community commitments: a dialogical analysis of a British woman's World War II diaries', *Journal of Community Psychology*, vol 36, no 1, pp 35–52.

Gray, M. and Gibbons, J. (2007) 'There are no answers, only choices: teaching ethical decision making in social work', *Australian Social Work*, vol 60, no 2, pp 222–38.

Guillemin, M. and Gillam, L. (2004) 'Ethics, reflexivity and "ethically important moments" in research', *Qualitative Inquiry*, vol 10, pp 261–80.

Hawes, S. (1998) 'Positioning a dialogic reflexivity in the practice of feminist supervision', in B.M. Bayer and J. Shotter (eds) *Re-constructing the psychological subject: Bodies, practices and technologies*, London: Sage, pp 94–110.

HCPC (Health and Care Professions Council) (2012) *Standards of conduct, performance and ethics*, London: Health and Care Professions Council.

Hermans, H.J.M. (2001) 'The dialogical self: towards a theory of personal and cultural positioning', *Culture and Psychology*, vol 7, no 3, pp 243–81.

Hick, P., Kershner, R. and Farrell, P.T. (2009) 'Introduction', in P. Hick, R. Kershner and P.T. Farrell (eds) *Psychology for inclusive education: New directions in theory and practice*, New York: Routledge, pp 1–10.

Kennedy, D. (2004) 'The philosopher as teacher: the role of a facilitator in a community of philosophical inquiry', *Metaphilosophy*, vol 35, no 5, pp 744–65.

Lindsay, G. (2008) 'Ethics and value systems', in B. Kelly, L. Woolfson and J. Boyle (eds) *Frameworks for practice in educational psychology*, London: Jessica Kingsley, pp 52–66.

Markova, I. (2003) 'Constitution of the self: intersubjectivity and dialogicality', *Culture and Psychology*, vol 9, no 3, pp 249–59.

Markova, I., Linell, P., Grossen, M. and Orvig, A. (2007) '*Dialogue in focus groups: Exploring socially shared knowledge*, London: Equinox.

Mockler, N. (2007) 'Ethics in practitioner research', in A. Campbell and S. Groundwater-Smith (eds) *An ethical approach to practitioner research*, Abingdon: Routledge, pp 88–98.

Nijhof, A., Wilderom, C. and Oost, M. (2012) 'Professional and institutional morality: building ethics programmes on the dual loyalty of academic professionals', *Ethics and Education*, vol 7, no 1, pp 91–109.

Petterson, T. (2011) 'The ethics of care: normative structures and empirical implications', *Health Care Analysis*, vol 19, pp 51–64.

Pring, R. (2002) 'The virtues and vices of an educational researcher', in M. McNamee and D. Bridges (eds) *The ethics of educational research*, Oxford: Blackwell, pp 111–27.

Rudnick, A. (2001) 'A meta-ethical critique of care ethics', *Theoretical Medicine*, vol 22, pp 505–17.

Rydderch, G. and Gameson, J. (2010) 'Constructing a flexible model of integrated professional practice: Part 3 – The model in practice', *Educational Psychology in Practice*, vol 26, no 2, pp 123–49.

Salgado, J. and Clegg, J.W. (2011) 'Dialogism and the psyche: Bakhtin and contemporary psychology', *Culture and Psychology*, vol 17, no 4, pp 421–40.

Scottish Executive (2002) *Review of provision of educational psychology services in Scotland*, Edinburgh: Scottish Executive.

Scottish Government (2008) *Getting it right for every child*, Edinburgh: Scottish Government.

Sherif, B. (2001) 'The ambiguities of boundaries in the fieldwork experience: establishing rapport and negotiating insider-outsider status', *Qualitative Inquiry*, vol 7, pp 436–47.

Shotter, J. (1993) 'Psychology and citizenship: identity and belonging', in B.S. Turner (ed) *Citizenship and social theory*, London: Sage, pp 115–38.

Somers, M.J. (2001) 'Ethical codes of conduct and organisational context: a study of the relationship between codes of conduct, employee behaviour and organisational values', *Journal of Business Ethics*, vol 30, no 2, pp 185–95.

van der Riet, M. (2008) 'Participatory research and the philosophy of the social sciences: beyond the moral imperative', *Qualitative Enquiry*, vol 14, pp 546–64.

Verhezen, P. (2010) 'Giving voice in a culture of silence: from a culture of compliance to a culture of integrity', *Journal of Business Ethics*, vol 96, no 2, pp 187–206.

Verkerk, M.J., Leede, J. and Nijhof, A.H.J. (2001) 'From responsible management to responsible organisations: the democratic principle for managing organizational ethics', *Business and Society Review*, vol 106, no 4, pp 353–379.

Warmington, P., Daniels, H., Edwards, A., Brown, S., Leadbetter, J., Martin, M. and Middleton, D. (2004) *Interagency collaboration: a review of the literature*, Bath: Learning in and for Interagency Working Project.

Weaver, G. (2006) 'Virtue in organizations: moral identity as a foundation for moral agency', *Organization Studies*, vol 27, no 3, pp 341–368.

Wegerif, R. (2011) 'Towards a dialogic theory of how children learn to think', *Thinking Skills and Creativity*, vol 6, no 3, pp 179–90.

Whittier, N.C., Williams, S., and Dewett, T.C. (2006) 'Evaluating ethical decision-making models: a review and application', *Society and Business Review*, vol 1, no 3, pp 235–47.

THREE

The organisational context of professional and interprofessional ethics

Bridget Hanna

The management of services is changing and staff are increasingly being asked to work 'interprofessionally' (Tope and Thomas, 2007; Cameron et al, 2009) and to come together in new configurations to deliver services in new ways (Baxter and Brumfitt, 2008). The term '**interprofessional** working' is often used when different professionals work together, and is also termed interprofessional practice (World Health Organization (WHO), 2010; Interprofessional Education Collaborative Expert Panel, 2011). Interprofessional working affects all organisational members and the very structures of the organisations that support them. As a result, leaders and managers in organisations are required to manage individuals with diverse professional affiliations and skills. This chapter presents a case study to highlight the potential tensions within interprofessional organisations when the professionals refer to their profession's code of ethics, which might be different from those of others. From the author's experience, despite increasing **regulation** in the workplace, interprofessional working is largely considered solely in relation to professionals delivering care, rather than the organisations they work within and across. Therefore, to confine an analysis of ethical behaviour to those staff formally recognised as professionals (or those working in teams) that deliver care ignores many of the organisational factors that underpin successful interprofessional working.

This chapter highlights the centrality of the organisational context in discussions of professional and interprofessional ethics, with some reference to personal ethics (see Figure 1.1). When considering ethics in the context of organisations, literature suggests that several ethical theories have been used to understand it. For example, Verbos et al (2007) have summarised the organisational theories based on normative and deontological ethical theories, such as stockholder theory, **stakeholder** theory and post-conventional corporate moral responsibility. The author has on purpose not used an ethical theory as the basis of this chapter, as ethics within an organisation is usually guided by the ethics of the leaders and staff in that organisation, and also because of the need to make this chapter relevant to the other chapters of this book, with their various ethical theories.

Interprofessional teams

Organisations have an important role to play in care delivered by interprofessional teams (Henneman et al, 1995; Zwarenstein and Bryant, 2000; McCallin, 2001; Melia, 2001; D'Amour et al, 2005). What makes a set of individuals a group or a team? There are certainly lots of designated teams in the workplace that do not work as teams. Salas et al (2009) suggest that examining teams through a process model is helpful. Salas and colleagues highlight that three developmental coordination mechanisms are important: shared mental models, closed loop communication and mutual trust. In organisations, the development of these three elements could be helpful for wider interprofessional working and perhaps, in turn, notions of ethics in interprofessional teams. Other important elements seem to be developing shared goals (Hackman, 2002), shared knowledge and respect (Bamber et al, 2009). In a concept analysis of **interdisciplinary** collaboration (Petri, 2010), support, both organisational and administrative, was also identified as key. This support could be in the form of resources, rewards, incentives (Baggs et al, 2004), time and scheduling (Smith et al, 2010). The significance of a supportive work group design has also been highlighted (Sicotte et al, 2002). The key point is that organisations can do much to support interprofessional working in a team structure.

Similarly, organisations have a responsibility to ensure that the management structure is set up to work interprofessionally. This is because managers have a key role in supporting wider collaboration. As organisations rarely specify the conditions around collaboration (Willumsen, 2008, Willumsen et al 2012), managers need to facilitate these both internally and externally (Hunter, 2004; Huxham and Vangen, 2005; Axelsson and Axelsson, 2006). Clearly, this implicates all levels of the organisation and all its organisational members in interprofessional working, and to really change the wider **organisational culture** it could be that all organisational members need to examine (and perhaps change) the way they relate to one another ethically and interprofessionally (Suchman et al, 2011).

Organisational culture

Organisational culture consists of the values, attitudes and history that underpin what is seen as ethical behavior within organisations. Schein (1992) defines organisational culture as: 'the set of shared, taken-for-granted implicit assumptions that members of an organisation hold and that determines how they perceive, think about and react to their various environments' (p 12).

Culture is the sum total of the organisation historically, up to and including present operations, whereas climate is more localised and short term. Ethics, as a consideration, is simply not present in much of organisational life. Worse still, the ethical culture may support poor behaviour. Making ethics part of the organisational conversation can contribute to a culture in which discussion can take place, and potentially support organisations in avoiding such situations.

Forsgarde et al (2000) examined the use of ethical discussion groups as an intervention to improve the culture of interprofessional work in Sweden. In this intervention, discussion groups offered a way to develop the ethical conversation. Interestingly this organisation's positive attitude to interprofessional working and participation in research around the development of ethical conversations suggests organisational engagement. It may be that the organisations that most need this type of ethical development are the least likely to engage in research or development around the concept. This suggests that interest in and research around interprofessional working may also offer a route for developing organisational ethical culture.

Management of ethics in organisations

Organisations are characterised by differences in ethical conceptions. The case study in Box 3.1 highlights the tensions of working in an organisation where the professionals have different professional codes of ethics, with no defined organisational view on what is ethical.

Box 3.1

Case study: an occupational psychologist's professional dilemma in an interprofessional context

A medium-sized organisation was interested in developing its leadership capabilities and appointed an occupational psychologist (OP) to design and run a leadership development centre. The managers took part enthusiastically, as they knew this could help them develop their careers. Some of the development involved thinking about their role in the organisation and reflecting on things that hadn't gone as well as hoped. Some of the participants were worried about this element and the OP and the Human Resources (HR) Director assured them that this exercise was designed solely to help with their development. The development centre was a great success. Two years later, however, the economic environment had changed and the organisation had to reduce its management staffing levels. The OP was asked to use the information provided by the managers to help select staff for retention and redundancy. The OP refused, on the basis that the managers had only participated in the development centre on the basis of confidentiality of their results. The HR Director who had originally appointed the OP had left and the newly appointed Director maintained that the organisation owned the results of the development centre, that it would be used to develop some of the managers and therefore they were justified in both having and using the outcomes. The OP was informed that they would no longer get any work from the organisation and that the HR Director would not give any future recommendations unless they gave the information back. When the OP refused on the basis of their requirement to adhere to their professional ethical framework, the company threatened legal action on the basis of theft of organisational information. Each party felt the other was acting unethically. The HR Director argued that the organisation was legitimately seeking to use information that it owned, as it would retain and develop the managers it felt best suited the business. The OP argued that the information was provided (as agreed) for specific purposes and that to use it elsewhere violated the agreement that the organisation had made with both the OP and its managers. Finally the organisation decided that it would not issue legal action and the two parties agreed not to work together.

When structures don't exist or are in conflict, professionals must then fall back on their professional practice, their professional training and the values that underpin their profession as criteria for judgement. Ethics as professional practice, therefore, emerges as more situated and subjective. Accountability at this level becomes more localised as professionals hold themselves to account. Professional colleagues and organisations can then hold professionals to account based on a utilitarian view of the impact of outcomes on themselves.

Further, people can behave differently at work (Elm and Nichols, 1993) and in their personal lives (Trevino, 1986; Weber, 1990; Hauptman and Hill, 1991), and be subject to multiple forms of ethical surveillance. Interestingly, some managers believe that ethics are not even relevant at work (Bartlett and Preston, 2000). Organisations act to manage this diversity through different strategies. Often organisations devolve some responsibility for ethical behaviour by recruiting only accredited individuals/professionals or by using organisational criteria (which may or may not include specific reference to ethics). Once hired, professionals can be managed through professional **regulatory** bodies or through internal performance management frameworks or both. Although for some organisational members – particularly those not termed 'professionals' – ethical behaviour can be managed only through a yearly appraisal process or, in the absence of even this strategy, through organisational policies.

Similarly, **competency frameworks** are also used to manage staff. The competency frameworks are themselves an indicator of the ethical culture of the organisations that use them. They indicate what organisations purport to value and support. Therefore, when organisations measure competencies, their intent is to drive behaviour in staff. This has important ramifications for behaviour and practice.

Competency frameworks

Competency frameworks define what is important in our future practice. If they are effective, they influence the way work is done. Therefore, it is important to understand their development. There are three key approaches: organisations can create their own frameworks, buy in consultants to produce a bespoke framework or purchase a standardised package. One reason why organisations use competencies, is that they are seen as acceptable and 'reasonable in community settings and have mutual agreement' (Young et al, 2000, p 322). Competencies can be used in recruitment, recognition and **accreditation**, appraisals, **supervision** and training (Pearson et al, 2002). Ethics in competency frameworks are generally conceptualised as a facet of individual performance. However, successful achievement of an ethical competency usually means an absence of any negative ethical information, rather than providing evidence of positive ethical behaviour. The issue here is that an ethical competency does not easily translate into every situation. For this reason, producing evidence that you have behaved ethically can be problematic and the way that **standards** are met can be ethically disputed.

Interpretation and **ethical judgements** are central to the process of behaving ethically (Wilhelmsson et al, 2012). In order to understand how to interpret standards, there is a need to look at who makes the judgements, what judgements have been made in the past and the results of those judgements. This is not dissimilar to the approach to law in the UK. However, ethics does not stand still and often what is considered ethical behaviour changes over time (Lindsay, 2009). Organisations and regulatory bodies use competencies because they focus directly on behaviour that is more amenable to measurement, but a key weakness of this approach is that it is usually evidenced by a lack of unethical behaviour.

Measures, however, are far from neutral. Whatever the measurable outcomes, the process of developing competencies is at heart a social one. They are often based on what (or who) is valued at a given time and on who is doing the creating. Although some codes of ethics make their theoretical basis clear (for example, see Chapter Two about the BPS code of ethics), most ethical frameworks and competencies rarely make their theoretical or historical basis clear. It is this ability to propagate models of practice (Kendall et al, 2011) that reveals information about the power structures that generated them. From the author's professional experience, the information on who had the power to define the 'agreed' model of practice is often obscured due to the collaborative nature of framework development and lack of transparency of individual accountability. If there are not clear processes (rather than policies) for resolving the ethical issue, the responsibility falls to the individual to make an ethical decision about what to do (see whistleblowing, below). In a complaint, the organisation's role is obscured by the method of assessment.

Interprofessional competencies

Interprofessional competencies (including interprofessional ethics) are widely hailed as important in delivering and improving modern healthcare (WHO, 2006) as well as in many other areas of care delivery. Ethics and working with others appears in almost all professional frameworks (for example, gerontological nursing and occupational therapy, see Chapter Sixteen). Sometimes these appear as standalone items, but they are often encapsulated as part of a wider definition of professional practice. The extent to which notions of interprofessional working are present evidences the importance placed on them by those who developed the framework.

As interprofessional working increases, new interprofessional competencies are emerging, including ethics that are truly cross professional. This is because a degree of convergence in content can be found in some disciplines, with many domains being similar across professional groupings with similar care contexts (Interprofessional Education Collaborative Expert Panel, 2011). To the extent that they do converge, similar conceptions of ethics seem to be supported within similar contexts. The increase in the measurement of such interprofessional competencies seems set to continue, although the evidence of their success in performance seems empirically limited.

Regulation, ethical elements of competency-based frameworks and **ethical codes** emerge from an empiricist view of ethics as independent of human action. Organisations hold professionals individually to account through judgements against these structures. Often the definition of what makes a field of practice a profession is that individuals are held to account through such structures (Cruess et al, 2004). This chapter argues that structures are necessarily only a starting point for the accountability of professionals and that dialogue around ethics should be supported in organisations to ensure the accountability of all involved in interprofessional working.

Ethical organisations

Verbos et al (2007), who contest that business ethics literature has focused on critical incidents and unethical behaviour, presented a 'living code of ethics' model in which they emphasised three aspects that interact to create an ethical organisation: authentic leadership, organisational processes and organisational culture. This implies that, to function ethically, organisations are reliant on ethical leadership, ethical staff, and organisational structures and systems.

Ethical leadership

The concept of ethical and authentic leadership is highly relevant to person-centred professions. Within the power dynamics of an organisation, an authentic leader is one who models ethical behaviour (see teachers in Chapter Five, for instance); whose ethical values and actions are transparent; who is consistent in decision making; and who involves others in ethical decision making, thus acknowledging the complexity of ethical decision making. As will be seen in later chapters, this authentic leadership is what helps members of an organisation in identifying with the organisational ethical identity and makes them willing to have an open ethical dialogue; with an understanding that lack of it leads to professionals feeling uncomfortable with the decision (see, for example, Chapters Seven and Eight).

It is important to remember, however, that the leaders are influenced by their own value base, life experiences, religion, culture and so on, like any other individual within the organisation (see Figure 1.1). Also, in an organisational set-up where they are managing staff from other disciplines with different professional codes, there might be tensions between their view of an ethical decision and those of the staff whom they lead and manage. Therefore, in such situations an ethical leader would manage ethical behaviour through on-going dialogue about organisational ethics and professional codes, supporting staff who are experiencing ethical dilemma, engaging in ethical dialogue about day-to-day issues and, most importantly, modelling ethical behaviour.

Ethical staff

For some professionals, the first ethical conversation they have at work only happens on disagreement with an enactment of a policy (such as a gift or honesty policy) or a standard encompassed in competency frameworks. The consideration of ethics has usually been part of the registration process, but this validation of professional registration may similarly be the first and last ethical conversation they have with their employing organisation. If there is no ethical framework on which to draw within an organisation, individuals must necessarily base their actions and decisions on their own personal or professional ethics. Regulated professionals must adhere to their professions' ethical framework (see Chapter One). Some professions require re-validation so as to demonstrate compliance with ethical standards. Re-validation often involves completing a form, continuing professional development (CPD), making a health declaration or even just signing a self-declaration of compliance. Self-surveillance is then the cornerstone of regulated professional ethical behaviour. A key weakness with this approach is that individuals may not be aware of issues, may ignore them or, in the case of health, be aware of the consequences of disclosure. Only if a complaint is made does the regulator step in. There may, however, be spot checks by employers of employee registration. Regulators may inform employers of registration status and may call a percentage of professionals for audit.

Unregulated professionals can only be guided by their profession's concepts of ethics within the workplace. For these organisational members, local conditions are critical in decisions about how to act. With no conceptions of ethics at an organisational level, the result is a proliferation of policies as organisations seek to regulate each behaviour separately. The problem with these approaches is the lack of on-going ethical conversations to guide future behaviour proactively. If no process for debating, understanding or resolving ethical dilemmas exists within organisations, conflict may occur. Conflicts around ethics may be especially difficult between professions where conceptions of ethics may differ. The competency frameworks used by professionals in their work are therefore critical in discussing on-going ethical behaviour at work.

Ethical professionals tend to engage in ethical dialogue with their colleagues when there are such clashes. Another way of managing ethical behaviour in an organisation is through whistleblowing. Whistleblowing is an important concept, as it lies at the intersection between professional and interprofessional ethics and the organisation. This is because professionals can manifest ethical aims through different forms of behaviour. Even when the aims of professional ethical standards or competencies are similar, what those aims mean in professional practice may be very different.

Whistleblowing 'refers to a warning issued by a member or former member of an organisation to the public about a serious wrongdoing or danger created or concealed with the organisation' (Dougherty, 1995, p 2552). Miceli and Near (1985) define whistleblowing as: 'the disclosure by organisation members (former or current) of illegal, immoral or illegitimate practices under the control of their employers, to persons or organisations that may be able to effect action' (p 4). Usually the aim is to stop the current behaviour and to prevent it in the future.

There is a common pattern of escalation with internal boundary disclosure, usually preceding external boundary disclosure. Disclosing internally allows the individual to demonstrate loyalty to the organisation and gives ethical justification for subsequent external disclosure (Dworkin and Bacus, 1998). It also gives the organisation an opportunity to act. Internal whistleblowing can take place hierarchically (up through the organisation), through peers or via professional groupings. Consequences for all parties increase as whistleblowing crosses organisational boundaries into the external environment. As the legal, social and financial consequences of whistleblowing can be high, organisations are putting in place whistleblowing policies.

Whistleblowing may represent a 'clash of values' at the individual, professional and organisational level in interprofessional working. Whistleblowing can be thought of as an attempt by an individual to locate their own complex ethics within the organisation milieu and to resolve the dissonance experienced from the event that prompted it. However, seen positively, internal disclosure offers real potential for organisational development and strategic advantage (Kaptein, 2011). The organisation could act to develop an ethical conversation that encompasses the whistleblower's concerns. However, more often there is a mobilisation to 'silence' the whistleblower. If internal disclosure does not develop into an ethical conversation, or if that conversation subsequently collapses, then external disclosure usually follows.

External disclosure can cause reputational damage, and organisations often mobilise to avoid this. External disclosure usually ruins the relationship between the employer and employee, due to perceptions of trust violation between them, or because the values of those involved are in serious conflict. Most whistleblowers are dismissed, with all the legal implications this act brings. If they are not dismissed, generally the work environment is such that the individual leaves anyway. Retaliatory actions can abound (Keil et al, 2010).

Whistleblowing may be linked to the importance of ethics to the individual or the role they occupy. The importance of ethics to the individual can be related both to their organisational role and to the perceived distance between them and client contact or service delivery (Figure 3.1). The salience of ethics to the individual can also be examined spatially by its importance to the person's job performance. These two dimensions, distance to client and role salience can be represented spatially (Figure 3.1). For some professions, although regulation is not required for job performance, there may be a voluntary framework, for example human resources professionals may sign up to the Chartered Institute of Personnel and Development framework.

Figure 3.1: Ethical conceptual distance

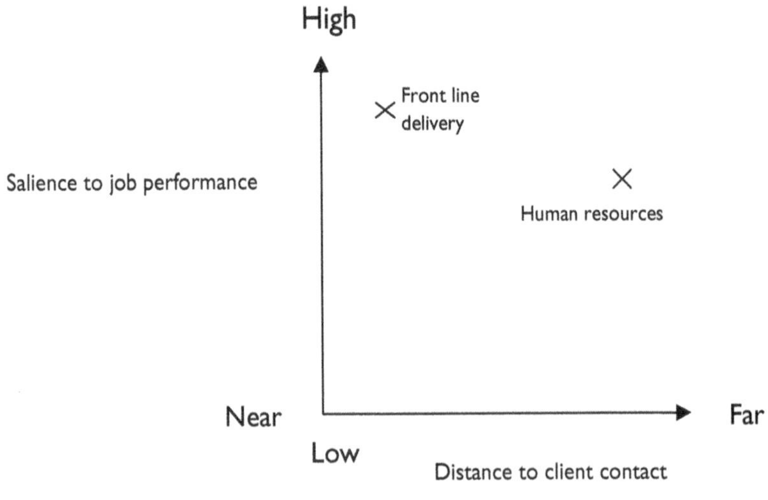

However, this is voluntary and some employees may feel that there are no ethical dimensions to their work.

The discourses around ethics within organisations are often aimed at those individuals who occupy organisational spaces that are high in importance to role or distance to client. The salience of ethics can be thought of as varying across two key dimensions: distance to client and salience to performance (Figure 3.1).

If a job role does not involve clients and the job holder does not recognise the relevance of ethics to their performance, then ethics is likely to be ignored by both the employee and the organisation. It is within and between all of these interprofessional relationships that the ethical conversation can collapse as opportunities for disagreement and misinterpretation within different values systems are multiplied (Fletcher et al, 1998). There is evidence that the organisational milieu plays an even larger role in whistleblowing than does the individual (Rothwell and Baldwin, 2007). Both the individual and the organisation suffer when ethical conversations decay. Both the individual and the organisation bear some of the consequences for whistleblowing, but the organisation contorts its own potential. As early as 1978, Argyris and Schön highlighted that keeping quiet can have negative effects on organisational learning and development. Rather than thinking about whistleblowing negatively, it could even be reconceptualised as a positive tool for organisational development (Loyens, 2012).

Organisational structures and systems

The author's reading of the evidence suggests that promoting interprofessional ethical development is important for all parties involved. One way to do this is through surfacing the implicit and explicit ethical values held by individuals (either personal or developed through professional training), and then prioritising ethical conversations across the organisation to support the development of shared perceptions around ethical behaviour and judgements. Supporting these processes and developing ethical conversations is the organisation's responsibility, as only the organisation operates at a structural level. Organisations should therefore look at how they support interprofessionality and, specifically, interprofessional ethics.

However, from the author's experience, in many organisations employees are directed to policies (often held in an online 'intranet') and asked to confirm reading and understanding as evidence of knowledge of the required ethical standards. Often policies in organisations are atheoretical. Those writing policies may have limited knowledge of the rich and diverse nature of ethics and are merely seeking to direct behaviour. Policies are characterised by an absence of an author, as they are seen as belonging to the organisation. They can be prompted through the occurrence of an unethical event for which guidance is not available. For some organisations, this can lead to a plethora of policies. As organisations cannot envisage every possible future scenario, the number of policies an organisation could have is potentially unlimited.

In the absence of any surfaced or agreed ethical values at an organisational level, individuals without professional frameworks must fall back on their own value base or draw from those in use in the culture surrounding them. This can lead to a clash between different individuals within the same organisation, depending on whether or not they have explicit professional frameworks and the extent to which those frameworks are in agreement.

The organisation and its policies (such as whistleblowing) can be thought of structurally. Imagine, for example, the devolvement of financial decisions. Time taken by overly robust financial signatories can impede efficiency but strengthen financial accountability. It is the outcome of designated process itself that reveals the operation of power. Whenever rhetoric is deployed by organisations in policies around interprofessional working, it is important to ask what their role is in doing so.

Conversations around ethics in organisations are key resources that individuals draw on when making ethical decisions. Each instance of ethical collapse is important, as these instances can act multiplicatively to form the basis of the organisation's future culture (see also Chapter Two). Organisations aiming to be ethical organisations have clear and transparent codes of ethics and return to them from time to time in discussion with all staff in the organisation, ensure there is a transparent decision making process, set up an ethics committee, provide on-going ethics training to staff and ensure that the whistleblowing mechanisms are clear.

Conclusion

One model that goes some way to explaining the interactions between the individual, their profession and the employing organisation is the attraction, selection, attrition model (Schneider, 1987). This theory suggests that individuals are attracted to professions and organisations with similar values to their own and that organisations, through selection mechanisms, promote the appointment of particular types. The concept of 'fit' can be thought of as underpinning organisational attrition. If either side of the employment contract perceives a poor fit, the individual is likely to exit the organisation either through internal dissonance or through organisational pressure (such as experienced in whistleblowing). There are a couple of important issues to highlight here. Firstly, in difficult economic times or certain geographic locations, individuals may not be able to 'choose' to apply only to organisations that they feel they would work well in. Secondly, organisations may promote themselves in particular ways that are inconsistent. If, when individuals join, there is a difference between the organisation's public face and the internal experience, then dissonance can be felt by all parties. Interested readers are directed to Kristof-Brown and Billsberry (2013) for a wide exploration of the concept of fit.

To end on a positive note, there is evidence that participating in interprofessional teams can be a professionally rewarding experience (see also Chapter Nine). Growth, it appears, can emerge from the enhanced learning and understanding the individual has gained from their efforts to work in the complex and challenging arena of working interprofessionally (DiPalma, 2004). If organisations want to develop, then learning from organisational events such as whistleblowing can help. Whistleblowing has much to teach organisations about the development of their conversations about ethics. Further, for an organisation to support an ethical culture, it is important that the three pillars – the ethical leader, ethical staff, and organisational systems and structures – are all working towards ethical conversations that could help the organisation and its members to develop wider and more integrated models of ethics across an interprofessional workforce.

References

Argyris, C. and Schön, D. (1978) *Organizational learning: A theory of action perspective*, Reading, MA: Addison-Wesley.

Axelsson, R. and Axelsson, S.B. (2006) 'Integration and collaboration in public health – a conceptual framework', *International Journal of Health Planning Management*, vol 21, no 1, pp 75–88.

Baggs, J.G., Norton, M.H. and Schmitt, C.R. (2004) 'The dying patient in the ICU: role of the interdisciplinary team', *Critical Care Clinics*, vol 20, no 3, pp 525–40.

Bamber, G., Gittell, J.T., Kochan, A. and von Nordenflycht, A. (2009) *Up in the air: How the airlines can improve performance by engaging their employees*, Ithaca, NY: Cornell University Press.

Bartlett, A. and Preston, D. (2000) 'Can business be ethical?', *Journal of Business Ethics*, vol 23, pp 199–209.

Baxter, S.K. and Brumfitt, S.M. (2008) 'Professional differences in interprofessional working', *Journal of Interprofessional Care*, vol 22, no 3, pp 239–51.

Cameron, C., Moss, P., Owen, C., Petrie, P., Potts, P., Simon, A. and Wigfall, V. (2009) *Working together in extended school and children's centres. A study of interprofessional activity in England and Sweden*, Sheffield: Department of Education.

Cruess, S., Johnston, S. and Cruess, R. (2004) '"Profession": a working definition for medical educators', *Teaching and Learning in Medicine: An International Journal*, vol 16, no 1, pp 74–6.

D'Amour, D., Ferrada-Videla, M., San Martin-Rodriguez, L. and Beaulieu, M.D. (2005) 'The conceptual basis for interprofessional collaboration: core concepts and theoretical frameworks', *Journal of Interprofessional Care*, vol 19, no 1, pp 116–31.

DiPalma, C. (2004) 'Power at work: navigating hierarchies, teamwork and webs', *Journal of Medical Humanities*, vol 25, pp 291-307.

Dougherty, C.J. (1995) 'Whistleblowing in health care', in W.T. Riech (ed-in-chief), *Encyclopedia of Bioethics* (rev edn), New York: Simon and Schuster Macmillan.

Dworkin, T.M. and Bacus, M.S. (1998) 'Internal vs external whistle blowers: comparison of whistle blowing processes', *Journal of Business Ethics*, vol 17, pp 1281–98.

Elm, D. and Nichols, M.L. (1993) 'An investigation of the moral reasoning of managers', *Journal of Business Ethics*, vol 12, pp 817–33.

Fletcher, J.J., Sorrell, J.M. and Silva, M.C. (1998) 'Whistleblowing as a failure of organizational ethics', *The Online Journal of Issues in Nursing*, vol 3, no 3, www.ispub.com/journal/the-internet-journal-of-law-healthcare-and-ethics/volume-6-number-1/whistle-blowing-in-healthcare-an-organizational-failure-in-ethics-and-leadership.html#sthash.6NAHnZ0L.dpuf.

Forsgarde, M., Westmas, B. and Nygren, L. (2000) 'Ethical discussion groups as an intervention to improve the climate in interprofessional work with the elderly and disabled', *Journal of Interprofessional Care*, vol 14, no 4 , pp 351–61.

Hackman, J.R. (2002) *Leading teams: Setting the stage for great performance*, Cambridge, MA: Harvard Business School Press.

Hauptman, R. and Hill, F. (1991) 'Deride, abide or dissent: on the ethics of professional conduct', *Journal of Business Ethics*, vol 10, pp 37–44.

Henneman, E.A., Lee, J.L. and Cohen, J.I. (1995) 'Collaboration: a concept analysis', *Journal of Advanced Nursing*, vol 21, no 1, pp 103–9.

Hunter, D. (2004) 'A structural perspective on health care reform', *Journal of Health Services Research & Policy*, vol 9, no 1, pp 52–3.

Huxham, C. and Vangen, D. (2005) *Managing to collaborate: The theory and practice of collaborative advantage*, London: Routledge.

Interprofessional Education Collaborative Expert Panel (2011) *Core competencies for interprofessional collaborative practice: Report of an expert panel*, Washington, DC: Interprofessional Education Collaborative.

Kaptein, M. (2011) 'From inaction to external whistleblowing: the influence of the ethical culture of organizations on employee responses', *Journal of Business Ethics*, vol 98, pp 513–30.

Keil, M., Tjwana, A., Sainsbury, R. and Sneha, S. (2010) 'Towards a theory of whistleblowing intentions: a benefit-to-costs differential perspective', *Decision Sciences*, vol 41, no 4, pp 787–812.

Kendall, E., Muenchberger, H., Catalano, T., Amsters, D., Doresett, P. and Cox, R. (2011) 'Developing core interprofessional competencies for community rehabilitation practitioners: findings from an Australian study', *Journal of Interprofessional Care*, vol 25, pp 145–51.

Kristof-Brown, A.L. and Billsberry, J. (eds) (2013) *Organizational fit: Key issues and new directions*, New York: Wiley-Blackwell.

Lindsay, G. (2009) 'Professional ethics in psychology', *Papeles del Psicólogo*, vol 30, no 3, pp 184–94.

Loyens, K. (2012) 'Towards a custom-made whistleblowing policy: using grid-group cultural theory to match policy measures to different styles of peer reporting', *Journal of Business Ethics*, http://rd.springer.com/article/10.1007/s10551-012-1344-0# doi: 10.1007/s10551-012-1344-0.

McCallin, A. (2001) 'Interprofessional practice: learning how to collaborate', *Contemporary Nurse*, vol 20, pp 128–37.

Melia, K.M. (2001) 'Ethical issues and the importance of consensus for the intensive care team', *Social Science and Medicine*, vol 53, pp 707–19.

Miceli, M.P. and Near, J.P. (1985) 'Characteristics of organizational climate and perceived wrongdoing associated with whistle-blowing decisions', *Personnel Psychology*, vol 38, pp 525–44.

Pearson, A., Fitzgerald, M., Walsh, K. and Borbasi, S. (2002) 'Continuing competence and the regulation of nursing practice', *Journal of Nursing Management*', vol 10, pp 357–64.

Petri, L. (2010) 'Concept analysis of interdisciplinary collaboration', *Nursing Forum*, vol 45, pp 73–82.

Rothwell, G.R. and Baldwin, J.N. (2007) 'Whistle-blowing and the code of silence in police agencies', *Crime and Delinquency*, vol 53, no 4, pp 605–32.

Salas, E., Rosen, M.A., Burke, C.S. and Goodwin, G.F. (2009) 'The wisdom of collectives in organizations: an update of competencies', in E. Salas, G.F. Goodwin and C.S. Burke, *Team effectiveness in complex organizations: Cross-disciplinary perspectives and approaches*, London: Routledge, pp 39–79.

Schein, E. (1992) *Organizational culture and leadership*, San Francisco: Jossey-Bass.

Schneider, B. (1987) 'The people make the place', *Personnel Psychology*, vol 30, no 3, pp 437–53.

Sicotte, C., D'Amour, D. and Moreualt, M. (2002) 'Interdisciplinary collaboration within Quebec community health care centres', *Social Science & Medicine*, vol 55, pp 991–1003.

Smith, K., Lavoei-Tremblay, M., Richer, M.C. and Lanctot, S. (2010) 'Exploring nurses' perceptions of organizational factors of collaborative relationships', *The Health Care Manager*, vol 29, no 3, pp 271–8.

Suchman, A.L., Sluyter, D.J. and Williamson, P.R. (eds) (2011) *Leading change in healthcare*, London: Radcliffe Publishing.

Tope, R. and Thomas, E. (2007) *Health and social care policy and the interprofessional agenda: Creating an interprofessional workforce*, www.caipe.org.uk/silo/files/cipw-policy.pdf.

Trevino, L. (1986) 'Ethical decision making in organisations: a person–situation interactionist model', *Academy of Management Review*, vol 11, no 3, pp 601–17.

Verbos, A.K., Gerard, J.A., Forshey, P.R., Harding, C.S. and Miller, J.S. (2007) 'The positive ethical organization: enacting a living code of ethics and ethical organizational identity', *Journal of Business Ethics*, vol 76, pp 17–33.

Weber, J. (1990) 'Managers' moral reasoning: assessing their responses to three moral dilemmas', *Human Relations*, vol 43, pp 687–702.

Wilhelmsson, M., Pelling, S., Uhline, L., Dahlgren, L.O., Faresjo, T. and Forslund, K. (2012) 'How to think about interprofessional competence: a metacognitive model', *Journal of Interprofessional Care*, vol 26, pp 85–91.

Willumsen, E. (2008) 'Interprofessional collaboration – a matter of differentiation and integration? Theoretical reflections based in the context of Norwegian childcare', *Journal of Interprofessional Care*, vol 22, no 4, pp 352–63.

Willumsen, E. Ahgren, B. and Odegard, A. (2012) 'A conceptual framework for assessing interorganizational integration and interprofessional collaboration', *Journal of Interprofessional Care*, vol 26, pp 198–204.

World Health Organization (WHO) (2006) *Working together for health, Report 2006, The 59th World Health Assembly* (WHA.59.23), Geneva: World Health Organization.

World Health Organization (WHO) (2010) *Framework for action on interprofessional education and collaborative practice*, Geneva: World Health Organization.

Young, A., Forquer, S., Tran, A., Starzynski, M. and Shatkin, J. (2000) 'Identifying clinical competencies that support rehabilitation and empowerment in individuals with severe mental illness', *The Journal of Behavioural Health Services and Research*, vol 27, no 3, pp 321–33.

Zwarenstein, M. and Bryant, W. (2000) 'Interventions to promote collaboration between nurses and doctors' (Review), *The Cochrane Library*, no 2, pp 1–12.

FOUR

The policy context: user involvement – a case study in health and community settings

Lesley Greenaway and Bridget Roberts

Introduction

Increasingly, professionals find themselves operating in a policy context where governments seek greater levels of community involvement and participation. For example, a **Scottish Government** consultation on a proposed Empowerment and Community Renewal Bill (Scottish Government, 2012) aims to 'ensure communities are able to have a greater role in determining how their local public services are delivered' (p 5). In Australia, partnership with health **service users** in planning, designing and evaluating healthcare is one of ten National Safety and Quality Health Service Standards (Australian Commission on Safety and Quality in Health Care, 2011).

The authors welcome this focus, but it does cause them to think about what they understand community involvement to mean, and to consider whether this matches the government view. And, for that matter, do the authors, with different professional cultures, share common understandings and beliefs? This is especially relevant where the values and ethics of involvement are a benchmark for professional practice. The Community Learning and Development (CLD) Standards Council in Scotland (2011), for example, describes a commitment to education as a prerequisite for democracy and citizenship, characterised by 'actively engaging those who are excluded from participation in key social processes that shape their lives' (p 18). In Australia, guidelines for the ethical conduct of evaluations (Australasian Evaluation Society, 2006) emphasise the involvement of all **stakeholders** and the need to take account of social differences and inequalities. Research and evaluation in health is guided by a national statement on participation (National Health and Medical Research Council and Consumers' Health Forum of Australia, 2004), which advocates a range of strategies to ensure that participation is embedded in policies and procedures and is adequately funded. This means that the long process of changing structures and attitudes is given enough time and commitment, and the crucial support from senior leadership.

Different types and levels of involvement exist, ranging from information sharing and consultation through collaboration to consumer control, in a 'ladder of participation' that implies increasing consumer empowerment (Boote et al, 2002). Arnstein's (1969) model of participation, still influential with practitioners and policy makers, emphasises that empowerment, and hence true participation, is achieved only through partnership and delegation. Strategies on the lower rungs of the ladder are described as passive involvement. This invites the question: who decides and controls the level of participation? This is particularly relevant where government policy, as previously described, aims to achieve higher levels of active involvement by individuals and communities. These seemingly contradictory '**top-down**' views of achieving social change can also hide problems with empowerment when actions which espouse empowerment have the effect of disempowering. For example, promises or suggestions of influence and change may lead to frustration when expectations are raised of improved services (Titterton and Smart, 2008); and how people are involved may lead to tokenism rather than authentic participation (Arnstein, 1969). There are ethical tensions for practitioners when their personal or professional moral code is tested by government policy and its multiple meanings and priorities. This issue of 'authentic involvement' is perhaps illustrative of Stajkovic and Luthans' (1997) (cited in Miner and Petocz, 2003) descriptive model of ethical decision making, where 'moral deliberation and behaviour' (Miner and Petocz, 2003, p 14) are influenced at three levels: the personal level, the organisational level and the institutional level. In this case, the institutional is reflected through government policy and priorities.

The increased attention to individual and community participation in government health and community initiatives raises a number of questions for professional practice:

- What is authentic involvement or participation?
- What ethical tensions and dilemmas does it raise?
- What can guide and support professional decision making?

In this chapter, the authors will explore these questions and challenges through examples from their professional experience and with reference to a range of relevant literature. Their proposition is a positive one that suggests that professionals, in any field, can benefit from sharing a deeper awareness of the implications for greater involvement and should be mindful of the likely tensions at play on the path to ethically sensitive and effective participation.

In line with the aim of Part One, this chapter considers the personal, professional and **interprofessional** dynamics experienced by the authors in differing policy contexts (see Figure 1.1). It uses the case studies of two different settings, namely health and community settings, to illustrate these dynamics. The authors identify with the ethical theories of utilitarianism as well as non-consequentialism, with virtue ethics playing a minor role.

The chapter begins by mapping the authors' professional journeys and initiating a reflexive conversation about how beliefs and principles, or moral code, have influenced their professional practice, and how this relates to wider ethical decision-making models. Then, with reference to the literature, the authors explore what might constitute authentic **user involvement**; and last, they use examples from their practice to show how ethical tensions and dilemmas manifest themselves in practical ways. An exploration of the risk of tokenistic or merely symbolic participation is followed by discussion of the dynamics of differing stakeholder agendas. The chapter concludes by suggesting some guiding principles for achieving and maintaining a balance between the personal, professional and interprofessional ethics of involvement.

Professional journeys – developing a moral code of involvement

The following story of the authors' professional journeys illustrates some of the personal and professional factors involved in ethical decision making. It is interesting to note an apparent shift from a simple model early on in the professional journey, where a particular situation raises a number of ethical issues. The authors, as practising professionals, draw on a number of reference points to triangulate decisions about the 'right' course of action. Early reference points included values and principles of outdoor learning and **experiential education** and a number of codes or rules governing, for example, risk and safety and environmental issues. As the authors changed direction into other professional settings, they transferred these founding influences, but experienced more complex ethical decision making where they encountered other environments, other settings, other professionals and other codes. It would seem that, as the professional develops and grows in confidence and experience, what emerges is an ethical decision-making model based on a developed moral philosophy that can encompass a much broader perspective.

Shared beginnings

The authors share a background in experiential education, having met and worked together on outdoor adventure-based courses focused on developing teamwork and leadership skills, whether for the young and labelled 'at risk' or for adults learning to be corporate managers. Earlier iterations of this type of education (such as Outward Bound) were dubbed 'character-building' and there remained in the skills-based, cognitive-behavioural approach a sense of developing internal moral resources (a virtue ethic, see Thiroux and Krasemann, 2009). The practice model in the authors' workplace can be summed up as 'plan–do–review–apply'. Participants were offered a series of challenging, small-group activities in the outdoors, the art room and the drama studio, as well as the experience of living together. Facilitated reviewing led to generalised learning (action points) to be taken forward into a future activity (Greenaway, 2004). Ethical issues permeate such work, such as assessing risks and benefits, paternalism and autonomy, environmental concerns, and weighing individual versus group benefits (Hunt, 1990).

Diverging professional pathways

For one of the authors, outdoor learning provided an intense education in the dynamics of ethics in practice. Taking on an outdoor adventure facilitation role with people experiencing serious mental illness, she encountered many situations where respect for a participant's decision-making rights had to be balanced with knowledge of the risks of harm to the participant or others. She had to be confident in her particular professionalism, especially when it might involve making decisions that could reasonably be challenged by another professional working with the same participants. For example, her confidence in taking a woman to a cliff top might not be matched by that woman's case manager, who was concerned about her history of attempted suicide. In that type of work, considerable effort went into talking with other professionals about how risks were assessed and managed in the outdoors, and the 'rights' philosophy that lay behind it. Mutual understanding was further aided when mental health professionals were able to take part in the outdoor experiences themselves, as fellow participants with 'their' clients.

For the other author, a different pathway led to involvement in youth work and **volunteering**, and applying the principles from outdoor learning to the indoor learning environment. This transfer of learning led to establishing new courses and programmes using a model of empowerment that built on participants' existing expertise. This introduced a new ethical challenge of creating learning environments where there was a sharing of expertise between the professional educator and the participants. The empowerment approach recognises the participant as expert and strives to establish a relationship of mutual respect and power sharing. However, this raises a question about the place of professional knowledge in relation to participants' knowledge, and can be seen as a challenge to professional identity and power.

Professional convergence

The authors' professional journeys have converged in the field of evaluation and research studies. Although they have different foci of interest (in community evaluation processes and in collaborative evaluation of health services), they encounter the ethical dilemmas and challenges that affect community involvement. In particular, can evaluation and research become a tool for enhancing participants' voices? Can authentic power-sharing relationships be established? Or is there a risk of tokenism where different agendas 'play' with the needs and priorities of participants?

The authors' **ethical practice**, or moral code, has been influenced by a number of factors during their professional journeys. Foundations of personal values and beliefs have been shaped by professional guidelines in outdoor learning and experiential education, and these early markers have been influential as they are applied in new professional settings. The authors conclude that they share a number of ethical principles that have evolved to inform their decision making in practice and that guide them when they meet contradictions or when ethical boundaries are crossed or tested. This moral map is consistent with utilitarianism (Thiroux and Krasemann, 2009), in that there is a focus on involvement as a means of achieving good outcomes, yet also an underlying sense of the rightness and wrongness of actions that fits with non-consequentialist (deontological) theories (Thiroux and Krasemann, 2009) that involvement is a human right and citizens should be involved, regardless of outcome. While their early outdoor learning experience had some roots in 'character-building' and therefore in the framework of 'virtue ethics' (Thiroux and Krasemann, 2009) and intuitive approaches to decision making, this is a minor influence. The authors' experience has reinforced a belief in:

- the potential of individuals to achieve in an environment of trust, respect and supported challenge;
- the role of and attitudes towards risk as a vehicle for mutual awareness, learning and growth;
- the rights of the individual to participate and contribute;
- the striving for equality and power-sharing relationships;
- the effective sharing of insights and decision making with other professionals as well as with the participant.

In this context, the authors take up the theme of authentic **user involvement**, and how moral codes are tested and challenged when engaging with complex practical settings and the policy context that shapes the directions of their work.

Defining authentic user involvement

At this point it is helpful to define who the candidates of 'user involvement' are and to highlight some conclusions from the literature on what might constitute authentic individual and community involvement and participation.

Key stakeholders in user involvement

The authors use a mix of terms to refer to the individuals and communities that governments and organisations wish to engage with as stakeholders. It is relevant to point out that different professions with different purposes employ different language. In health and **social services**, the term 'consumer' is often reluctantly settled on. Alternatives include **service user**, client, customer, citizen or a receiver of care (Boote et al, 2002) (See Chapter Sixteen for a similar discussion of terminology). The training and learning environment uses 'participant' or 'learner'; and the community learning and development (CLD) profession refers to its primary 'constituents' of young people, adult learners and community organisations. People representing these groups through community organisations, networks or campaigning and self-help groups (Oliver et al, cited in Boote et al, 2002) also play a role as representatives and advocates. The stakeholders of user involvement, then, are individuals, community groups and advocacy organisations. Further, how these stakeholders are labelled may or may not suggest the governing professional or personal ethic in a given situation; people identified by the term 'consumer', for example, may be fully engaged in the involvement process.

Theoretical perspectives on authentic user involvement

Freire (1972), Heron (1981) and Reason (1994) highlight some original and important indicators for authentic involvement. These are the need to establish collaborative power-sharing relationships, the need to design processes that facilitate involvement and the need to prioritise the voice of the primary constituent. The work of Freire (1972) advocates emancipatory meanings for involvement to happen. He emphasises the empowerment of individuals and communities as they become conscious of and influential in their own destiny. He refers to authentic dialogue as a process for articulating individual experience and reality, and is concerned that dialogue is achieved best when it is in collaboration and cooperation with others. This involves a process of co-creation of knowledge, learning and understanding that gives more authority to the voices of transformation. Heron (1981), through the notion of 'experiential research', provides a guiding template for designing consultation, evaluation and research projects where the 'subjects contribute not only to the content of the research that is the activity that is being researched, but also to the creative thinking that generates, manages, and draws conclusions from the research' (p 153). This collaborative approach, like Freire's, is an attempt to alter the traditional power relations between researcher and researched that emphasise the role of participants to contribute beyond a more conventional (and passive) respondent role. Reason (1994), on the theme of power, asks 'Who owns the knowledge, and thus who can define the reality?' (p 325). He is making clear that when we engage in consultation, evaluation and research, it is important to be aware of the different power relationships that influence the process and the outcomes. Wadsworth (2001) also endorses this importance of wider stakeholder involvement in evaluation as more than 'a nice democratic idea' (p 46). The evaluator and the evaluation participants become partners in a collaborative inquiry, and there is an expectation that evaluation will be useful and used as a means for influencing social change, developing skills and capacity or for improving organisational practice (Wadsworth, 2001).

The concept of collaborative power sharing has accrued varied interpretations. Current thinking on authentic user involvement focuses on empowerment for change. Titterton and Smart (2008) emphasise empowerment in terms of skills and personal development 'by giving participants a voice in improving local services' (p 61). Ghaye (2000) has described empowerment as problematic 'in that it means different things to different people' (p 67). In part, he is referring to how empowerment relates to particular individual experiences and contexts. For example, it can mean being on a management committee or being part of decision-making processes, it can mean setting up a self-help group to address a personal need, it can mean getting a job or accessing education. It is clear that empowerment, in all its interpretations, is linked to the relationship between participants and their different interests, and these relationships are most often governed by relationships between the powerful and the powerless. Ghaye (2000) and Titterton and Smart (2008) are aligned to authentic user involvement through their concern with challenging existing power relations to enable other voices to be heard. Ghaye (2000) also highlights the voice of the professional practitioner, especially in relation to fields like health and education, where services are being transformed with the explicit aim of enabling users and practitioners to become more influential in the services that affect them. There is also a subtle aspect to empowerment that needs careful consideration. The professional's role can *facilitate empowering situations*, but to *empower people* is a mistaken idea, as it suggests a more powerful person giving power to a less powerful person or, in effect, taking their power.

In the authors' professional context, these ideas about power and participation are evident in professional codes of ethics. For example, the Community Learning and Development Standards Council for Scotland (2011) emphasises the capability of constituents to assess and act on their interests, enabling them to clarify and pursue their priorities, building skills in decision making, making power relations open and clear and supporting constituents in holding accountable those with power. Guidelines for consumer participation in research (National Health and Medical Research Council and Consumers' Health Forum of Australia, 2004) highlight overlapping concepts of 'collaboration' and 'partnership': active partnership means doing research *with* rather than *for, at* or *to* consumers, and service users and researchers work in partnerships based on understanding, respect and shared commitment to conducting research that will improve health. Such statements, however, are only one step towards addressing the challenges of different ways of knowing, of unequal power and the conditions needed for authentic user involvement.

Ethical tensions and dilemmas

In this section, the authors examine hurdles that need to be understood and negotiated professionally and interprofessionally to achieve authentic involvement. Questions of tokenism and differing agendas are each considered and illustrated through a practice example.

The risk of tokenism

Achieving authentic user involvement remains a work in progress. While commissioners and funding bodies may stipulate user involvement in policy consultation and project briefs, and project leaders may have good intentions, the necessary expertise, time, funding and other resources are far from assured. If consumer involvement is required as a condition of funding, this can result in a scramble to find consumers, tokenism and little sharing of power. In the case of consumers leading research (**community researchers**), barriers to involvement include funders' expectation of particular kinds of governance and of 'gold standard' methods and types of evidence (Hanley, 2005), as well as negative attitudes towards consumers. In the initial stages of a project, human research ethics committees may not understand community researchers' philosophy or approach, and when it comes to dissemination, publication in academic journals may be hampered by a lack of consumer researchers to conduct peer reviews (Hanley, 2005).

At a pragmatic level, through their involvement, consumer or community researchers may become more deeply connected to local projects, but may be frustrated when expectations of change and action are unmet. Titterton and Smart (2008) highlight the dilemma of raising expectations: the challenges of how to continually involve community members and to generate trust within communities where there is a reluctance to take part. Indeed, community participants may find themselves sandwiched between different political agendas being pursued from above and below. In the following example, an organisation uses a community researcher approach to find meaningful ways to engage with stakeholders. Despite the efforts to empower the community researchers and to value their voices, there is an ethical question about whether it is right to raise hopes when these voices will not be heard in a wider political and policy context.

Community researchers as an approach for making local voices heard

This approach involved the recruitment, training and support of a small team of **volunteer** researchers drawn from the organisation's constituents. The project involved volunteers learning about their role and boundaries as researchers, practising interview skills and creating and piloting questions. With the support of an external evaluator, the volunteers carried out interviews with local people, community representatives and strategic partners, and came back together to reflect on their experiences. The outcome of this approach was that the organisation gathered rich stakeholder feedback, the respondents reported feeling more at ease and were more honest being interviewed by local people, and volunteers developed skills and confidence in a new role. The project created benefits for everyone concerned, but does raise a question as to whether the voice of local people could make a difference, or was there a risk of tokenism. For example, the goals of the evaluation were driven by the organisation; and the design of the evaluation was driven by the evaluator. What was the driving force for the volunteer researchers? They did report benefits from being involved, but their involvement was limited to the practical experiences of the evaluation, and this was unlikely to have a direct effect on local issues and change.

The ethical decision making in this scenario involves weighing the risk of a diluted or unmet promise of influence and voice with a range of 'good' outcomes such as the potential of individuals to achieve in an environment of trust, respect and supported challenge. This approach might achieve a 'good' outcome, but does it miss the point and fudge the more critical social goal of challenging unequal power relations? It focuses on a softer personal development approach that potentially maintains the status quo in terms of who influences what.

The clash of different agendas

Any given project may bring together stakeholders with both common and varying values and assumptions and language in which these are expressed. The tension between different agendas can be seen in many settings, but is particularly marked in government-sponsored research and evaluation concerning indigenous people, which has a long history of being seen as about the 'other' and associated with colonisation and dispossession. There is a need to build or rebuild trust, to respect the diversity of indigenous cultures, to take responsibility for learning appropriate ethical behaviour, to do work that is relevant and influential and to build in reciprocity through appreciating the contribution of participants and feeding back project findings (Markiewicz, 2012). Culturally based evaluation theories and frameworks can be worked out that are congruent with broader evaluation theory (Kerr, 2012; Price et al, 2012). Challenges arise from the frequent fact that evaluations are conducted by outsiders with limited resources and time, such that principles cannot be put into practice. The following example touches on the effectiveness of early consultations with community leaders and a preparedness by the evaluator to renegotiate a project with its government commissioners so that the community's priorities were better acknowledged.

Finding and listening to community leaders

An evaluation team working for a mainstream (that is, non-indigenous) non-governmental organisation accepted a government commission to evaluate the effectiveness of a programme that funded indigenous community alcohol- and drug-worker positions in a number of Aboriginal community-controlled health services (Berends and Roberts, 2003). Before starting work (and throughout the project), the lead evaluator consulted an elder who could offer guidance on the implications of the evaluation in the context of tense relationships between the communities, the research and evaluation field and the government. This led to preliminary consultations with other relevant leaders. Informed by the elders' perspectives, the evaluator returned to the government to negotiate a change to the project brief and key evaluation questions. Thus, an emphasis on accountability for narrowly defined outcomes gave way to an evaluation that was strengths based and developmental. This process helped to ensure that community participants, although still alert for signs of a hidden government agenda, were willing to contribute to building a full and accurate picture of the ways in which the programme was meeting community needs, as well as recommendations for improvement. The evaluation team discussed draft findings with stakeholder organisations some weeks before delivering a final report to government representatives at a closing celebration. While the evaluation fell some way short of the criteria for empowerment or emancipatory evaluation (Hanley, 2005), the evaluator was able to modify the approach to achieve some resolution of inherent tensions among the parties and a greater respect for community voices.

The ethical decision making in this scenario is focused on the position of the professional evaluator between two different agendas, and faced with balancing the needs and interests of the local group with the expectations and timetable of the somewhat distant evaluation commissioner. The identification of pressures on the individual from self and others is recognised by Miner and Petocz (2003) as an important dimension that defines an ethical situation. The added pressures of authentic user involvement might emphasise the rights of the individual and a striving for equality and power sharing, but this may not be a 'good' outcome for the commissioner. This example highlights how there are times when the professional may have to work hard to retain the integrity of their moral map in the face of different interests.

These examples illustrate how, in striving for authentic user involvement, the practitioner is engaged directly with the moral deliberation and behaviours of ethical decision making. It is clear that there is no single 'right' response, but a need for weighing up or balancing of multiple outcomes and interests. This interplay between personal and professional ethics, the pressures on the individual from self and others, and a wider understanding of ethical decision making within complex professional situations is recognised in a comprehensive ethical decision-making model proposed by Miner and Petocz (2003, p 22). This model has been adapted to show the interplay of these dimensions in relation to authentic user involvement (Figure 4.1).

Figure 4.1: Factors influencing ethical decision making for authentic user involvement

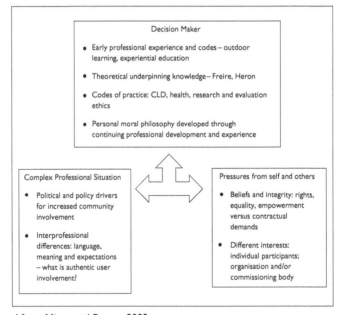

Decision Maker

- Early professional experience and codes – outdoor learning, experiential education

- Theoretical underpinning knowledge – Freire, Heron

- Codes of practice: CLD, health, research and evaluation ethics

- Personal moral philosophy developed through continuing professional development and experience

Complex Professional Situation

- Political and policy drivers for increased community involvement

- Interprofessional differences: language, meaning and expectations – what is authentic user involvement?

Pressures from self and others

- Beliefs and integrity: rights, equality, empowerment versus contractual demands

- Different interests: individual participants; organisation and/or commissioning body

Adapted from Miner and Petocz, 2003

Conclusion: guiding and supporting ethical decision making

The authors have based their reflections in this chapter on their shared and separate careers in experiential education, community learning and development, health services and evaluation and research. The stories they have chosen illustrate just some of the ways in which the lens of authentic user involvement adds complexity to the everyday work of ethical decision making. Emergent themes were the need to manage expectations sensitively, taking into account stakeholder hopes and the reality of the resources available; the building of relationships with community leaders that can drive a challenge to dominant agendas; and the acceptance that only small steps towards authentic participation are sometimes feasible. An additional dimension in ethical decision making is introduced where governments and an increasing policy emphasis seek greater levels of community involvement. This increases the pressures on the practising professional and tests their core values and principal belief in what constitutes authentic user involvement. It is clear from the examples used that different agendas and priorities are part of this complex interaction.

The authors close with three key concepts for day-to-day ethical decision making that have emerged from their dialogue and writing.

Relationships

Guidelines and the ethical instruction of practitioners are necessary, valid and useful, but not sufficient for supporting ethical behaviour. The authors emphasise the need for creating respectful relationships in each new endeavour and context, enabling practitioners and stakeholders to learn together. Partnerships with communities move beyond the **neoliberal** view of radical individualism, bringing moral concepts such as mutuality or reciprocity and a genuine respect for difference into traditional white, male, Eurocentric practice (Wallwork, 2008).

Power

Acknowledging and doing something about unequal relationships in human interactions is vital. This entails mindfulness about the dynamics of power so that even in small ways our actions open up new emancipatory paths. Further, reflexivity should help practitioners to be alert to how they exert their own economic or social power in seeking to redress power imbalances. Again, dialogue is essential – internally and with participants, professional networks and beyond.

Readiness

As practitioners, we need to develop our ability to work within the social environment in a way that crafts or seizes opportunities for:

- primary constituents to be the focus;
- constituents to review and reflect on their experiences;
- timely dialogue among professions and with constituents on key decisions, for example how risks are assessed and managed;
- gaining practical insights into other professional worlds.

The qualities and skills that we need to be able to summon up include flexibility, empathic neutrality, the courage to challenge long-held assumptions and, as was required in outdoor learning, the willingness to observe, engage with and adapt to the (metaphorical or actual) weather of the day.

References

Arnstein, S.R. (1969) 'A ladder of citizen participation', *Journal of American Institute of Planners*, vol 35, no 4, pp 216–24.

Australasian Evaluation Society (2006) *Guidelines for the ethical conduct of evaluations*, Victoria, Australia: Australasian Evaluation Society.

Australian Commission on Safety and Quality in Health Care (2011) *National Safety and Quality Health Service Standards*, Sydney: Australian Commission on Safety and Quality in Health Care.

Berends, L. and Roberts, B. (2003) 'Evaluation standards and their application to indigenous programs in Victoria, Australia', *Evaluation Journal of Australasia*, vol 3, pp 54–9.

Boote, J., Telford, R. and Cooper, C. (2002) 'Consumer involvement in health research: a review and research agenda', *Health Policy*, vol 61, pp 212–36.

CLD Standards Council for Scotland (2011) *A learning culture for the community learning and development sector in Scotland*, www.cldstandardscouncil.org.uk/files/CPD_Strategy_for_CLD.

Freire, P. (1972) *Pedagogy of the oppressed*, London: Penguin.

Ghaye, T. (2000) 'Empowerment through reflection: is this a case of the emperor's new clothes?' in T. Ghaye, D. Gillespie and S. Lillyman, (eds) *Empowerment through reflection: The narratives of healthcare professionals*, Dinton, Wilts: Quay Books, pp 65–91.

Greenaway, R. (2004) 'Touching base at Brathay – what are the theoretical foundations of Brathay's mainstream work?', conference paper: *Old Traditions and New Trends: Examining what is continuous and what is changing in young people's lives and outdoor experiential learning, EOE Conference 15–19 September 2004*, Brathay, UK.

Hanley, B. (2005) *Research as empowerment? Report of a series of seminars organised by the Toronto Group*, York: Joseph Rowntree Foundation.

Heron, J. (1981) 'Experiential research methodology', in P. Reason and J. Rowan (eds) *Human inquiry: A source book of new paradigm research*, Chichester: John Wiley and Sons, pp 153–66.

Hunt, J.S. (1990) *Ethical issues in experiential education* (2nd edn), Boulder, CO: The Association for Experiential Education.

Kerr, S. (2012) 'Kaupapa Māori theory-based evaluation', *Evaluation Journal of Australasia*, vol 12, no 1, pp 6–18.

Markiewicz, A. (2012) 'Closing the gap through respect, relevance, reciprocity and responsibility: issues in the evaluation of programs for indigenous communities in Australia', *Evaluation Journal of Australasia*, vol 12, no 1, pp 19–25.

Miner, M. and Petocz, A. (2003) 'Moral theory in ethical decision making: problems, clarifications and recommendations from a psychological perspective', *Journal of Business Ethics*, vol 42, no 1, pp 11–25.

National Health and Medical Research Council and Consumers' Health Forum of Australia (2004) *A model framework for consumer and community participation in health and medical research*, Canberra: Commonwealth of Australia, www.nhmrc.gov.au.

Price, M., McCoy, B. and Mafi, S. (2012) 'Progressing the dialogue about a framework for Aboriginal evaluations: sharing methods and key learnings', *Evaluation Journal of Australasia*, vol 12, no 1, pp 32–7.

Reason, P. (1994) 'Three approaches to participatory inquiry', in N.K Denzin and Y.S. Lincoln (eds) *Handbook for qualitative research*, London: Sage Publications.

Scottish Government (2012) *Consultation on the proposed Empowerment and Community Renewal Bill*, http://www.scotland.gov.uk/Publications/2012/06/7786.

Thiroux, J.P. and Krasemann, K.W. (2009) *Ethics theory and practice* (10th edn), New Jersey: Prentice Hall.

Titterton, M. and Smart, H. (2008) 'Can participatory research be a route to empowerment? A case study of a disadvantaged Scottish community', *Community Development Journal*, vol 43, pp 52–64.

Wadsworth, Y. (2001) 'Becoming responsive and some consequences for evaluation as dialogue across distance', *New Directions for Evaluation*, vol 92, pp 45–58.

Wallwork, E. (2008) 'Ethical analysis of research partnerships and communities', *Kennedy Institute of Ethics Journal*, vol 18, no 1, pp 57–85.

FIVE

The education context: strategies for well-being and ethically sustainable problem solving in teacher–student interaction

Tiina Soini, Janne Pietarinen, Kirsi Pyhältö and Kirsi Tirri

Introduction

The complexity of teachers' work is primarily due to the varying social interactions that teachers encounter and are constantly challenged to reflect on as part of their professional practice. They relate to others and regularly deal with highly complex and emotional situations that expose them to both emotionally draining and ethically ambiguous experiences. This is one reason why teachers are vulnerable to burn-out. Teachers' professional ethics may be understood in social terms, moral justification arising from the question as to whether teachers' actions are beneficial or harmful to social interaction, the community and, eventually, the democratic society (Mead, 1962; Dewey, 1964). Teachers' ethical decision making in a socially complex school environment is based on professional values and experiences, manifested eventually in professional judgement *in situ*. Therefore, a teacher's moral judgement is embedded in social action and interaction, and moral theory implied may not be explicit and distinctive for the observer or for teachers themselves (Miner and Petocz, 2003). In that sense, the authors' view on teachers' professional ethics represents a pragmatist view, emphasising situational problem solving and aiming for moral growth at both individual and community level (Dewey, 1964; Alhanen, 2013). The approach of this chapter is congruent with the idea of a synthesis of moral philosophical positions and ethical approaches, and aims at the development of new models and theories (see Chapter One).

The teaching profession differs, for example, from the medical profession in that, in order to be a good professional, a teacher cannot keep a social distance nor maintain a knowledge gap between the students and themselves. On the contrary, the teaching profession is based on the reciprocal effort of the teacher and the students (Colnerud, 2006), and a school is always a community aiming at moral growth. Moreover, problem solving in complex and ambiguous social situations is the core of both effective pedagogy and moral character building (Dewey, 1897). Accordingly, it has been argued that resolving stressful social situations at teachers' work, for example problems with students, also requires shared professional judgement constituting ethically sensitive and sustainable pedagogy (Hanhimäki and Tirri, 2009). In this chapter, the relationship between teachers' professional ethics and **occupational well-being** is explored by looking at the strategies teachers use during burdening episodes that simultaneously challenge their ethical standards and compromise their well-being.

Considerable evidence suggests that experienced **socio-psychological well-being** regulates both students' and teachers' learning at school (for example, Kristersson and Öhlund, 2005; Hakanen, et al, 2006). Accordingly, experienced well-being has been shown to have a significant impact on the whole of pedagogical practice, for example on an individual's ability to concentrate and observe his/her environment, to perceive affordances and to interpret and learn from feedback (Antonovsky, 1987; Deci and Ryan, 2002; Pallant and Lae, 2002). Teacher burn-out has been found to have significant implications in terms not only of a teacher's motivation, health and job satisfaction, but also of student behaviour and learning (Dorman 2003; meta-analysis by Montgomery and Rupp, 2005). It has been shown that teacher burn-out is related to an increased use of performance-oriented teaching practices (Retelsdorf et al, 2010) which are related, for example, to increased cheating behaviour (Anderman and Midgley, 2004), consequently resulting in ethical problems in pedagogical practices.

Ethically sustainable problem solving is the solving of problems in a way that takes ethical matters and consequences as well as the perspectives of different actors into account. It can be viewed as a precondition for well-being in the school community. Further, caring school communities with good-quality interaction have been found to foster moral development. This refers to a two-fold function of ethics in the teaching profession; teachers do not follow moral conduct just as a part of the professional way of interacting with people: they also aim to inspire and teach students to behave ethically (Colnerud, 2006). This requires teachers to have learned to conduct ethical education (for example, Integrated Ethical Education (IEE) model, Narvaez, 2006) and act as moral experts (see Chapter Fourteen for information on the teacher education programme in Finland). The aspects of **moral expertise** – ethical focus, skills of **ethical judgement** and sensitivity and competence in ethical action (Table 5.1) – are present in the ethical decision-making process (Miner and Petocz, 2003). In teachers' professional practice, ethical education calls for the intentional use of specific action strategies such as socially constructive measures aimed at creating shared understanding and coherence in the school community (Tirri, 1999; Hanhimäki and Tirri, 2009). Moreover, findings indicate that ethically sustainable action in pedagogical work is crucial to attaining educational goals both in the classroom and at the school community level, as well as in terms of teachers' well-being. Little is known, however, about the dynamics between teachers' well-being and ethically sustainable problem solving. In line with the aim of Part One (Figure 1.1), this chapter concentrates on examining interrelations between teachers' well-being and professional ethics in the context of professional–**service user** interactions, using teacher–student interaction as the case study. The authors provide examples from their research to highlight the voice of the teacher and take a moral theory approach. This chapter highlights the importance of the congruence of personal and professional ethics for a professional's well-being.

Tensions and frictions of school life

Teacher–student interaction is an arena of varying interests and negotiation (Tirri and Husu, 2002; Soini et al, 2012). Accordingly, encounters may evoke conflicting ethical concerns in teachers and students, concerning for example the proper ways of discipline. Moreover, the complexity of the school environment exposes teachers to situations where 'right and wrong' ways of acting are not explicit but, rather, there is an element of uncertainty (Dewey, 1966). Hence, tension and friction are always present between students and the school environment. However, friction may either promote (constructive friction) or hinder (destructive friction) meaningful learning (Vermunt and Verloop, 1999). In constructive friction, the tensions, for example differences of perspectives, are recognised and even utilised as a source of learning. On the other hand, in destructive friction a tension goes unrecognised or the conflicting interests are ignored. A teacher may, for example, emphasise the learning goals related to a specific subject, and simultaneously fail to recognise problems within students' peer groups that are highly significant and ethically challenging to them. According to the experience of students, concentrating on learning outcomes alone may neglect the social aims of education, which in turn may

Figure 5.1: An integrative approach to teachers' moral expertise and problem-solving strategies

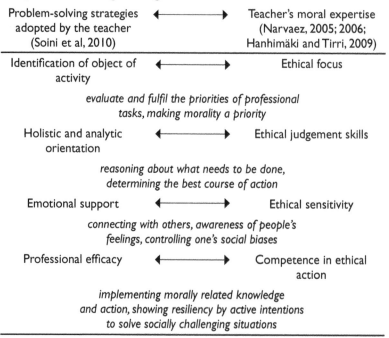

Problem-solving strategies adopted by the teacher (Soini et al, 2010)		Teacher's moral expertise (Narvaez, 2005; 2006; Hanhimäki and Tirri, 2009)
Identification of object of activity	⟷	Ethical focus

evaluate and fulfil the priorities of professional tasks, making morality a priority

| Holistic and analytic orientation | ⟷ | Ethical judgement skills |

reasoning about what needs to be done, determining the best course of action

| Emotional support | ⟷ | Ethical sensitivity |

connecting with others, awareness of people's feelings, controlling one's social biases

| Professional efficacy | ⟷ | Competence in ethical action |

implementing morally related knowledge and action, showing resiliency by active intentions to solve socially challenging situations

Source: Based on Narvaez, 2005, 2006; Hanhimäki and Tirri, 2009; Soini et al, 2010

eventually cause destructive friction. On the other hand, by creating a relaxing atmosphere and using means of oversight that emphasise trust rather than external control, a teacher is likely to promote positive, constructive friction between students and their learning environment and create opportunities for ethical and moral reasoning and growth (Dewey, 1966). The opportunity to participate in and contribute to the community is the key to the type of friction created between students and their learning environment.

While teachers recognise the importance of making it easier for students to play an active role in learning, they often still offer quite traditional and passive roles to them with regard to school practices (Ahonen et al, in press). Although students may anticipate a more active role, they see adapting to the practices and norms set by teachers as the primary strategy for success at school (Ulmanen et al, 2012). Consequently, the moral rules manifested in the teacher's action play a key role in creating a climate, for example in the classroom, which in turn has a strong moral influence on the students (Fenstermacher, 2001). Because of their professional stance, teachers can be considered responsible for promoting constructive friction at a fruitfully dynamic level, adjusting their strategies and managing situations in ways that facilitate both ethical sensitivity and well-being in students. Some very successful pedagogical attempts have been made to involve students in constructing an ethically sensitive community. For example, in Tirri's studies (2011), a special curriculum was introduced to attract students with similar interests, and it provided them with both the cognitive and emotional skills necessary for their personal growth. The students were given an opportunity to process their worldview and discuss it with both scientific and religious components in mind. Even though the students were encouraged to express their own values and worldviews, they showed a respect for and tolerance of diversity as well as a readiness to engage in dialogue with others who held worldviews different from their own (Tirri, 2011).

Results from the study of Finnish **comprehensive school** teachers suggest that teachers perceive interaction with students to be the most significant aspect of their well-being with respect to pedagogical work. Further, they describe both empowering and stressful experiences related to socially challenging pedagogical situations with students, such as dealing with bullying, loss of study motivation and disturbing behaviour. In most cases, challenging situations in teacher–student interaction seem to embody dimensions of well-being as well as ethical matters. Teachers feel that solving these problematic situations is a core task of their work and at the same time highly demanding (Soini et al, 2010; Pyhältö et al, 2011):

> "That you kind of have to get a hold of the pupil so that you make contact, some sort of a contact with them, a 'plus' contact. If it's negative, if you have to scold the kid and remind them all the time, and, well, scold them over and over again, that you're late again, you haven't done your homework again, then after all this negative scolding you've got to find that huge plus for them somewhere. And if you can't find it, the kid will just fade away, so … So that the kid won't be left with a feeling that the teacher didn't care for them enough. Like when I think about my own situation, that have I just let it go too easily too many times, then yes, sometimes I feel like I have and it bothers me, but then I remember the supervisory aspect, that wait a second, it's not like I'm supposed to be able to do everything." (Class teacher cited in Soini et al, 2010, p 11; Soini et al, 2012, p 742)

Yet, at the same time, the more general goals of supporting and facilitating students' growth have also been found to be very important in terms of teachers' work engagement and sense of purpose. In difficult cases, concentrating on the best interest of the students gives teachers hope for the future and the resilience to continue their work, regardless of challenging situations (Tirri and Husu, 2002). Teachers' images of ideal school practices are ways to access teachers' sense of purpose. A particular vision can provide inspiration and motivation to teachers as well as guide them to reflect on their work (Husu and Tirri, 2007). According to Darling-Hammond (1990), one of the most powerful predictors of a teacher's commitment to teaching is the sense that he or she is making a positive difference in the lives of students. However, in order to have an impact on the school reality, these visions need to be congruent with the pedagogical solutions and strategies that teachers use in pursuing their professional goals.

In Finland, teachers' professional autonomy is strong and the ethical basis of the work is the general principle of human rights (see Chapter Fourteen). Challenges faced in teacher–student interactions are often reflected onto the meaning-making and problem-solving process within the professional community. The process of pedagogical meaning making, which is searching with colleagues for optimal strategies to meet perceived challenges, includes more or less conscious professional negotiations about ethically sustainable strategies for developing teacher–student interaction in the school. Due to this, a teacher's professional interests might diverge from the views of other colleagues, and confrontation between professionals and their views about pedagogical aims might occur. Such destructive friction often also significantly hinders teachers' opportunities to engage in pedagogical processes as active educational experts employing moral expertise. In this process the burdening of a teacher increases, and feelings of cynicism and/or insufficiency may deepen (Pyhältö et al, 2011).

The authors argue that strategies for proactively anticipating confrontations and solving potential problems, as well as promoting ethically sustainable pedagogy, can be learned and developed in the school community. However, this calls for action strategies and intentional pedagogical solutions that are not self-evident or easy to achieve. In the next section, the authors explore the relations between teachers' **well-being strategies** and ethically sustainable problem solving. The explorations are based on research findings from both international and, in more detail, two recent Finnish school research projects.

Teachers' well-being strategies and professional ethics

When confronted with stressful situations, both individual teachers and teacher communities can use a variety of strategies; they can, for instance, ignore, adapt to, or fully take on the challenges raised by the situation. The decision about what strategy to use includes professional ethical judgement on the desired outcome. The strategies may be viewed as self-regulated, co-regulated or both (Salmela-Aro, 2009). They can also be more or less functional in terms of both burdening and ethical decision making. For example, the use of active and optimistic social strategies is likely to facilitate meaningful goal orientation and goal attainment, and hence reduce burn-out (Butler, 2007; Salmela-Aro et al, 2011; Devos et al, 2012). Moreover, optimistic social strategies promote social efficacy beliefs which are likely to increase one's determination in the face of challenges (Baumeister et al, 2003). Positive emotions, furthermore, have been seen as promoting a more flexible use of strategies (Fredrickson, 2001) as well as a willingness to employ new innovative ideas to resolve situations (Lyubomirsky et al, 2005), and hence facilitate teacher learning.

Research has shown that teachers' self-efficacy, emotional involvement, motivational structure and work engagement are interrelated and have an effect on the practices a teacher adopts (Ryan et al, 1998; Pelletier et al, 2002; Butler and Shibaz, 2008). This, in turn, affects the goals and strategies adopted by students, such as seeking help. More specifically, skilled and motivated teachers are likely to promote active and functional learning strategies, and thus achieve the best learning outcomes (Hoekstra et al, 2007; Hoy et al, 2008). A teacher's will and ability to regulate interaction and use a suitable strategy are also crucial in ethically sustainable problem solving. More specifically, a teacher's capacity to interpret moral/social situations (ethical sensitivity), reason about what needs to be done (ethical judgment skills) and evaluate and fulfil various professional tasks (ethical focus and competence in ethical action) is challenged in burdening situations (see Figure 5.1).

It seems that problem-solving strategies vary in different contexts of teachers' work. For example, Soini et al (2010) found that teachers most often used active, holistic and multifaceted strategies to solve problematic situations with students, and a more passive approach was adopted in problem solving with colleagues. The authors also know from research with early education and elementary school teachers that ethical problems involving students are the easiest to solve, but that problems involving colleagues and the whole community are more difficult and in many cases remain unsolved (Tirri and Husu, 2002).

Moreover, a teacher's career stage influences the ethical-sensitivity skills that also play a role in problem-solving strategies. Recent empirical findings show differences between experienced and novice teachers' self-estimated ethical sensitivity, which is in line with assumptions included in Narvaez's (2006) IEE model: teachers with more experience exhibited greater ethical sensitivity than did novice teachers (Kuusisto et al, 2012).

An integrative approach

The context-dependent nature of ethical reasoning and well-being strategies discussed above suggests that teachers' professional ethics are not fixed entities of rules that could, for example, be learned by rote in teacher education. Rather, they seem to evolve in complex interactions between teachers and their working environment, changing from one context to another as well as during an entire teaching career. However, learning moral expertise requires not just accumulating experiences but also reflecting on them and regulation of one's action (Dewey, 1960). According to research, some orientations and core strategies seem to produce more sustainable pedagogy, in terms of both well-being and ethics, irrespective of context or subject matter. Figure 5.1 shows that teachers' problem-solving strategies for reducing work-related stress have components similar to moral expertise in the educational professions.

Empirical results from both teachers and students support the importance of a holistic approach to school pedagogy (Tirri, 2011). In Soini, Pyhältö and Pietarinen (2010), when teachers described using a holistic and analytic orientation they referred to utilising the whole school community as well as resources outside the school in their problem solving.

> "I feel really good here. We have a very good, a very good team here, a caring team. They, we here, we have our hearts in this work and I experienced it immediately when I arrived here. And I still feel the same, people here really do a good job. And if you think about the background, the background of the pupils here in XXX [a part of the city], it's not the easiest, just thinking about the families that live here. So really a job well done. Me, I like it, I just do my thing and I like it. Of course, every community has their issues, something causes disagreement, but I just take

it as a sign that we actually do some thinking here." (Class teacher, unpublished quote from research conducted for the studies published in Soini et al, 2010; Pyhältö et al, 2011; Soini et al, 2012)

Moreover, they used these resources to identify and specify the object of the activity. These first two strategies are tightly combined, since the holistic orientation in education and pedagogical work almost inevitably includes ethical elements and forces identifying the ethical focus of the problem at hand. This phase of recognising the problem as ethical (Miner and Petocz, 2003) requires a strategic orientation that combines both co- and self-regulation. In teachers' professional problem-solving, this may require expanding their collaboration outside the school and at the same time relinquishing the role of sole authority. For example, in cases where teachers' professional ethics with regard to control and discipline and the cultural norms of students' families differ, the use of discourse strategies (that is, enabling constructive friction) has been identified as a more appropriate way of solving moral dilemmas at the school than the authoritative, single-handed decision making (that is, causing destructive friction) adopted by a teacher (Oser, 1991; Tirri, 1999; 2003; 2010).

To meet the aims of holistic pedagogy, teachers need to identify and verbalise the educational goals and meanings of their teaching. It also seems that ethically sustainable pedagogy is highly embedded in learning to master the central concepts in each subject taught that provide students with the vocabulary they need for this kind of discussion and reflection. These often include ethical reasoning and value judgements. Further, this requires sufficient competence in translating these intentions into action (Tirri, 2011).

To facilitate ethical reflection, teachers have to have learned it themselves. Soini, Pyhältö and Pietarinen (2010) showed teachers also describing the diversity of opportunities for professional development and experiences of efficacy that are provided by teacher–student interactions. In fact, the teachers often saw the insight or better understanding gained from challenging situations vis-à-vis students as a cause of empowerment and engagement which, in turn, is likely to promote more ethically sensitive interaction with students.

"It's, well if I think of it now, it's those times when a pupil comes to you to tell about their problems, things that are really difficult for them, so you have to have time for them. It's not like you can tell them you're sorry and that you

actually should be in charge of monitoring the break or that you have this and that going on, so come back tomorrow. It may be that it's the last time they ever try to talk to you. So you need to be like sensitive to these situations, be there when the kid comes to you and says his or her father didn't come and pick them up although it was their turn. Or something. You just have to be like, alert, present ..."
(Class teacher, unpublished quote from research conducted for the studies published in Soini et al, 2010; Pyhältö et al, 2011; Soini et al, 2012)

Research indicates that offering adequate emotional support to students is a key element in promoting students' well-being. Studies on well-being in pedagogical processes (Pyhältö et al, 2010) have shown teachers and students emphasising the emotional, social, moral and spiritual aspects of education. Moreover, Tirri (2011) found that, despite students being very cognitive and science oriented, they required significant social and emotional support for their personal growth. Reflecting on values and purposes is thus an important aspect of all school pedagogy and learning.

Based on these findings, ethically sustainable and well-being-supportive pedagogy can be seen as holistic in many ways: it recognises the importance of the social contexts and relations both in and outside of school and also appreciates students and teachers as complex human actors. It is also in line with the ideas of the school as a form of community life, and education as a social process where students are taught (stimulated and controlled) through the life of the community, rather than by a single teacher (Dewey, 1897; Törmä, 1996). The authors argue that to succeed in this kind of pedagogy, teachers should be given opportunities to learn analytic *self-regulation strategies* together with the possibility and ability to use the social resources of the school environment, that is, *co-regulation strategies*. Learning to identify and vary these regulation strategies as a part of teachers' professional practices can protect teachers from being burdened and enable them to identify and resolve ethical dilemmas in their work.

Discussion

This chapter draws on research into teachers' ethical expertise and occupational well-being, and proposes an integrative model for developing both well-being-promoting and ethically sustainable pedagogy in school. The authors argue that, in the context of teacher–

student interaction, the strategies of well-being and of ethically sound pedagogy are in some fundamental ways very similar and intertwined. These strategies adopted by teachers and pupils are not personal dispositions but, rather, socially learned skills and readiness. Moreover, they are continually reconstructed during the process of identifying and elaborating the burdening and ethically charged features of salient school episodes and applying suitable, context-sensitive strategies to them. In the learning processes of ethically sustainable problem solving, teachers reflect on their vision and everyday problem solving, and also identify the consequences of their actions in ethically challenging and potentially burdening situations. This is a process of professional development through self- and co-regulation, aiming at ethical coherence in a teacher's professional practices and at optimal interaction between teachers and students.

Teachers' work is becoming more and more collaborative, and schools are becoming multi-professional organisations, for example due to the progress of inclusive education. Consequently, teachers' professional ethics are increasingly negotiated in the school at both a professional and an **interprofessional** level. The school community will not only profit from, but requires a values-clarification approach where common values are identified and made clear to everyone (Husu and Tirri, 2007). The shared planning and reflection process simultaneously offers an arena for the learning of self-regulation and co-regulation strategies for teachers, and paves the way to pedagogy in which students are given the necessary skills and concepts to discuss as well as reflect upon all subject matter taught at school. This argument is consistent with increasing recognition of the notion that dealing with the implicit and explicit values characterising students' lives is an essential facet of effective learning. Due to this, dealing with moral conflicts in schools seems to require specific pedagogical intentions and interventions that involve all people related to a particular moral dilemma and utilise the community beyond the school (Oser and Althof, 1993; Tirri, 2003).

To conclude, the authors argue that ethical reflection and the construction of well-being should be seen as skills and professional action strategies to be learned and constructed at school every day in the interaction between different **stakeholders**, teachers and their students and peers. The best interest of students is most optimally established and served through high-quality interaction between all groups. The well-being strategies, ethical skills and work orientations of teachers are learned not only during teacher education but also in the school, as continuing professional development, and also in conjunction with the collective learning of interprofessional ethics and problem solving in the community. In order to promote well-being and ethically sustainable pedagogy, teachers should therefore be given an opportunity to reflect on their everyday work and action strategies together. They should be encouraged to do this not only in connection with formal learning outcomes, but also by perceiving it as ethical professional activity that creates well-being and a sense of meaningful and coherent pedagogical practice both for students and for themselves.

References

Ahonen, E., Pyhältö, K., Pietarinen, J. and Soini, T. (in press) 'Teachers' professional beliefs about their and pupil's roles in the school', *Teacher Development* .

Alhanen, K. (2013) *Deweyn kokemusfilosofia* [Dewey's philosophy of experience], Helsinki: Gaudeamus.

Anderman, E.M. and Midgley, C. (2004) 'Changes in self-reported academic cheating across the transition from middle school to high school', *Contemporary Educational Psychology*, vol 29, no 4, pp 499–517.

Antonovsky, A. (1987) *Unraveling the mystery: How people manage stress and stay well*, San Francisco: Jossey-Bass.

Baumeister, R.F., Campbell, J.D., Krueger, J.I. and Vohs, K.D. (2003) 'Does high self-esteem cause better performance, interpersonal success, happiness, or healthier lifestyles?', *Psychological Science in the Public Interest*, vol 4, no 1, pp 1–44.

Butler, R. (2007) 'Teachers' achievement goal orientations and associations with teachers' help seeking: examination of a novel approach to teacher motivation', *Journal of Educational Psychology*, vol 99, no 2, pp 241–52.

Butler, R. and Shibaz, L. (2008) 'Achievement goals for teaching as predictors of students' perceptions of instructional practices and students' help seeking and cheating', *Learning and Instruction*, vol 18, no 5, pp 453–67.

Colnerud, G. (2006) 'Teacher ethics as a research problem: syntheses achievement and new issues', *Teachers and Teaching: Theory and Practice*, vol 12, no 3, pp 365–85.

Darling-Hammond, L. (1990) 'Teacher professionalism: why and how?', in A. Lieberman (ed) *Schools as collaborative cultures: Creating the future now*, London: Falmer Press, pp 25–49.

Deci, E.L. and Ryan, R.M. (2002) *Handbook of self-determination research*, Rochester, NY: The University of Rochester Press.

Devos, C., Dupriez, V. and Paquay, L. (2012) 'Does the social working environment predict beginning teachers' self-efficacy and feelings of depression?' *Teaching and Teacher Education*, vol 28, no 2, pp 206–17.

Dewey, J. (1897) 'My pedagogic greed', *School Journal*, vol 54, pp 77–80.

Dewey, J. (1960) *How we think*, Massachussetts: D.C. Heath & Company.

Dewey, J. (1964) *Democracy and education*, New York: The Macmillan Company.

Dewey, J. (1966) 'Three independent factors of morals', *Educational Theory*, vol 16, pp 197–209.

Dorman, J.P. (2003) 'Relationship between school and classroom environment and teacher burnout: a LISREL analysis', *Social Psychology of Education*, vol 6, no 2, pp 107–27.

Fenstermacher, G.D. (2001) 'On the concept of manner and its visibility in teaching practice', *Journal of Curriculum Studies*, vol 33, pp 639–53.

Fredrickson, B.L. (2001) 'The role of positive emotions in positive psychology: the broaden-and-build theory of positive emotions', *American Psychologist*, vol 56, no 3, pp 218–26.

Hakanen, J., Bakker, A. and Schaufeli, W. (2006) 'Burnout and engagement among teachers', *Journal of School Psychology*, vol 43, pp 495–513.

Hanhimäki, E. and Tirri, K. (2009) 'Education for ethically sensitive teaching in critical incidents at school', *The Journal of Education for Teaching*, vol 35, no 2, pp 107–21.

Hoekstra, A., Beijaard D., Brekelmans, M. and Korthagen, F. (2007) 'Experienced teachers' informal learning from classroom teaching', *Teachers and Teaching: Theory and Practice*, vol 13, no 2, pp 189–206.

Hoy, A., Hoy, W.K. and Kurz, N.M. (2008) 'Teachers' academic optimism: the development and test of a new construct', *Teaching and Teacher Education*, vol 24, pp 821–35.

Husu, J. and Tirri, K. (2007) 'Developing whole school pedagogical values – a case of going through the ethos of "good schooling"', *Teaching and Teacher Education*, vol 23, no 4, pp 390–401.

Kristersson, P. and Öhlund, L.S. (2005) 'Swedish upper secondary school pupils' sense of coherence, coping resources and aggressiveness in relation to educational track and performance', *Scandinavian Journal of Caring Science*, vol 19, pp 77–84.

Kuusisto, E., Tirri, K. and Rissanen, I. (2012) 'Finnish teachers' ethical sensitivity', *Education Research International* (in press).

Lyubomirsky, S., King, L.A. and Diener, E. (2005) 'The benefits of frequent positive affect', *Psychological Bulletin*, vol 131, pp 803–55.

Mead, G.H. (1962) *Mind, self and society*, Chicago: University of Chicago Press.

Miner, M. and Petocz, A. (2003) 'Moral theory in ethical decision making: problems, clarifications and recommendations from a psychological perspective', *Journal of Business Ethics*, vol 42, pp 11–25.

Montgomery, C. and Rupp, A.A. (2005) 'A meta-analysis for exploring the diverse causes and effects of stress in teachers', *Canadian Journal of Education*, vol 28, pp 458–86.

Narvaez, D. (2006) 'Integrative ethical education', in M. Killen and J. Smetana (eds) *Handbook of moral development*. New Jersey: Lawrence Erlbaum Associates, pp 703–34.

Oser, F. (1991) 'Professional morality: a discourse approach (the case of the teaching profession)', in W. Kurtines and J. Gerwirtz (eds) *Handbook of moral behavior and development*, vol 2. New Jersey: Lawrence Erlbaum Associates, pp 191–228.

Oser, F. and Althof, W. (1993) 'Trust in advance: on the professional morality of teachers', *Journal of Moral Education*, vol 22, no 3, pp 253–75.

Pallant, J.F. and Lae, L. (2002) 'Sense of coherence, well-being, coping and personality factors: further evaluation of the sense of coherence scale', *Personality and Individual Differences*, vol 33, pp 39–48.

Pelletier, L.G., Legault, L. and Séguin-Lévesque, C. (2002) 'Pressure from above and from below as determinants of teachers' motivation and teaching behaviours', *Journal of Educational Psychology*, vol 94, pp 186–96.

Pyhältö, K., Pietarinen, J. and Salmela-Aro, K. (2011) 'Teacher working-environment fit as a framework for burnout experienced by Finnish teachers', *Teaching and Teacher Education*, vol 27, no 7, pp 1101–11.

Pyhältö, K., Soini, T. and Pietarinen, J. (2010) 'Pupils' pedagogical well-being in comprehensive school – Significant positive and negative school experiences of Finnish nine graders', *European Journal of Psychology of Education*, vol 24, pp 447–463.

Retelsdorf, J., Butler, R., Streblow, L. and Schiefele, U. (2010) 'Teachers' goal orientations for teaching: associations with instructional practices, interest in teaching, and burn-out', *Learning and Instruction*, vol 20, no 1, pp 30–46.

Ryan, A.M., Gheen, M.H. and Midgley, C. (1998) 'Why do some students avoid asking for help? An examination of the interplay among students' academic efficacy, teachers' social-emotional role, and the classroom goal structure', *Journal of Educational Psychology*, vol 90, no 3, pp 528–35.

Salmela-Aro, K. (2009) 'Personal goals and well-being during critical life transitions: the four C's – channelling, choice, co-agency and compensation', *Advances in Life Course Research*, vol 14, pp 63–73.

Salmela-Aro, K., Tolvanen, A. and Nurmi, J.-E. (2011) 'Social strategies during university studies predict early career work burnout and engagement: 18-year longitudinal study', *Journal of Vocational Behavior*, vol 79, no 1, pp 145–57.

Soini, T., Pyhältö, K. and Pietarinen, J. (2010) 'Pedagogical well-being – reflecting learning and well-being in teachers' work', *Teaching and Teachers: Theory and Practice*, vol 16, no 6, pp 765–82.

Soini, T., Pietarinen, J., Pyhältö, K., Westling, S.-K., Ahonen, E. and Järvinen, S. (2012) 'Mitä jos opettaja etääntyy työstään', *Nuorisotutkimus*, vol 30, no 2, pp 5–20.

Tirri, K. (1999) 'Teachers' perceptions of moral dilemmas at school', *Journal of Moral Education*, vol 28, pp 31–47.

Tirri, K. (2003) 'The teacher's integrity', in F. Oser and W. Veugelers (eds) *Teaching in moral and democratic education*, Bern: Peter Lang, pp 65–81.

Tirri, K. (2010) 'Teachers' values underlying their professional ethics', in T. Lovat, R. Toomey and N. Clement (eds) *International research handbook on values education and student well-being*, New York: Springer, pp 153–63.

Tirri, K. (2011) 'Holistic school pedagogy and values: Finnish teachers' and students' perspectives', *International Journal of Educational Research*, vol 50, no 2, pp 159–65.

Tirri, K. and Husu, J. (2002) 'Care and responsibility in "the best interest of the child": relational voices of ethical dilemmas in teaching', *Teachers and Teaching*, vol 8, no 1, pp 65–80.

Törmä, S. (1996) 'Kasvun mahdollisuus' [Opportunity for growth], *Acta Universitatis Tamperensis*, series A vol 496, University of Tampere.

Ulmanen, S., Soini, T., Pietarinen, J. and Pyhältö, K. (2012) 'Strategies for academic engagement perceived by 6th and 8th graders in Finland', Paper presented at *European Conference on Educational Research, Annual meeting, September, Cadiz, Spain*.

Vermunt, J.D. and Verloop, N. (1999) 'Congruence and fiction between learning and teaching', *Learning and Instruction*, vol 9, 257–80.

PART TWO

Personal–professional ethics

The social work–criminal justice context: personal and professional ethical tensions

Jane Fenton

Background

The historical changes in Scottish **criminal justice social work** (CJSW) have been well documented (for example McNeill, 2004; McNeill and Whyte, 2007), but require some attention in this chapter as they are important for understanding possible '**disjuncture**' and for contextualising the respondents' comments from the research study explored later in the chapter. The Social Work (Scotland) Act 1968 was responsible for the reorganisation of **social work** in Scotland, including the incorporation of work with offenders within generic social work, and Section 12 of the Act puts a duty on social work departments to promote welfare for all **service users**. Furthermore, the International Federation of Social Workers (IFSW) states that:

> The social work profession promotes social change [...] Principles of human rights and social justice are fundamental to social work. (IFSW, 2012, p 1)

Therefore, social work should be concerned with helping people with their welfare needs *and* with understanding and promoting social justice (see Chapter Sixteen for further details about social work values). Social work departments in Scotland operationalise these values via the **Scottish Social Services Council** (SSSC), the **regulatory** body for social services in Scotland, and its Codes of Practice, which state that social workers must 'protect the rights and promote the interests of service users and carers' (SSSC, 2009, p 22). Because work with offenders is part of mainstream social work in Scotland, it is based on the same values and should be concerned with the same things. This chapter, therefore, takes a utilitarian approach to the exploration of ethical tensions in CJSW, because a utilitarian theoretical framework is very congruent with the above welfare-based, social work approach to work with offenders. The chapter uses a vignette to illustrate the disjuncture that a social worker might experience. The chapter is part of Part Two and focuses on the dynamics of personal and professional ethics (see Figure 1.1). It also refers to some of the **interprofessional** perceptions and tensions to provide a context for the dilemmas faced by the social work profession and the social worker who might have to work in a manner not congruent with their personal beliefs.

Garland (2001) states that the dominant ideology in criminal justice in the Western world has, from the beginning of the 20th century, been characterised by a penal welfare ethos. **Penal-welfarism** has rehabilitation at its centre, and is underpinned by the axiom that as material circumstances improve for people, so crime should reduce (Garland, 2001). There is, therefore, congruence between a penal welfare approach, the value base of international social work (IFSW, 2012) and the legal and value base of Scottish social work. Helping people to improve their circumstances is a welfare-based approach, and endeavouring for a more materially comfortable society for everyone is a social justice aim. The good fit between social work in general, and social work with offenders in particular, would therefore lend itself to social work with offenders sitting comfortably within social work departments, and having clear legitimacy for undertaking helping and welfare work.

This comfortable arrangement, however, has changed over the decades and Garland (2001) states that even as early as the end of the 1970s, 'no-one could unabashedly support the old model' (p 62), that is, the 'old' penal welfare model. Feeley and Simon (1992) explain that that there is now a 'new, strategic formation in the penal field' (p 449) in the Western world, which they refer to as the **'new penology'**. The new penology is concerned with managing and controlling groups of offenders according to the level of risk they pose. This is a managerial endeavour, unconcerned with change or rehabilitation – the central concerns of the 'old penology'. Garland suggests that the new penology can be located within a broader socioeconomic development in post-modern, western society, when 'a reactionary, all-encompassing' turn against traditional penal-welfarism emerged (Garland, 2001, p 452). The neoliberal ideology that welfare is an expensive luxury, benefiting the undeserving, leads seamlessly to the suggestion that penal-welfare, 'helping' work with offenders is 'absurdly indulgent' (Garland, 2001, p 76). An alternative discourse of a 'wicked' offender who needs to be risk-managed and held accountable emerges. Any suggestion that welfare or issues related to social justice might deserve attention is seen as indulgent and 'soft'.

So, what had happened in the criminal justice field in the 1970s? Firstly, several reports were produced, the most well-known of which was *What works? Questions and answers about prison reform* by Martinson (1974). These reports were critical of criminal justice policy and approaches and culminated in a loss of faith in probation and rehabilitation. At the same time, radical thinkers in the UK and US objected to the 'coercive nature of the rehabilitative ideal' (Bottoms, 1980, p 3), suggesting that discretionary sentencing and treatment based on compliance were discriminatory (Bottoms and McWilliams, 1979). So, traditional penal welfare-based probation approaches began to lose purchase, due to these criticisms, and subsequently a reactionary discourse of punishment and retribution added to their demise (Garland, 2001). After a decade of probation in England at its lowest ebb, the 1990s heralded the advent of '**What works**' informed programmes, with their central tenets of cognitive-behavioural group work and risk classification of offenders (Andrews et al, 1990). 'What works' was unreservedly welcomed by the Home Office, and is credited with rescuing the probation service (Mair, 2004). Furthermore, 'What works' thinking fitted well into the new penological framework; offenders were risk-classified and managed, were subject to 'correctional' treatment for thinking 'wrongly' and there was little room for welfare-based work. In other words, the focus of attention had become solely the individual offender and the systemic 'management' of him or her, with no attention being given to his or her social environment.

Changes in Scottish CJSW

The effects of 'What Works' soon began to be felt in Scotland with the adoption of cognitive-behavioural programmes and structured risk assessments (McCulloch, 2005). This resulted in a shift in the legitimate targets for work with offenders from traditional welfare and 'helping' issues to internal 'thinking errors' and other psychological characteristics of offenders. Also, the adoption of *National Objectives and Standards in the Criminal Justice System* (NOAS) (Social Work Services Group, 1991) 'signified a recalibration of the underlying ideology of CJSW' (McCulloch and McNeill, 2011, p 186). No longer was welfare unquestioningly the priority; rather, a 'responsibility model' had taken its place. Offenders were to be held to account for their actions and their thinking was to be 'corrected'. Organisational change then took place, with CJSW becoming 100% funded by the then **Scottish Executive**

(McNeill and Whyte, 2007), which separated it economically and influentially from the wider social work department. Furthermore, McNeill (2005) points out that by the mid-1990s the issue of public protection had moved centre stage, with legislative changes leading to more 'high risk' offenders on social workers' case loads. As McNeill states, advances in public protection policy and practice from then on were rapid, and when *The Tough Option* (Scottish Office, 1998) was published, public safety was stated as the priority aim of CJSW. As Croall (2005) stated, 'many fear that Scotland's welfarist tradition is under threat' (p 177). A parallel development was the increasing attention to the system itself, with a focus on key performance indicators, audit measures and efficient functioning. In a 'new penological' framework, these are the important measures (Slingeneyer, 2007).

At this point, then, we can see that penal-welfarism (congruent with social work values) and the new world of CJSW, based on a new penology, were diverging more and more. The creation of the Scottish Parliament (operational in 1999) might well have been optimistically welcomed by CJSW departments as a chance for the resurrection of a penal welfare value base. The new parliament, however, was dominated by a Labour Party heavily influenced by policies underpinned by **popular punitivism**, an approach developed by the preceding Conservative government and retained by New Labour to avoid being branded 'soft' on crime (Croall, 2005). In essence, popular punitivism is the belief that offenders simply choose to commit crime and that explanations of contributory social factors such as poverty or disadvantage have no validity. Individual responsibility, a feature of neoliberalism and the new penology, therefore still dominated. McNeill and Whyte (2007), however, point out that at the same time the government made explicit its continuing commitment to penal welfarist-based rehabilitation and the reduction of prison numbers (unlike the rest of the UK), although the authors, and McNeill (2004, p 426), also note that the government was 'quiet and discreet' about doing so, possibly in recognition of the significant influence of popular punitivism.

The next important development for CJSW was the Management of Offenders etc (Scotland) Act 2005, which created **Community Justice Authorities** (eight groupings of CJSW local authority areas) and gave explicit instruction about defining and managing 'high risk' offenders. **Multi Agency Public Protection Arrangements** (MAPPA) were adopted in Scotland as a mechanism for operationalising the Act (Scottish Government, 2007). This is a very explicit example of *managing* offenders classified by risk and of putting public protection at the heart of criminal justice work, and, as such, is entirely congruent with a new penology.

Finally, the Criminal Justice and Licensing (Scotland) Act 2010 was passed, replacing old probation orders with new **community payback orders**. In essence, there is more emphasis on reparation in the form of unpaid work, but the tensions that exist around how to engage and actually work with offenders are still just as acute.

At this point in time, then, we can see that the developments in CJSW in Scotland have led to a real divergence between social work values/penal welfarism and the neoliberal value base characterised by the management of offenders within a new penology. This leads us to question whether social workers in CJSW might feel frustrated in the expression of their traditional social work value base.

Disjuncture

Students in Scotland who want to work with offenders undertake the same generic social work qualification as those who want to work with other service user 'groups'. There is an assumption, then, that those students who successfully qualify as social workers after four years of study have a personal value base in sympathy with the value base of social work. When social workers are in practice, therefore, what happens when they feel thwarted in their desire to base their practice on their values?

Di Franks (2008) distributed 500 questionnaires to a random sample of social workers in the US who were all members of the National Association of Social Workers. The main purpose of the questionnaire was to measure the social workers' belief in the NASW Code of Ethics; their behaviour in implementing it; and disjuncture. **Disjuncture** is defined as the ethical stress experienced when a worker cannot base their practice on their value beliefs, and Di Franks did, in fact, find that social workers scored high for disjuncture when their belief scores and their behaviour scores were discordant. So, when social workers could not behave in a way that was congruent with their social work value beliefs, they felt stress. A further exploration of the literature identifies that a key factor that influences the extent to which workers experience disjuncture is whether or not they feel that they can get to know and 'help' service users when they want to (Fenton, 2012a). In essence, then, if workers feel that they can build relationships with people; can help where they feel it is warranted; and generally feel a congruence between their values and their actions, they will experience minimal disjuncture.

Is it reasonable at this point to question whether social workers in CJSW might experience disjuncture? If their value base is congruent with penal welfarism and with a wider social work belief in welfare and social justice, and if the suggestion that CJSW has diverged significantly from this is a valid one, then it is extremely possible that workers will experience ethical stress or disjuncture. The case study should help to illuminate this.

Case study

A social worker in CJSW in Scotland is working with a young man, Billy, who has been involved in a series of assaults on other young men when under the influence of alcohol. The social worker's job is to work with him to change his offending behaviour. In a context dominated by **risk management** and cognitive behavioural work, the social worker would make sure all the risk assessment and management paperwork is done; might draw up a contract which instructs Billy to avoid certain public houses (minimising the risk); might instruct him to attend a generic 'offending behaviour' group to change his thinking about offending; and instruct him to attend alcohol counselling sessions. However, the social worker might also know that Billy has spent years in various foster homes; wants to repair his relationship with his estranged mother; and has a pregnant girlfriend with whom he is desperate to create a stable family. He also says he wants to stop offending (his girlfriend will not put up with it any longer). The social worker has to, in effect, deprioritise all of these circumstances to work on the risk management plan as outlined, as the primary task. If Billy were asked how he could be helped to stop offending, he might say he wanted help for himself and his girlfriend to find a new flat; wanted relationship counselling with his girlfriend, as she was finding it hard to trust him; wanted to work on re-contacting his mother; wanted to pursue working with cars, or wanted help with other things he perceived as important. Not being able to help with these issues might well cause a social worker to experience disjuncture.

Desistance

One way of addressing the above tensions and stresses lies in the adoption of a **desistance** approach to work with offenders. A comprehensive examination of the desistance literature is not possible within this chapter, but is available elsewhere (for example McNeill, 2006; McCulloch and McNeill, 2009). In essence, desistance is the personal and individual journey a person makes to stop offending. The desistance literature promotes an approach to social work practice that supports this process, rather than one that is characterised by doing something *to* someone to stop them offending, as per the cognitive-behavioural approach of 'What works'. For example, Farrall's (2002) theory of desistance proposes that the factors that support desistance are those changes in a person's life that they most value. Therefore, the value that the person attaches to a change (for example, employment or a relationship) is of central importance, and this means that the offender must be the key player in deciding which changes are to be worked towards. McNeill (2006) suggests that because desistance is primarily a complex and individual process, CJSW services should be a secondary service, supporting the offender's own journey.

Key Practice Skills (McNeill et al, 2005) was commissioned by the then Scottish Executive and draws significantly upon the desistance literature. An approach to working with offenders based on desistance principles would encompass genuine, warm and **therapeutic relationships** with offenders, and explicit attention to the importance of 'helping' work within those relationships. Clearly, this approach is also congruent with social work and penal welfare values, and would thus relieve the tension inherent in the work as outlined earlier. The social worker for Billy, for example, would be guided by him in what the priority tasks were in regard to supporting his own desistance attempts.

As the literature review was commissioned by the Scottish Executive, it would be logical to think that there was government support for the adoption of such an approach. However, as McCulloch and McNeill (2009) observe, 'the *muted impact* that the desistance literature has had on policy and practice is both surprising and problematic ...' (p 155, emphasis added). If this is the case, and desistance welfare work is being eclipsed by correctional, managerial approaches described earlier in the chapter, then criminal justice social workers will still struggle to base their work upon the social justice, penal welfare values they were trained in.

Ultimately, we can see that the direction from the government is inconsistent, perhaps contributing to the 'muted impact' of the desistance literature on practice. Another factor may be that desistance approaches necessitate social workers having discretion and autonomy to respond to service users in the individual ways required. This type of responsive practice is not one that can be wholly prescribed by policy or practice guidelines, is less suited to measurement, audit and defence and, thus, may well cause anxiety for managers within agencies. It is much 'safer' for the agency if the social worker can demonstrate due diligence by a procedural and rule-following approach to practice (Fenton, 2012b).

Double marginalisation of CJSW

It can be seen from the discussion thus far, that CJSW practice expectations have changed significantly and that there is uncertainty and inconsistency in relation to the governmental direction of the work. Furthermore, the actual positioning of CJSW in relation to relevant interprofessions might also exacerbate the situation. CJSW is economically and perhaps ethically separated from the rest of the social work department, but is *also* marginalised from the legal world of the courts. Social workers in CJSW are conscious of this to the extent that they often try to status-seek in the reports they write for the court, so as to achieve credibility with those whom they perceive as having higher status (for example sheriffs) (Halliday et al, 2009). As McNeill et al (2010) state, social workers in CJSW 'also revealed a sense of "double-marginalisation"; both from generic social work ... and from the law-profession dominated world of the courts' (p 37).

In terms of interprofessional values, then, criminal justice social workers are worried that 'their professional discourse of welfare and care would be undervalued as "namby-pambiness"' (Halliday et al, 2009, p 422). So, workers in CJSW not only are having their values eroded by changes in the penal landscape and the formation of an influential new penology, but also worry that their adherence to traditional penal welfare and social work values will actually be viewed disparagingly by allied professionals with higher status (see Chapter Twelve for similar concerns among police officers as being seen to be weak if they express an emotional response to their work). McNeill et al (2010) also point out that a further consequence of 'double-marginalisation' is that 'criminal justice social workers may themselves tend to look inwards, to identify with their traditions, their teams and their peers' (p 40). This may well mean that CJSW workplace cultures are self-perpetuating, with new workers socialised into a 'new penological' way of working with offenders. To explore this further, we can draw on Schein's (2010) three levels that he applies to workplace cultures: artefacts, 'espoused beliefs and values' and 'basic underlying assumptions' (Schein, 2010, p 27). Artefacts are the parts of the culture actually experienced by people (for example **supervision**, office discussion and so on) and espoused beliefs are the articulated values of the agency, which may, in reality, be aspirational and at odds with the actual practice. In relation to CJSW, espoused values are likely to be traditional social work and penal welfare values as per workers' social work education, although these would indeed be at odds with the actual practice within agencies. The further, deeper level, 'basic underlying assumptions', is concerned with a fundamental belief, for example in the nature of people, that permeates the two upper levels. Herein lies the nub of the CJSW position. The old, basic assumptions were penal welfarist: we should help people with their problems, understand structural disadvantage and fight for more justice. Offenders are, it could be argued, **victims** of an unfair society. The question is, are the new underlying basic assumptions brought about by the advent of neoliberalism and the reactionary turn against penal welfarism? Are the basic underlying beliefs now concerned with the responsibility, containment and punishment of the offender? Additionally, is there a belief that there is little we can do to effect change, and so we should be primarily concerned with the efficient functioning of the system and with doing the accountability 'tasks' properly? If so, then the intraprofessional clash with the underlying basic assumptions of the wider social work department is indeed very significant.

Underpinning ethical theories

According to Garland (2001, p 49), penal welfarism embodied a collectivist form of governance, defined by 'the distinctive combination of humanitarian and utilitarian motivations that characterised the relations between ruling groups and subordinate classes'. Referring back to Chapter One and to the introduction to this chapter, penal welfarism can be easily understood as located within a utilitarian framework, based as it is on the premise that if material circumstances improve, crime should lessen. Clearly, the case for 'welfare' herein is that the greatest good for the greatest number of people will be achieved by attaining a reasonable standard of comfort and opportunity for all members of a society. If this is achieved, the 'good' for society should be further enhanced by the reduction of crime. In this way, the associations between utilitarianism, penal-welfarism and social work's concern with 'principles of human rights and social justice' (IFSW, 2012, p 1) can be understood in ethical terms.

What of the 'new penological' approach to the management and control of offenders, then (Feeley and Simon, 1992)? According to Slingeneyer (2007), the new penology is not concerned with the 'ends' of probation. The outcome measures of reduced re-offending or increased welfare are not the central aim of the new penology. Instead, the system itself and measures of efficient system functioning (that is, managing risk-classified groups of offenders) have become the ambitions of the system. If this is the case, the new penology has become dislocated from its underpinning philosophy of utilitarianism in the same way that it became dislocated from penal welfarism. It is no longer about achieving the greatest good for the greatest number (Parrott, 2010), but is about professional people following rules and procedures within a system that aims to show due diligence in its practices. In reference to Chapter One, then, it seems that the practice of criminal justice social workers within this new system is characterised by deontology: workers doing their 'duties' and following the procedures, with less interest in the impact of their actions (Parrott, 2010). Indeed, Barry (2007) found that workers were concerned, as a priority, about showing they had followed the policies and procedures correctly, rather than about really engaging with the service user. In conclusion, then, what do these ethical and practice shifts mean for social workers in terms of 'disjuncture'?

Research

As part of a wider (as yet unpublished) PhD study, the author distributed questionnaires to social workers in four local authority criminal justice departments. One hundred completed questionnaires were returned. The questionnaire concerned workers' experiences of disjuncture/ ethical stress and the factors that contributed to this. For the purposes of this chapter, the author will draw on illustrative quotes concerning whether social workers in CJSW believe that they are working in a context where penal welfare and traditional social work values still have purchase:

> "Being unable to spend more/quality time with clients due to constant sorties of new procedures and new policies and practices which are fuelling a culture of 'ticking boxes'."

> "I think the agency struggles with 'measuring' the value of a helping/welfare approach, is unsure of its political acceptability and therefore is reluctant to embrace it openly."
> (Fenton, 2013)

Many other comments of this type were made, illustrating that, as suggested, penal welfarism is indeed being eclipsed within CJSW agencies. Workers' comments demonstrate that a downgrading of welfare work has taken place and, as suggested above, efficient functioning and measuring of the system itself has become a more important priority. Furthermore, as the next set of quotes demonstrates, any welfare work that can be done is very clearly identified by workers as secondary to public protection/risk/paperwork/accountability work. The vast majority of comments made stated that there was no instruction for agencies not to undertake welfare work, and in fact agencies and workers still believed in the worth of this, *but* it would only happen if there was any time available after the priority tasks had been completed:

> "Public protection is seen as our utmost aim; however, my agency still values the welfare of clients."

> "The thing stopping me from doing welfare work is lack of time and resources rather than a mandate not to do this." (Fenton, 2013)

The above comments demonstrate that social workers have, to an extent, absorbed the requirements for the prioritisation of risk and public protection work without completely abandoning their welfare affiliations. The consistent message is that they simply do not have time to undertake the welfare work they would want to. In a study by McNeill (2000), workers were found to have reconciled the requirements for a sharper focus on re-offending by re-inscribing their welfare work as the means to bring about that end. In the current study, there is a clearer divide between the risk/public protection work and welfare work, with the latter being done only when there is time. In other words, McNeill's social workers *were* concerned with the aims and purposes of their work, while current practice appears to focus more on workers *doing* the tasks properly. Comments were also made such as "I believe the service a client receives is largely dependent on the individual worker and their knowledge and motivation". In other words, social workers will undertake welfare and helping work when there is time and when the social worker has the inclination to do so. The implication of this is that no one will be very perturbed if the welfare work does not happen, as long as the priority *tasks* are done. This is not wholly at odds with a penal welfare approach, but the emphasis on helping is undoubtedly diluted. Therefore, is there value conflict between their traditional social work values, and the diluted and new-penological version of those values? Some comments were made as follows:

> "Conscience pricks me when I have to do lengthy admin[istration] tasks when time could be better spent working with people."

> "My agency encourages good practice but prioritises criminogenic needs. My ethics as a social worker are in conflict with this at times." (Fenton, 2013)

Clearly, for some social workers, disjuncture is generated, although these types of comments were vastly outnumbered by an acceptance that CJSW is about *both* welfare *and* public protection (see Chapter Five for impact of disjuncture on well-being). According to those respondents, heavy workloads and lack of time, which do not leave time for 'real' social work, are the actual problem.

In summary, then, an analysis of the comments demonstrates that there is surprising clarity in the *doing* of the job in CJSW. The priority tasks are clear for social workers and they go along with them without much complaint. This calls into question the 'espoused values' (Schein, 2010, p 27), about which several comments were made, for example, "my agency still values the welfare of clients" and "I feel we can, and do, consider [social work] values". The aspirational nature, as opposed to real expression, of those values will be apparent in the 'artefacts' level of culture (Schein, 2010). Supervision, team discussions, informal case discussions and so on will be concerned with the explicit demonstration of public protection as a priority that, in an inward-looking, self-perpetuating agency, will gain momentum as new workers arrive and are socialised into the agency (Smith et al, 2012).

Conclusion

In conclusion, it is clear that there is tension between the value base of CJSW and the value base of generic social work, even though CJSW retains its place within the wider social work field and, as such, should share the same value beliefs in the promotion of welfare and the pursuit of social justice, based on utilitarian principles. The adoption of a desistance approach would address this situation, as well as providing a plurality of benefits. The benefits would include a research evidence base that demonstrates that such an approach is effective in helping people to stop offending; that it is a very good 'fit' with social work education (which gives significant attention to welfare, anti-oppressive practice and structural discrimination) and so should be easily adopted by social workers; that it would reduce disjuncture for workers; and that it would re-affirm that CJSW's value base is congruent with the value base of wider social work, based on underlying penal welfare, utilitarian assumptions. In turn, this would help welfare/helping work to reclaim its place as a legitimate and worthwhile social work endeavour, no matter what label has been given to the service user.

References

Andrews, D.A., Zinger, I., Hodge, R.D., Bonta, J., Gendreau, P. and Cullen, F.T. (1990) 'Does correctional treatment work? A clinically relevant and psychologically informed meta-analysis', *Criminology*, vol 28, pp 369–404.

Barry, M. (2007) *Effective approaches to risk assessment in social work: An international literature review.* Edinburgh: Scottish Government.

Bottoms, A.E. (1980) 'An introduction to "the coming crisis"', in A.E. Bottoms and R.H. Preston (eds) *The coming penal crisis: A criminological and theological exploration,* Edinburgh: Scottish Academic Press, pp 1–24.

Bottoms, A.E. and McWilliams, W. (1979) 'A non-treatment paradigm for probation practice', *British Journal of Social Work*, vol 9, no 2, pp 159–202.

Criminal Justice and Licensing (Scotland) Act 2010, www.legislation. gov.uk/asp/2010/13/contents.

Croall, H. (2005) 'Criminal justice in the devolved Scotland', in G. Mooney and G. Scott (eds) *Exploring social policy in the 'new' Scotland,* Bristol: Policy Press.

Di Franks, N. (2008) 'Social workers and the NASW Code of Ethics: belief, behaviour and disjuncture', *Social Work*, vol 53, no 2, pp 167–76.

Farrall, S. (2002) *Rethinking what works with offenders: Probation, social context and desistance from crime,* Portland: Willan Publishing.

Feeley, M. and Simon, J. (1992) 'The new penology: notes on the emerging strategy of corrections and its implications', *Criminology*, vol 30, pp 449–74.

Fenton, J. (2012a) 'Bringing together messages from the literature on criminal justice social work and "disjuncture": the importance of helping', *British Journal of Social Work*, vol 42, no 5, pp 941–56.

Fenton, J. (2012b) 'Risk aversion and anxiety in Scottish criminal justice social work: can desistance and human rights agendas have an impact?' *Howard Journal of Criminal Justice*, doi: 10.1111/j.1468-2311.1012.00716.x, ISSN 0265-5527.

Fenton, J. (2013) 'Ethical stress in Scottish criminal justice social work: social workers' views', unpublished doctoral thesis, Dundee: University of Dundee.

Garland, D. (2001) *The culture of control: Crime and social order in contemporary society*, Chicago: Oxford University Press.

Halliday, S., Burns, N., Hutton, N., McNeill, F. and Tata, C. (2009) 'Street level bureaucracy, interprofessional relations and coping mechanisms: a study of criminal justice social workers in the sentencing process', *Law and Policy*, vol 31, no 4, pp 405–28.

International Federation of Social Workers (IFSW) (2012) 'Definition of social work', http://ifsw.org/policies/definition-of-social-work/.

Mair, G. (2004) 'The origins of "what works" in England and Wales: a house built on sand?' in G. Mair (ed) *What matters in probation?* Cullompton, Devon: Willan Publishing.

Management of Offenders etc (Scotland) Act 2005, www.legislation.gov.uk/all?title=Management%20of%20Offenders%20%28Scotland%29%20Act%202005.

Martinson, R. (1974) 'What works? Questions and answers about prison reform', *The Public Interest*, vol 35, pp 22–54.

McCulloch, T. (2005) 'Probation, social context and desistance: retracing the relationship', *Probation Journal*, vol 52, pp 8–22.

McCulloch, T. and McNeill, F. (2009) 'Desistance-focused approaches', in S. Green, E. Lancaster and S. Feasey (eds) *Addressing offending behaviour: Context, practice and values*, Cullompton, Devon: Willan Publishing.

McCulloch, T. and McNeill, F. (2011) 'Adult criminal justice', in R. Davis and J. Gordon (eds) *Social work and the law in Scotland* (2nd edn), Milton Keynes: Palgrave Macmillan, pp 184–200.

McNeill, F. (2000) 'Defining effective probation: frontline perspectives', *The Howard Journal*, vol 39, pp 382–97.

McNeill, F. (2004) 'Desistance, rehabilitation and correctionalism: developments and prospects in Scotland', *The Howard Journal*, vol 43, pp 420–36.

McNeill, F. (2005) 'Remembering probation in Scotland', *Probation Journal*, vol 52, pp 23–38.

McNeill, F. (2006) 'A desistance paradigm for offender management', *Criminology and Criminal Justice*, vol 6, pp 39–62.

McNeill, F. and Whyte, B. (2007) *Reducing re-offending: Social work and community justice in Scotland*, Cullompton, Devon: Willan Publishing.

McNeill, F., Burnett, R. and McCulloch, T. (2010) *Culture, change and community justice,* Report No 02/2010, Edinburgh: The Scottish Centre for Crime and Justice Research.

McNeill, F., Batchelor, S., Burnett, R. and Knox, J. (2005) *21st century social work, reducing re-offending: Key practice skills*, Edinburgh: Scottish Executive.

Parrott, T. (2010) *Values and ethics in social work practice* (2nd edn), Exeter: Learning Matters.

Schein, E.H. (2010) *Organisational culture and leadership* (4th edn), Hoboken, NJ: Jossey-Bass.

Scottish Government (2007) *Criminal Justice Directorate Circular 15/2006*, www.scotland.gov.uk/Publications/2007/10/03110820/0.

Scottish Office (1998) *Community sentencing: The tough option – review of social work services*, Edinburgh: Scottish Office.

Scottish Social Services Council (SSSC) (2009) *Codes of practice for Scottish social service workers and employers*, Dundee: SSSC.

Slingeneyer, T. (2007) 'The new penology: a grid for analyzing the transformations of penal discourses, techniques and objectives', *Penal Field*, vol 4, http://champpenal.revues.org/7798.

Smith, L., Amiot, C., Callan, V., Terry, D. and Smith, J. (2012) 'Getting new staff to stay: the mediating role of organizational identification', *British Journal of Management*, vol 23, pp 45–64.

Social Work (Scotland) Act 1968, www.legislation.gov.uk/ukpga/1968/49.

Social Work Services Group (1991) *National objectives and standards for social work in the criminal justice system*, Edinburgh: The Scottish Office.

SEVEN

Personal and professional ethical dilemmas in the context of developing teacher leaders in Australia

Allie Clemans, John Loughran and Amanda Berry

The context of ethical dilemmas

In line with the aims of Part Two, this chapter focuses on the dynamics of personal and professional ethics (see Figure 1.1). It takes up an intellectual exploration of the ethical tensions and practices that emerged for the authors during their leadership of a **professional learning** programme for teachers in government-funded schools over a three-year period. The authors present and examine their lived experiences and draw on the writing of teachers involved in the programme to illustrate the ethical dilemmas they confronted and the consequent decision-making approach they adopted.

The authors were educators and researchers within the education faculty of an Australian research-intensive university. They were contracted by the state's Ministry of Education to develop and conduct a professional learning (PL) programme for teachers who were appointed as **professional learning leaders** in their schools. The contract required the programme leaders to design and implement a PL programme for over 200 primary and secondary teachers, the Leading Professional Learning (LPL) programme. The authors led and implemented the programme over the three years. That work required **interprofessional** collaboration between the **teacher leaders** who participated in the programme, the government department that funded the programme and the team of academics that jointly delivered the programme over the three years.

In this chapter, attention is focused on the conditions through which this programme unfolded and, in particular, on the ethical dilemmas that such conditions raised for the authors as 'contractors' and researchers.

Unlike their previous work, which attends to the experiences of teacher leaders in the programme and its impact on them (Clemans et al, 2010, 2012; Loughran et al, 2011), here the authors reflect on themselves as leaders of the programme and identify the shifting 'ethical' ground on which they found themselves standing.

Hardy and Lingard's (2008) analysis of a professional learning programme in another state of Australia suggests that policy imperatives can often override the ways in which the professional principles may drive professional learning programmes designed to support teachers' professional growth, autonomy and forms of inquiry. Their analysis resonates with the authors' experiences of leading this programme. However, before progressing with the chapter, it is important to define the use of the term 'ethical dilemma'. Duignan and Cannon (2011) used the term to refer to times 'when all seems to be in constant crisis and when strategic direction seems to be swamped by short-term emergencies, [at that time] leaders need to focus on core values and moral purpose' (p 26). The ethical dilemmas refer to the authors' normative sense of what felt 'right' or 'wrong' during work in this programme and the ways in which these norms informed their actions and relations with the professionals with whom they collaborated. Importantly, the notion of dilemma is crucial to these feelings because a dilemma is something that is managed, not necessarily solved. Therefore, these ethical dilemmas ebbed and flowed with the programme to the extent that the authors managed their influence and impact on their work – and the work of the teacher leaders involved in the LPL programme.

This chapter explores the lived experience of these dilemmas through consideration of a number of data sources that emerged through, and as a result of, the LPL project. In this exploration, excerpts of data from teacher leaders' writing generated through their participation in the programme, data from interviews held with teachers on their completion of the programme, data from formal evaluations of the programme and the authors' reflection on events are woven together.

Consideration of these sources highlighted three areas around which professional and ethical dilemmas were identifiable. The first dilemma is associated with the ways in which a research-led approach to professional learning, which informed the design of the LPL programme, clashed with the imperatives of the funding agency. For example, while the authors viewed the teacher leaders as 'active knowers' and 'generators of knowledge', the funding agency positioned them as passive consumers of others' knowledge. Clearly, these contradictory positions created real concerns about the ways in which the authors' talk of 'valuing teachers' might be interpreted by the participants. The second dilemma is linked to the ways in which teacher leaders in the programme were supported to articulate, for themselves and their professional communities, that which they had come to know about leadership. Despite the fact that the teacher leaders came to see and understand their practice as problematic, the funding agency preferred to portray participants' experiences through the lens of 'cause and effect', which situates the experiences of leading within a school context as rather linear and solution driven – or more so, a desire to find the 'correct' (bureaucratic/policy directed) solution. The third dilemma is embedded in an overarching concern about the relationship between PL 'interventions' and their contribution to authentic and sustainable change in the teachers' organisational contexts, namely, in their schools. This situation stems from compromises forced onto the LPL programme that diminished opportunities for meaningful longer-term change; that is, change was mandated by the bureaucracy rather than driven by professional needs and concerns brought to the surface through the programme.

As is no doubt evident, these descriptions (above) prompt a question that this chapter now explores: 'what did managing these dilemmas mean for the authors as ethical researchers and educators leading the learning of other professionals?'

The Leading Professional Learning programme

To discuss the dilemmas outlined above, a brief description of the LPL programme is provided. The programme was designed to support teachers who were responsible for leading professional learning in their respective schools. The term 'teacher leader' refers to these participant teachers, who described themselves as new to, or only slightly experienced in, leadership. As new appointees to the leadership position, their school-based responsibilities included being both a classroom teacher and a leader of professional learning for their school. For teachers, making the transition is neither simple nor straightforward, as is well illustrated in the academic literature (for example, Taylor et al, 2011). Taking that into account, the LPL programme targeted the development of teacher leaders' leadership (and the transition associated with doing so), assisting them to explore issues and dilemmas in their own practice and document the professional knowledge they developed over the course of the programme.

Design principles: working *with* rather than *on* teachers

The programme design was intentional and explicit. The use of the term 'professional learning' (PL), rather than 'professional development' (PD), reflected the evidence-led view of the nature of teacher learning (Mockler, 2005; Wei et al, 2009), which supported a deep and sustained approach to PL. In short, PD could be viewed as working *on* teachers so that they were 'upskilled' and able to do what was expected in their practice (in order to implement mandated policies or prescribed changes in curriculum and/or teaching), while PL is about working *with* teachers to help them develop their skills, knowledge and abilities in ways that are responsive to *their* pedagogical concerns, issues and needs. The distinction is crucial, as it not only framed the way the LPL programme was conceptualised and conducted but it also made clear where ownership of learning should reside (that is, within the individual participant).

The LPL programme was built on two principles. First, it was formally constructed as a PL programme that placed teacher learning, schools and leadership contexts at its core. Second, the LPL programme positioned teachers as producers of knowledge rather than receivers of the wisdom of (more knowledgeable) others. This meant that the LPL programme seriously viewed teachers as learners whose learning was driven by a set of contextually and personally relevant and recognisable dilemmas. The growth of teachers' capacities to inquire and investigate their own leadership practices was therefore valued as a programme outcome. However, meetings held with the funding agency prior to each of our workshops imposed a set of intentions and outcomes that clashed with these programme and design principles.

The outcomes that drove the programme were set by the government funding agency and, in sum, they aimed to build the participating teacher leaders' capability to design, implement and evaluate effective school-based professional learning to support improved teaching and learning. The government view of leadership at that time was based on the well-documented work of Sergiovanni (1996). Essential to this leadership conceptualisation was the desire to enable teacher leadership based on a connection between teacher quality and classroom/student outcomes. This is something that also 'falls into the category of "easy to say, hard to do"' (Groundwater-Smith and Mockler, 2009, p 95), but the government funding body was determined for this link to be asserted and for teacher leaders to do their part in forging it.

Thus, the LPL programme was pulled between the authors' intentions about constructive notions of the value of teacher learning for leadership (Berry et al, 2007; Poeckert, 2012) and the granting body's expectation of (what was considered to be elusive) evidence of a direct link between teacher learning and student outcomes. The tension between these two perspectives meant that the funding agency's ambitions for the programme were grand, and the content expected to be covered in a short amount of time was expansive. Part of this involved developing participants' understanding of a policy initiative current at the time, the *Principles of Highly Effective Professional Learning* (DEECD, 2005). The predictable result was that the programme vacillated between being one in which programme leaders 'told' teacher leaders what they needed to know, and challenging and supporting them to inquire into and critically reflect on their needs. For programme leaders, the tension between what the funding agency expected and their own understanding of PL created a sense of discomfort and unease that ebbed and flowed throughout the programme. For the researchers, it stands out as an ethical dilemma that is considerably more apparent now that the pragmatic demands of programme delivery are past.

As is evident in the nature of the dilemma noted above, the competing expectations within this situation challenged a key design principle of professional learning that was underpinned by the concern to work *with* rather than *on* teachers. Conceptually, the authors were of the view that constructing teachers as 'knowers' signalled to the teacher leader participants that their situated knowledge of leadership-generated knowledge was both worthy and important to share. So much so, that space was purposely made for this knowledge generation in the programme through a one-day case-writing day, in which teacher leaders were supported in writing an account of their learning as leaders of professional learning (for a full description, see Clemans et al, 2012). The resulting cases drew not only on what participants were learning but also on the ways in which their learning played out in the social situation of leading PL in their schools. Clearly, this process hinged on participants generating their own professional knowledge of leading. The case-writing process prompted reflection by surfacing their tacit knowledge, reframing ideas and '[t]hrough this process, new theory [was] constructed' (Raelin, 2007, p 506).

Importantly, in the process of knowledge building and consolidation, and writing a case as the expression of that process, these teacher leaders were repositioned as professional and confident knowers who had developed contextual knowledge about leadership that was of value to express and, ultimately, to share. Juggling this with the funding agency's need to tell teachers leaders how to lead created dilemmas for the programme leaders. Awareness of these contradictions had varied implications.

It meant that programme leaders were confronted by their multiple roles and the need to balance the competing practices inherent in their identities as researchers, educators and 'contractors' (Davis and Ferreira, 2006). While the awarding of the contract for the delivery of this programme to the faculty endorsed its research-led capacity in, and professional experience of, professional learning, contracting to the project signalled a role as consultants, with the obvious expectation that they 'delivered' on the client's outcomes. Part of that 'delivery' – success, as measured by the clients – had more to do with the reproduction of particular knowledge among the teacher leaders than with the knowledge-building activities the programme had envisaged.

Managing the varying roles associated with the work on the project created complexity in ways not previously envisaged. It was not as simple as programme leaders being cast in a way that demanded a different identity but, rather, their moving between multiple identities, necessitating discernment about who they were expected to be, when and for what purpose, and the moral and professional values that were perceived to be embedded in these roles. Some writers have noted such shifts for academics as university business in a global market place is transformed and academics are reconstructed (Davis and Ferreira, 2006, p 40). Negotiating these different relationships invoked ethical complexity. The traditional separation of the roles of researcher, educator and consultant, familiar within universities, did not play out as neatly in this contract work of developing and implementing the LPL project. For example, there were times when there was a need to 'educate' the funding partner, as much as the teacher leaders, about what an inquiry-driven approach to leadership meant – not just theoretically but also practically. The tangible impact of the situation was evident when programme leaders were confronted by a need to justify certain programme approaches that played out in concrete ways as 'points of no-compromise', that is, where the authors were not prepared to contradict the underlying programme principles in practice. Navigating these 'points of no-compromise' presented ethical dilemmas as they impacted on the type of professional learning programme the leaders were able to deliver.

Dilemma-driven work

Like Larson and Walker (2010, p 338), the LPL programme was constructed with the aim of supporting teacher leaders' learning of leadership by structuring the programme as a series of 'dilemmas of practice' rather than as a set of fixed concepts that had to be acquired. In many ways, this mirrored the authors' own experience of working with the funding agency.

The dilemma-driven aspect of teacher leaders' work was explicitly built into the programme as a catalyst for learning through case writing (for full details of case writing see Shulman, 1992). Each teacher wrote a case that articulated their experiences of working with their dilemmas of practice. Analysis of the content of those cases for one particular year of the programme (Clemans et al, 2010) identified the ways in which these teacher leaders began to reframe their role through the lived experiences of their leadership. That analysis showed that they saw themselves not as 'fixers' of problems but as leaders who negotiated and managed dilemmas. As these teacher leaders made the transition from classroom educator to leader, an increased sense of vulnerability emerged for them around their perceived lack of authority and expertise in this role. Some of their case writing attests to this:

> For some reason, accepting a leadership role makes you feel like you have to fix it or make it work; it's actually hard to view it as a dilemma, something that is managed, not necessarily resolved. (Case 11, 2007)

> What exactly is my role? I wish there was an easy and transparent way for me to resolve this type of dilemma … (Case 15, 2007)

It is argued (above) that in the process of consolidating knowledge and writing a case as the expression of that knowing, these teacher leaders were repositioned as active knowers. 'Knowing' was not necessarily an easy stance to adopt for these teacher leaders. Part of what they came to know and write up in their cases centred on their knowing about the problematic and messy nature of leadership and coming to understand that as being legitimate rather than a sign that they did not know (enough). Interviews conducted with teachers six months after their participation in the programme highlighted that case writing validated for them that "[things were] confusing at times … but thought provoking" (Teacher K); and that "it is okay to make mistakes and to learn from them" (Teacher S1). This view of leadership was something they came to understand over time; it was not how they necessarily viewed their role at the outset.

In this writing process, teacher leaders came to terms with how it felt to be a professional learning leader. They recognised, as the authors do now with the reflective hindsight of writing this chapter, that an identity founded on vulnerability and born of on-going learning was, indeed, the basis of professional expertise. As Stronach et al (2002) wisely remind us: 'Professionals walk the tightrope of an uncertain being. It is important, then, for theories of professionalism to hold on to these notes of ambivalence and contradiction, rather than try to reduce or resolve them …' (p 121). In many ways, the programme was encouraging the teacher-leader participants' knowledge development by supporting and valuing what Munby and Russell (1994) described as their 'authority of experience'. However, such a view of learning and of professional identity formation was not always equally appreciated by the funding agency. The agency tended to view knowledge development from the opposing perspective of 'authority of position' (Munby and Russell, 1994), which therefore cut across the process and products that the programme sought to deliver. Once again, the authors' stated approach and underpinning principles were directly challenged by an opposing perspective of the funding agency. Their ethical dilemmas were very real.

'Smoothing out' dilemmas

Tensions between the funding agency and leaders of the programme intensified toward the end of each year of the three-year programme. The programme design had always rested on case writing as a significant dimension of the programme and a crucial aspect of participants' learning. Using a case-writing methodology, participants constructed their cases, shared and discussed their drafts and then, through collaboration with their **Peer Network Leaders**, further edited, refined and collated their cases for inclusion in a published Case Book (Berry et al, 2008; Clemans et al, 2009).

In the first year of the programme, financial responsibility for this initiative was assumed by the programme leaders, as it had always been seen it as a key learning outcome of the programme. Further, it was believed the publication was a significant representation of the worthiness of teacher leaders' professional learning and an explication of their developing professional knowledge. The funding agency had not, at first, anticipated the value of this aspect of the publication (despite its being an element of the programme design that originally attracted a great deal of their attention). The agency did not seem to grasp how the case process and book could promote its support for teachers' professional learning as well as convey their efforts to focus on current policy directions. On completion of the first book, this became strikingly apparent to it. So, too, did an edge of vulnerability around its lack of control over the content of the cases that concerned it and created some discussion about what cases portrayed and the level of openness the funding agency felt comfortable with in the light of its bureaucratic guidelines.

In the second year, how the publication process was to be managed/controlled changed. The funding agency saw the value of case writing and unilaterally mandated that all of its other funded professional learning programmes should similarly lead to the production of cases. However, it decided that it would take control of publishing and distributing the resulting book. In wresting control of this aspect of the programme, the funding agency redefined the work that comprised this aspect of the programme. Once again, the authors were confronted by a challenge to the programme intent that had not been anticipated.

The value of cases has been well recognised in the research literature as a powerful real-world, practice-based approach to fostering discoveries about teaching and learning at both a theoretical and a practical level (Loughran and Berry, 2011). Cases highlight the complexity and messiness of educational work in ways that are readily identifiable by professionals (Levin, 2002), thus creating an engaging narrative for others to read. The funding agency, however, rebadged these 'cases' as 'case stories', stripping away the professional knowledge-building traditions and dilemma-driven nature of these in an attempt to recast them in ways not fully consistent with the original formulation of such work. Further, they chose to edit the cases and adapt those accounts that were at odds with current policy directives, or that exposed less favourable accounts of schools and their systems, so that there was a 'smoothing out' of the situations or, as some teachers described it, ensuring case stories complied with policy directives. For example, there was quite some negotiation between the funding agency and a teacher leader who wrote a case poignantly titled 'Closed for business: Gone surfing', that ended with the writer's expressed intention to leave his post at the school as a result of his feeling devalued and unrecognised as an educational professional. Negotiations ensued around 'restorying' the case so that it ended on a more optimistic note. This troubled the programme leaders for a number of reasons. The first was that the intent and method of cases was being changed to suit a different outcome agenda; the second was that it appeared that participants' learning was being 'politically managed', and that third was that the programme leaders' response to the situation, although ethically driven to maintain fidelity with method and support for participants' stated learning outcomes, was at odds with the bureaucratic expectations and management/policing system of the funding agency in relation to 'sign off' and acceptability for 'system branded' documents.

Sustaining learning

A core ethos of the programme was that the development of learning should be experienced within school-based practice settings and a key support mechanism for so doing was through establishing professional learning communities of peers. **School-based Professional Learning Projects** were conducted by the teacher leaders in their respective schools. The LPL project included this small school-based project as a way of being both organisationally responsive and professionally valuable for the individual teacher leader. Groundwater-Smith and Mockler (2009) recognised that such small-scale projects of this nature may be scaled up, depending on the support and engagement of the system, school and staff. It was known that logistical issues such as lack of time and material and symbolic support for such work were barriers to active collaboration, often reducing it more to rhetoric than reality (Armour and Yelling, 2007; Power, 2011). Formative and summative evaluations of each of the workshops run over the three years showed consistent results. The four factors ranked highest by teacher leaders identifying aspects that limited their leadership related to their sense of lack of support, time, collegial interest and resourcing for their projects, with insufficient time as the most highly ranked aspect.

The evaluation data highlighted the difficulties in connecting the impact of individual teachers' growth to the schools in which they were located. This was borne out in the interview data gathered from teachers six months after their participation in the programme. While teachers themselves affirmed the growth in their 'confidence' to lead, the absence of the organisational support to absorb the professional learning and knowledge they had acquired meant that their growing confidence withered. While it could be said that the programme had an impact on individuals, the impact of the programme on the educational system was diluted because of the lack of institutional or systemic continuity around the programme – a paradox within a government-funded programme. These 'fault lines' constrained the programme and, despite unsuccessful attempts to work with the funding agency to strengthen these areas over the three years, the loss had to be reconciled. Again, what was sought for the programme and what the funding agency was prepared to give were not always congruent.

Conclusion: learning to live with and lead through ethical dilemmas

Reflecting on the professional experiences of working collaboratively and contractually with government and teacher professionals has highlighted points of tension that emerged for the authors as leaders of professional learning. In the cut and thrust of action, the authors aspire to act ethically but often take for granted what professional ethics look and feel like. Ethical dilemmas prompted the authors to reframe (Schön, 1983) some taken-for-granted assumptions about their practice and interactions with the funding agency. It is interesting that the ethical dilemmas that emerged for them through reflection and articulation in writing this chapter in many ways mirrored those that emerged for the teacher leaders through the programme. In the same way that the teacher leaders in the LPL programme were drawn to a level of honesty in their case writing in order to convey their knowledge with authenticity, so too the present act of writing has caused the authors to 'notice' things differently. As one of the teacher leaders noted:

> "[my] initial reaction when I put pen to paper was to make myself look good ... but once you step back from it and read ... [you] think 'hang on, that's not what happened at all' ... [it] was [a] really powerful moment." (Teacher S3)

As for the teacher leaders, for the programme leaders enacting professional responsibilities ethically meant a need to confront the messy nature of leadership as 'value laden and value driven' (Norberg and Johansson, 2007, p 278). Ethical professional practice involved 'valuing, selecting and acting' (p 279) and the values that drove choices were informed by the authors' identities as educators, researchers and contractors in this process. The professional learning programme was guided by a set of principles which were themselves value based. How these played out in a government-funded professional learning programme was complex, compromised and, at times, uncomfortable. As Atkinson (2004) acknowledges:

> we are living in a simulacrum of education constructed by the rhetoric of policy makers and reinforced by our own collusion as researchers and practitioners.... A dangerous

> position that brings with it ... vital ethical questions to be
> answered ... (p 114)

It is interesting to note how, through reflecting on the authors' experiences as developers and implementers of the LPL programme, this chapter has highlighted the nature of the ethical standpoints that underpinned the essential elements of relationships with, and responsibility to, the teacher leaders at the centre of the programme. As is evident in the above account, the interplay of personal and professional ethics guided the leaders' ethical decision making in accord with Ehrich et al's (2011) description. In this case, the leaders' professional ethics was not so much an adherence to a code governing their profession (as described in Chapter One) but, rather, a form of ethical alignment or 'like-mindedness' based on their implicit professional values, manifested in the way the leadership team considered and valued their profession and, in this case, their practice in fostering the learning of others.

The challenges experienced by the authors of this chapter to their deeply ingrained personal and professional ethical perspectives were mirrored for the teacher leaders. This is what Zenni (2001) refers to as the essential ethics of practitioner research. As Zenni noted, in such cases:

> Ethical guidelines need to be rethought for the special case of research by practitioners in their own workplaces ... [which] ... most often brings ethical dilemmas. If our journals remain private ..., we can inquire with equanimity. But though we document our own practice, we rarely work in isolation.... Dilemmas of responsibility and ownership arise, and the academic codes of conduct are silent. (Zenni, 2001, p 153)

The practitioner research that the teacher leaders conducted with the explicit support from the programme leaders was, in effect, bound up in the Aristotelian notion of 'phronesis' – moral practical knowledge or practical wisdom of which an ethical component is intrinsic (Hughes, 2001). So, too, the actions at the heart of the authors' experiences were voluntary responses based on their ethical deliberations in the given situation. They were driven not by a pre-ordained universal (scientific) approach to the situation but, rather, by what might be described by Aristotle as ethical perceptions of the particular situation. There was not a correct choice to make, but a personal response gained through the experience. This chapter brings to the fore the personal responses inherent in the lived experience of this professional work and the tacit nature of the phronetic knowledge that guided the leaders' work as they were confronted by the dilemmas they encountered. While the management of these dilemmas was underpinned by professional 'like-mindedness', it does likewise suggest that articulating one's personal and professional ethical standpoints is a core dimension of professional practice.

In developing and conducting the LPL programme, the authors were forced to transition between their identities as educators, researchers and contractors and to consider ethical dilemmas from these differing standpoints. Through examination in, or after, the action, it was personal and professional values that determined the next moves to be made, although it could well be argued that the articulation of these as the basis of ethical decision making was not always clear at the time, but certainly became clearer in retrospect. What was learned about leading professional learning was that leadership is not always about resolving situations by making the 'right' or 'wrong' decisions, but about managing dilemmas that such relationships and activities brought to the surface. Leading, as the teacher leaders learned, was about knowing ourselves amidst shifting identities – what we stood for, what we could surrender and what we chose not to lose. Such were the ethical dilemmas of the authors' professional practice as they led a path of negotiation through conditions of compliance, 'collusion', compromise and uncertainty.

References

Armour, K. and Yelling, M. (2007) 'Effective professional development for physical education teachers: the role of informal, collaborative learning', *Journal of Teaching in Physical Education*, vol 26, pp 177–200.

Atkinson, E. (2004) 'Thinking outside the box: an exercise in heresy', *Qualitative Inquiry*, vol 10, pp 111–29.

Berry, A., Blaise, M., Clemans, A., Loughran, J., Mitchell, I., Parr, G., Riley, P. and Robb, D. (eds) (2008) *Leading professional learning: Cases of professional dilemmas*, Melbourne: DEECD and Monash University.

Berry, A., Clemans, A. and Kostogriz, A. (eds) (2007) *Dimensions of professional learning: Identities, professionalism and practice*, Rotterdam, Netherlands: Sense Publishers.

Clemans, A., Berry, A. and Loughran, J. (2010) 'Lost in transition: the professional journey of teacher educators', *Journal of Professional Development in Education*, Special Issue, vol 36, no 1, pp 211–28.

Clemans, A., Berry, A. and Loughran, J. (2012) 'Public anticipation yet private realisation: the effects of using cases as an approach to developing teacher leaders', *Australian Journal of Education*, vol 56, no 3, pp 287–302.

Clemans, A., Berry, A., Keast, S., Loughran, J., Parr, G., Riley, P., Robb, D. and Tudball, T. (eds) (2009) *Willing to lead. Leading professional learning*, Melbourne: DEECD.

Davis, J. and Ferreira, J. (2006) 'Higher Education Inc.: the personal and professional dilemmas of environmental educators undertaking research with/for private corporations', *Australian Journal of Environmental Education*, vol 22, no 1, pp 39–47.

DEECD (2005) *Professional learning in effective schools: The seven principles of highly effective professional learning*, www.eduweb.vic.gov.au/edulibrary/public/teachlearn/teacher/ProfLearningInEffectiveSchools.pdf.

Duignan, P. and Cannon, H. (2011) *The power of many: Building sustainable collective leadership in schools*, Victoria: ACER.

Ehrich, L.C., Kimber, M., Millwater, J. and Cranstone, N. (2011) 'Ethical dilemmas: a model to understand teacher practice', *Teachers and Teaching*, vol 17, no 2, pp 173–85.

Groundwater-Smith, S. and Mockler, N. (2009) *Teacher professional learning in an age of compliance: Mind the gap*, Rotterdam: Springer.

Hardy, I. and Lingard, B. (2008) 'Teacher professional development as an effect of policy and practice: a Bourdieuan analysis', *Journal of Education Policy*, vol 23, no 1, pp 63–80.

Hughes, G.J. (2001) *Aristotle on ethics*, London: Routledge.

Larson, R.W. and Walker, K.C. (2010) 'Dilemmas of practice: challenges to program quality encountered by youth program leaders', *American Journal of Community Psychology*, vol 45, pp 338–49.

Levin, B. (2002) 'Dilemma-based cases written by preservice elementary teacher candidates: an analysis of process and content', *Teaching Education*, vol 12, no 2, pp 203–18.

Loughran, J.J. and Berry, A. (2011) 'Making a case for improving practice: what can be learned about high quality science teaching from teacher produced cases?', in D. Corrigan, J. Dillon and R. Gunstone (eds) *The professional knowledge of science teachers*, Dordrecht: Springer, pp 65–82.

Loughran, J., Berry, A., Clemans, A., Keast, S., Miranda, B., Parr, G. and Tudball, E. (2011) 'Exploring the nature of teachers' professional learning', in A. Lauriala, R. Rajala, H. Ruokamo and O. Ylitapio-Mantyla (eds) *Navigating in educational contexts: Identities and cultures in dialogue*, Rotterdam: Sense Publishers, pp 93–102.

Mockler, N. (2005) 'Trans/forming teachers: new professional learning and transformative teacher professionalism', *Journal of In-service Education*, vol 31, no 4, pp 733–46.

Munby, H. and Russell, T. (1994) 'The authority of experience in learning to teach: messages from a physics method class', *Journal of Teacher Education*, vol 4, no 2, pp 86–95.

Norberg, K. and Johansson, O. (2007) 'Ethical dilemmas of Swedish school leaders', *Educational Management Administration & Leadership*, vol 35, no 2, pp 277–94.

Poeckert, P.P. (2012) 'Teacher leadership and professional development: examining links between two concepts central to school improvement', *Professional Development in Education*, vol 38, no 2, pp 169–88.

Power, A. (2011) 'Against short term professional learning', *Issues in Educational Research*, vol 21, no 3, pp 295–309.

Raelin, J. (2007) 'Toward an epistemology of practice', *Academy of Management Learning and Education*, vol 6, no 4, pp 495–519.

Schön, D.A. (1983) *The reflective practitioner: How professionals think in action*, New York: Basic Books.

Sergiovanni, T.J. (1996) *Leadership for the schoolhouse. How is it different? Why is it important?* San Francisco: Jossey Bass.

Shulman, J. H. (1992) *Case methods in teacher education*, New York, NY: Teachers College Press.

Stronach, I., Corbin, B., McNamara, O., Stark, S. and Warne, T. (2002) 'Towards an uncertain politics of professionalism: teacher and nurse identities in flux', *Journal of Education Policy*, vol 17, no 1, pp 109–38.

Taylor, M., Goeke, J., Klein, E., Onore, C. and Geist, K. (2011) 'Changing leadership: teachers lead the way for schools that learn', *Teaching and Teacher Education*, vol 27, no 5, pp 920–29.

Wei, R.C., Darling-Hammond, L., Andree, A., Richardson, N. and Ophanos, S. (2009) *Professional learning in the learning profession: A status report on teacher development in the US and abroad*, Dallas, TX: National Staff Development Council.

Zenni, J. (ed) (2001) 'Epilogue', in *Ethical issues in practitioner research*, New York: Teachers College Press, pp 153–65.

EIGHT

Child protection social work in times of uncertainty: dilemmas of personal and professional ethics

Lynn Kelly and John Young

Introduction

As part of Part Two, this chapter focuses on dynamics of personal and professional ethics (see Figure 1.1). It considers the moral challenges to social workers and focuses on the role of the child protection social worker in particular. The authors take a moral philosophy and virtue ethics approach to highlight the importance of the concept of 'role' as the basis of a morally adequate and readily applicable response to these challenges. They draw upon a case study to highlight the moral and ethical dilemmas that the lead author faced in her own practice – challenges that are representative of the difficulties faced by other professional child protection workers.

The authors acknowledge the influence of Mayo's conceptualisation of the moral agent (Mayo, 1968) in laying out what they consider to be the moral and, more broadly, the philosophical dimensions of 'role', and in linking this to the philosophy of mind and in this respect to the structuring of self-consciousness. Mayo reminds us of the need to regard the differences between virtue and rule or principle related ethical approaches as being in large part a question of emphasis. His examination of the ethical dimensions of 'role' prompts the presentation of a few clearly interlinked but very basic questions of relevance to thorough moral reasoning in the shifting contexts of day-to-day practice. These questions might, with various modifications, be fashioned along the following lines: 'In this situation what ought I to *do as* a practitioner?' 'In this situation what ought I to *be as* a practitioner, or *as* a professional person or more broadly still *as* a moral agent?' Broadly then, the authors see the role of the social worker as encompassing the character of the individual and shaped by the ethical demands arising from practice and not merely confined to being seen *as* or being expected to be 'implementers' of technical and procedural aspects of tasks. Clark regards the 'currently re-emerging emphasis on character as a partial reference back to the early concepts and ideals of personal social service that were lost sight of during the ascendancy of "competence" as the yardstick of professionalism' (2006, p 87). In essence this development has provided an alternative standpoint from which to view, and to challenge, the dominance of competence based thinking in the definition of what it is to be a 'good' social worker.

Child protection social work: proceduralism and standardisation

Before considering the case example, the authors want to consider the current political and organisational context in which most child protection social workers find themselves working, by arguing that the environment and landscape are changing. Never before has the need for us to understand the nature and scope of the educational needs, skills and knowledge that child protection practitioners require been so important.

'Social work with children and families involves critical decisions' (Akister, 2006, p 159). Akister believes that inquiries into child deaths focus almost exclusively on the procedural aspects of the cases, including the coordination of services and professionals, and fail to adequately address the family system or environment in which the child lived. Eileen Munro, in her response to Akister's paper, advocates a more radical use of the systems framework in which the family is only one subsystem and analysis is directed at the interaction of *all* the subsystems that are influencing the efforts of front-line workers to help children and parents (Munro, 2006, p 164). While the authors agree with Munro, it is argued that social workers today are not adequately prepared or supported to be able to conduct such complex assessments. Social workers who practise in a child protection context are required to have the highest levels of analysis and reflection to fully understand and assess the complex, dynamic and at times chaotic lives of children and families. Both qualifying and post-qualifying education and training must therefore address not only the technical and procedural aspects of the social work role but also the conceptual, analytical and ethical dimensions of the role. Smith (2001) argues for a return to a position where the public have trust in professionals, especially social workers, rather than the current position that relies on a less trustworthy confidence in systems. In relation to burgeoning systems, Parton (2012) argues that the growth of central government guidance, targets and rules have 'severely limited the ability of practitioners and managers to stay child centred ...' (p 152). The Munro report, in the document *Working Together to Safeguard Children* (Her Majesty's Government, 2010), adds to this concern by highlighting the growth in unnecessary 'guidance'. Munro (2011) went on to recommend that this document should 'remove unnecessary and prescriptive advice and focus on only essential rules for effective multi-agency working' (p 7).

In a response to what appears to be the intractable problem of children dying while under the care and protection of **social services** departments, policy makers and governments have endorsed the concept of '**interprofessional** working' as the panacea for tackling all the difficulties and complexities of the problem. However, in a note of caution, McLaughlin (2013) reminds us that interprofessional practice is a 'complex and contested term' that means different things to different workers and these tensions need to be more closely examined. McLaughlin (2013) also points out that interprofessional working can tend to focus on the process of professional working and the nature of professional relationships, rather than on the voice of the **service user**. This omission can lead to distorted understanding of the needs of children and their families and the risk that they become mere 'objects' of investigation rather than partners in identifying solutions. Another neglected aspect of interprofessional working is the nature of professional education and training. Kelly and Jackson (2011) recognise that recommendations for training and education consistently form a major part of the political response to child abuse inquiries. They argue that this push inevitably calls for more specialist training for social workers and for more opportunities for interprofessional working. However, very little consideration is given either to the actual content of this training or to how professionals from different disciplinary backgrounds might learn and train together. Without any clear parameters for professional education in child protection, the authors find themselves in a position where both the concept of what it means to be a professional and what constitutes high quality and relevant interprofessional education and training lacks any real meaning. Instead of being a panacea for the failings of the child protection system, it can be argued that interprofessional working has yet to establish itself as a credible alternative to sound **ethical judgement**.

Philosophical considerations

The question which concerns the authors now is the individual practitioner's responsibility for the definition and defence of his or her role *as* practitioner. This question requires consideration of one's role as a moral agent, a role that transcends professional settings and encompasses questions relating to what might be said to do with our conceptualisation of personal autonomy. Mayo takes issue with what he describes as the 'over-simplified' (Mayo, 1968, p 48) and frequently encountered contrast that is made between the ethics of rule and the ethics of character, and in particular Kant's ethical thinking and that of Aristotle. As Mayo puts it: 'One does not just do things; one does the sort of things one does because one is the sort of person one is. And, as Aristotle stresses, one becomes the sort of person one is by doing the sort of things one does' (Mayo, 1968, p 48).

It may be argued that whatever the success of his efforts to ground moral autonomy in reason, Kant is weak on the question of the moral justification of resistance to the misuse of power. Kant does not, contrary to the impression conveyed in caricatured accounts of his work, neglect questions to do with the function of virtue in the morally directed life. His 'Doctrine of Virtue' forms a significant part of his *Metaphysics of Morals* (2005 [1797]). Virtue is clearly regarded by him as a capacity for fortitude in dealing with the '[i]mpulses of nature [which] involve *obstacles* within the human being's mind to his fulfilment of duty and (sometimes powerful) forces opposing it, which he must judge that he is capable of resisting and conquering by reason ...' (p 513). It could be argued that duty defines what is to be taken as a virtue. But for Kant duty is not merely the centrepiece of any attempt to answer the questions 'What ought I to do?' and 'What ought I to be?'; it also is intimately interlinked with the duty to pursue self-perfection and the need to attend to the underlying intentions relating to the life one ought to lead (Louden, 1997). In essence, it also assists the moral agent to answer the question 'What ought I to become?'

As outlined above, Kant fails to provide adequate guidance in the moral justification of resistance in the public sphere of life. This failure is instructive in the development of the present argument. What part should reason play in our thinking about 'role' and in the justification of resistance to policy, to discourses and practices that are ideological rather than rationally grounded? Kant's much-quoted statement regarding the central importance of personal rationally grounded autonomy in *What is Enlightenment?* (2005 [1784]) is immediately followed in his reference to 'private reasoning' and what amounts to a justification of the curtailment of the public expression of views inconsistent with one's role or public office (p 18). The justification touches on Kant's fear that resistance, which finds an echo even today, about speaking outside one's role is tantamount to threatening the cohesion, proper functioning even survival of an organisation. In his *Common Saying* (2005 [1793]), after considering the significance of the contract between subjects and ruler, which is the foundation of the rights of subjects, he dismisses the subject's right of resistance to the will of the ruler on the grounds that such resistance 'would take place in conformity with a maxim, that made universal, would annihilate any civil constitution and eradicate the condition in which alone people can be in possession of rights generally' (p 298). Even if the ruler is tyrannical, rebellion remains 'the highest and most punishable crime within a commonwealth because it destroys its foundation' (p 298), that is, the contract between subjects and ruler. The link between resistance and the fear of political and social collapse has an ideological basis that still resonates in contemporary public service. It is grounded in assumptions about who the custodians of 'reason' in public life are or ought to be.

Applying this to the present discussion, one can say that moral autonomy implies the need for role choice. 'What ought I to be in this situation?' Choice as to role is intimately linked to choice as to the structuring of 'self' in one's consciousness and to the possibilities and implications of adopting the role of 'resister', implications that in turn may demand displays of virtues, including courage.

The dominant discourse

Returning to the authors' concerns, the growing influence of the *Getting it Right for Every Child* (**GIRFEC**) (Scottish Executive, 2006a) policy illustrates how the **Scottish Government** has been able to direct, and at times dictate, the practice of the social worker and other professionals in their working relationships with children and families. This policy was introduced in response to the Child Protection Reform Programme that was introduced following the publication of '*It's Everyone's Job to Make Sure I'm Alright': report of the Child Protection Audit and Review* (Scottish Executive, 2002). The title of the policy identifies an ideological shift from 'child protection' towards a more inclusive focus on 'all children'. Across Scotland, this policy has heralded the introduction of a common assessment framework and a new emphasis on interprofessional working and new systems for sharing information. The aim of GIRFEC is to identify children who may be 'in need' at an early stage and that services should be able to intervene early enough to prevent this 'need' becoming a more significant 'risk'. While the benefits of early intervention and interprofessional working are recognised, there are concerns that GIRFEC fails to recognise that alternative ways of 'doing' and interpreting experience need to be considered.

The domination of the GIRFEC practice framework in Scotland also raises some interesting questions about the social construction of child poverty, abuse and neglect. Hoyle's (2008) critique of the *Every Child Matters: Change for Children* report (DfES, 2004) raises important issues about the discourse and inherent judgements contained within the policy, and the extent to which these are socially constructed. Hoyle highlights what Thorpe (1994, p 73) refers to as 'situated moral reasoning', that is, the unconscious relationship between the internal cognitive processes of the social worker and the external, political, social and organisational context in which they work. In the UK, these norms predominantly mean white, middle class and heterosexual. This means that decisions or judgements that are made can often reflect the values of the system or culture and not necessarily represent the reality of the child or family that is being assessed. This manifests itself most clearly in relation to national and local government strategies for cutting costs and reducing services. Workers from all disciplines will have less direct contact time with children and their families, while parents themselves are facing increasing financial difficulties that will undoubtedly impact on their ability to provide the 'healthy start' that the government wants for children. Within the framework of GIRFEC, poverty is largely neglected as a contributory factor, but the consequences of living in conditions of poverty are regarded as blameworthy. Jack and Gill (2003) argue that most agencies and workers still continue to focus most of their attention on internal family issues, failing to adequately account for the impact of poverty or social class on the family and child. This emphasis on what Bronfenbrenner (1979) calls the 'microsystem' locates the cause of child abuse within the family, without regard to the wider issues. The authors argue that in the current climate of public spending cut-backs, the government's commitment to prevention is disingenuous and serves only to place the responsibility onto the family and the child protection worker, leaving policy makers free to criticise and accuse both families and child protection social workers when things go wrong.

The system

Child protection systems in the UK have become overly concerned with performance indicators and targets. This emphasis on performance indicators and targets has forced social workers to focus on process at the expense of the quality and effectiveness of their practice (Munro, 2011). In our view, this approach creates an environment that encourages practitioners to see themselves as if they are part of a bigger 'superorganism' in which the ethical justification for practice is grounded in the need to ensure the survival and functioning of this entity, rather than serving the needs of vulnerable children. This surrendering of individual responsibility to the greater wisdom of the 'superorganism' has resulted in a generation of social workers who no longer consider that they have a duty to act morally in the Kantian sense (Kant, 2005 [1785]). Of more concern to the authors, however, is the failure of the 'superorganism' or, more generally, the state, and those charged with educating social workers to fully consider the role and merit of moral and ethical practice and that this can bring about a culture and approach to practice that is not only ethical but disciplined and well considered. Social work ethics is traditionally associated with codes of ethics and usually comprises of lists of values, principles, **standards** and rules for the implementation of principles in practice. Banks (2008) argues that this approach provides a false picture of ethics as being a rational process. While recognising that this narrow or descriptive view of ethics is being challenged (Banks, 2008), the authors consider that there is an growing need for those working in the increasingly complex area of child protection to be able to consider the ethical dimensions of their practice in a more conceptual way, to consider the fundamental role of virtue ethics, particularly courage, and ethical resistance and to better understand what people should do in terms of ethical practice.

In the authors' view, the day-to-day working situations encountered by practitioners in the field of child protection cannot be isolated or insulated from the wider organisational environment that in turn is the product of government policy and initiatives. Ecological frameworks tell us that the wider influences, trends and habits of thought permeate the way in which we behave (Bronfenbrenner, 2005). This in turn has implications for the shaping of the practitioner's role and is highly significant for the process of moral reasoning. The authors believe that, with ever greater degrees of uncertainty in the work place, social workers will need, if they continue meaningfully to regard themselves as social workers, to ensure that their practice and their decisions are ethically directed. Failure to attend to this will see the profession either become so fragmented that it will literally disappear, or prove itself and make such an invaluable contribution that it will thrive as a profession, wherever it finds itself (Cree, 2003).

The case study

We return to the question regarding the growing and unchallenged influence of government in the day-to-day task of the social worker engaged in child protection social work, and our interest in ethical duty. To help clarify the dilemma facing the social worker, a case study has been introduced to assist the reader to understand better the practice context of the authors' concerns. This case study illustrates a real-life tension experienced by the lead author of the chapter. The situation highlighted for her questions about role and resistance in relation to the authority of her employer. These questions led to a dialogue with the co-author, who has a strong interest in the role of ethics in social work practice and education. The scenario illustrates the linkages between role and resistance in relation to matters of knowledge and its application in practice contexts and, in particular, in relation to the tension mentioned above between expectation of proceduralised and codified knowledge and practice experience. The issue is not that the dilemmas arise, nor is it about blaming the manager, as they too are faced with similar dilemmas on a regular basis; rather, it is that there is little or no opportunity for the professional social worker to rehearse and consider their position under similar sets of circumstances. The authors believe that there is no longer any explicit or transparent moral or ethical position in relation to role and resistance in the current social work context and therefore pose this question: has resistance or the requirement to question become problematic, or has the discourse shifted to view resistance as criticism?

The lead author's practice scenario

The author was a social worker in a children and family team working with a complex family including two female children who had disabilities. A third child was in foster care. The family relied on state benefits and was housed in an area of high social and economic deprivation. The mother had severe mental health problems, including bi-polar disorder, and self-medicated using cannabis and alcohol. The father of the two girls was a regular heroin user, unemployed, did not live with the family and had only intermittent contact with his children. There was no other close family support. The author was instructed to prepare a report for a child protection case conference regarding concerns about the oldest child. Extensive child protection training and education had been undertaken and the author believed that she should use the range of assessment tools that she had the knowledge and experience to utilise. These frameworks included some that were specific to the mother's mental health and the disabilities of the youngest children. The author also felt unable to influence the social and economic environment that the family inhabited and did not believe that the generic assessment framework as outlined in the GIRFEC practice framework, and as adopted by her employer, was sufficient for understanding and analysing the uncertain future, complex environment or level of risk that was present for the children. However, she had been advised by her line manager that all social workers must use the same assessment format and was strongly encouraged not to go beyond the areas outlined in the GIRFEC practice framework. After some consideration, she informed her manager that she did not feel that she could adequately assess the children's situation using only the required assessment framework and clearly outlined her reasons for this view. She was nevertheless instructed to conform. The author indicated that she would comply but that her report would (a) express her reservations about its limited scope and (b) would incorporate conclusions based on other assessment frameworks. The author stated that if these conditions were not accepted then she would request that her manager attend the case conference with her to argue the management position. The manager agreed to her conditions.

The essential consideration in this scenario is the centrality of 'the situation' and how a professional might respond to it. It has been stated previously that attempts to draw a sharp dividing line between personal and professional is unhelpful and that the need to consider a 'whole person' response to the challenges presented is vital. Traditional treatments of moral theory make this difficult, in that they tend to be shaped around consideration of how 'rules' are applied – for example, compliance with codes of ethics – ignoring the equally important ethics of character, which concerns itself with what it is to be a good person. If one follows Mayo, then role presents itself as a key moral concept – the hub in the wheel as it were – that can be used to integrate the practitioner's attempts to draw together the answers to the questions mentioned above. Being true to the role of professional may require actions that display courage and acts of intellectual virtue such as curiosity and an open-minded pursuit of truth and knowledge. Without these personal attributes, the professional role might be diminished (see Chapter Nineteen for further discussion around identity and professionalism).

This scenario can be superficially read as simply a conflict regarding best practice, or it can be regarded as the product of differing perceptions regarding roles: the social worker as a functionary, an implementer of organisational directives; or else as a reflective, self-understanding practitioner who incorporates a duty to use their knowledge of assessment resources effectively. To summarise, the fundamental ethical decision involves a choice between two differing, indeed conflicting, sets of expectations that underlie the tension illustrated in this scenario – the perception of role assigned by the employer, and the other adopted by the self-aware professional.

The authors' view is that these role conflicts face child protection social workers and managers on a more regular basis than is often recognised and that the route taken is usually to 'comply' with the dominant discourse, whether this is in the form of a specific set of guidance such as the GIRFEC practice framework or in other practice areas of tension such as resource allocation.

This scenario broadly illustrates the tension between the social worker who regards her role as encompassing the need to exercise best professional judgement and the expectation of the state, through her managers, that her practice comply with a standardised framework governing intervention. It also illustrates the issue of when and how to 'resist' the authority of an employer when the latter runs contrary to professional judgement and expertise. This tension is in part the product of the perception that, at the level of individual child care, the GIRFEC framework fails to give anything other than the most general of guidance and, further, that it is inadequate in determining how measures of success or otherwise are to be constructed. In relation to the environmental and wider family considerations, the framework is also found wanting in that it relies on descriptive observations rather than indicators for ways of improving the life of the child and family. The scenario serves to illustrate the linkages between role and resistance in relation to matters of knowledge and its application in practice contexts and, in particular, in relation to the tension between expectation of proceduralised and codified knowledge and expertise.

In this scenario the worker represents a role that stands in conflict with the role that the organisation, for various reasons, would wish to assign to her. The role adopted is consistent with what might be regarded as 'professional' but is one that also allows the worker to 'be true to herself' as moral agent. The insistence that workers should rely exclusively on standardised frameworks for assessment rests on the assumption that the latter have a well-grounded basis in knowledge and are informed by robust research findings. This has not been adequately determined and therefore cannot be relied upon in relation to informed ethical practice. Furthermore, the role of the professional requires the exercise of constructive scepticism and, while it is unacceptable to resist the authority of those in management positions just for the sake of it, it is important that there is a shared contract of understanding that recognises that the occupancy of a management role does not in itself imbue a person with expertise or render a person competent to pronounce on issues related to the application of knowledge.

Conclusion

The continued lack of debate or consensus within both the academy and the profession generally about what social workers 'do', what social workers 'are' and what they need to know, and how this is justified and legitimised within a transparent framework of ethics, has created a vacuum that has been filled by the state. The social work academy in Scotland has not brought any clarity to this situation, in fact, by adopting the under-theorised and poorly conceptualised *Key Capabilities in Child Care and Protection* (Scottish Executive, 2006b); the academy has forgone any claim to academic independence. The very notion of a '**competency**'-based approach to the very complex and contested area of child protection is problematic. Kelly and Jackson (2011) highlight the fact that 'this approach to education and training has continuously been criticised for its lack of ability to produce practitioners who have the capacity to work in complex situations' (p 486). Lymbery (2003) also alerts the reader to the fact that competency models do not produce practitioners who can deal with the 'milieu of uncertainty and ambiguity' (p 105) (see Chapter Three for another perspective on competencies). The authors, in short, recommend a shift towards a way of learning and knowing that puts ethically defensible conceptualisation of role at its core and assigns procedures, competencies and codified ways of being to the margins of the social work learning experience.

References

Akister, J. (2006) 'A systems approach: back to the future – response to Munro, E. (2005) "A systems approach to investigating child abuse deaths"', *British Journal of Social Work*, vol 36, no 1, pp 159–61.

Banks, S. (2008) 'Critical commentary: social work ethics', *British Journal of Social Work*, vol 38, no 6, pp 1238–49.

Bronfenbrenner, U. (1979) *The ecology of human development: Experiments by nature and design*, Cambridge, MA: Harvard University Press.

Bronfenbrenner, U. (ed) (2005) *Making human beings human: Bioecological perspectives on human development*, Thousand Oaks, CA: Sage Publications.

Clark, C. (2006) 'Moral character in social work', *British Journal of Social Work,* vol 36, pp 75–89.

Cree, V. (2003) *Becoming a social worker*, London: Routledge.

DfES (Department for Education and Skills) (2004) *Every child matters: Change for children, London:* DfES.

Her Majesty's Government (2010) *Working together to safeguard children: a guide to inter-agency working to safeguard and promote the welfare of children* (PDF), Nottingham: DCSF (Department for Children, Schools and Families) Publications.

Hoyle, D. (2008) *Problematizing every child matters: A critique,* http://www.infed.org/socialwork/every_child_matters_a_critique.htm

Jack, G. and Gill, O. (2003) *The missing side of the triangle,* Barkingside: Barnardo's Childcare Publications.

Kant, I. (2005[1784]) 'An answer to the question: what is enlightenment', in M.J. Gregor (ed and trans), *The Cambridge edition of the works of Immanuel Kant: Practical philosophy,* Cambridge: Cambridge University Press, pp 15–35.

Kant, I. (2005 [1785]) 'Groundwork of the metaphysics of morals', in M.J. Gregor (ed and trans), *The Cambridge edition of the works of Immanuel Kant: Practical philosophy,* Cambridge: Cambridge University Press, pp 41–108.

Kant, I. (2005 [1788]) 'Critique of practical reason', in M.J. Gregor (ed and trans), *The Cambridge edition of the works of Immanuel Kant: Practical philosophy,* Cambridge: Cambridge University Press, pp 137–271.

Kant, I. (2005 [1793]) 'On the common saying: that may be correct in theory but it is of no use in practice', in M.J. Gregor (ed and trans), *The Cambridge edition of the works of Immanuel Kant: Practical philosophy,* Cambridge: Cambridge University Press, pp 274–309.

Kelly, L. and Jackson, S. (2011) 'Fit for purpose? Post qualifying social work education in child protection in Scotland,' *Social Work Education,* vol 30, no 5, pp 480–96.

Louden, R.B. (1997) 'Kant's Virtue Ethics', in D. Statman (ed) *Virtue Ethics: A Critical Reader,* Edinburgh: Edinburgh University Press, pp 286–99.

Lymbery, M.E.F. (2003) 'Negotiating the contradictions between competence and creativity in social work education', *Journal of Social Work,* vol 3, pp 99–117.

Mayo, B. (1968) 'The moral agent', *The Royal Institute of Philosophy Lectures Volume 1,* London: Macmillan, pp 47–63.

McLaughlin, H. (2013) 'Motherhood, apple pie and interprofessional working', *Social Work Education: The International Journal,* vol 32, no 7, http://dx.doi.org/10.1080/02615479.2012.709841.

Munro, E. (2006) 'Eileen Munro's response to Jane Akister's comment on Munro, E. (2005) "A systems approach to investigating child abuse deaths", *British Journal of Social Work*, 35(4), 531–46', *British Journal of Social Work*, vol 36, pp 163–4.

Munro, E. (2011) *The Munro review of child protection: final report: a child-centred system)*. Norwich: The Stationery Office (TSO).

Parton, N. (2012) 'The Munro review of child protection: an appraisal', *Children and Society*, vol 26, pp 150–62.

Scottish Executive (2002) *'It's everyone's job to make sure I'm alright': Report of the child protection audit and review*, Scottish Executive: Edinburgh.

Scottish Executive (2006a) *Getting it right for every child: Proposals for action*, Edinburgh: Scottish Executive.

Scottish Executive (2006b) *Key capabilities in child care and protection*, Edinburgh: Scottish Executive.

Smith, C. (2001) 'Trust and confidence: possibilities for social work in high modernity', *British Journal of Social Work*, vol 31, pp 287–305.

Thorpe, D. (1994) *Evaluating child protection*, Buckingham: Open University.

PART THREE

Professional–interprofessional ethics

Professional and interprofessional ethics: an intellectual disabilities perspective in an interprofessional health context

Eleanor Brewster and Lorna Strachan

Introduction

In line with the aims of Part Three (see Figure 1.1), this chapter explores professional and **interprofessional** ethics from the perspective of professionals working within an **Intellectual Disabilities (Learning Disabilities)** team. Vignettes based on lived experiences of people with intellectual disabilities (ID) and the teams working with them have been used to illustrate the dilemmas faced by multidisciplinary teams. The authors draw upon medical ethics and moral ethics theory to frame their discussion.

Multidisciplinary and multi-agency working is well established in ID, though different professional backgrounds and cultures can lead to disagreement between practitioners and debate over the ethically correct approach to contentious situations. Examples from practice will be used to illustrate these concepts. The development of ID as a health speciality, recent legislative change and the resulting overarching obligation of ID workers to consider the impact of **incapacity** and vulnerability will also be described. Effective interprofessional and **interagency** working are integral to intellectual disabilities practice and must be utilised to promote optimal care. The authors will comment reflectively on current practice and suggest strategies for developing shared understanding.

The terminology used to describe people with arrested or incomplete cognitive development is varied and includes ID, learning disability and mental retardation. For consistency, the term ID will be used throughout this chapter.

Background to current practice

ID is defined as a condition of arrested or incomplete development of the mind, characterised by impairment of skills that contribute to the overall level of intelligence, that is cognitive, language, motor and social abilities. This skills deficit is manifested during the developmental period (World Health Organization, 1993). This intellectual impairment is consistent with having a measured intelligence quotient (IQ) below 70, and will typically mean that the person will need a degree of support to manage in society. People with ID are also more likely to experience various physical and mental health conditions; people with **profound and multiple learning disabilities** have been shown to be particularly **vulnerable** to the detrimental impact of a multiplicity of conditions on quality of life (Garrard et al, 2010).

In Scotland in 2011, 26,036 people were recognised by their local authority as having an ID, equating to around six in every 1,000 people. There were also 2,992 adults identified as being on the **autistic spectrum**, of whom 2,369 (79%) also had an ID (**Scottish Consortium for Learning Disabilities**, 2011).

History

From a historical perspective it can be argued that people with intellectual disabilities have been subject to restrictions in how they can behave and live, to a greater extent than other members of society. Segregation from wider society in institutional care was common and abuses occurred. This history tends to lead to staff teams that are acutely aware of the potential both for **abuse**, and for a perception of over-control and paternalism. Complex ethical issues are common, and **interdisciplinary** teams have to be willing to consider these in an objective and non-partisan way in order to arrive at a treatment and support plan that safeguards the patients' well-being and their autonomous wishes.

Legislation

The three main legislative instruments that affect practice in intellectual disabilities in Scotland are the Adults with Incapacity (Scotland) Act 2000 (AWIA), the Adult Support and Protection (Scotland) Act 2007, and the Mental Health (Care and Treatment) (Scotland) Act 2003. The AWIA provides a framework for enabling the care of people who lack **capacity** to make decisions for themselves. It enables healthcare to be received by people who are not able to give informed **consent** to treatment, and can also allow '**guardianship**', where an individual is nominated to make decisions on behalf of the person whose incapacity prevents them from making informed choices for themselves. This may include welfare issues such as where to live or the degree of support needed, and also financial matters. For the purposes of the Act, being 'incapable' (lacking capacity) means being incapable of: acting on decisions; or making decisions; or communicating decisions; or understanding decisions; or retaining the memory of decisions in relation to any particular matter due to mental disorder; or inability to communicate because of physical disability (Adults with Incapacity Act 2000). The Adult Support and Protection (Scotland) 2007 is a legislative tool aimed at facilitating the assessment of people who are thought to be vulnerable and supporting vulnerable people in avoiding situations and circumstances that can lead to exploitation.

The Mental Health (Care and Treatment) (Scotland) Act 2003 allows for compulsory treatment of people with mental disorder if certain legal criteria are met and the person is unwilling to consent to this themselves. ID is a mental disorder for the purposes of the Act. The Act supports the principle of least restriction, thereby encouraging care in the community if possible, rather than in hospital.

The Adult Support and Protection (Scotland) Act 2007 and AWIA state that professionals coming into contact with adults with ID have a **duty of care** as well as a legislative responsibility to promote the safety of vulnerable adults by integrating strategies, policies and services relevant to abuse. Professionals should be trained in identifying and reporting abuse, and have an awareness and understanding of personal safety and protection among the vulnerable adults they work with. Professionals also have a responsibility to develop increased awareness of safety and protection in adults with ID.

There is an overarching legal framework that aims to protect liberty that is of relevance to people with IDs. There is a presumption in **common law** that people cannot usually have their freedom restricted or receive medical treatment without consent, a position supported by the Human Rights Act 1998. The above legislation, together with policy and strategy documents such as *The Same As You?* (Scottish Executive, 2000), reinforce the need to recognise issues of capacity, improved personalisation, greater choice and control, a commitment to independent living and increased protection from harm. The United Kingdom has also signed agreement to adhere to the UN Convention on the Rights of Persons with a Disability, an international human rights instrument of the United Nations that is intended to protect the rights and dignity of persons with disabilities. 'Fiona's case' (Box 9.1) raises the question whether the professionals, in ensuring her physical health on account of their good intentions and professional responsibility, were perhaps overlooking the issue of her choice and dignity? Parties to the Convention are required to promote, protect and ensure the full enjoyment of human rights by persons with disabilities and to ensure that they enjoy full equality under the law. Was the change in their focus from 'feeding her' to the quality of life essential to ensure that Fiona's human rights were being protected? These issues are more complex, as will be discussed later.

The various statutory instruments tend not to conflict with each other, and can be utilised together if needed to provide the best support for the patient. The legislation can be complicated and can be a source of confusion, particularly for those who encounter it infrequently. The provisions of a certain piece of legislation may be desired for a greater number of people than those for whom the legal tests for implementing those powers apply. This has the potential to lead to conflict if an action that may be felt desirable to protect a person is not available, for example if guardianship is desired but the person is felt to be capable of making those decisions for themselves. As seen in Fiona's case, often the desire to act as an advocate for a person with ID and to promote what is viewed as their best interests is compelling, and paternalism must be guarded against. At times, colleagues may disagree on the use of the legislation, though this could be viewed as positive, in terms of healthy debate and minimising restriction. While there may be discussion around the application of legislation in general, professional roles in terms of implementation of legislation are well defined, so most debate focuses on the best way to utilise legally available powers, rather than on whether or not those powers apply.

Defining ID

Holland (2004) argues that in distinguishing between people with and without ID there is a danger of objectification of people with lowered intellectual functioning, and while classification can be useful for scientific and research purposes, it can also be harnessed as a way of oppressing this group. Deciding who in the population is classified as having ID can be challenging, since, as previously described, this involves making a definite distinction between two groups (those with ID and those without), where in reality the highest-functioning member of the ID group will, in practical terms, be indistinguishable from the lowest-functioning person without ID. Even skilled professionals may disagree about exactly which side of the line a particular person may fall, creating a recurring ethical dilemma.

At a fundamental level there are many similarities between people described as having ID and those with borderline intellectual functioning (for example, an IQ between 70 and 80). While professionals working 'on the ground' are able to identify client needs, it may be that organisational systems and service boundaries impact on how such needs can be met. This is not merely a matter of academic interest, but has significant practical implications for the individual concerned in terms of accessing appropriate care services, supported employment opportunities, welfare benefits and supported accommodation. Such individuals are at risk of 'slipping through the cracks' that divide current service design, resulting in a repeat cycle of crisis intervention involving health, **social work** and police services that is both detrimental to the individual and costly to the economy. At this time of increased pressure on public service budgets, it is essential that the best use is made of resources to achieve good outcomes for people, including those most at risk of poor health, isolation and abuse.

Service organisation

In Scotland, care services for people with ID are typically provided by multiple agencies. The main agencies are Social Care and Health, though independent sector organisations are also involved in the delivery of care and support. The **Scottish Government** (2012) has proposed legislation to increase joint working between Health and Social Care agencies: the Integration of Adult Health and Social Care Bill, which would aim to agree joint outcomes and budgets between health and social care agencies.

Healthcare teams providing a specialist ID service will typically include nursing, psychology, occupational therapy, speech and language therapy and psychiatry. Each professional group comes from a distinct professional background, **regulatory** system and ethos. There are various independent sector organisations that provide care, and these care packages are typically funded by local authority social work departments, but may also be wholly health funded or a combination of the two, depending on which needs predominate. A multi-agency approach brings with it a richness and diversity of approach and knowledge, though it can also lead to conflict arising from different ethos and prioritisation; this theme is explored later in this chapter.

Elements of concordance and conflict in interprofessional working

Interdisciplinary and **interagency** working is well established in IDs, though differing professional backgrounds and cultures can lead to disagreement. Conflicting interpretations of ethical principles and professional best practice can lead to discord between practitioners and confusion over the ethically correct approach to contentious situations.

Rennie et al (2007) explored the differences between **morals** and ethics within healthcare settings. They suggest that morals are culturally sensitive rights and wrongs. Ethics, on the other hand, are a set of principles including duty, rights, consequence and virtue. As can be seen, this definition of ethics tries to encapsulate various ethics theories such as consequentialist (teleological), non-consequentialist (deontological) and virtue ethics. In making ethical decisions, healthcare professionals must ask what is the **duty of care** to the individual, what rights the individual has and what the consequences are of actions or inaction. Then, finally, they must act with an integrity based on ethical decision making (EDM) (Miner and Petocz, 2003). Miner and Petocz conclude that outcomes may differ from what is expected or planned, but if a robust process of professional ethical decision making was undertaken, such outcomes will stand up to scrutiny.

Conflict and tensions can develop between members of an interagency team; they need to have a willingness to understand the roles of different professionals and agencies in order to work together successfully, and not to stick rigidly to delineated lines of responsibility. Each professional will be working on their own priorities for intervention; for some, the focus will be on preventative work, while for others crisis intervention dictates the priorities, all of which must be squared within the boundaries set by available resources (see Chapters Ten and Sixteen for a similar discussion). Within ID services there is also a potential for tension to arise between the wishes of the individual and those of carers (professional or family members). Current changes in service delivery that are being led by the Scottish Government pose challenges and opportunities in equal measure to clients, professionals and carers.

Boxes 9.1 and 9.2 present two 'real-life', though anonymised, examples of ethical challenges faced by ID services that provide some context to the issues involved in the field of ID and highlight the importance of open communication and team working. They will be reflected on in this chapter to contextualise and illustrate the pertinent ethical issues.

Box 9.1
Fiona's case study

Fiona is 26 years old, with moderate ID following birth injury. She has significant mobility problems and a history of depression. Fiona has an involved family. She lives in a supported tenancy with a 24-hours staff presence. She has positive relationships with her support team.

Fiona has long-term difficulties with food intake and cannot eat food thicker than a soft mashed consistency, and support staff have frequently had to be imaginative in finding foods that Fiona will eat. Her BMI is typically in the range 16–18. Percutaneous endoscopic gastrostomy (PEG) tubes have twice been inserted to attempt to supplement oral intake, but Fiona is frequently unsettled, with a tendency to pull at clothing, and has on both occasions removed her PEG tubes. About 18 months ago Fiona developed a respiratory infection from which she was not expected to survive. Eventually she did recover, but became physically frail and oral intake was inconsistent.

There has been extensive interdisciplinary input. Dietetics and speech and language therapists worked together to find safe and appealing foods to try to encourage oral intake. However, the gastroenterology team did not feel that a PEG replacement was viable. A psychiatric professional was involved in a regular review of Fiona's mental state, which has been consistently bright and cheerful. The Community Learning Disability Nursing teams has been involved throughout, providing advice and support to Fiona and her support team, who spent much of their time offering food and fluids to Fiona.

Although professionals were concerned that Fiona might starve, they were aware also that in spending so much time encouraging food intake they were causing distress and depriving Fiona of other activities that she might enjoy more. In recognition that the situation was not sustainable in the long term, an interdisciplinary meeting was held to ensure that Fiona's family and everyone involved in her care were fully aware of the situation. Despite the difficulty in accepting a course that could result in her death, her family and professionals were able to debate this honestly and frankly. A change in emphasis was made, with an emphasis on quality of life, and with food and fluid offered once, but not repetitively.

Against all expectations, Fiona's weight stabilised. Net oral intake remained extremely low, and Fiona was bedbound, but she was happy and taking in enough food to maintain her current state.

Box 9.2

Stephen's case study

Stephen is a 20-year-old young man with moderate ID who lives with his parents and attends day-care services. He has a history of petty theft and his family have concerns that this behaviour is increasing, despite various different strategies devised to deter it, including ensuring that Stephen has enough money to pay for purchases.

Recently, Stephen was caught taking sweets out of a local supermarket without paying, and when store detectives approached him, Stephen became upset and verbally abusive. The store staff called the police on this occasion, due to the repeat nature of the offence, and Stephen was escorted home by the police and given a formal warning in front of his parents.

Subsequently Stephen did not attend day care for four weeks, and missed other events. Concerned staff members had difficulty contacting the family and, when eventually a home visit was undertaken by Stephen's advocacy worker, family members advised him that "Stephen will not be going back to his classes until he learns how to behave himself". Stephen's father advised that the young man's 'punishment' for stealing and getting into trouble with the police was to stay in his room for a month, and his mobile phone contract had been cancelled.

Professional staff were notified and both health and social work professionals attended the house to discuss the situation with Stephen's family and also to speak to Stephen and check on his welfare. It was felt that the restrictions placed on Stephen were excessive and inappropriate, as Stephen was unable to understand the connection between taking sweeties from a shop without paying and not being allowed to go swimming. The 'punishment' failed to address why Stephen was displaying such behaviours and risked resulting in additional undesirable behaviours, low self-esteem, poor motivation and reduced confidence.

Tensions arose between agencies; the advocacy worker, while concerned, did not wish to 'damage' the relationship between himself and the family. Health staff wished to introduce family therapy in order that Stephen and his family should receive support to explore the reasons why Stephen might be stealing and to propose strategies to prevent further incidents of theft; while social work staff had serious concerns relating to issues of adult support and protection and felt that there were grounds to immediately remove Stephen from the home situation. Stephen's future remains uncertain. It has been proposed that he should move into supported living accommodation in the longer term, but at present he remains at home in the care of his father, although he has now resumed attendance at day care and professionals are working to increase their engagement with the family.

Ethical principles

There are many different ethical principles that apply in the care of people with ID, and balancing them in order to support the best outcome for the person is one of the most important aspects of this area of work. It is essential that members of multidisciplinary teams working with people with intellectual disabilities are comfortable with openly discussing areas of ethical difficulty and willing both to raise issues and also to consider concerns raised by others. Based on the authors' own lived experience, there follows a description of some of the common themes that challenge ID teams.

Choice and risk management

As the example of Fiona demonstrates, at times appropriate decision making and the making of an informed choice can be a contentious issue. The core principles of medical ethics are classically described by Beauchamp and Childress (2008) as being autonomy, **beneficence**, **nonmaleficence** and justice. Autonomy is often viewed as being the most important; however, a focus on autonomy is useful only when the person is able to make meaningful choices. If people are not able to do this, then they may potentially endanger themselves by making choices that they do not understand. This would not be a true exercise in autonomy, and it is important to note the distinction as to whether or not a decision is made with capacity. The emphasis on autonomy brings with it the risk that people who may never be able to operate in an autonomous manner may therefore be viewed as lacking an important human attribute. In a system that prioritises autonomy, they may also find then that they are treated within an ethical paradigm that is irrelevant to their situation and from which they can therefore struggle to benefit.

Reinders (2000) suggests that prioritising 'autonomy' beyond the point where a person can make an informed choice can mean a loss of protection for people with ID. Carers and professionals working within ID services will be familiar with occasions when the lack of a patient's ability to make an autonomous choice has not been noted and the patient has therefore been left to make inappropriate choices – for example, choosing to spend all their money on fast food, with resulting gross obesity and no finances to pay essential bills. Equally, there will be times when the input of health services may be seen as being controlling and not maximising autonomy. Clegg (2004, p 106) challenges the prevailing ethical convention: 'Concepts such as autonomy, anti-discrimination and empowerment may appear to be self-evidently ethical goods for people with ID, but they merely express the dominant assumptions of liberal culture and are open to critical evaluation.'

The need to ensure that choices are underpinned by appropriate capacity applies to situations where the individual may inflict harm on themselves and also on others. Forensic services for people with ID are particularly concerned with the prevention of harm and with trying to achieve a balance between public protection and individual liberty (Brewster, 2012). **Risk management** and the theoretical foundations that underpin this are themselves open to debate. This applies both at a lay level, with the general public tending to form strong associations between ideas of mental disorder and dangerousness, and also at a professional level, with a consistent over-estimation of risk (Link et al, 1999) (see Chapter Six for a similar discussion).

There is a need for balance between over-estimating risk – as in the case of Stephen, with the potential to unfairly restrict people on the basis of what might happen – and failing to predict violent incidents. A risk assessment that incorrectly suggests that a person is at high risk of violence can lead to involuntary in-patient or out-patient treatment, including medication, and also the loss of other civil liberties (Cocozza and Steadman, 1976). The example of Stephen also shows the adverse consequences that can occur when risk is over-estimated or is not addressed in a meaningful way.

Risk is an inescapable part of life and work, and it is never possible to entirely eliminate risk. A tendency towards risk aversion is at odds with the current policy emphasis on more enabling relationships between people and services, and the drive towards encouraging increased independence. However, there is still a requirement to balance positive risk taking with ethical and legal requirements regarding both Adult Support and Protection and Child Protection responsibilities to implement Multi-agency Public Protection Arrangements (MAPPA), care standards and health and safety legislation.

Stigma and public perceptions

Stigma is particularly relevant in ID, especially amongst those who may be felt to present a risk to others. The way in which the formerly technical words used to define people with impaired intellectual function – namely idiot, imbecile – have become stigmatised and appropriated as terms of abuse is further illustration of this.

A person with ID is more likely to be a **victim** of crime rather than a perpetrator, and people with ID are at significantly higher risk of being victims of crime than are the general population (Petersilia, 2001). In 2011, the Equality and Human Rights Commission published the findings of a formal inquiry into disability-related harassment, *Hidden in Plain Sight*. The findings revealed that many disabled people experience harassment, bullying and abuse, including verbal and physical abuse, on a recurring and frequent basis. Systematic failings by public authorities to recognise such incidents and to act to prevent their occurrence are highlighted within the report and the role that health services play in tackling these issues is explored. One of the key areas for improvement is that of effective interagency working. More recently events at a private hospital for people with ID, Winterbourne View, have brought these concerns into sharp focus (Flynn, 2012).

Treatability

The potential success of treatment is relevant to consideration of the ethics of compulsory treatment, or treatment that the person is not capable of consenting to. This applies particularly to people with ID, as the ID itself cannot be cured and there may be no improvement, with treatment, in the person's presentation.

In 2010, Lillywhite and Haines examined the clinical practice evidence for occupational therapists working with people with IDs. They noted that measuring outcomes was a particular challenge and that improvements in quality of life were often hard to quantify, due to the limited number of tools that accurately indicate change.

Care is improved when a good working relationship exists between the individual with ID, family, carers, support workers and other team members. Open communication between all parties is vital when identifying the valued and meaningful elements of an individual's life and facilitates good decision making and conflict resolution. Where so-called 'ethical conflicts' arise, a more formal process may be required and professionals will require to be guided by a robust frame of reference, namely, professional guidelines.

As Fiona's case demonstrates, difficult situations can provoke anxiety and questioning within staff teams. Differences in background, ethos and understanding must be identified and acknowledged, with the opportunity then to seek further advice and clarification so that everyone can have enough confidence in the care plan to be able to deliver it in a consistent manner.

Professional guidelines and the way forward

A typical IDs team will be comprised of many different staff groups with different professional ethos and guidelines. This can include nursing, psychology, occupational therapy, speech and language therapy, dietetics, psychiatry and close working relationships with **care management**.

Health and social care professionals have their standards of practice defined and scrutinised by a range of regulatory bodies, including the Care Quality Commission, General Medical Council and Nursing and Midwifery Council. The Health and Care Professions Council (HCPC) has overall responsibility for ensuring that all relevant health professionals meet certain given standards in order to be registered to practice in the United Kingdom. Such standards act as a source of information and as an audit tool that provides a framework for individuals to develop and maintain high-quality current practice. Members of the HCPC are required to maintain 14 standards of conduct, performance and ethics in order to remain 'fit to practise' (Health and Care Professions Council, 2012). Despite such a seemingly robust system of regulation, there remain alarming numbers of incidents where vulnerable individuals fail to receive the required care, respect and dignity and, in the worst cases, are victims of shocking abuse and neglect, as highlighted in Mencap's (2012) *Death by Indifference* report.

Different agency backgrounds can also lead to conflict. Separate budgets and management of health and social care organisations, and a scarcity of resources, can lead to attempts to preserve resources that may in the long run be more expensive for the country as a whole. For example, if someone is a hospital in-patient but is ready to be discharged to a care setting, then their care is at that point being funded by the health service. It may be that a social care setting would be less costly, but from a **social services** perspective it may be difficult to justify allocating resources to move someone out of hospital to a community setting when there may be others competing for the same scarce resources and who are not being safely cared for. There may also be disagreements about the balance of funding for a care placement when a person has both health and social care needs, and discussions about joint funding can in themselves be time consuming and therefore costly. Such dilemmas are also divisive, creating a focus on the difference between agencies and the aspects of care covered, rather than on the commonalities. It might be that a system of a shared budget for health and social care would lead to a more acute focus on the needs of the person.

Conclusion

As can be seen from this chapter, the care offered to a person with ID can come from a complicated web of different staff from a number of different organisations and professional backgrounds, thus influencing the ethical standpoint of the practitioners. This combines with the complicated and multifaceted nature of the difficulties associated with ID to create an exceptionally challenging and satisfying framework within which ID practitioners have the privilege of serving their client group.

In a rapidly changing society, economically and socially, social care and healthcare services are being challenged to deliver new models of care within limited resources. The need to work in partnership with other agencies is, therefore, even more pressing. Unintentional discrimination and overt abuses of trust continue to occur. The value of working within a shared, ethically sound framework of good practice is now of even greater importance, and at the heart of considerations must be the needs of individuals with ID themselves.

References

Adults with Incapacity (Scotland) Act 2000, http://www.legislation.gov.uk/asp/2000/4/contents.

Adult Support and Protection (Scotland) Act 2007, http://www.legislation.gov.uk/asp/2007/10/contents.

Beauchamp, T. and Childress, J. (2008) *Principles of biomedical ethics*, Oxford: Oxford University Press.

Brewster E.B. (2012) *Public protection: An analysis of the legal approach to people with learning disabilities who pose a risk to others*, Charleston: CreateSpace.

Clegg, J. (2004) 'How can services become more ethical?', in W.R. Lindsay, J.L. Taylor and P. Sturmey (eds) *Offenders with developmental disabilities*, Chichester: Wiley, pp 91–108.

Cocozza, J. and Steadman, H. (1976) 'The failure of psychiatric predictions of dangerousness: clear and convincing evidence', *Rutgers Law Review*, vol 29, pp 1084–101.

Equality and Human Rights Commission (2011) *Hidden in plain sight: Inquiry into disability-related harassment*, www.equalityhumanrights.com/uploaded_files/disabilityfi/dhfimain.pdf.

Flynn, M. (2012) *Winterbourne View Hospital: A serious case review*, http://hosted.southglos.gov.uk/wv/report.pdf.

Garrard, B., Lambe, L. and Hogg, J. (2010) *Invasive procedures: Minimising risks and maximising rights: improving practice in the delivery of invasive procedures for people with profound and multiple learning disabilities. Project report and recommendations*, Dundee: White Top Research Unit.

Health and Care Professions Council (2012) *Standards of conduct, performance and ethics*, www.hpc-uk.org/publications/standards/index.asp?id=38.

Holland, A.J. (2004) 'Criminal behaviour and developmental disability: an epidemiological perspective', in W.R. Lindsay, J.L. Taylor and P. Sturmey (eds), *Offenders with developmental disabilities*, Chichester: Wiley.

Human Rights Act 1998 www.legislation.gov.uk/ukpga/1998/42/contents.

Lillywhite, A. and Haines, D. (2010) *Occupational therapy and people with learning disabilities; Findings from a research study*, London: College of Occupational Therapists.

Link, B.G., Phelan, J.C., Bresnahan, M., Stueve, A. and Pescosolido, B.A. (1999) 'Public conceptions of mental illness: labels, causes, dangerousness, and social distance', *American Journal of Public Health*, vol 89, no 9, pp 1328–33.

Mencap (2012) *Death by indifference: 74 deaths and counting. A progress report 5 years on*, London: Mencap.

Mental Health (Care and Treatment) (Scotland) Act 2003, www.legislation.gov.uk/asp/2003/13/contents.

Miner, M. and Petocz, A. (2003) 'Moral theory in ethical decision making: problems, clarifications and recommendations from a psychological perspective', *Journal of Business Ethics*, vol 42, pp 11–25.

Petersilia, J.R. (2001) 'Crime victims with developmental disabilities: a review essay', *Criminal Justice and Behavior*, vol 28, pp 655–94.

Reinders, R.S. (2000) *The future of the disabled in liberal society*, Notre Dame: University of Notre Dame Press.

Rennie, I., Nichol, H. and Carmichael, J. (2007) 'Morals or ethics: which should you rely on?' *British Journal of Healthcare Assistants*, vol 1, no 8, pp 372–4.

Scottish Consortium for Learning Disabilities (2011) *Statistics release: Adults with learning disabilities-implementation of 'The same as you?' Scotland 2011*, http://www.scld.org.uk/sites/default/files/final_2011_esay_statistics_release_-_learning_disability_statistics.pdf.

Scottish Executive (2000) *The same as you? A review of services for people with learning disabilities*, Edinburgh: Scottish Executive.

Scottish Government (2012) *Integration of Adult Health & Social Care Integration Bill – programme for government 2012–13*, www.scotland. gov.uk/About/Performance/programme-for-government/2012–13/ Adult-Health-Bill.

World Health Organization (1993) *The ICD-10 classification of mental and behavioural disorders: Diagnostic criteria for research*, Geneva: World Health Organization, F70–F79.

TEN

Protecting unborn babies: professional and interprofessional ethical considerations for social work and midwifery

Ann V. Hodson and Ruth Deery

Introduction

In this chapter the authors consider pre-birth child protection assessment and intervention from the perspectives of **social work** and midwifery to highlight some of the ethical issues inherent for both professions. Both social work and midwifery have international codes of ethics that shape and guide practice, and in this chapter these **ethical codes** have been considered from the theoretical perspectives of utilitarianism and value-based ethics.

Child protection practice in the UK is directed by law, policy and guidance that seek to promote the well-being of the child and its family. Where there are significant concerns for a child's well-being or safety, a multi-agency assessment must occur. The information gathered and analysed in an assessment is complex and may be used to inform decision-making processes or to justify expensive packages of family support. When conducting a **pre-birth assessment**, social workers and midwives may be part of a multi-agency or court process that ultimately decides if it is safe for a mother to retain care of her baby or if the baby is to be removed from her care at birth. The consequences of such decisions can be enormous for all concerned, and so it is essential that professionals have an understanding of the ethical principles underpinning their actions and the tensions therein. Pre-birth assessment in social work has received minimal research or literary attention (Hodson, 2011), and yet findings from serious case reviews in England between April 2007 and March 2011 highlighted shortcomings in the timeliness of pre-birth assessment (Ofsted, 2011). As a consequence of the lack of research, the ethical tensions that are inherent within pre-birth assessment have been under-explored. This chapter seeks to open debates around professional ethics as a vehicle for enhancing or changing practice.

This chapter, which is a part of Part Three and focuses on professional and **interprofessional** ethics (see Figure 1.1), begins by considering the ethical base of social work and midwifery, looking at the common ground underpinning both professions and factors influencing and impacting on professional ideology. It then moves on to look at how terminology such as 'unborn child' highlights some of the ethical tensions and moral arguments central to this area of child protection practice, before finally considering how refocusing on the needs of pregnant women may ultimately enhance pre-birth assessment. Drawing on quotes and a case study from practice, the real-life experiences of front-line professionals are used to highlight the experience of this complex area of practice (all names have been changed to protect anonymity).

A common ethical starting point

In the United Kingdom, child protection concerns can be raised by professionals, members of the public or family members before a baby is born. A referral to a **children's services** department will then prompt a pre-birth assessment, which will be conducted using holistic assessment tools such as the Framework for the Assessment of Children in Need and Their Families (DoH, 2000). Pre-birth assessment can take place at any stage of a woman's pregnancy and may be a short initial information-gathering process that identifies whether minimal or no additional support is needed beyond that provided by the midwife. However, where significant concerns are identified a more comprehensive process of assessment will take place drawing on information from the family as well as information from the 'relevant' multi-agency network. The 'relevant' multi-agency network will be different for each family; however, the core composition will be social workers, because of their role in the assessment process, and midwives, because their professional knowledge and skills are paramount in supporting the pregnant woman.

While it is in a minority of situations that the child protection risks are such that the mother and baby are separated at birth, the enormity of that decision cannot be understated (Hart, 2010; Hodson, 2011). As the Honourable Mr Justice Munby declared, 'removal of a child from his mother at or shortly after birth is a draconian and extremely harsh measure which demands extraordinarily compelling justification'

(England and Wales **High Court** (Administrative Court) Decisions 15 April 2003, point 44.ii). Identifying also that such applications to Court must be detailed and compelling, Justice Munby called for professional evidence to be supported by articulated reasoning (England and Wales High Court (Administrative Court) Decisions, 15 April 2003). With social workers and midwives being the key professionals involved in compiling information for pre-birth assessments, it is therefore paramount that they should understand the inherent ethical tensions if they are to recognise and present articulated reasoning for such decisions.

Approaches to practice for social workers and midwives are based upon the same ethical principles, creating a clear starting point for **interdisciplinary** assessment. The International code of Ethics for Midwives states: 'This code acknowledges women as persons with human rights, seeks justice for all people and equity in access to health care, and is based on mutual relationships of respect, trust, and dignity of all members of society' (International Confederation of Midwives, 2008, p 1).

Likewise, the International Federation of Social Workers code of ethics identifies respect for human dignity and human rights as core to the profession (International Federation of Social Workers, 2012). Central to both codes of ethics are principles surrounding the value of human life, working in partnership and empowering those who receive, directly or indirectly, midwifery and social work services.

Given that both midwifery and social work are underpinned by common professional ethics, it seems logical that their approaches to pre-birth child protection and assessment and intervention will also be similar. However, as highlighted in Chapter One by Hannah and Jindal-Snape, professional bodies have established codes of conduct and ethics designed to protect professional and public interest, but these of themselves are not sufficient. The interplay and interrelationship between personal and professional ethics is significant and an important consideration. It is not simply a matter of identifying the importance of human rights when considering pre-birth assessment, primarily because there is a potential ethical conflict between human rights as they pertain to the mother and human rights as they pertain to the unborn child. Moreover, professional responsibilities created by legal and organisational requirements can create complex contradictions that mitigate against the professional ethical value base. The chapter will now explore some of the professional responsibilities and issues to highlight some of the ethical tensions presented to social workers and midwives when undertaking pre-birth child protection assessments.

Professional ideology

Woman-centred care is an ideological preference for social rather than medical approaches to birth and something that most midwives would claim that they work towards. It aspires to empower women by engaging with them to identify their needs and preferences and enabling them to make choices. Thompson (2004) has stated that the ethics of midwifery practice lies in the engagement between mother and midwife and, more importantly, understanding the exercise of power that medical professionals may have within that relationship. A woman-centred midwife is therefore able to offer a professionally empowering approach to women that can, in turn, give midwives greater professional autonomy. Research has shown that women are appreciative of woman-centred care (Kirkham, 2010), but an unsettling climate of continual reorganisation of services within the National Health Service, where labour and birth are now increasingly centralised into larger maternity units, means that maternity services described as 'woman centred' are often run according to an industrialised, conveyor-belt model. The result is a fragmented relationship with women, with no opportunity for continuity of relationship between woman and midwife. Institutional dominance and practices (Thompson, 2004) result in conflicting values and, rather than being able to develop a woman-centred approach and concentrate on developing interprofessional relationships, midwives become interchangeable workers who must prioritise keeping the system running (Deery and Kirkham, 2006). An increased emphasis on quantifiable targets, efficiency savings and the rationalisation of service delivery, along with the processes of reorganisation, has produced workplace practices that leave workers swamped by immediate demands and unable to afford the time to stand back and reflect on how they work (Deery, 2005; Bryson and Deery, 2010). Another more fundamental result is the strengthening of a culture that directly conflicts with the intangible and unquantifiable processes of relationship where a midwife often has to negotiate with other professionals and to help and support women so that they can be facilitated to value their own knowledge of their body during pregnancy (Deery and Fisher, 2010).

In child protection-based social work, the backdrop of practice development has been shaped by many factors, not the least of which is public accountability. Social and political ideology relating to child protection has at its core notions of identifying, or predicting, the 'risk of harm', focusing social work assessment toward measurable risk indicators. Following the death of Victoria Climbié, the inquiry by Lord Laming placed emphasis on systemic failures across agencies responsible for protecting children (Cm 5730, 2003). As a consequence, Lord Laming recommended, greater accountability of agencies was needed, along with strengthening of interagency recording procedures and increased management of front-line professionals (Cm 5730, 2003; Corby 2006) (see also Chapter Twelve). However, the Munro report (DfE, 2011), an independent review of child protection in England, identified that managerial systems had become burdensome and prescriptive, limiting the capacity of front-line workers to engage with families. Hodson (2011) considered national statutory guidance, assessment frameworks and child protection procedures in England and found that unclear frameworks surrounding pre-birth assessment existed. As a consequence, social workers were left to develop approaches based on implicit knowledge and practice wisdom drawn from post-birth assessments work rather than on specific knowledge pertinent to the unique issues presented by pregnancy (Hodson, 2011).

An underpinning professional ethical stance is emergent whereby social workers and midwives strive to provide services that engender mutual trust and promote dignity. A woman-centred approach promotes the needs, rights and choices of the mother, and the child protection approach places emphasis upon the needs and risks present for the unborn child. Ethically, the two are not mutually exclusive, and indeed they should be mutually supportive, but procedural and political emphasis on targets, efficiency and measurable quantifiable indicators of service delivery contradicts the core of social work and midwifery approaches.

The morality and ethical basis for managerial forces provides an interesting backdrop to the debate here, as it highlights how utilitarian perspectives can influence planning and decision making. The principle inherent within a utilitarian approach is that social rules are needed and must be developed in order protect and promote the greater good for all concerned. In the case of pre-birth child protection, the 'all' is wider society, which has a collective interest in the 'production' of healthy members of society who will grow and develop and ultimately sustain the status quo. Pressure to ensure the greater good of all is affected by the need to share finite resources such as access to medical services and health costs, not the least of which is the midwives' and social workers' time. As a consequence, managerial approaches require emphasis on efficient and accurate decision making as a means of ensuring both the safety and well-being of all members of society. However, from a social work and midwifery perspective, adopting this utilitarian approach can contradict the importance of understanding the individual needs and rights of the pregnant woman and so it sits in direct contrast with a virtue-based ethical stance that may impact on the assessment process.

Virtue-based ethical theories place less emphasis on the rules people should follow in society and instead adopt a theoretical approach, focusing on helping people to develop good character traits, for example, kindness and generosity (Armstrong, 2006). Virtue-based ethical theorists also emphasise the need for people to learn how to lead more moral lives. From a pre-birth assessment perspective, notions of 'good' character traits and moral lives are especially interesting, as there is potential for expectations to be focused on pregnant women concerning how they 'should' live their lives, particularly in relation to choices or actions that may have a direct impact on the developing foetus. For example, the use of substances such as alcohol may be debated in relation to the impact on wider society, with sliding scales of concern from occasional social drinking not being a concern to high intake levels posing greater concern. For pregnant women, however, this scale changes, as the issue becomes one not simply of the impact on society, but of the impact on the developing foetus. On the one hand, a virtue-based approach may equate to emphasis being placed on support for the pregnant woman to enable to her to develop an approach regarded as 'good' for her baby. Such an approach sits comfortably with health-promotion strategies such as eating a healthy diet and cessation of smoking. On the other hand, a pregnant woman who consumes alcohol or any other substance known to have a detrimental impact on the developing foetus may also be regarded as morally 'bad'. In turn, the professional's perception of morality may then translate into a health-deficit approach by contextualising a pregnant woman as not being able to place the healthy needs of her baby before her own 'unhealthy' needs. An assets-based approach would focus on, and value, the capacity, skills and knowledge of the pregnant woman rather than solely focusing on her needs, deficits and problems (Morgan and Ziglio, 2007). What is important is recognising that during pregnancy a woman cannot be regarded only in relation to the risks she may or may not pose to the developing foetus; her own experiences, needs and wishes also need to be taken into account. There is no sliding scale of morality along which a pregnant woman can be measured; instead, morality and virtues are multi-dimensional concepts that must be regarded within much wider frameworks. Pre-birth assessment therefore cannot be reduced to simple notions of 'good' and 'bad' but must consider a multitude of complex issues and then consider how these issues may or may not impact on the future care of the baby.

Definition of the 'unborn child' and the impact on ethical practice

Definition of the 'unborn child' is a significant aspect of pre-birth assessment that impacts on how professional roles and responsibilities are shaped. In England, procedure and guidance have focused on children aged from birth to 18 years and have not considered the unique issues and debates relevant to pregnancy. As a consequence, pre-birth assessment has been contextualised within frameworks that have evolved to protect children rather than the foetus, ignoring scientific and theological debate surrounding the point at which life begins.

Scientific knowledge about human development has created debate around issues such as human fertilisation, foetal experimentation, the termination of pregnancy and human rights. Growing understanding of the physiological development of the foetus has had an impact on social and legal perspectives and on how life is defined from the moment of conception (Brinsden, 2009), and enhanced medical technology has resulted in the ability to keep extremely premature babies alive, thus impacting on the point at which a foetus is regarded as 'viable'. Kaczor (2011) considers the far-reaching ethical issues associated with abortion, highlighting in particular the issues of human rights and justice as well as the impact that language has on our perception of the foetus. Faced as we are with many factors influencing our understanding of pregnancy and human development, the terminology of 'unborn child' seems somewhat simplistic and potentially misleading.

The 'abortion debate' is interesting from the perspective of professional ethics and pre-birth assessment because it particularly highlights how the terminology of 'unborn child' generates significant ethical tensions. Kaczor (2011) refers to the 'loaded language' of abortion often used in debate to heighten awareness of either the foetus or the mother. In use of the term 'unborn child', a bias toward an anti-abortion stance is created because midwives and social workers are bestowed with professional responsibility to protect children. Consider the following example from an interview with a child protection team manager:

"Sandra came to the office demanding to see me. We were in the final stages of proceedings to have her child adopted and here she was again pregnant! She said point blank, 'will you take this one off me?' She said she couldn't go through that again and demanded an early assessment. She made it clear if the assessment was negative she would rather have an abortion than go through the loss of adoption again." (Steve, 2009, unpublished data in the context of Hodson, 2011).

Steve was faced with an assessment that might end the pregnancy, ending an 'unborn' child's life; an action clearly in direct conflict with procedural ideology that directs the protection of children. Equally, Steve needed to consider his own ethical and moral position on abortion and how this might impact on his decision making. However, from Sandra's perspective, her approach was appropriate in terms of considering the impact of her loss.

Regardless of the terminology used, for many legal systems around the world the status of personhood is not bestowed pre-birth. As a consequence, the phrase 'unborn child' is an oxymoron with potential to hide the importance of maternal rights. Corner (1997) undertook a small-scale study of parents who had been involved in pre-birth child protection assessments and pointed out: 'In pre-birth risk assessment practice the primary user is the unborn child. This poses considerable ethical problems, particularly as the expectant parents are involuntary **service users** participating in a process which it is assumed they would much prefer to avoid' (Corner, 1997, p 16).

Corner's words highlight fundamental principles for the social worker to understand, namely that their primary focus is the unborn child and this is their only reason for assessing and being involved with the family. However, this is not to suggest that attention to the family's needs, and particularly to the pregnant woman's wishes, should be ignored. Hart (2010), when writing about pre-birth assessment practice, identified the overarching rights of the mother and made the following statement: 'A pregnant woman is not a human incubator, but retains autonomy over her own body and as a consequence that of her baby' (Hart, 2010, p 237).

In England, pregnant women retain the right to refuse medical treatment even if doing so may cause harm to the woman or the child. A landmark case involved Ms S, who refused medical treatment during her pregnancy, knowing that this decision might place her and the unborn child in real danger. Having undergone an enforced caesarean operation, she subsequently took legal action and the judicial review of the case (England and Wales Court of Appeal (Civil Division) Decisions, 30 July 1998) ruled in her favour on the grounds that the Court had been misinformed with regard to her ability to **consent**. While this was an extreme case, it lays the legal foundation for the principle upon which all pre-birth assessments should be conducted, as the Honourable Mr Justice Munby declared: 'No matter how serious the concerns for the unborn child, the same principles that allow a mother to refuse medical intervention, apply to refusing to take part in an assessment'

(England and Wales High Court (Administrative Court) Decisions, 15 April 2003, point 44.ii).

Therefore, while the focus for social work intervention may be the unborn child, maternal rights must not be ignored. Ethical tension is created as a consequence of the professional responsibility to intervene using child protection procedures and the woman's absolute right to not comply, and it is not difficult to imagine how fear and anxiety may cause noncompliance. However, it is also hard to imagine how not involving the woman could equate to a thorough and comprehensive assessment. Midwifery therefore has much to offer to pre-birth child protection practice in social work, particularly as a consequence of the relational, woman-centred basis of midwives' work.

Refocusing on the needs of pregnant women

Munro (DfE, 2011) highlighted that trends toward managerial systems limit engagement with families and create a space within which oppressive practice can develop. As the case study in Box 10.1 highlights, time is needed not only to engage directly with families but also to enable professionals to negotiate their roles and responsibilities relevant to the individuals they are supporting and assessing. Considering policy in Australia that, at the time, contained a push toward developing standardised risk-assessment practice, Goddard et al (1999) highlighted that ethical and moral issues abound in child protection and that standardisation is often regarded as a means of reducing the margin for error. Likewise, Broadhurst et al (2010) found that managerial systems that attempted to increase accountability potentially created conditions for error as social workers' focus turned to developing systems to manage the procedures rather than to spending time with children. As a consequence of managerial environments, professional practice can be reduced to form filling, ticking boxes and categorising similarities rather than understanding individual circumstances (Goddard et al, 1999). There are similar situations in midwifery where midwives have expressed concerns that attempts to standardise care result in a tick-box approach (Kirkham et al, 2002). Managerial approaches to form filling 'require' a particular professional to complete a particular form and to do so in a particular way. Considering the case study in Box 10.1, it was the freedom of the professionals to work directly with Sarah that enabled a safe and appropriate conclusion; a conclusion that might not have emerged if each professional had regarded their primary responsibility to be completing the relevant paperwork. For pre-birth child protection, managerial emphasis is even more concerning if it occurs in addition to existing practice that negates ethical understanding of pregnant women's rights. Consequently, awareness of and adherence to an ethical basis of practice may actually serve to empower not only pregnant women who undergo pre-birth assessment, but also the professionals responsible for conducting them.

Box 10.1

Sarah's case study

During an antenatal appointment Sarah spoke to her midwife about physical and verbal abuse from her husband. Although the violence was severe and sustained, Sarah was reluctant to seek support for fear that this would increase her husband's anger. The midwife discussed the impact of domestic violence on babies and explained her child protection responsibility to contact the social work department. This increased Sarah's level of anxiety, prompting her to fear that her baby would be removed from her care.

Negotiation between the midwife and the social worker resulted in the midwife taking the primary role in discussing child protection concerns and possible support plans with Sarah. Gradually Sarah began to trust the support she was being offered and eventually she indicated her wish to leave her partner. In consultation with Sarah, the midwife identified that support via a women's refuge would be most appropriate. The social worker took responsibility for organising a support package and, once Sarah was placed in the refuge, began working with her to enable her to achieve a safe and secure future for herself and her baby.

In terms of empowering pregnant women who undergo a pre-birth assessment, the underlying principle is that the woman herself is best placed to identify solutions to the concerns raised by social workers. When midwives are able to place emphasis on a woman-centred approach, organisational context becomes secondary (Kirkham, 2010). Engendering this principle in child protection social work would require skills and time directed toward developing mutual trust and, as Thompson (2004) highlights, when this relationship is central, trust and respect will form, leading to mutually beneficial outcomes – the woman is not seen as merely a vessel for a child at risk. The principle of woman-centred child protection requires social workers to emphasise and work with women's rights, appreciating that during the course of pregnancy women will experience many physiological and emotional changes. Women's responses to pre-birth assessment are therefore likely to change during pregnancy, as are feelings about their body or their baby. It is therefore important to recognise the way in which these changes can impact on the capacity to change behaviour or circumstances that may present risks to the new-born baby. In turn, emphasis is placed not on predicting risk but on working with the woman to identify solutions to identified risks.

It is not suggested that such an approach is only considered in situations where the long-term plan is to implement post-birth packages of support. In those situations where the outcome is to recommend the removal of the baby from the mother's care at birth it seems even more important that principles of trust are engendered in interpersonal and interprofessional relationships. As one social worker said:

> "She just sobbed and sobbed. I wanted to help her but I didn't know how to. So we [social worker and midwife] just waited. She had known for ages the plan was to remove her baby but now she wanted to know the detail, exactly what did that mean. The midwife explained that she would get to cuddle and feed her baby, and he would be with her whilst she was in hospital, but she couldn't leave the hospital with him." (Carla, 2008, unpublished data in the context of Hodson, 2011)

This was an emotional situation and one in which difficult discussions needed to happen. A working relationship that is built on trust enables discussion around decision making and its management as well as the provision of physical and emotional support.

This leads us to consider the ways in which a woman-centred approach might also empower professionals. At first, adopting a woman-centred approach to pre-birth assessment might appear incongruous, relative to some of the statutory aspects of child protection, particularly those that direct professionals toward formal decision-making arenas such as child protection conferences or the Courts. Essentially, a woman-centred approach shifts the emphasis to choice for women, enabling them to identify solutions and thus impacting on the power balance. Professional autonomy to intervene to protect the child appears to be weakened because the pregnant woman retains full control over her situation and may well refuse to cooperate. However, as identified earlier, the unborn child has no status of personhood and legal redress cannot actually be applied pre-birth. A woman-centred approach means that professional responsibility to protect the long-term health and well-being of the child is not negated but is refocused on spending time on building relationships and developing an understanding of the individual woman and her circumstances, rather than on responding to the pressure to reduce complex information to a tick-box format.

The refocusing onto the pregnant woman's needs also engages social workers in the longer-term support and health needs of the child. As noted earlier in this chapter, science and medicine have provided information about the developing foetus that has enabled increased understanding of the importance of maternal health in promoting the health of the baby (Kent, 2000). **Abuse** in all forms impacts on post-birth child development, but in recent years there has been increasing evidence that maternal drug and alcohol use during pregnancy can also have significant developmental and physical consequences for the child (Ward and Glaser, 2010). As Moe and Slinning (2002) note, it is not possible merely to isolate substance use as a concern, because prenatal drug exposure is often associated with other factors, including poor nutrition, poverty, stress, domestic abuse and chaotic lifestyles. Such assertions are unlikely to be a surprise to social work and midwifery practitioners, but thinking about child development from the point of conception highlights the importance of ensuring that appropriate and adequate support is available during pregnancy to benefit both maternal and foetal health. However, the current emphasis on prenatal health is subject to differing responses within the structural, organisational and professional cultural environments of the two professions.

Policy emphasis on early intervention in children's lives is developing because it is recognised that preventing the escalation of problems is beneficial for children, rather than responding only when the concerns are such that intervention is necessary (C4EO, 2011). Responses to the early intervention agenda tend to be located in the universal childcare services (health and education) and the voluntary sector, and for midwives this has resulted in development of their public health role in order to promote a positive impact on the health of women. The life circumstances of women, and an evidence-based approach to care, are taken into account when supporting vulnerable families, and the existing focus of midwifery on issues such as breastfeeding, domestic abuse and smoking cessation has been further developed through networking with other statutory and voluntary organisations.

The professional challenge for social work is not to become associated with intervention only when there is what C4EO (2011) refers to as an 'escalation of problems', but to recognise and embrace the role of supporting pregnant women and therefore supporting the long-term well-being of the child. A woman-centred approach to child protection could embrace ethical principles of human dignity and engagement, potentially enabling social workers to justify intervention from early pregnancy and to extend the process of assessment over a longer and more involved time frame. The ethical tension is not, therefore, the challenge of balancing the 'unborn child's' needs against maternal rights, it is in challenging the impact of managerialism. This approach focuses on utilitarian principles that strive to share finite resources, engaging with strong **ethical practice** that recognises the rights and needs of individuals.

Conclusion

In situations when child protection concerns arise during pregnancy, a pre-birth assessment is the mechanism for identifying the risks and protective factors likely to prevail at birth and during the first few weeks, months or years of life. Social workers and midwives are key professionals in the process of assessment, by virtue of their knowledge, skills and responsibilities in relation to women and children's health, well-being and safety. Starting from the same ethical basis that embodies principles of justice, mutual relationships, respect, trust and dignity, these two groups of professionals have experienced influence and, at times, constraint from the organisational, procedural and sociopolitical contexts within which they practise. Professional perspectives have evolved that have resulted in midwifery practice that emphasises and encompasses **woman–centred care** as the preferred ideological approach, and child protection social work has been influenced by notions of risk and **risk management** and the context of post-birth assessment and intervention.

Managerialism is evident in social work and midwifery, impacting on professional practice and heightening the challenge that professionals face in adhering to central ethical principles. Added to this, terminology such as 'unborn child', if used within the context of pre-birth child protection, creates a potential for confusion and further tension, implying that a pregnant woman is merely a vessel for a child at risk. Complexity abounds in child protection generally, and more so in pre-birth assessment because of the unique circumstances surrounding pregnancy and the interrelated needs of the pregnant woman and the foetus. Within the confines of complicated legal, political and organisational constructs, social workers and midwives are required to make decisions that can have life-changing consequences for all concerned. In doing so they must draw on professional knowledge and experience, but also recognise how their personal knowledge, experience and belief systems may impact on their decision-making process. A fundamental understanding of ethical principles is essential to help make some sense of what is required of them and how they approach pre-birth assessment. Therefore, despite, or possibly because of, the impact of managerialism, emphasis must shift toward ensuring that approaches to practice are appropriate and relevant. In this respect, the woman-centred approaches central to midwifery practice have much to offer to social work practice.

The surface of the ethical debate has only been touched upon and more is needed, particularly in relation to encompassing how culture and religion inform our approaches to pregnancy and childbirth. However, this chapter has entered into the ethical debate about pre-birth assessment and in doing so has identified how recourse to the professional ethical value base can serve to empower both the women who experience pre-birth assessments and the professionals who undertake them. Moreover, the chapter has highlighted how learning can be drawn from existing midwifery approaches to women-centred care and applied to social work approaches to pre-birth assessment so as to refocus practice on the needs of pregnant women, while not negating the needs of the child.

References

Armstrong, A.E. (2006) 'Towards a strong virtue ethics for nursing practice', *Nursing Philosophy*, vol 7, pp 110–24.

Brinsden, P.R. (2009) 'Thirty years of IVF: the legacy of Patrick Steptoe and Robert Edwards', *Human Fertility*, vol 12, no 3, pp 137–43.

Broadhurst, K., Wastell, D., White, S., Hall, C., Peckover, S., Thompson, K., Pithouse, A. and Davey, D. (2010) 'Performing "initial assessment": identifying the latent conditions for error at the front-door of local authority children's services', *British Journal of Social Work*, vol 40, pp 352–70.

Bryson, V. and Deery, R. (2010) 'Public policy, "men's time" and power: the work of community midwives', *The British National Health Service, Women's Studies International Forum*, vol 33, pp 91–8.

C4EO (2011) *Grasping the nettle: Early intervention for children, families and communities*, www.c4eo.org.uk/themes/earlyintervention/files/early_intervention_grasping_the_nettle_full_report.pdf.

Corby, B. (2006) *Child abuse: Toward a knowledge base* (3rd edn), Berkshire: Open University Press.

Corner, R. (1997) *Pre birth risk assessment in child protection*, Social Work Monographs, Norwich: University of East Anglia.

Cm 5730 (2003) *The Victoria Climbié Inquiry Report*, London: The Stationery Office.

Deery, R. (2005) 'An action research study exploring midwives' support needs and the effect of group clinical supervision', *Midwifery*, vol 21, no 2, pp 161–76.

Deery, R. and Fisher, P. (2010) 'Switching and swapping faces: performativity and emotion in midwifery', *International Journal of Work Organization and Emotion*, vol 3, no 3, pp 270–86.

Deery, R. and Kirkham, M. (2006) 'Supporting midwives to support women', in L. Page and R. McCandlish (eds) *The new midwifery: Science and sensitivity in practice* (2nd edn), London: Elsevier, pp 125–40.

Department for Education (DfE) (2011) *The Munro review of child protection: Final report*, London: The Stationery Office.

DoH (Department of Health) (2000) *The framework for the assessment of children in need and their families*, London: The Stationery Office.

England and Wales Court of Appeal (Civil Division) Decisions (30 July 1998) *MS, R (on the application of) v Collins & Anor* [1998] EWCA Civ 1349, [1999] Fam 26.

England and Wales High Court (Administrative Court) Decisions (15 April 2003) I*n the matter of unborn baby MR* [2003] EWHC 850 (admin) case number CO/1814/2003.

Goddard, C.R., Saunders, B.J. and Stanley, J.R. (1999) 'Structured risk assessment procedures: instruments of abuse?', *Child Abuse Review*, vol 8, pp 251–63.

Hart, D. (2010) 'Assessment prior to birth', in J. Horwath (ed) *The child's world, assessing children in need* (2nd edn), London: Jessica Kingsley Publishers, pp 229–40.

Hodson, A.V. (2011) 'Pre-birth assessment in social work', unpublished PhD thesis, University of Huddersfield.

International Confederation of Midwives (2008) *International Code of Ethics for Midwives, Core Document CD2008_001*.

International Federation of Social Workers (IFSW) (2012) *Statement of ethical principles*, http://ifsw.org/policies/statement-of-ethical-principles/

Kaczor, C. (2011) *The ethics of abortion: Women's rights, human life and the question of justice*, New York: Routledge.

Kent, J. (2000) *Social perspectives on pregnancy and childbirth for midwives, nurses and caring professionals*, Buckingham: Open University Press.

Kirkham, M. (ed) (2010) *The midwife–mother relationship* (2nd edn), London: Palgrave Macmillan.

Kirkham, M., Stapleton, H., Thomas, G. and Curtis, P. (2002) 'Checking not listening: how midwives cope', *British Journal of Midwifery*, vol 10, no 7, pp 447–51.

Moe, V. and Slinning, K. (2002) 'Prenatal drug exposure and the conceptualization of long-term effects', *Scandinavian Journal of Psychology*, vol 43, pp 41–7.

Morgan, A. and Ziglio, E. (2007) 'Revitalising the evidence base for public health: an assets model', *Promotion and Education*, vol 14, pp 17–22.

Ofsted (2011) *Ages of concern: Learning lessons from serious case reviews.* Report number 110080, www.ofsted.gov.uk/resources/ages-of-concern-learning-lessons-serious-case-reviews.

Thompson, F. (2004) *Mothers and midwives, the ethical journey*, London: Elsevier.

Ward, H., and Glaser, D. (2010) 'The developmental needs of children: implications for assessment', in J. Horwath (ed) *The child's world, assessing children in need*, London: Jessica Kingsley Publishers, pp 160–73.

ELEVEN

Professional and interprofessional ethical considerations for practising psychologists in Australia

Christopher Boyle

Introduction

As part of Part Three, this chapter focuses on the dynamics of professional and **interprofessional** ethics (see Figure 1.1). The author uses a real-life case study, namely the Tarasoff case, to illustrate these dynamics. The chapter draws on moral philosophy and consequentialism to debate issues of **ethical practice**.

The **standards** of ethical practice will inevitably vary among people and professions and by country. Ethics can take on many theoretical perspectives but, in essence, it is, fundamentally, about knowing what is right and what is wrong in any given situation and exercising appropriate **ethical judgement** to act accordingly in new and developing situations (Margison and Shore, 2009). Two principal components that should always be expected to hold steadfast in ethical standards are those of **nonmaleficence** (to do no harm) and of **beneficence** (doing good) (APS, 2007). Ethical and moral standards are intertwined and it would be foolhardy in a professional context to attempt to separate the two; however, Francis (2009, p 25) suggests that the distinction lies in ethics being a '...codified set of value principles which have application to a nominated subset of people', while moral standards are related to known rules about behaviour that are not formally recorded, that is, not set down in a code. Ethically, professionals should attempt to conduct their professional lives with the utmost integrity and selflessness. As Koocher and Keith-Spiegel (2008) suggest, ethics are about knowing good from bad and right from wrong, and this will be based on an ethical understanding of what constitutes each component. It is about understanding where psychologists should be in relation to

social responsibility (Davidson, 2010), especially considering the '**vulnerable** group' that seeks professional support. In short, adhering to an **ethical code** is attempting to do what *ought* to be done in any given professional situation.

The Australian Psychological Society (APS) Code of Ethics

For psychologists to practise in Australia, they must be registered with the national **regulatory** body, the Australian Health Practitioners Regulation Agency (AHPRA), which has adopted the **APS** *Code of Ethics* (2007, hereafter referred to as the Code) (see Chapters Two and Eighteen for discussion of codes of ethics and conduct for psychologists working in the UK). The general purpose of any professional ethical code is to provide a uniform guide to good practice, which covers appropriate conduct in various general situations. It is what the practitioner should endeavour to do in any given situation; it is aspirational but not fixed and must be interpreted differently depending on the particular event. No ethical code can ever be expected to cover all eventualities or apply to all situations and, in the case of the APS, it is also designed to be the *minimum* standard required from practitioners (Allan, 2011). The Code is split into three separate sections, which are referred to as the 'general principles' and cover the areas of *respect*, *propriety* and *integrity*.

The Code expects psychologists to behave in such a way that there is both beneficence and nonmaleficence toward the client. It is the optimum position, where psychologists aspire to practise with the best of intentions. The Code assists by providing a benchmark and a guide as to what is regarded as good practice. Of course, it should not be taken as a guide that includes all that should or should not be done. Fronek et al (2009) state this well when they suggest that 'codes provide a framework for discipline specific practice, however, do not necessarily provide clear cut answers with consistency within and across disciplines' (p 18). The Code stands for a general consensus across the profession as to what is appropriate behaviour in professional situations. Only a fool would expect it to be a step-by-step guide to good practice.

Complementing the Code, Australian psychologists also have *Ethical Guidelines* (APS, 2009), which are provided to supplement and to clarify the more technical and legalistic language that is used in the Code. The Guidelines provide various sections such as:

- on **confidentiality**
- for working with people who pose a high risk of harm to others
- for managing professional boundaries and multiple relationships.

There are a total of 23 separate guidelines, and although the 9th edition was published in 2009, several of the individual sections have been updated separately and are available on the APS website (www.psychology.org.au). This is more in line with providing a guide through different potentially foreseeable ethical difficulties so that the practitioner can be proactive in avoiding issues that may become ethically problematic. As with ethical standards and codes of conduct for professionals, it seems that the question of whether you acted ethically or not may arise only if a complaint or challenge is made against your professional practice. At that point one must be able to show that one has behaved within the stipulated and accepted protocols of the registered profession. Contemporary society can be somewhat litigious, and therefore bearing in mind that one's practice can be challenged legally and/or professionally should ensure that practitioners take cognisance of their respective ethical codes and guidelines. The point being that one's behaviour should be ethical not because one is concerned about breaching the Code per se but because this should be what the professional aspires to. It should not be that one is frightened of falling foul of ethical principles, as this would take us into Plato's Ring of Gyges, which is discussed in the next section.

Philosophical ethics

The ethical codes of most (if not all) professions have their grounding in the philosophical underpinnings of a moral code. According to Ford (2006), there are two major theories in Western philosophy: 'Kant's ethical formalism and utilitarianism' (p 55). The former is the underlying knowledge of what is good and that, in order to do good, there should be an underlying knowledge of the universal necessity. In other words by doing good one is acting not out of individualism but for the good of humanity. Utilitarianism, in its simplest form, is based on the notion that the outcome is more important than the process. So, if the ultimate result is good, then this would suggest a positive ethical outcome. This is a consequentialist approach that, as the name suggests, takes into consideration the consequences of the action (Healy, 2007). From the perspective of the APS *Code of Ethics*, it could be suggested that the Code is based on consequentialist principles, thus taking cognisance of the outcomes of the person's actions. An example would be the need to disclose information (that is, to breach confidentiality) to a third party, in which case it would be based on the outcome of the action and the ramifications from there onwards.

Plato's story of the Ring of Gyges illustrates his fear that human nature can essentially be good unless they think that 'nobody is watching', and then they can act without fear of retribution or besmirching their own character, thus with impunity. In the story described in Plato (1955), Gyges finds a ring that, he discovers, can make him invisible. He finds that through his new-found invisibility he is able to listen to what others say about him. Gyges takes this further and eventually gains much material wealth and riches by successfully manipulating situations to his advantage. Of course, Gyges acts unethically because *he can*. Plato (1955, 360c) suggests that 'there is no one, it could commonly be supposed, who would have such iron strength of will as to stick to what is right and keep his hands from taking other people's property'. If we follow this suggestion, then we consider that humans are predisposed to find it difficult to maintain ethical standards if a seemingly perfect opportunity to circumvent the rules arises. Clearly, Plato laid the foundations for ethical codes, as he foresaw the vulnerability of the human character, which is exemplified in the need for ethical codes in some form across all professions.

In essence, ethical conduct or appropriateness exists only because of the fear of one's reputation becoming damaged. This is a point that can be seen to exist in present-day ethical conduct. In psychology and other professions there are many examples of serious breaches of ethical standards causing individual professionals to face issues such as loss of professional **accreditation**, financial earnings, possible prosecution and, maybe most significantly, the loss of reputation, especially if that is one of eminence in the field of practice. Maybe this is why ethical codes, including the Hippocratic Oath, have their roots in moral and ethical philosophy.

Good ethical practice

The philosopher Immanuel Kant (1724–1804) suggested that good ethical practice was based on ethical duty and on logical thinking that would, therefore, lead to absolute ways of reasoning and thus behaving morally (Hill, 2006). This absolutist approach to an ethical code is not what a code for psychologists or other professionals should be about. As mentioned earlier in this chapter, it cannot be a logical progression model of how to act in *any* given situation. It needs to provide a guide as to what is generally expected of professional practitioners. What is acceptable practice in the professions will vary by code; however, in Australia there is an additional consideration: that of the rurality of many of the population. Anderson et al (2011, p 1) ask a very pertinent question: 'should we play basketball with clients?' This is an issue that practitioners in various professional fields have to consider in day-to-day practice, even if it is not broached in such terms. The blurring of boundaries in the client–professional relationship can be problematic and is usually best avoided. However, the scenarios can become more blurred when we consider the theme of the question posed above. If the situation arises in an urban setting, then it is clear that this would be a breach of most ethical codes, in that playing basketball with a client, outside of a therapeutic environment, would not be regarded as an ethically sound decision. If the scenario was situated in a rural setting, then the decision might become more difficult.

The study by Anderson et al (2011) comprised 410 participants who worked as psychologists across the state of Victoria in Australia. The main finding was that psychologists working in rural areas were more inclined to have experienced dual relationships. Examples could be being members of the same sports club or having children in the same school. Anderson et al (2011) found that when the population was less than 5,000, all psychologists had experienced some form of overlapping of position. However, the researchers emphasised that this did not lead to a relaxation of standards, but in fact heightened awareness of the potential for breaches of the ethical code. In a small population you may be the only social worker, psychologist, physiotherapist (among other professions); therefore you are ethically obliged to provide a professional service to the client. A study of New Zealand psychiatrists also found that there was more likelihood of rural practitioners meeting clients (past and present) at social activities or in general day-to-day activities, for example, at the supermarket or a children's football match (Scopelliti et al, 2004).

In many rural areas the option of not taking on a client because you play basketball with them may not be available. In a more urban area, with more human resources, referral to a professional colleague would be the ethically acceptable method of dealing with this potential conflict. An interesting anecdote relating to the potential problems for rural practitioners is related by Hammond (2010), where the psychologist (in this case, but equally applicable to any professional) is attending a dinner party with her husband and coincidentally finds herself sitting opposite one of her current clients. In order to avoid the potential for a boundary violation the psychologist had to leave, which caused a 'marital discussion' with her husband, who clearly did not understand why they had to leave. Even more frustratingly, it was not possible to inform the husband of the true reason, as this could have been construed as a breach of confidentiality in respect of the client.

Interprofessional good practice

Interacting with other agencies is a necessary component of the caring professions and this is certainly the case with psychologists. Ensuring that procedures are followed with regard to a code of ethics of one's own profession is paramount. Variations in accepted procedure can take place; however, it would not suffice to say to a professional discipline board that you followed the ethical code of another profession, despite there being an interprofessional linkage. Arguably one of the most infamous cases in professional ethics, and especially relating to the practice of psychology, is the Tarasoff case (Supreme Court of California, 1976). It is not within the scope of this chapter to provide full details of the case (for a wider discussion the reader is referred to Borum and Reddy, 2001; Fisher, 2013), but a synopsis is relevant to give the reader a perspective on the sharing and disclosure of confidential information among professionals.

Tatiana Tarasoff was an American student who was murdered by a fellow student in California in 1969. In a case that has become the central topic of discussion for ethics classes around the world, the main issue centred on the duty to disclose confidential material to a third party. In the Tarasoff case, Prosenjit Poddar, who eventually killed Tarasoff, had been attending sessions with the university psychologist. In one of the sessions he disclosed that he intended to kill Tarasoff, who was not named directly but was identifiable (Borum and Reddy, 2001). Poddar was detailed enough in his descriptions of violent intent for the psychologist to believe that this was a serious threat and he, in consultation with the supervising psychiatrist, contacted the police and Poddar was arrested. However, Poddar was released after the police interviewed him and did not believe that he was actually going to carry out his threat.

Some months later Poddar did indeed murder Tarasoff (Supreme Court of California, 1976). He carried out his threat, which had been taken seriously by the case psychologist who saw fit to breach confidentiality, as it was a threat to the life of a third party. From a professional ethics perspective, the psychologist could have been considered to have done all that was necessary in that a client's threat was taken seriously and the supervising psychiatrist was informed, with the subsequent decision made to contact law enforcement. However, the psychologist and other university staff were successfully sued in Court, despite having taken action on account of their (as it turned out) correct belief that the perceived threat from Poddar was more than an idle threat. It was decided by the Court that these actions had been insufficient because nobody had warned Tatiana Tarasoff about the potential danger, thus meaning that she was not able to protect herself, as she had no knowledge that any sort of threat existed or had been made against her.

The case hinged on the psychologist having a duty to warn a third party, and in the 1976 ruling the police were exonerated, despite their release of Poddar. Here we can see a clash in the interprofessional standards where it could be legitimately argued that a health professional passing on this type of information to an appropriate body (in this case, law enforcement) is an acceptable breach of client confidentiality. However, it seems that this ruling has meant that the responsibility to warn a third party lies with the information-receiving professional. It is up to that person to follow up with whatever authority is necessary so as to ensure that appropriate protection measures have been taken. Koocher and Keith-Spiegel (2008) noted that a subsequent argument was put forward in 1979 by the Director of the American Psychological Association. He suggested that if client confidentiality had not been breached by the case psychologist, then Poddar might have remained in psychotherapy, thereby continuing to receive treatment and thus, possibly, reducing his propensity to commit a violent act. Whether this would have been the case or not will never be known, but it is a salient point for all practitioners in the caring professions in that, once confidentiality has been broken with a client, there is no going back. This is especially the case where the breach of confidentiality has not been intimated to the client prior to its taking place. In these circumstances the client can no longer be expected to have trust in the professional, thus signalling the end of the **therapeutic relationship**.

A study by Mason et al (2010) of professionals in England working in the forensic field indicated some interesting findings in relation to Tarasoff liability. Across the professions of **social work**, psychiatry, psychology and nursing there was an agreement regarding the necessary duty to inform a significant other. Mason et al (2010) highlight a difference in how the reporting was done. Nursing staff reported pushing it further up the food chain, whereas the other professionals reported laterality in their reporting. It was found that 'the nurses felt that they were blameless once the information had been passed to the psychiatrists' (Mason et al, 2010, p 553). The psychologists, psychiatrists and social workers felt that, after passing on the information, they were still professionally responsible. If we consider these findings under Tarasoff liability, it should be considered that passing information 'upwards' could not be taken as being the end of the matter. Effective follow-up so as to ensure that whoever has been informed has acted appropriately in a situation and dealt with it at an ethically satisfactory level (as deemed by the original professional) is an ethical responsibility, no matter what the professional status. It seems fair to suggest that all staff in the helping professions have equal responsibility in this regard, but does this happen in the various types of professional practice?

Many professional groups in Australia have clear ethical guidelines about practice, but the teaching profession does not, according to Teaching Australia (2008), which states that, 'there is however no overarching code of ethics which applies to teachers and principals in their professional capacity, wherever they are employed' (p 16). The author of this chapter has worked both as a teacher and as a school psychologist, and it was clear from those experiences that there was an interesting dichotomy between the role of school psychologist and that of teacher. Considering that many psychologists work in school settings and have very clear ethical codes, as described above, this is an interesting interprofessional dynamic. In this setting students will be referred to the school psychologist by a staff member involved in pastoral care or student guidance, but teachers will expect feedback on how the 'counselling' is progressing. This request for feedback may also be more formalised in psychology–teacher liaison meetings.

Confidentiality is a fundamental principle in the psychologist's ethical code but, as there is no overarching code of ethics for teachers (Teaching Australia, 2008), this may present difficulties for psychologists who disclose information, as the ethical boundaries may not be as robust and secure as they should be. The main point about sharing information among professional colleagues is that an agreement (or contract) is negotiated between the client and professional before any meaningful therapeutic relationship is undertaken. This is best practice and ensures that the (quite often) necessary sharing of information between professionals can take place without fear of breaching client confidentiality.

Comparing some aspects of the Australian Association of Social Workers (AASW) *Code of Ethics* (2010) with the psychologists' Code, it is interesting to note that the former refers in various places to the importance of linking with colleagues in other professions. This is not reflected in the psychologists' Code, where the only mention of interprofessional conduct relates to portraying the profession in a good light, and not to interaction with other professions. It could be suggested that the AASW recognises that much of social work involves liaising with other professions, whereas psychology can quite often be practised at an individual level with only limited input from others (for example, general practitioner (GP) referral). However, it could be counter-argued that insufficient cognisance is given to interprofessional working because other professions such as social work or teaching are not seen as being of equivalent standing in the professional community.

Confidentiality and blurred boundaries

One of the most controversial aspects of the psychologists' Code is the matter of confidentiality and when it is necessary, and indeed proper, to breach the confidentiality between client and therapist. Confidentiality is important because 'Right to privacy is predicated on the principle of autonomy – self-determination – because it involves individuals being free to make the decision to be le[f]t alone, provides protection from undue, arbitrary interference or intrusion by others into one's personal affairs ...' (Davidson et al, 2010, p 78). Being able to maintain confidentiality is the cornerstone of any helping professional's approach to working with a client. It is clearly a fundamental part of a psychologist's role, such that a strong psychotherapeutic relationship with the client can be fostered. Having a **rapport** with a client is recognised as one of the fundamentals of practice that is recognised as being more important than the type of therapeutic approach that is actually used (Houser et al, 2006; Boyle, 2007).

The Code states that there are various reasons why confidentiality should not be maintained, including client agreements to divulge certain information to another party, for example referring GP, parent or carer, among others. In Australia the psychologist is required to provide privileged information if 'there is a legal obligation to do so' (p 15), for example, if subpoenaed by a court. As has been discussed elsewhere in this chapter, a serious consideration for various professionals is that of a duty to disclose certain information with or without the **consent** of the client. Best practice would dictate that an attempt should be made to have the client in agreement that this course of action is best. For example, if an adolescent (under 18 years) discloses to a professional that she is pregnant, that professional's **code of conduct** will dictate how this information is dealt with. Consideration should be given to how the therapeutic relationship can be maintained if a disclosure is made without client agreement. In this example the social worker may be aware of serious familial issues that may put the adolescent in danger if the information is divulged to the parents. However, passing the information on to a supportive person in the school or to a medical practitioner can ensure that the client's well-being is still paramount despite, the technical breach of confidentiality.

The most likely reason to break a client's confidentiality in the field of psychology is 'if there is an immediate and specified risk of harm to an identifiable person or persons that can be averted only by disclosing information' (APS, 2007, p 15). This goes along with the Tarasoff case, where it is clear that a third party is in danger and information must be passed on to an appropriate agency. This may be the only occasion when agreement with the client is not forthcoming prior to disclosure of information. How a person acts in these circumstances will depend on the profession that is involved. The only way for a helping professional to protect him or herself is to rigorously follow the relevant Code of Practice, because if they are challenged in court the Court will use this as the basis for determining whether criminality or negligence occurred.

The blurring of boundaries in professional settings can be common, depending on the practice and the location of such practice. In a country such as Australia, which has a large geographical expanse and where there are many isolated and remote communities, it is quite possible that there will be an overlapping of professional practice. There is also more chance that there will be a connection between client and professional, as was discussed earlier in the chapter. In the various fields of forensic psychology and social work, among others, there is always the potential for conflicts of interest that will have little to do with geographical matters.

The most obvious of these is when a psychologist or social worker is instructed to provide a forensic report to a Court on the basis of their professional opinion. If this is requested as an independent report and the client is fully aware that the purpose includes providing information to the Court, then there should be nothing of concern about this engagement. However, if the professional is also providing some form of therapeutic service to the client, then it could be argued that this is clearly a breach of 'good practice' and ethics. There is the possibility of deceiving the client. Consideration needs to be given to the original contractual obligation between the professional and the client as to what is an acceptable outcome with regard to the service that they can be expected to receive. If a psychologist or social worker, without a subpoena, subsequently provides information to the Court in the form of a report, then this could be regarded as ethically problematic, as it was not an agreed outcome between the client and the professional. In other words, there could be a **conflict of interest** where the professional might not be acting in the best interests of the client.

Conclusion

This chapter has highlighted some of the main issues for practising psychologists in Australia, including when working with other professionals. Acting ethically is about what you *ought* to do and the various ethical codes that exist are there to provide something akin to a uniform guide to good practice. The Tarasoff case, despite being almost 45 years old, remains a crucial debate in deciding what to do in certain situations, especially when considering the protection of third parties from violent acts. If disclosure is necessary, thus breaching confidentiality, then best practice is to always attempt to get an agreement with the client that such action is necessary. If this is obtained, then there is a chance of the therapeutic relationship continuing. However, as was discussed in relation to the Tarasoff case, as soon as the breach takes place the therapy will usually cease, and thus breaking confidentiality will not be done without serious consideration of the ramifications. Interprofessional training in many areas, and especially that of ethics, has been suggested to be an important step in ensuring strong inter-ethical approaches to **casework**.

Psychologists, social workers and other members of the helping professions receive specialist training through university or other accredited courses, and so it should follow that ethical training is a core product of the course. In Australia, in order to gain professional accreditation as a psychologist, it is compulsory for students to take a class in professional ethics. Fronek et al (2009, p 18) state that 'Proficiency in ethical decision making is essential to the maintenance of healthy boundaries'. Fronek et al suggest that a linking of ethical training is essential in order to ensure that interprofessional linkage is based on robust and similar ethical principles. The crux of their argument is that some training on boundary issues for healthcare professionals seems to be perfunctory and that this causes problems when working with clients (patients) in the later stages. In short, the staff have not been adequately trained to deal with these everyday dilemmas that all professional staff in the helping professions will face on a regular basis.

References

Allan, A. (2011) 'The development of a code for Australian psychologists', *Ethics & Behaviour*, vol 21, no 6, pp 435–51.

Anderson, R., Pierce, D. and Crowden, A. (2011) 'Should we play basketball with our patients? Professional boundaries and overlapping relationships in rural Australia', paper presented at *11th National Rural Health Conference, 13–16th March 2011, Perth*, Australia.

AASW (Australian Association of Social Workers) (2010) *Code of ethics*, Canberra: AASW.

APS (Australian Psychological Society) (2007) *Code of ethics*, Melbourne, Victoria: APS.

APS (2009) *Ethical guidelines: Complementing the APS code of ethics (9th edn)*, Melbourne, Victoria: APS.

Borum, R. and Reddy, M. (2001) 'Assessing violence risk in Tarasoff situations: a fact based model of inquiry', *Behavioural Sciences and the Law*, vol 19, pp 375–85.

Boyle, C. (2007) 'The challenge of interviewing adolescents: which psychotherapeutic approaches are useful in educational psychology?', *Educational and Child Psychology*, vol 24, no 1, pp 36–45.

Davidson, G.R. (2010) 'Exploration of psychologists' social responsibilities: how does the 2007 code of ethics measure up,', in A. Allan and A. Love (eds) *Ethical practice in psychology: Reflections from the creators of the APS code of ethics*, Chichester: John Wiley & Sons Ltd, pp 103–22.

Davidson, G.R., Allan, A. and Love, A.W. (2010) 'Consent, privacy and confidentiality', in A. Allan and A. Love (eds) *Ethical practice in psychology: Reflections from the creators of the APS code of ethics*, Chichester: John Wiley and Sons Ltd, pp 77–102.

Fisher, C.B. (2013) *Decoding the ethics code: A practical guide for psychologists* (3rd edn), Thousand Oaks, CA: Sage.

Ford, G. (2006) *Ethical Reasoning for mental health professionals*, Thousand Oaks, CA: Sage Publications.

Francis, R. (2009) *Ethics for psychologists* (2nd edn), Chichester: BPS Blackwell.

Fronek, P., Kendall, M., Ungerer, G., Malt, J., Eugarde, E. and Geraghty, T. (2009) 'Towards healthy professional–client relationships: the value of an interprofessional training course', *Journal of Interprofessional Care*, vol 23, no 1, pp 16–29.

Hammond, S. (2010) 'Boundaries and multiple relationships', in A. Allan, and A. Love (eds) *Ethical practice in psychology: Reflections from the creators of the APS code of ethics*, Chichester: John Wiley and Sons Ltd, pp 103–22.

Healy, L.M. (2007) 'Universalism and cultural relativism in social work ethics', *International Social Work*, vol 50, no 1, pp 11–26.

Hill, T.E. (2006) 'Kantian normative ethics', in D. Copp (ed) *The Oxford handbook of ethical theory*, New York: Oxford University Press, pp 480–514.

Houser, R., Wilczenski, F.L. and Ham, M. (2006) *Culturally relevant ethical decision-making in counselling*, Thousand Oaks, CA: Sage Publications.

Koocher, G.P. and Keith-Spiegel, P. (2008) *Ethics in psychology and the mental health professions: Standards and cases* (3rd edn), New York: Oxford University Press.

Margison, J.A. and Shore, B.M. (2009) 'Interprofessional practice and education in health care: their relevance to school psychology', *Canadian Journal of School Psychology*, vol 24, no 2, pp 125–39.

Mason, T., Worsley, A. and Coyle, D. (2010) 'Forensic multidisciplinary perspectives of Tarasoff liability: a vignette study', *Journal of Forensic Psychiatry and Psychology*, vol 21, no 4, pp 549–54.

Plato (1955) *The republic*, trans D. Lee, Middlesex: Penguin Books.

Psychology Board of Australia (2010) *Guidelines for mandatory notifications*, www.psychologyboard.gov.au/documents/default.aspx?record=WD10%2F1339&dbid=AP&chksum=pgFDZiMYViF6U eZvxTMO5w%3D%3D.

Scopelliti, J., Judd, F., Grigg, M., Hodgins, G., Fraser, C., Hulbert, C., Endacott, R. and Wood, A. (2004) 'Dual relationships in mental health practice: issues for clinicians in rural settings', *Australian and New Zealand Journal of Psychiatry*, vol 38, nos 11–12, pp 953–59.

Supreme Court of California (1976) *Tarasoff v Regents of the University of California* 7 Cal. 3d 425, 551 P.2d 334, 131 Cal. Rptr. 14 (Cal. 1976), California: Supreme Court of California.

Teaching Australia (2008) *National professional standards for advanced teaching and for principals*, Canberra: Australian Institute for Teaching and School Leadership Ltd.

Personal, professional and interprofessional ethics

TWELVE

Personal, professional and interprofessional ethics in policing in a child protection context

Dawn MacEachern, Edward Miles and Divya Jindal-Snape

This chapter presents findings from a number of serious case reviews in the UK as case studies to highlight the need for professionals involved in child protection to work collaboratively with professionals from other disciplines. In line with the aim of Part Four (see Figure 1.1), these cases are used as a lens to understand the multiple dynamics of personal, professional and **interprofessional** ethics experienced by professionals working in this area, with a focus on the perspectives of police officers, elicited through research conducted by the first author.

A police officer, especially in the field of child protection, domestic **abuse** and the investigation of serious sexual assaults, can often have a silent inner ethical conflict with regard to the desire to protect the rights of the child and the professional duty to protect the rights of the **accused**. In child protection incidents and sexual crime, the scales of justice are often seen to be weighted heavily towards the human rights of the suspect/accused, sometimes to the detriment of the **victim**. There is potential for conflict when the police are working in an increasingly interprofessional context involving **social work**, law and health services where each profession may have different priorities and professional codes of ethics. This chapter will explore this personal, professional and interprofessional ethical tension to protect the rights of the victim and accused within a legislative context, using the philosophical approach to ethics (see Chapter One).

The legislative framework and tensions between personal and professional ethics in policing

In Scotland the police have a statutory responsibility under the Police (Scotland) Act 1967 (Scottish Office, 1967) and the Children

(Scotland) Act 1995 (Scottish Office, 1995a) to protect children, prevent crime and detect offenders. The **criminal justice systems** of most countries around the world are permeated by the notion of balance, as symbolised by the 'Scales of Justice'. Kamlasabayson (2003), Sri Lankan Attorney General, asserts that on the one hand the system is meant to ensure that an innocent suspect is not unfairly prosecuted or convicted; and on the other hand the interests of the victim are protected, and taken cognisance of, in having the perpetrator prosecuted and punished. To this end, police forces around the globe are tasked with carrying out the defined policing functions delineated in their country's legislation; in principle, to detect offenders and bring them swiftly to justice. When conducting investigations the police have to perform a number of duties. These range from obtaining full witness statements for the prosecution to providing sufficient evidence and interviewing the suspect, while taking cognisance of their human rights and incorporating fairness. In performing both roles, the police aim to ensure that the scales of justice are evenly balanced, in a climate where there is an ever-increasing perception that the scales have tipped in favour of the rights of the suspect/accused, to the detriment of the victim. The following case provides a background to the changes in Scottish law and practice.

The Cadder Case and Lord Carloway's review

Peter Cadder was detained on suspicion of serious assault under section 14(1) of the Criminal Procedure (Scotland) Act 1995 (Scottish Office, 1995b) in May 2007, and interviewed by two police officers in Glasgow. In line with **statute**, he was advised that he did not have to answer any questions other than those related to factual information about his identity. Police followed procedures and informed him that he was entitled to have a solicitor informed of his detention. However, he chose not to do so. During the interview he made a number of admissions. In an identity parade the victim was unable to identify him. Therefore, in the Court case, to prove him guilty, the Crown had to rely on admissions made by Cadder during the police interview. He was convicted. However, he was able to successfully appeal that not having had a solicitor present at the police interview was a breach of Article 6(1) (right to a fair trial) of the European Convention on Human Rights (ECHR).

In 2010, following the decision of the United Kingdom Supreme Court in *Cadder v HM Advocate*, the Cabinet Secretary for Justice, Kenny MacAskill, **MSP**, requested a single **High Court** Judge to be nominated to lead an independent review of the key elements of Scottish law and practice. In November 2010, Lord Carloway commenced work on the review, which involved public consultation in 2011. Lord Carloway (2011) reported that the review was mindful of the need for the protection of the rights of suspects as well as those of victims and the general public. He highlighted a number of relevant principles derived from the ECHR, namely Article 5 (right to liberty), Article 6(1) (right to a fair trial) and others such as the right to silence and privilege against self-incrimination. This led to the fundamental principles of Scots law being questioned as never before, with centuries-old procedures and practices being challenged by human rights legislation in the Cadder case.

However, according to child protection professionals, the criminal justice system in Scotland causes its own tensions. According to MacEachern (2011), **detective** officers commented on their exasperation with the criminal justice system. A particular detective officer stated:

> "Lack of sufficient evidence to prosecute a person in position of trust who allegedly involved a 5 year old female child to perform oral sex on him. Despite having limited forensic evidence it was insufficient for the **Procurators Fiscal** to proceed which was extremely disappointing and caused frustration in the Unit [Family Protection Unit]." (p 119)

It could be argued that police officers have to perform conflicting functions when investigating cases of child abuse, serious sexual assault and suspicious child deaths, resulting in them experiencing **disjuncture** (see Chapter Six). Their inner conflict involves balancing the rights of child victims and/or survivors of serious sexual crimes against the rights of an accused or suspect. For example, MacEachern (2011) reports that detective officers who work within dedicated police units investigating cases of child protection and sexual assault often experience such conflicts, as one detective officer indicated:

> "After interviewing a 10 year old child re sexual abuse, I had to view a video recording previously made which contained images of the abuse. I supported the family throughout the enquiry and was present during the sentencing. The conclusion was positive for me as I saw the reaction of the

family as the perpetrator received a custodial sentence."
(p 118)

Another detective officer reported:

> "A recent historical sexual abuse enquiry involving two
> sisters abused by their father. From my time in the FACU
> [Family and Child Unit, now Family Protection Unit] the
> abuse was the most horrific and degrading that I have dealt
> with and being the first person both sisters had told in detail
> I felt a real sense of 'wanting to get justice for them', while
> not showing my disgust of what they had been through."
> (p 120)

A further detective officer commented:

> "A be-friender of a handicapped male, sexually abused him
> (the suspect was working for the SW dept), he laughed all
> the way through the interview, was conceited and knew
> there was nothing we could do. He had chosen one of the
> most **vulnerable** in our community to abuse, he really
> sickened me." (p 120)

These quotes clearly demonstrate the tensions that police officers may
experience as a result of a conflict between their personal values/
beliefs and the need to follow their profession's code of ethics and
related legislation. Officers articulated their need to 'do justice' for the
children they were interviewing. For the majority of police officers,
justice is achieved when a custodial sentence is handed down by the
courts to the perpetrator and they can no longer abuse their victims.
However, to achieve fairness, the suspect must be treated in line with
the **Lord Advocate's** guidelines for the interviewing of suspects. As
mentioned earlier, any indication that a suspect's rights have been
violated or insufficient evidence has been collated to prove the guilt of
an accused beyond all reasonable doubt could result in a case being lost
or abandoned or a **'not proven'** verdict. As such, officers must ensure
that both the victim's and the accused's rights are finely balanced and
that any personal views and beliefs that they hold do not interfere
with their professional judgement, which may jeopardise the case.
These tensions appear within an **organisational culture** of being
able to do the job without being affected by the cases. MacEachern
(2011) noted in her research that officers commented on the problem

of openly acknowledging the effect that child protection work might have had on them, and its implications. A detective officer appeared to hold the view that by "admitting" that he considered certain incidents "significant" or "operationally challenging" would be seen as a sign of being unprofessional or of weakness on his part. Another reported:

> "I have not dealt with an incident that has had a significant impact on me; I detach myself from incidents and deal with them in a professional manner, rather than allow them to affect me personally." (p 121)

There are concerns of their 'professionalism' being questioned. However, when using **detachment** techniques, officers could be seen as being cold or impersonal, which could negatively affect any **rapport** built up between the witnesses or the suspect/accused and the detective officer, and consequentially have a negative impact on the quality of evidence obtained. As a result, the tensions for working in a professionally efficient manner increase.

This detachment and the need to be seen to be unaffected by ethical dilemmas have often led to police officers feeling stress, especially as the organisational culture is perceived not to be empathetic to such feelings. In the MacEachern (2011) study it was found that of the 63 who responded, 24% of detective officers conducting child protection enquiries were experiencing 'mild' levels of **Secondary Traumatic Stress** (STS), 16% were experiencing 'moderate' levels, and a minority were experiencing 'high' (n=3, 5%) to 'severe' (n=4, 6%) levels of STS. Although 40 respondents (63%) indicated that they had experienced an incident that they considered had had a significant impact on them, 51 respondents (81%) had never used the formal support mechanisms offered by the organisation. Interestingly, those who did access support through the organisation found it to be effective. There were both positive and negative perceptions about the support offered by supervisors and line managers. Several police officers stated that they relied on peer support during these tensions, and dialogues with them provided another perspective on the issues.

Tensions due to interprofessional and interagency work

Increasingly, since 2000, the ability of the world's media to broadcast live coverage of policing incidents and individual officers' actions has brought about renewed interest in ethics within the police service.

Police ethics have been further challenged by a number of high-profile cases of police corruption, unethical behaviour and alleged inappropriate use of force; for example Rodney King being beaten by police officers in Stockton, California in 2001 and the death of Ian Tomlinson during G20 demonstrations in London in 2009. Further, in recent times, the issue of child protection and the actions of **interagency** professionals have progressively become the subject of increased media interest and public scrutiny.

Since the early 1970s, a number of high-profile child deaths in the US and the UK have been widely publicised, and the circumstances surrounding the deaths have been made public knowledge, such as through the inquiries into the deaths of Victoria Climbié (2002) and of Jessica Chapman and Holly Wells (2004). Aspects of a number of these cases will be considered to provide evidence for the argument about the victim's rights versus the accused's rights, as well as to emphasise the importance of interprofessional practice.

Victoria Climbié Inquiry report

On 25 February 2000, Victoria Climbié died in North Middlesex. On 12 January 2001, Victoria's great-aunt, Marie-Therese Kouao, and Carl John Manning were convicted of her murder. Lord Laming (2003) commenced an Independent Statutory Inquiry in 2001 into circumstances surrounding Victoria's death. It found that, leading up to Victoria's death, there had been contact with a number of services including two National Health Service (NHS) hospitals, two Metropolitan Police Service child protection teams and numerous **social services**. In his report Lord Laming expressed the view that 'none of the agencies with a duty to protect children emerged from the Inquiry with much credit ... the death of Victoria was a gross failure of the system ... It is clear to me that the agencies with responsibility for Victoria gave a low priority to the task of protecting children' (Lord Laming, 2003, p 3). He stated that to safeguard the well-being of children and families effectively, it was important that different agencies should share relevant information with each other. This view is now evident as a golden thread running through the **Scottish Government**'s **GIRFEC** approach (discussed later in the chapter).

The Bichard Inquiry and Sir Christopher Kelly's Serious Case Review

On 17 December 2003, Ian Huntley was convicted of the murders of Jessica Chapman and Holly Wells. There was widespread public disquiet when it became clear he had been known to the authorities over a period of years. Huntley had become known to Humberside Police in relation to eight separate allegations of sexual offences between 1995 and 1999, and had been the subject of another investigation. This information had not emerged during the vetting check carried out by Cambridgeshire **Constabulary** at the time of Huntley's appointment to Soham Village College in June 2001.

The Home Secretary at that time, the Right Honorable David Blunkett, MP, requested Sir Michael Bichard to lead an independent inquiry into child protection measures, record keeping, vetting and information sharing in Humberside Police and Cambridgeshire Constabulary. Sir Michael Bichard (2004) identified that one of the key failings was the inability of Humberside Police and Social Services to quickly identify Huntley's behaviour pattern, viewing each case in isolation, and the failure to share information effectively, blaming systemic and corporate failures. In addition, the report was critical of Cambridgeshire Constabulary's handling of Huntley's vetting check, and these misgivings were also referred to in Sir Christopher Kelly's Serious Case Review (2004). It is clear from Sir Christopher Kelly's report that the failure to share information between police force and social services was identified as a major shortcoming.

As can be seen, in these cases problems with information sharing between professionals and agencies were identified as significant factors contributing to failures to keep the children safe. In an interprofessional context, in view of differences in priorities and **ethical codes** with regard to when to maintain confidentiality and when to share information, it is perhaps not surprising that these incidents happened. These cases have led to a thorough review of policy and services. Throughout the UK, including in Scotland, children and young people are high on the priority and agendas of the UK government and Scottish Government (formerly Scottish Executive). The Scottish Executive (2004a, p 5) stated that 'Children and young people should be protected from abuse, neglect and harm by others at home, at school and in the community. This is one of the first commitments in the Scottish Government's vision for children and young people in Scotland and reflects the priority we give to keeping them safe and improving their protection.' Not only did the Scottish Executive author a Children's

Charter; it went further by creating *Protecting Children and Young People: A Framework for Standards* (Scottish Executive, 2004b).

In 2007, the way in which policy was developed and implemented in Scotland changed, primarily as a result of a **Concordat** between the Scottish Government and local government (Scottish Government and **COSLA**, 2007). The Concordat included a joint focus on the delivery of a national performance framework, achieved through 15 national outcomes, indicators and targets, enhancing the role that local government played. A number of the national outcomes under the Concordat relate to children and young people. The Scottish Government's *Getting It Right for Every Child* (GIRFEC) framework (Scottish Government, 2008) seeks to underpin the outcomes, in particular aiming to ensure that young people are successful learners, confident individuals, effective contributors and responsible citizens. The framework goes further by seeking to integrate children's services; creating a shared vision of professionals working together in partnership, with children and young people at the centre; engaging families; and using a common GIRFEC language throughout Scotland, common to all professionals involved in working with children, young people and their families.

In Scotland, police forces, NHS boards and **local authorities** (LAs) are the key agencies with responsibility for working together to identify and commission child protection activities. Each organisation has a statutory duty to develop effective safeguarding measures with robust systems, policies, procedures, protocols, interagency procedures, structures, resources and personnel. Each is vital to the child protection process (Scottish Executive, 2004b).

In 2003, the Local Government in Scotland Act 2003 placed a duty on public services in Scotland's 32 LAs to work in partnership to tackle local issues together, creating **Single Outcome Agreements** (SOAs). The development of SOA, has given Scotland's LAs greater freedom to set their own priorities, setting out the outcomes which each LA is seeking to achieve with its community planning partners. These reflect local needs, circumstances and priorities, but relate to the relevant national outcomes. Underpinning the Concordat is the concept of partnership working in order to achieve improved outcomes. This partnership approach must be reflected at the community planning level with a recognition that, for it to be successful, the needs of individuals and communities have to be addressed collectively.

The ability of Scotland's statutory agencies to work together in an interprofessional context in terms of conducting child protection investigations, like that of their English counterparts, has not been without its problems. Each organisation has a different remit and role in a case, whether investigative, therapeutic and support or health of the family. Such varying remits have historically led to a lack of understanding, blurring of roles and **mission creep**, resulting in dilemmas and tensions between professionals and organisations, with problems being highlighted in the majority of serious case reviews into child deaths. One police officer quoted in MacEachern (2011) voiced his feelings of anger and frustration when investigating a case that involved another partner agency:

> "enquiry involved a social work mess... children were historically subjected to abuse ... in care ... these enquires give rise to a great feeling of anger and frustration from myself as the children had a difficult life prior to being taken into care ... anger is generally my initial feeling ..." (p 182)

He further added:

> "I want things done as soon as possible ... with efficiency ... some of our partners are slow, inefficient and expect the police to baby sit them ... drive things forward all the time ... I would really appreciate other agencies taking the initiative."(p 182)

However, it could be argued that although the training undertaken by the police and social workers (at times interagency) focuses on child protection issues and the gathering of evidence, the evidence gathering can be for very different end purposes. Social workers have a more therapeutic and long-term involvement with not just the child victim(s) but the whole family. At times this may include work with the alleged offender following proceedings or non-prosecution case disposals (see also Chapter Six). In comparison, the police have a remit of bringing offenders to justice and, acting as agents of the Crown, to present all relevant evidence before the Courts to allow the consideration of a prosecution. This may lead to perceived conflicts between the professions and frustration caused by a lack of understanding of each other's roles.

Similar feelings of frustration were expressed by detective officers in relation to the Procurator Fiscal's Office in MacEachern (2011):

> "after a 19 month enquiry where foster carers had been abusing a young female from the age of about 6 ... child's

hair falling out and showing signs of forms of distress …
PF [Procurator Fiscal] not willing to proceed … obviously
upset the complainer who is now 15 … this was so
frustrating." (p 183)

Decisions as to whether or not criminal proceedings should be initiated
are based on three main factors (following consultation with the
Procurator Fiscal or Scottish Children's Reporter Authority): whether
or not a criminal prosecution is in the best interests of the child; in the
best interest of the public; and sufficiency of evidence. Having reported
an offender, police officers have no part in the decision to prosecute
that person, nor do they have any part other than as witnesses if a
prosecution should take place. This can cause tensions for officers who
are "wanting to get justice" for the children and family they have been
working with, and for a legal system whose professional code wants to
ensure that the scales of justice are carefully balanced.

An ethical approach that could be argued to best fit with policing
principles and values and form the foundation of Scots law is the
'philosophical approach' (see Chapter One). Such an approach, Cranston
et al (2003) and Thiroux and Krasemann (2009) assert, prescribes
and makes value judgements as to the 'right' and 'wrongs' of human
behaviour and reactions to situations. The Police Service of Scotland
acts to enforce the **common law** and legislation of Scotland, reporting
cases to the Procurators Fiscal for consideration of a prosecution. It
could be argued that consequentialist theories of morality (Thiroux and
Kraseman, 2009) are fundamental to the process when considering the
actions of suspects and accused. However, the reality of the influence
of both forms of utilitarianism (act and rule) (Thiroux and Kraseman,
2009) cannot be overestimated; when alleged crimes and offences
are investigated, the actions of suspects and accused are examined in
detail, looking at the situation and context of individuals' actions and
reactions, while taking cognisance of the 'rules' of the land, that is,
Scots law. In this regard, the reality for police officers is that ethics and
moral codes are very much entrenched in legislation, police policy,
Standard Operating Procedures (SOPs) and memoranda, and at
times are dictated by police powers – that is, unconditional (can arrest
without any conditions being applied), conditional (can only arrest
if certain conditions are not met, identity cannot be confirmed and
so on) and silent (no mention of any conditions) powers of arrest.
The hierarchical nature of the police, with line manager/supervisor
responsible for checks, balances and inspection of officers' actions and
decision making, has led over time to officers' discretion being reduced,

resulting in a greater number of children, young people and individuals being reported for minor crimes and offences to the Scottish Children's Reporters Administration (SCRA) and the Procurator Fiscal (PF). As a direct consequence of primary and secondary legislation, with associated unconditional, conditional or common law powers of arrest and police SOPs influencing an officer's decision making, personal ethical and moral values are less likely to impact on their personal judgement as to how to manage a situation. However, the Scottish Government's drive for early and effective interventions, reducing offending and reoffending, has given officers back their discretion to decide the police measures most suitable for dealing with the offender/accused at the lowest level. With regard to serious and sexual crime investigations, it is clear from officers' reflections that personal moral values, although present and felt, are not permitted to interfere with their professionalism or impact/impinge on the progress of an investigation or its ability to be brought to justice, which could result in a failure of justice to be done.

Conclusion

As can be seen, one organisation alone cannot achieve the best outcomes for children and young people. Professionals must have the skills, knowledge, understanding and values that allow them to work together to meet the individual needs of children and young people, respecting the different strengths that each service brings. This has to happen in authentic partnership, without 'mission creep' and blurring of roles and with a true understanding of individual organisations' roles and remits. It is not without its difficulties, but is what all local authorities and child protection organisations aspire to.

It is clear that tensions exist as a consequence of interprofessional working and adhering to Scottish Law, taking cognisance of the rights of all Scotland's citizens. The dual role that the police perform in investigating the circumstances of cases, in terms of working with both the witnesses/victims and the suspects/accused, adds to the inner tensions that officers experience. This dual function can often cause inner conflict, of which officers have to be aware, while remaining impartial and unbiased so as to secure and ensure continued public confidence of all members of society.

Acknowledging the tensions that exist requires organisations to examine the cause of those tensions; and, having acknowledged these tensions, it is imperative that organisations address the issues. The training and educational programmes that professionals undertake when entering the profession are important to ensure a well-trained and informed workforce. Kennie (1998) argues that, in order to keep up with the 'rapid pace of change', embracing **continuous professional development** (CPD) training is increasingly central to a professional's and organisation's success. Kennie further argues that CPD is essential to good professional practice, to personal effectiveness, when new knowledge is applied, to improving skills and to developing personal qualities. Previous serious case reviews have also identified the CPD of all childcare protection professionals as being critical. However, Kelly and Jackson (2011) question whether the current child protection training is fit for the current dynamic environment. The matter of CPD is also relevant for supervisors who are expected to support police officers during the tensions they experience. Bernotavicz and Muskie (1997) consider the role of the supervisor in the child welfare agency as critical. They further argue that not only should supervisors have a knowledge base in child protection and issues that place children at risk of harm; but they should also possess a skill set including teaching, negotiating and motivational skills, and an understanding of law, ethics, policy, procedures and interagency working. There are numerous example of good practice in terms of interagency training in Scotland, namely **Joint Investigative Interview Training** for both practitioners and supervisors; and the CPD programme of seminars offered at the Scottish Police College to non-police professionals and hosted by **interdisciplinary** professionals.

The Scottish Government's GIRFEC approach advocates such an interprofessional approach to ensure that practitioners aim at the outset to reduce bureaucracy; adopt a common language; and work together to get it right for Scotland's children, young people and their families. Once fully implemented and embedded in the policies, practices and cultures of child protection agencies, in particular the Police Service of Scotland, the subject of ethics and inner conflicts resulting from the application of the GIRFEC values and principles would be worthy, in its own merit, of being the topic of future research and empirical studies from, both a national and an international perspective.

A common thread identified in many incidents nationally and over a wide range of agencies has been the lack of communication and information sharing between organisations. Information sharing has been identified in a number of serious case reviews and inquiry reports as being vitally important in terms of protecting children and being able to identify early and effective intervention opportunities at the right time to meet the needs of children, young people and their families. The key themes identified are reminiscent of similar findings in a number of high-profile child murders in the UK, where services primarily considered their work to be with the parents as opposed to the child. The long-established doctrine of **Integrated Emergency Management** that has been utilised for some time in Scotland might suggest a way forward, the aim being to develop flexible and adaptable arrangements for dealing with emergencies. It is based on an interagency approach and the effective coordination of those resources. The doctrine is underpinned by five key activities, namely, Assessment, Prevention, Preparation, Response and Recovery. These principles, contained in a 2012 Government publication entitled *Preparing Scotland*, espouse the full exploration of the benefits of collaborative working and utilising the skills of a wide range of participants in efficient partnership working.

As an **Emergencies Procedure Advisor** with the police, the second author has often attended the scene of a critical or major incident to provide advice or assistance to a **Police Incident Commander**. At such scenes, it is the duty of the police to coordinate the resources present, even though the police may not have primacy. At such scenes there are a series of interagency meetings organised, with set objectives discussed at each meeting within the time frame of the incident until resolution with a return to normality. It is clear that the doctrine has established excellent partnership working and allows each organisation present to do its duty with the maximum collaboration of its partners. This is of course based upon the scene of a critical or major incident, whether foreseen or unforeseen; however, this partnership working, and exchanging and sharing of information is crucial for any work. Plans, protocols and processes are in place for these types of incidents and it may be that the incorporation of the above principles in day-to-day work could be vital in reducing the incidences of lack of communication between respective professionals dealing with child protection incidents.

As discussed, the police officers at times suffer in silence because they are concerned that their tensions and dilemmas, and acknowledgement of being affected by the stories of children and families, might be seen as a sign of weakness and inability to do their work professionally. For professionals who are not always able to discuss tensions between their personal and professional ethics within their organisation, the barriers in an interprofessional context will be even bigger. It was also observed that this had a negative impact on the well-being of these professionals, with several experiencing **post-traumatic stress disorder**, while others who had come forward and sought support found it useful. Therefore, an organisational culture shift is required within the police force and allied professions that, instead of forcing professionals to hide behind the perceived mask of 'professionalism', would allow space for debate and discussion about dilemmas related to any clash between personal, professional and interprofessional ethics. Positive messages have to be given about the benefits of supervisory or other organisational support available. This would not only ensure the well-being of the professionals, it would also lead to more effective work with children and families.

References

Bernotavicz, F. and Muskie, E.S. (1997) *Retention of child welfare caseworkers: A report*, http://muskie.usm.maine.edu/helpkids/pubstext/retention.htm

Cranston, N., Ehrich, L. and Kimber, M. (2003) 'The right decision? Towards an understanding of ethical dilemmas for school leaders', *Westminster Studies in Education*, vol 26, no2, pp 135–47.

Kamlasabayson, K.C. (2003) *Balancing rights of the accused with rights of the victim, The 13th Kanchana Abhayapala Memorial Lecture by Attorney General K.C. Kamlasabayson*, http://www.alrc.net/doc/mainfile.php/documents/432/.

Kelly, C., Sir (2004) *Serious case review – Ian Huntley*, www.nelincs.gov.uk/council/local-safeguarding-children-board/read-north-east-lincolnshire-serious-case-reviews/serious-case-review-ian-huntley/.

Kelly, L. and Jackson, S. (2011) 'Fit for purpose? Post qualifying social work education in child protection in Scotland', *Journal of Social Work Education*, vol 30, no 5, pp 480–96.

Kennie, T.J.M. (1998) 'The growing importance of CPD', *Continuing Professional Development*, vol 1, no 4, pp 112–19.

Local Government in Scotland Act (2003), www.legislation.gov.uk/asp/2003/1/contents.

Lord Carloway (2011) *The Carloway Review: Report and recommendations*, www.scotland.gov.uk/Resource/Doc/925/0123001.pdf.

Lord Laming (2003) *The Victoria Climbié Inquiry: Report of an inquiry*, London: HMSO.

MacEachern, A.D. (2011) 'An exploration into the experiences of police officers that investigate child protection cases and secondary traumatic stress', unpublished Doctoral Thesis, Dundee: University of Dundee.

Scottish Executive (2004a) *Protecting children and young people – the charter*, www.scotland.gov.uk/Publications/2004/04/19082/34410.

Scottish Executive (2004b) *Protecting children and young people: Framework for standards*, www.scotland.gov.uk/Publications/2004/03/19102/34603.

Scottish Government (2008) *A guide to 'Getting it right for every child'*, www.scotland.gov.uk/Resource/Doc/238985/0065813.pdf.

Scottish Government (2012) *Preparing Scotland – Scottish guidance on resilience*, www.scotland.gov.uk/Publications/2012/03/2940.

Scottish Government and Convention of Scottish Local Authorities (COSLA) (2007) *Concordat between Scottish Government and local government*, www.scotland.gov.uk/publications/2007/11/13092240/concordat.

Scottish Office (1967) *Police (Scotland) Act 1967*, www.legislation.gov.uk/ukpga/1967/77.

Scottish Office (1995a) *Children (Scotland) Act 1995*, www.legislation.gov.uk/ukpga/1995/36/contents.

Scottish Office (1995b) *Criminal Procedure (Scotland) Act 1995*, www.legislation.gov.uk/ukpga/1995/46/contents.

The Bichard Inquiry (2004), http://image.guardian.co.uk/sys-files/Society/documents/2005/03/15/Bichardfinalreport.pdf

Thiroux, J.P. and Krasemann, K.W. (2009) *Ethics theory and practice* (10th edn), New Jersey: Prentice Hall.

Personal, professional and interprofessional ethical issues in the context of supporting children affected by bereavement

Steve Sweeney and Per Boge

This chapter explores some of the ethical issues involved in supporting children and young people who have experienced **bereavement**, highlighting personal, professional and **interprofessional** dilemmas in line with the aims of Part Four (see Figure 1.1). The authors present cases of children who were bereaved and not effectively supported by adults, whether their own family or professionals. These narratives and the importance of children's rights are discussed using the frame of moral theory.

When an adult is bereaved they can draw upon a life's-worth of experiences and make use of their cognitive abilities to discern what needs are to be met so as to bring about positive results for their health and well-being (Deci and Ryan, 2002). The adult can then plan a course of action that may be helpful in seeking support in their **grief** and mourning. In the context of the UK, support could be obtained, for instance, by self-referral to a National Health Service general or mental health practitioner, to the private or voluntary sector, to a work-based counsellor and so on. The adult will attend their appointment, taking with them information that can be communicated to the counsellor or support worker in order to devise a suitable support plan.

Children and young people, on the other hand, are entirely dependent upon adults to take care of them and know what to do. According to Dyregrov (2008, p 15), 'Children's understanding of death develops in parallel with the child's cognitive maturing through childhood' and, due to the relationship of dependency upon adults, children and young people are vulnerable if adults do not know how to respond. The range of responses that children and young people may receive are: no response or acknowledgement; little or minimum information; false information; mixed information from varying sources; changing information over time; detailed information. The varied responses given to children may result in some receiving helpful support, but others not. To ensure equitable and easy access to support it could be argued, from a prescriptive ethical perspective with a focus on consequentialism as a normative moral theory (Miner and Petocz, 2003, pp 11–12), that all children and young people should have the right to be consulted about their bereavement needs as a protective measure, because without such provision there may be a risk to their well-being and healthy development.

Some professionals (who may also be parents) believe that it is acceptable for parents to withhold information from their children. The authors consider that there is a potential for personal, professional and interprofessional conflict to arise when other professionals believe that it is not acceptable for children and young people to be unable to gain access to information about their bereavement circumstances.

Worden (2003, p 162) states that 'children need clear information about death, its causes and circumstances'. If information is not given in terms that they can understand, children will make up a story to fill in the blanks; a story that is often more frightening or bizarre than the truth. We have to be skilful with our language when we communicate with children, who may struggle to merge the abstract and concrete. For example, telling a child that **angels** took daddy away may cause more fear than comfort. Children need the truth of facts, but not necessarily the details that are privy to the adults. These can be shared as the child naturally requests such information. Telling the truth also prevents the erosion of trust, should children accidentally learn about events from other sources.

Statistics kept in one bereavement service showed that children had to wait for long periods of time before they were able to access support. In the case of children referred in 2008–09 who were affected by murder and suicide, the average length of time from the event of death until referral was nine years. Case notes reveal the factors involved in why this was the case:

- anxiety not to make things worse by talking about 'it' to the children
- observing children and concluding they were 'doing OK' because they appeared fine
- misdiagnosing traumatic avoidance symptoms with 'doing fine'
- not having a coordinated system of support that recognised **traumatic bereavement** as a priority area of need
- no professional body being responsible or held accountable for children affected by bereavement.

A cultural norm such as believing that grief is a family matter and therefore should stay within the family is potentially a risk factor for children. For some children it is only when their grief is acted out in concerning ways such as violence and aggression, self-harming, running away and so on that support from professionals is sought. Professionals have a role in deciding a course of action that could be considered best practice, and the interplay between personal, professional and interprofessional ethics will determine how any decision is derived at. The authors therefore determine that ethics should form a part of a conscious decision-making process where thought processes are transparent and can be utilised as part of debate in relation to culture, systems and practice; for example, when working in a context of early intervention, child protection, education, mental health and well-being.

While the Children (Scotland) Act 1995 (p 17) places a duty on **local authorities** to make provision for children 'in need', this guiding moral principle has appeared to be insufficient in influencing key professional behaviour to act specifically in support of children who are bereaved. The authors consider it important to discuss the utility of any legislative guidance when any such legislation, policy or guidance fails to act in the best interest of all members of society. The Education (Support for Learning) (Scotland) Act 2004 (amended in 2009), however, does recognise bereavement as a potential barrier to learning, and bereavement falls under the term 'additional support needs'. This Act places the local authority under a duty to make adequate and efficient provision for each child or young person with an additional support need. Further to this provision, the **Scottish Government** supports the guidance entitled *Getting It Right for Every Child* (**GIRFEC**) (Scottish Executive, 2007), in which all agencies are encouraged to practise the 'SHANARRI' principles of keeping children Safe, Healthy, Achieving, Nurtured, Active, Respected, Responsible and Included.

As part of a programme being piloted across a school cluster within one Scottish local authority, a working group consisting of professionals from **social work**, education, the voluntary sector and health met to discuss how bereavement support policy should be developed and implemented in schools. A suggestion from one member that a letter be sent out to all parents/carers in one school community requesting them to inform the school if their child had experienced significant bereavement and would like support was met with great anxiety and initial opposition. There were concerns stemming from an anticipated overwhelming response with the potential ethical dilemma in terms of resources and the capacity to respond. A question raised for the group was, 'is it better to know or not to know how many children are bereaved in the community?'. The group was forced to consider the consequences of answering either 'yes' or 'no'. The stronger influence in the discussion swayed eventually in favour of doing the right thing for children by answering 'yes' regardless of the possible enormity of the task. To answer 'no' would be to maintain the status quo where children largely have their bereavement needs unrecognised by the majority of the adult population. As it transpired, there was a 2% return of requests for support from a community of approximately 800 pupils. There were no referrals from children with a **Looked After** status or from any black or ethnic minority groups, highlighting that extra efforts would be needed in order to reach these extra vulnerable groups.

Miner and Petocz (2003, pp 21–2) propose a model for decision making that 'rather than supplying decisional rules ... would outline the tasks and choices in which the decision maker must exercise moral judgment'. The authors welcome this approach to a process of supporting professionals to consider and, it is to be hoped, reach consensus about what must be done to support grieving children in their mental health outcomes. However, unless such a tool is employed to advise the strategic development of policy and guidance concerning the rights of children to access information, then unresolved tensions and **disjuncture** may persist due to the range of personal and professional values that can be evoked in bereavement circumstances. The potential dilemma concerning the protection of children and young people by withholding or providing information could be dealt with by increasing awareness among the adult population that bereaved children, alongside other support measures, require age and stage appropriate information contained within trusting relationships to process grief.

While it is normal for children and young people in the initial stages of grief to express shock, numbness and a feeling of confusion when relaying their narrative about the death of someone important to them, it is concerning if this is still occurring years after the event (Worden, 2003; Dyregrov, 2008). From observations in practice, it is clear that large numbers of children and young people are not being given the opportunities to learn about grief and to express their experiences in a safe and structured way. The lack of a strategy and support for children and young people affected by bereavement makes it tempting to argue, from a rule utilitarianism perspective (McHugh, 2006), that professionals should act to produce good outcomes for children, as the consequences of inaction may be to maintain the adversities and risks previously mentioned. However, in a pluralistic society (Hugman, 2012, p 2) professionals have to work with people who comply with very personalised sets of rules across a range of cultures, and 'not everyone agrees what is the right thing to do'. What is a right or wrong action becomes very difficult to prescribe, and to attempt to do so would risk creating further adversity for children living with parents who might not subscribe to certain rules, thus placing them at odds with any professional consensus.

In Denmark, the OmSorg (dealing with bereavement) Project (Boge and Dige, 2005) aims to support children by helping adults to recognise their responsibilities and providing action plans for schools to support children and young people who are bereaved. A randomised survey among all Danish primary schools between 1997 and 2012 showed that the proportion of schools with a written action plan had grown from 4% to 96%. There has been similar development in kindergarten settings, where the increase between 2003 and 2012 was from 21% to 86%. One of the reasons behind this success was the publication of children's narratives about their experiences of indifference, rejection and confusion in circumstances of bereavement.

One OmSorg resource is the following poem by a child who experienced multiple bereavements (included here with his permission); he was 11 years old when his father died, 12 years old when his grandmother died and aged 13 years when his mother died. No one ever talked to him about his losses, but he was showered with material possessions.

Why Me?

Why me exactly?
Why me?
I don't get it.
Why not somebody else?
I just don't get why it had to be me that had to suffer.
That my mum and dad had to die.
It could've been somebody from another country who
   died of cancer.
All of a sudden things moved fast.
Cancer ate my mum and dad.
Deep down inside I think it's my fault.
Because the doctors did a lot for them.

Clearly, this child has a lot of questions that need answering. This could be achieved with appropriate psycho-education. However, it might take some time to support this child in terms of his negative perception that he was the cause of the deaths, for which there a number of possible reasons, one being his stage of cognitive development, which is that of magical thinking, whereby he believes that he is at the centre of the world and is the cause of events. If this is the case, he will need transitional support, over a period of time, during his sequential cognitive development and understanding of death. The authors wonder if this case could have been avoided if there had been an opportunity to discuss with him issues relating to loss, grief and cancer. In terms of the professional agencies that can be involved with children who become orphans (legal, health, social work and education), the authors suggest that there should be clear interprofessional guidance on the pathway of care in such circumstances, and a system of accountability for practitioners in relation to their respective **ethical codes** of conduct; for example, ensuring that there is a lead coordinator to organise bereavement support.

Another contribution to OmSorg publications was from a child who told that even though her terminally ill brother was treated at home, no one ever talked to her about what was happening. Not even while he was dying or during the two following years did anyone speak to her. Finally, she wrote a very lengthy and detailed letter to her class teacher entitled 'My Dead Brother'. The only feedback she received was 'good job but you have to work on your spelling'. A month later, then aged 14 years, she sent a letter to the Danish Cancer Society in which she said: 'Here where I live no one seems interested in talking with me about my dead brother. I thought perhaps this letter could be useful to you in your work.'

Stories such as these highlight the need for adults to overcome personal barriers such as their own unresolved grief, or discomfort at the thought of talking about death, which may prohibit helpful responses. A group of multi-agency staff in a Scottish city were asked how effective they considered their interventions to be when supporting bereaved children (Jindal-Snape and Sweeney, 2011). On average they rated their effectiveness in bereavement support interventions to be at 3.5 on a scale of 10, where 10 represented the most effective. This suggests a tension between personal issues and professional roles. It may be that professionals require support in order to manage their personal discomfort in ways that will allow them to organise and to deliver effective support. This would begin to remove the barriers for children accessing quality support.

In a Scottish region in 2005, an unpublished survey of **children's service** providers across staff in health, education, social work and the voluntary sector asked to where staff would refer a child if they discovered that the child was bereaved. Twenty-three different services were named, including:

- child adolescent mental health
- counsellor
- educational psychologist
- family centre
- general practitioner
- guidance teacher
- health visitor
- Macmillan nurse
- psychiatrist
- psychologist
- school health nurse
- social work
- support for learning
- various adult charities
- various children's charities
- various local authority young people's services, such as support for youth justice, non-school attendance, drugs and alcohol misuse.

The survey highlighted a haphazard system that lacked understanding and coordination among professionals in terms of bereavement support. The findings suggest that professionals refer on to other professionals, in the belief that other professionals are more appropriate, are better equipped or are the experts who are more able to provide bereavement support. This, in effect, cancels out any professional as a potential source of bereavement support. For example, school health nurses said they would refer to guidance; guidance staff said they would refer to school health, and so on. A professional in any of these roles may or may not feel able to provide support based upon their self-perceived levels of confidence, knowledge and skills on the subject of death. It would therefore make sense to the authors for training to be provided to deal with these issues.

One of the questions asked in the consultation entitled 'Dead Right N.O.W. (No Opinions Wasted)' (Sweeney, 2009) held with 313 children and young people across Scotland was 'Do adults get it right when supporting children and young people in their bereavement needs?' The response was mixed, with as many participants saying that they had a good experience as reporting a negative one. This suggested an inequality of available support and variability in the quality of support offered. Another extremely important message from this group of participants was that they wanted adults to consult with them further on bereavement matters as part of a school-based curriculum.

In one school, a mother – who broke down in front of the head teacher – explained that her child, currently aged 8 years, had experienced bereavement three years previously when the father had died. The mother accepted the head teacher's advice to make a referral to a bereavement support service. The bereavement support worker met with the mother, who said that she wanted her child to be supported but did not want the child to know the circumstances of the father's death (suicide). The support worker had to manage the tension of balancing the rights and needs of the mother and the child, and did so by engaging from the ethical position of acting in the child's best interests. The worker used skilful means to avoid collusion and help the mother to see that sharing information, although a painful thing to do, is crucial to healthy grieving. The mother was able to agree that her initial desire for collusion had been linked to her denial and her need to protect herself from facing the painful facts. She stated that, at the time, she had felt that her child was too young to know about such things and she had lied to her, saying that her father had died from a heart attack. She wanted to tell her child the truth some day, but the right time never seemed to arrive and now that she had lied she felt that she could not talk about it at all. The mother described how she had discovered her husband's body and could not erase the image from her mind. The mother was screened for post-traumatic stress and received treatment to alleviate the symptoms, thus helping her to become a more emotionally and cognitively available parent to her child. The mother acted on the advice that it is never too late to sit down with children and explain how events unfolded and to make the effort to restore and build trust.

The mother did not say it was 'ethically correct' to tell the child, but she did mention wanting to share the facts as being the best way forward. Unfortunately, overcome by anxiety, she was unable to do so. Having worked hard to contain the situation for three years contributed towards her 'breaking down'. She told the head teacher about her wish not to tell the child the truth and the head teacher agreed because it might have been too upsetting for the child and might have opened up old wounds. Both the mother and head teacher had an expectation that the bereavement support worker and the entire school staff would comply with the mother's request not to share with the child the cause of death. When the support worker learned that the head teacher believed that the parent had the right to withhold information from the child and had colluded with the parent, the support worker had to work with the head teacher to consider the matter of professional integrity, now that the mother had decided that she was, after all, going to tell the child the truth. It could be said that professionals should operate within an ethical framework that provides strategic cohesion across professions with regard to safe/good practice, not just for children but for professionals too. Extensive work on this has been carried out in the arena of child protection. Is there an ethical argument to incorporate the good practice of obtaining the child's views, for example, following bereavement? If this became standard practice then it could go a long way to balancing potential adversities and vulnerabilities in cases where information had not been provided or false information had been given to the child. A situation would then occur in which helpful conversations could take place, mapping out the best way forward for all parties.

The decision of the head teacher to collude with the parent may have been a well-intentioned one in a situation where there was no agreed bereavement support policy, but in fact it was experienced by some staff who disagreed with the strategy as uncomfortable, disempowering and stressful. However, the situation was retrievable, due to the head teacher's willingness to accept the situation as a learning opportunity and move forward with an intention to develop bereavement support guidance.

In schools, as in many families, the subject of death can be open or closed. There are numerous examples in practice of tension among staff groups when they have to deal with children who have not been given accurate information or sufficient explanation about a death and the resulting anxiety spills out into the classroom. Children naturally enquire from a range of sources about what happens when you die, where do you go, is there a god, do you believe in god and do you know how my daddy died. The authors believe that it is not ethical to isolate children and put them in a position where they are unable to share their information with adults, who are operating within a closed system.

It could be said that, when parents make decisions for or about children, along with a notion of responsibility there is also a perception of power and ownership. Parents may say, "They are my children and I will do as I like with them"; "You can't tell me how to bring up my child". These are quite defensive/aggressive statements and demonstrate that the parent is reacting to a perceived threat with a fight/flight response. The perceived threat may be a childcare professional suggesting, in the best interest of the child, that bereavement information should be shared. The professional advocating on behalf of the child may be acting on an ethical belief that children have a right to self-determination but can exercise it only when equipped with the facts.

A common element, which appears to be an inhibiting factor in people being able to discuss bereavement, is the degree of shame, blame or guilt attached to the narrative. Culturally, there may also be an element of not wanting to speak ill of the dead and so, for example, if a child asks why his/her mother died and the adult knows that it was as a result of excessive alcohol and drug misuse, the child may be told that the mother died from cancer, so as to prevent the child from thinking the worst of his/her parent. It is when the child persists in asking more specific questions, like "what kind of cancer?" that adults find themselves weaving more elaborate misinformation into the narrative. From practical experience we know that children are able to work out they are not being told the truth and in terms of modelling culture from adults to children, children may learn that this is a norm and it is the way to deal with children in bereavement circumstances. If this norm is not challenged, there is a potential risk to further generations of bereaved children being cared for by adults who were bereaved as children and who experienced this style of support.

Some parents may request support in the form of wanting their child to be 'fixed', but without having to provide any input themselves. This is always difficult for professionals, as their role is not to carry out parental responsibilities. Professionals can support parents in moving towards the fulfilment of parental responsibilities, but this requires a far more resource-intensive systemic intervention.

One primary school-aged boy presented as being depressed and continually brought the class round to speaking about death. It seemed that all the staff had tried everything to help the situation and the last hope was referral to the bereavement support worker. It became clear that everyone in the family was suffering from **post-traumatic stress** after witnessing the death of a family member. All of the family members except for the primary school-aged boy had a predominant **trauma symptom of avoidance**. The boy was the opposite, and he sought out opportunities to speak and to find out details of the death. The other family members experienced this boy as a source of threat and actively avoided meeting his needs. The parents hoped he could be 'fixed' as a means to resolving their own needs not to be re-exposed to **traumatic material**. The care and support offered to the parents by educational psychology, school staff and the bereavement support agency were unable to shift the parents from this position. The parents then perceived these professionals as a threat and requested that the child be placed in another school. The education department then had to deal with the problem of collusion by deciding whether or not to meet the request. The parents eventually decided to move away with the situation unresolved.

These narratives may provide explanations as to why some professionals consider that it is correct for parents to withhold information in stigmatising circumstances when:

- parents are defensive/aggressive
- parents/professionals view bereavement as solely a private/family matter
- parents have the power to control situations even when the law and guidance supports children's rights to access services with factual information
- professionals do not feel particularly empowered and are unable to make use of supporting legislation and guidance
- professionals have not had the opportunity to think through the consequences of holding such views.

Figure 13.1: The relationship between preparedness and outcomes

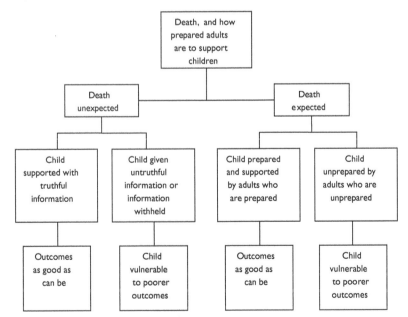

The authors suggest that it is a good idea to plan for the inevitability of death and how it affects large numbers of children and young people. According to Fauth et al (2009), around 1 in 29 children and young people currently of school age have experienced the death of a parent or sibling, and many more are affected by the death of someone else close to them. Only by being prepared will it be possible to model to children how to deal with grief and manage distressing information.

Consider Figure 13.1. The authors believe that if improved outcomes are desired for children and young people, then a cultural shift from a reactive to a proactive position is required.

Working groups need to be set up with responsibility for the coordination, development, implementation and evaluation of effective, measurable, equally accessible and integrated bereavement support throughout the education, health and welfare systems of local authority areas/society. The remit for this group would be to focus on partnerships, policy and guidance that support staff to support children and young people who are bereaved. Outcome tools could be used to evaluate the short-, medium- and long-term benefits for all concerned, in the context of early intervention.

Within their own professional associations, practitioners are required to be responsible for their continuing professional development (for example, the British Association of Social Workers Code of Ethics; Policy, Ethics and Human Rights Committee, 2012). By developing and maintaining the attitudes, knowledge, understanding and skills to provide quality services, professionals need to educate themselves in how to inform people, particularly children and young people, about healthy grieving. Offending behaviour, alcohol and drug misuse, running away, self-harming, violence and aggression and engagement in under-age sex are often linked to a history of unresolved trauma and loss (Mental Health Foundation, 2012). The authors suggest that children and young people need to be equipped with information that will enable them to relate their narrative of loss within a context of cause and effect, where therapeutic intervention as part of a support plan can lead to increased safety and well-being.

Grief is not an event but a process that happens over time and it may affect a child's physical, social, educational, emotional, spiritual and psychological development (Black, 1998; McCarthy and Jessop, 2005). All professionals in Scotland are encouraged to use 'The Child's World Triangle' framework within GIRFEC, which links the triad of developmental needs, environment and adult responsibilities in an interprofessional partnership. For example, teachers are not just educators; they have to consider pupils' ability to learn in adverse mental health circumstances such as bereavement, but they need the support of other professionals in this task (Cole et al, 2009).

Children require new information as their awareness develops that death is irreversible. Renewed inputs from adults are needed to update the narrative of bereavement so that it is congruent with the child's developing cognitive abilities. Bereavement support plans for children not only have to be updated through each developmental stage but also have to follow the child through the transitions from nursery to primary, secondary and higher educational settings. Forming a narrative of events is crucial in coming to terms with change, and settling down and restoring normal functioning (Lovett, 1999). From birth, children develop resilience or the ability to self-soothe, based upon the quality of their attachments or relationships with caregivers (Howe, 1995). They learn to trust and to anticipate whether their needs will be met or not. Good parenting and professional practice are about being able to anticipate and meet the needs of children, thus supporting them to become independent and resourceful contributors to society.

In grief we are faced with the psychological task of accepting the new reality that the person significant to us has died. If it is our best hope to be as happy as we can be, then we have to adjust accordingly to the new reality. However, we can only adjust in relation to what is known to us at any given point in time. If a 'reality' is constructed on the basis of information that is not true, then it could be argued that a person is not living in the same reality as others who have access to the truth. How ethical is this? In the authors' view, it may be useful for interprofessional training to be available to encourage debate and reflection on such issues.

Mindful and reflective practitioners may learn from experience that it is their collective responsibility to protect children with the truth rather than with a lie or false information. Children naturally want to learn how the world works, and it is the adults' responsibility to help them to understand for healthy survival. Children and young people also need to know what grief is and that it is a normal response to loss. It is never too late to share information that has been withheld and to restore trust through honesty and bravery. Examples from practice show that children and young people appreciate this approach and respect such efforts. They also experience relief in finally having a solid base from which to work.

References

Black, D. (1998) 'Coping with loss: bereavement in childhood', *British Medical Journal*, vol 316, pp 931–33.

Boge, P. and Dige, J. (2005) *OmSorg: Dealing with bereavement: inspiration and resources for teachers and others who want to help grieving children*, Copenhagen: Danish Cancer Society.

Children (Scotland) Act (1995), London: HMSO.

Cole, S.F., Greenwald O'Brien, J., Geron Gedd, M., Ristuccia, J., Luray Wallace, D., and Gregory, M. (2009) *Helping traumatized children learn: Supportive school environments for children traumatized by family violence: a report and policy agenda* (6th edn), Massachusetts Advocates for Children: Harvard Law School.

Deci, E.L. and Ryan, R.M. (2002) *Handbook of self determination research*, Rochester: University of Rochester Press.

Dyregrov, A. (2008) *Grief in children* (2nd edn), London: Jessica Kingsley.

Education (Support for Learning) (Scotland) Act (2004), London: HMSO.

Fauth, B., Thompson, M. and Penny, A. (2009) *Associations between childhood bereavement and children's background, experiences and outcomes. Secondary analysis of the 2004 Mental Health of Children and Young People in Great Britain data*, London: NCB.

Howe, D. (1995) *Attachment theory for social work practice*, London: Macmillan Press Ltd.

Hugman, R. (2012) *Culture, values and ethics in social work: Embracing diversity*, New York: Routledge.

Jindal-Snape, D. and Sweeney, S. (2011) 'S.T.A.G.E.S. (Support: trauma and grief – enabling schools) bereavement support project – Pilot evaluation', Dundee: Barnardo's Scotland Rollercoaster Service.

Lovett, J. (1999) *Small wonders: Healing childhood trauma with EMDR*, New York: The Free Press.

McCarthy, J.R. and Jessop, J. (2005) *The impact of bereavement and loss on young people*, Joseph Rowntree Foundation, London: National Children's Bureau.

McHugh, P.J. (2006) 'Act and rule utilitarianism', *http://www.tere.org/assets/downloads/secondary/pdf_downloads/ALevel/RuleUtilNotes.pdf*

Mental Health Foundation (2012) *Mental health, children and young people and the year*, http://www.mentalhealth.org.uk/help-information/mental-health-a-z/C/children-young-people/

Miner, M. and Petocz, A. (2003) 'Moral theory in ethical decision making: problems, clarifications and recommendations from a psychological perspective', *Journal of Business Ethics*, vol 42, pp 11–25.

Policy, Ethics and Human Rights Committee (2012) '*The code of ethics for social work: Statement of principles*. British Association of Social Workers', in S. Banks (ed) *Ethics and values in social work* (4th edn), Basingstoke: Palgrave Macmillan, p 16.

Scottish Executive (2007) *Getting it right for every child, guidance on the child's or young person's plan*, Edinburgh: Scottish Executive.

Sweeney, S. (2009) 'Dead right N.O.W. (No Opinions Wasted): a national consultation report on the views of young people on trauma, bereavement and loss', Dundee: Barnardo's Scotland Rollercoaster Service.

Worden, J.W. (2003) *Grief counselling and grief therapy* (3rd edn) East Sussex: Brunner-Routledge.

Professional and interprofessional ethics in multicultural and multinational contexts

Framing the professional and interprofessional ethical landscape in education: Finnish and English perspectives on teachers' moral selves

Andrea Raiker and Matti Rautiainen

Introduction

The focus of this chapter is the interrelationship of personal and professional ethics in education, and the effect of differing political contexts on the development of the 'moral self' of teachers. In line with the aims of Part Five (see Figure 1.1), this is done in the context of two countries as case studies, namely Finland and England. The authors define 'ethics' as being the values that direct decision making and behaviour. The chapter considers the degree to which the values governing ethical decision making and behaviour in education are 'out there', a reality to be discovered through reasoning and attention to experts in the field, to be viewed in terms of skills learned and objectively applied. The opposing position, that ethical values in education are personal constructs central to all thought and action, is also explored.

The chapter considers these positions through the application of Bourdieu's (1990) concepts of 'habitus' and 'field' to Rest's (1986) four dimensions of moral development – moral sensitivity, moral judgement and moral motivation leading to moral character – to suggest a framework for considering teacher identity as moral self. The discussion is illustrated with reflections on the authors' lived experiences in England and Finland (see also Chapter Five).

According to Max Horkheimer, modern societies are concentrating on content at the expense of form. In his *Eclipse of Reason* the analysis is clear and sharp:

> It seems that even as technical knowledge expands the horizon of man's thought and activity, his autonomy as an individual, his ability to resist the growing apparatus of mass manipulation, his power of imagination, his independent judgement appear to reduce. (Horkheimer, 2004, p v)

Horkeimer's perspective reflects that of the philosopher and political theorist Hannah Arendt, who, writing over 50 years earlier, describes the state of humanity as degradation: people are not interested in common things but act principally for their own self-interest. According to Arendt (1958), consumption had conquered the public sphere, without being public, because the nature of consumption was private and did not require justification. It was easy to lose ethical perspective because humans lived in a world where there was no need to talk. 'Men in the plural, that is, men in so far as they live and move and act in this world, can experience meaningfulness only because they can talk with and make sense to each other and to themselves' (Arendt, 1958, p 4). In a technologised world, meaninglessness in existence through not talking is an even greater threat to ethical perspective and understanding of form.

The authors' initial position is that a teacher's mission is to support children's growth through education as individuals and as members of society. Because education in school is directed by outcomes, and these outcomes have a political component, education addresses such questions as the importance of form relative to content, and the relationship and interrelationship between individual interest and the interests of community. In other words, the authors are considering the basic questions of ethics: what is a good life, what values result in a good life and therefore how people should act.

The conceptual framework

The authors have suggested that a framework for considering the teacher as moral self could be created by considering Bourdieu's (1990) concepts of 'habitus' and 'field' in terms of Rest's (1986) four dimensions of moral development – moral sensitivity, moral judgement and moral motivation leading to moral character. Reynolds (2006) argues that multi-step conceptions of morality begin with individual moral awareness or the identification by an individual of a moral issue. **Morals** can be defined as internalisations of the predominant ethical system of socially accepted principles of right and wrong; they have an individual and a social component. This division resonates with Bourdieu's conceptions of 'habitus' and 'field'. 'Habitus' is an internal structure, the totality and embodiment of an individual's thoughts and experience organised into perceptions of correctness of practices. 'Field' is an external structure, the particular social reality in which 'habitus' finds itself at any point in time. So Rest's categorisation has to be seen in the context of an individual coming to terms with social conceptions of right and wrong. He recognises that this involves interpretation when the individual, or 'habitus', becomes aware that s/he is in a situation that requires a response requiring a moral decision, or that a theoretical problem has a moral dimension. Such recognition is indicative of moral sensitivity, the first of Rest's four categories. However, which comes first – morals as an internal state of knowing, as part of 'habitus', or morals resulting from an external compulsion connected with 'field' to conform to social standards of behaviour? Vygotsky's (1978) general genetic law of cultural development states the primacy of the social in that development: 'every function in the child's cultural development appears twice: first on the social level, and later, on the habitus level' (p 57). Therefore moral values in the 'field' generate interpretations of morality in the 'habitus', and this occurs through reasoning and results in moral judgements – Rest's second category. When considering teacher education, the authors would suggest that a role for teacher educators in the 'field' of the university is to challenge students to externalise their moral values and examine them so as to determine their epistemological implications through reasoning – in other words, to achieve moral consciousness. According to Butterfield et al (2000), an individual's reflection on the outcomes of her/his actions on the well-being and prospects of her/himself or others can be a strong motivator for changes in behaviour – Rest's third category. This in turn develops sensitivity towards the moral dilemmas present in everyday life, greater awareness of the implications of moral choices and understanding of the need for commitment to taking personal responsibility for moral outcomes. In teacher education, the authors argue, the development of moral character, or consciousness, is part of the process of students developing their professional selves, in other words, their identities as teachers. However, as habitus is everything an individual is at a given point in time and place, teacher professionalism, including the moral character identified by Rest, is part of habitus. A teacher's moral self will always be present in the field of the classroom. It will always be present elsewhere because of the 'nesting' of fields within fields; the field of the classroom is nested within the field of the school, which is nested within that of the community, and within that of society. However, Finland and England are societies arising from differing social, political, historical and economic backgrounds. This suggests that there could be differences in their respective education systems in how student teachers are taught about ethics and morality, and how these perspectives are manifested as 'habitus' in the 'field' of the classroom.

Ethical dimensions in teacher education in Finland

Finnish teachers have broad pedagogic autonomy in their work, as compared to international colleagues. This has arisen from socio-democratic principles based on equality, cooperation and political freedom. There is a long-established tradition of a 'positive circle of recognition' in recruiting students to the profession (Heikkinen and Huttunen, 2004). Finnish teachers are highly regarded and are trusted because their pupils achieve well in international tests such as the **Programme for International Student Assessment** (PISA) (OECD, 2012). This heightens the status of teaching, resulting in more young people wanting to become teachers. Universities are able to select the best trainees in terms of academic achievement and motivation to study. They achieve good results, and so the cycle continues. However, teaching in Finland is also a very independent profession. The Finnish school culture is characterised by limited cooperation between teachers. Also, a teacher's work is focused on students in the classroom. Involvement in extra-curricular activities is low (Nikkola et al, 2008).

This situation raises tensions because changes in society have been so significant since the late 1980s that teachers are unable to cope with working on their own (Innola et al, 2005). Although teachers' pedagogic autonomy has a long tradition, changes in the 1990s strengthened what Finnish educators call '**teacherhood**'. Teachers' duties became more demanding than in earlier decades. Particularly, the changes that took place in the 1980s and 1990s have entailed a change in pedagogical approaches, putting greater focus on the ethical dimension in teacher education. Through teaching and interactions with educators, both inside the university and in schools, it became evident to the Finnish author of this chapter that the dynamism of work-related changes was putting pressure on the 'traditional' professional skills of the teacher. Established traditions were making way for a constructivist orientation that presupposed constant assessment and renewal of one's work (for example, Lauriala, 2000). The national core curriculum lost its prescriptive element and became guidelines for school-based curricula. Also, the national school inspection system and inspection of school textbooks were abolished. At the same time there was extensive discussion of basic concepts associated with learning and the status of the school. The idea of collaboration in its various forms was spreading in Finland, concurrently with the shift to school-based curricula that resulted from the curricular reform (for example, Koppinen and Pollari, 1993; Sahlberg and Leppilampi, 1994). The resultant rise of responsibility and autonomy required broader reflections on professional ethics and teachers' responsibility for the morality of their practices.

Reflection on the theory–practice relationships outlined above raises some interesting questions about professional ethics in Finland. A school's ethical basis is defined in the core curriculum for basic education, but how can it be assured in a system where professional autonomy is strong, that teachers act according to these principles, and also according to the ethical principles defined by the professional community itself? In Finland all teachers are members of the same trade union (OAJ – Trade Union of Education in Finland), and the OAJ has defined the ethical principles of the teaching profession. These principles are based on the United Nations Universal Declaration of Human Rights. The OAJ's Code of Ethics (OAJ, 2012) is the principles according to which the teacher should act in his/her work. The organisation emphasizes the strong autonomy of Finnish teachers: ethics is not based on coercion or external control, but on internalisation of moral complexity. The basic values underlying these principles are human dignity, truth, justice, responsibility and freedom (OAJ, 2012).

Teacher education in Finland is defined by university schools and departments of education over a five-year Masters in Education course. This was the experience of the chapter's Finnish author, as this is the only way to become a teacher in Finland. Because in-service teacher training is fragmentary and unplanned in Finland, initial teacher education has an ethical responsibility for the moral character of students. Internalisation of moral complexity must occur in teacher education, because after a Master's degree the student is a fully authorised teacher.

University schools and departments of education collaborate to establish and maintain standards for entry into the teaching profession. This includes close relationship between university educators, of which the Finnish author is one, and teacher training school supervisors in the university-based schools (very few training schools have a non-university location). Academically and in practice, student teacher autonomy is encouraged. As teachers, students will be expected to act according to laws or rules that they have made for themselves. It is the role of teacher education 'to educate pedagogically thinking teachers who are able to become aware of and to evaluate the grounds and ethical premises of their teaching' (Jyrhämä and Syrjäläinen, 2009, p 3). So, in Finland there are opportunities to introduce comparable curricula to develop personal ethics throughout the country. Are these opportunities taken?

The authors analysed all class-teacher training and subject-teacher training curricula in Finnish universities in terms of the degree to which teacher education courses included professional ethics through examining the course unit descriptions, and the role professional ethics has in the curriculum through a general overview of curricula. Only those courses where an ethical point of view was dominant were selected.

As Tables 14.1 and 14.2 demonstrate, the number of ethics-oriented courses is small. This is because there is an implicit belief, arising from cultural attitudes and expectations, that an ethical dimension will naturally underpin all studies. It is an inseparable element of teachers' work. For example, the course information for class-teacher education at the University of Jyväskylä states: 'Teacher education's aim is to support students' professional development to become autonomous, ethically responsible and critical reformative experts' (JYU, 2012). The only course focused on ethics in Jyväskylä is 'Teacher's ethics and educational philosophy'. The aims of this course are

> To become aware of ethical aspects of teaching and differentiate one's own education and teaching philosophy. To evaluate the student's qualities as a teacher on the basis of his/her teaching practice experience. Aim is that students understand the limits and responsibilities of professionalism. The course also deals with the feelings aroused in students by the experience of entering working life and becoming a responsible adult. (JYU, 2012)

From experiences as an academic and teacher, the Finnish author can confirm that students are encouraged to identify, articulate and address ethical issues during teaching practice (see also Chapter Nineteen for similar discussion in the healthcare practice context). In the final teaching practice (fifth year) students are expected to act responsibly and autonomously in dealing with questions of ethics. One of four main objectives of the final teaching practice is for students to demonstrate that they have the ability to work according to teachers' professional ethical principles.

Table 14.1: Courses focused on professional ethics in class-teacher education

University	Courses	Credit	Level (B = Bachelor; M = Master)
University of Helsinki			
University of Jyväskylä	1	3	M
University of Turku (Turku)	1	3	M
University of Turku (Rauma)			
University of Tampere			
University of Oulu (Oulu)	1	4	B
University of Oulu (Kajaani)	2	5	B (3 European Credit Transfer and Accumulation System credits: ECTS); M (2 ECTS)
University of Eastern Finland (Joensuu)	1	3	M
University of Eastern Finland (Savonlinna)	1	3	M
University of Lapland			

Table 14.2: Courses focused on professional ethics in subject-teacher education

University	Course	Units
University of Helsinki		
University of Jyväskylä	1	4
University of Turku		
University of Tampere		
University of Oulu	1	4
University of Eastern Finland	1	3

In conclusion, the approach to student class-teachers in professional ethics at the University of Jyväskylä can be modelled in three parts. First, ethical growth is seen as an integral part of the entire training across all courses. Second, students' university experience involves developing a theoretical perspective through which to analyse and conceptualise ethical thinking focused on theoretical perspectives of ethics, a process involving the development of moral sensitivity and judgement. Third, moral motivation is encouraged through addressing ethical issues in authentic, everyday teaching situations as part of teaching practice. The end result is the moral character of 'habitus', a personal interpretation and demonstration of ethical competencies based on the values of Finnish society.

Ethical dimensions of teacher education in England

From the perspective of Jean-Paul Sartre's (2010) ethical thinking, English teachers are agents who have far less political and moral freedom than do their Finnish colleagues. For Sartre, morals and human responsibilities are revealed through actions in the world; they are not simply written principles. Politics and morals are inseparable. So the programmes of study followed by student teachers in England, which have been devised and published by the Secretary of State for Education to meet criteria known as the *Teachers' Standards* (TS) (Department for Education (DfE), 2012), will become moral actions when practised by teachers. The TS, which replaced the standards for Qualified Teacher Status (QTS) and the core professional standards previously published by the Teacher Development Agency (TDA), apply to nearly all teachers, regardless of their career stage, including students and newly qualified teachers as well as experienced teachers and those charged with misconduct.

The preamble to the TS states:

> Teachers make the education of their pupils their first concern, and are accountable for achieving the highest possible standards in work and conduct. Teachers act with honesty and integrity; have strong subject knowledge, keep their knowledge and skills up-to-date and are self-critical; forge positive professional relationships; and work with parents in the best interests of their pupils. (DfE, 2012, p 6)

Finnish educators would agree with the spirit of the TS's preamble, but there is one crucial word that demonstrates a fundamental difference in the perspective on teacher education: 'accountable'. The Finns would substitute the word 'responsible'. They do not need to be told the nature of their role by a government minister. The sentiments and values expressed in the TS's preamble are embedded in teacher education programmes and the standards of behaviour expected by families and the wider Finnish community, as discussed earlier. Illingworth (2004) calls this the embedded approach to ethics in which:

students study ethics indirectly, by considering some broader conception of professional identity, which has a significant ethical dimension. The theoretical approach begins with a study of moral theory, and considers real-life situations in terms of the application of that theory. Although teachers may employ methods drawn from more than one category, the context in which students first encounter ethics influences their perception of the subject and its relationship to professional values and behaviour. (p 7)

In England and Wales, a pragmatic approach is taken to ethics. According to Illingworth (2004), this involves the establishment of a framework of rules and procedures. For education in England and Wales, such a framework has been established and prescribed by the Secretary of State for Education to raise or maintain professional standards. In the 'Personal and Professional Conduct' part of the TS (DfE, 2012, p 10), ethics is defined as including the maintenance of dignity and mutual respect between teachers and pupils, 'at all times observing proper boundaries appropriate to a teacher's professional position', and safeguarding pupils' well-being 'in accordance with statutory provisions'.

As a teacher with experience in both school and university sectors, the chapter's English author strongly suggests that the boundaries of the ethics of teacherhood are determined by government. What is more, the ethics of 'habitus' are defined in deficit terms, suggesting that they are not naturally part of student teachers' culturally generated 'habitus'; in other words, students are not intrinsically morally sensitive. For example, the TS states that teachers will demonstrate high standards by 'ensuring that personal beliefs are *not* [italics added] expressed in ways that exploit pupils' vulnerability or might exhort them to lead the law', and that teachers will demonstrate high standards of ethics 'by *not* [italics added] undermining fundamental British values, including democracy, the rule of law, individual liberty and mutual respect, and tolerance of those with different faiths and beliefs' (DfE, 2012).

Student teachers will have to demonstrate at the end of their courses that they have met all the standards expressed in the TS, and providers of initial teacher education are accountable to government to provide evidence through documentation and inspection that this has been done. These standards came into force in September 2012, and at the time of writing an evaluation of their impact on student teachers' moral sensitivity cannot be given in this chapter. However, it is clear that government, acting through the Secretary of State for Education and the Teaching Agency, has control of teacher professionalism and the ethical position on which it is based. The reasons for this are historical and political, and are rooted in the period of experimental education known as 'progressive education' practised in the 1960s. In both Finland and the UK, selective schools were replaced with **comprehensive schools** (though **public schools** and some **grammar schools** in the UK avoided this replacement). However, whereas in Finland collaboration at all levels and by all **stakeholders** ensured the development of a cohesive education system with a shared understanding of required standards and their method of application, there was no such interconnected approach in the UK. As a result, 'progressive education' had powerful detractors. For example, Labour Prime Minister James Callaghan's 1976 Ruskin College speech launched his 'Big Debate' on education and began the end of teacher and teacher-educator autonomy. Public respect for teaching as a profession decreased. In 1983, the Conservative government's White Paper *The Content of Initial Training* signalled the end of university control of teacher education. As a school teacher practising during these years, the English author remembers vividly the struggle to master lengthy and detailed, highly prescriptive volumes on each subject resulting from the English Education Act of 1988. When the 1994 Education Act established the Teacher Training Agency in England to control teacher-training supply, funding and content, and teacher and school education, educators recognised these activities as manifestations of government ideology. That ideology is now commonly known as neoliberalism, defined by competition, compliance and political control.

This being the case, reflections on theory and practice suggest difficulties in giving ethics and moral philosophy a high profile in English teacher education. In comparison with Finland, where all teachers attain Masters' qualifications to teach, English students can engage in teacher education in a diversity of courses. Additionally, postgraduate certificate of education (PGCE) courses are only a year long and are heavily orientated to teaching practice. There is little time to externalise, reflect upon and consider the implications of moral positions in line with the progression given by Rest's stages. Another factor impeding reflection on moral issues by English student teachers is the movement of initial teacher education out of universities and into schools so that students can be more directly involved in the 'craft' of teaching as part of certification. However, the authors maintain that a way must be found to engage student teachers in England in the ethics and values of their profession. The authors suggest that a way forward may be in moving away from a focus on accountability and towards responsibility, as in Finland. Research by Patall, Cooper and Wynn (2010) into the effect of choice on intrinsic motivation, endeavour, engagement with task and perceived confidence has shown that responsibility in making decisions has positive results in all four areas. In addition, responsibility as manifested in autonomy and relatedness improves motivation and performance outcomes, according to self-determination theory (Ryan and Deci, 2000). In other words, responsibility enhances quality. If student teachers and teachers are given the responsibility of externalising their values through considering the praxis of their professional identities, it is argued, they are much more likely to find relevance and meaning in the ethical dimensions of their roles, and thus to embed them within their practices and their lives.

A suggested framework for developing ethics in education

It would be naïve to suggest that the approach to developing moral consciousness in teacher education in Finland could be transferred to England. Political contexts and government requirements must be acknowledged, and integrated with understanding of the impact that autonomy and responsibility can have on engagement and motivation. We suggest that an answer might lie in a relational constructive approach being adopted to raise the profile of ethics in the teacher-education curriculum. Constructions of moral self and identity cannot be detached from one another (Lapsley and Narvaez, 2004): they are constructed by 'habitus' and then restructured through its relations in continuous evolution. Also, Wenger argues that 'There is a profound connection between identity and practice' (Wenger, 1998, p 149). So teachers' moral selves are embedded within their identity. The values prescribed by government connect through the practice of the workplace, the school. Therefore, it is important for teacher employability that the identities of employer and teacher relate, that there is shared understanding of what is required so that the teacher can enter workplace practice determined by descriptors of ethics and behaviour prescribed by the TS. It can be argued that such relational constructivism is a form of social constructivism that has its roots in Vygotskian thought (Vygotsky, 1986) and Wenger's community of practice theory (1998), but there is close alignment with Bourdieu's conception of structuring structure (1990). In terms of teacher identity, this means that 'habitus' is involved in structuring the 'field' of teaching through its relations with it.

The model in Figure 14.1 has been developed from Holmes (2006, p 10) to illustrate possible relationships between conceptions of teacher identity.

Figure 14.1: Dimensions of teacher identity

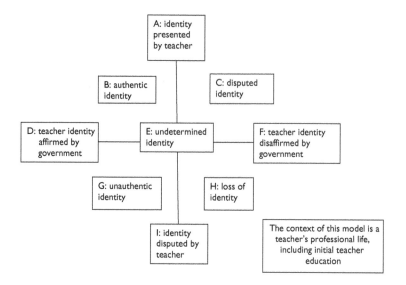

Source: Adapted from Holmes, 2006

When discussing his model, Holmes argues that people do not have identity as such, but a self-identity that is perceived by others as a particular sort of person. This is recognised in Figure 14.1, being in line with Sartre's thinking and illustrated by his 'man at the keyhole' metaphor (Sartre, 2010, p 261). The man at the keyhole has his identity, but when he is surprised by, say, his wife and becomes embarrassed he takes on the identity of a voyeur; if his sister comes along and is intrigued and wants to join in, he becomes an instigator of fun. However, according to Heideggerian thought (Heidegger, 1996), identity is not the product of 'others'; it is created by 'being-in-the-world' (*dasein*). The authenticity of an individual's identity becomes increasingly unauthentic if s/he takes on the identity given or desired by others. As identity is inseparable from moral self, and morals are internalisations of socially accepted principles of right and wrong, then Illingworth's embedded approach, in which students study ethics indirectly as an integral aspect of professional identity, is to be supported. This chapter proposes that teachers, both pre-service and experienced, should be encouraged to develop their moral selves in having explicit, critically evaluated perspectives on what is right or wrong as an essential part of teacher identity (Figure 14.1, Box A). This includes being aware that relations with government value systems through the TS will necessitate presentation and affirmation of particular identities and values (Box D). This is not promoting unauthenticity (Box G), but foregrounding particular characteristics of an individual's moral self that are valued by both the teacher and the government in the form of requirements of the TS (Box B). In this, the authors move away from Heidegger (1996). While recognising the importance of *dasein*, the authors suggest that a more persuasive framework is provided by the suggested figure. The authors suggest that it is the role of teacher educators to ensure that, in the process of acquiring identity, student teachers do not fall into the area of disputed, and loss of, identity denoted by Boxes C and H, with resulting loss of confidence, motivation and self-belief.

Conclusion

Sartre's famous phrase 'condemned to be free' (2010, pp 461–2) means that people have to create morals through their activities, and through activities they create what it is to be human. Thus the habitus of the teacher creates reality, including the values and morals of education, through personal choices that are at the same time personal and concerning all people. We have argued that in both Finland and England ethics in education has individual and social components. In Finland, the interpreter and instigator of moral values in practice is the individual, 'habitus'; in England, it is the socio-political 'field' in the form of government. So, in England the values governing ethical decision making and behaviour in education are 'out there', a reality to be discovered through reasoning and attention to experts in the field, to be viewed in terms of skills learned and objectively applied. The implications of such a moral rational approach are that professional ethics in education should have a place in curricula as a discrete subject to be taught, the understanding of which can be applied when desired, but put aside if tensions occur with personal ethics. We suggest that the framework given in Figure 14.1 could be used as a starting point to identify key aspects of an ethics curriculum. The opposing position considered is that ethical values in education are personal constructs, central to all thought and action. This approach suggests that personal and professional ethics are indivisible, and professional ethics in education are simply a particular feature in a personally perceived ethical landscape. Therefore in Finland, tutors could attempt to facilitate students' greater understanding of professional ethics through structured and supported personal development involving activities that engage their personal and social as well as academic and classroom-based ethical experiences. In comparing **ethical practices**, both authors have discovered insights that will enhance the moral perspectives of not only their course curricula but also their moral selves.

References

Arendt, H. (1958) *The human condition*, Chicago: University of Chicago Press.

Bourdieu, P. (1990) *The logic of practice*, trans R. Nice, Oxford: Polity Press.

Butterfield, K.D., Trevino, L.K. and Weaver, G.R. (2000) 'Moral awareness in business organizations: influences of issue-related and social context factors', *Human Relations*, vol 53, pp 981–1018.

DfE (Department for Education) (2012) Teachers' standards, www.gov.uk/government/uploads/system/uploads/attachment_data/file/208682/Teachers__Standards_2013.pdf

Heidegger, M. (1996) *Being and time*, trans J. Stambaugh, Albany: State University of New York Press.

Heikkinen, H. and Huttunen, R. (2004) 'Teaching and the dialectic of recognition', *Pedagogy, Culture and Society*, vol 12, no 2, pp 163–73.

Holmes, L. (2006) 'Reconsidering graduate employability: Beyond possessive-individualism', paper presented at *Seventh International Conference on HRD Research and Practice, 22–24 May 2006, University of Tilburg*, The Netherlands.

Horkheimer, M. (2004) *Eclipse of reason*, London: Continuum.

Illingworth, S. (2004) *Approaches to ethics in higher education: Learning and teaching in ethics across the curriculum*, Leeds: University of Leeds.

Innola, M., Kyrö, A., Mikkola, A. and Väyrynen, P. (2005) 'Opettajatarpeet nyt ja Tulevaisuudessa' [The present and future requirements in the teaching profession], in M. Kumpulainen and S. Saari (eds) *Opettajat Suomessa*, Helsinki: National Board of Education.

Jyrhämä, R. and Syrjäläinen, E. (2009) '"Good pal, wise dad, nagging wife" – and other views of teaching practice supervisors', in papers from the *ISATT 2009 Conference, Navigating in educational contexts: Identities and cultures in dialogue, Rovaniemi*, Finland.

JYU (University of Jyväskylä) (2012), www.jyu.fi/edu/laitokset/okl/opiskelu/luokanopettajakoulutus/luoko_ops_2010_13

Koppinen, M.-L. and Pollari, J. (1993) *Yhteistoiminnallinen oppiminen. Tie tuloksiin* [Collaborative learning. The road to results], Helsinki: WSOY.

Lapsley, D.K. and Narvaez, D. (2004) 'A social-cognitive approach to the moral personality', in D.K. Lapsley and D. Narvaez (eds) *Moral development, self and identity*, Mahwah NJ: Erlbaum.

Lauriala, A. (2000) 'Opettajan ammatillinen uudistuminen: sosiokulttuurinen näkökulma opettajan oppimiseen' [Teacher's professional renewal: a sociocultural perspective on a teacher's learning], in K. Harra (ed) *Opettajan professiosta. Okka vuosikirja 1 (2000).* [On the profession of teacher. Okka Yearbook 1], pp 88–97.

Nikkola, T., Räihä, P., Moilanen, P., Rautiainen, M. and Saukkonen, S. (2008). 'Towards a deeper understanding of learning in teacher education', in C. Nygaard and C. Holtham (eds) *Understanding learning-centred higher education,* Copenhagen: Copenhagen Business School Press.

OAJ (Trade Union of Education in Finland) (2012), www.oaj.fi/portal/page?_pageid=515,447767&_dad=portal&_schema=PORTAL.

OECD (Organisation for Economic Co-operation and Development) (2012) *OECD Programme for International Student Assessment (PISA),* www.oecd.org/pisa/.

Patall, E.A., Cooper, H. and Wynn, S.R. (2010) 'The effectiveness and relative importance of choice in the classroom', *Journal of Educational Psychology,* vol 102, no 4, pp 896–915.

Rest, J.R. (1986) 'An overview of the psychology of morality', in J. Rest (ed) *Moral development: Advances in research and theory,* New York: Praeger, pp 1–27.

Reynolds, S.J. (2006) 'Moral awareness and ethical predispositions: investigating the role of individual differences in the recognition of moral issues', *Journal of Applied Psychology,* vol 91, no 1, pp 233–43.

Ryan, R.M. and Deci, E.L. (2000) 'Intrinsic and extrinsic motivations: classic definitions and new directions'. *Contemporary Education Psychology,* vol 25, pp 54–67.

Sahlberg, P. and Leppilampi, A. (1994) 'Yksinään vai yhteisvoimin? Yhdessäoppimisen mahdollisuuksia etsimässä' [Alone or together? In search of opportunities for learning together], Helsingin: yliopisto Vantaan täydennyskoulutuslaitos.

Sartre, J.-P. (2010) *Being and nothingness,* London: Routledge.

Trade Union of Education in Finland (OAJ: 2010) *A teacher's professional ethics and ethical principles,* http://www.oaj.fi/pls/portal/docs/PAGE/OAJ_INTERNET/01FI/05TIEDOTTEET/03JULKAISUT/ENG_ETIIKKA_SIVUITTAIN.PDF.

Vygotsky, L.S. (1978) *Mind in society: Development of higher psychological processes,* Harvard, MA: Harvard University Press.

Vygotsky, L.S. (1986) *Thought and language,* trans A. Kazulin, Cambridge, MA: Massachusetts Institute of Technology.

Wenger, E. (1998) *Communities of practice: Learning, meaning and identity,* Cambridge: Cambridge University Press.

FIFTEEN

Professional and interprofessional cross-cultural ethics in trauma recovery programme implementation by UK professionals in the Middle East

Ian Barron and Ghassan Abdullah

Background

This chapter, a part of Part Five (see Figure 1.1), explores the dynamics of professional and **interprofessional** ethics when working across countries with significant cultural differences. It uses the case study of a trauma recovery programme delivered by UK professionals in Palestine to illustrate the potential tensions and dilemmas. The chapter then takes an ethical decision making (EDM) approach to suggest ways of resolving any issues inherent in such work.

The occupied Palestinian territories (oPt) are a dangerous place for children and adolescents. A recent survey found that children in Nablus experience on average at least 13 different types of war event (Barron et al, 2013). These events include witnessing the death, injury, detention and torture and/or abuse of someone close to them, be it family member or friend, or experiencing similar events themselves. Similar to other studies, higher levels of domestic violence were found, as compared to non-war contexts (Al-Krenawi et al, 2009). Srour (2005) observes that children in Palestine live in a multi-traumatic environment that includes not only the events of violent military occupation but also the impact of trauma on the adults who care for them. In short, trauma is fracturing the protective shield of childhood in this part of the world (Punamäki et al, 2001).

The consequences for children and adolescents are many, complex and enduring. Along with a high rate of **post-traumatic stress disorder** (PTSD) – as high as 65% – high numbers of children experience depression and **traumatic grief**. Children display difficulties in school, including motivation and concentration problems and relational difficulties with parents, peers and teachers. Zakrison et al (2004) conclude that children under occupation in Palestine display complex symptoms more akin to **developmental trauma** than PTSD.

In addition to war events, children's lives are negatively impacted by the deteriorating economic, social and health conditions of the occupied territories. Shortages of water, food and medical supplies; intermittent electricity; restrictions on movement; and the creation of imprisoned towns all add to the stress and trauma of living on a day-to-day basis (UNWRA, 2009). High levels of adults are unemployed (UNICEF, 2011), and those in work do not always have the guarantee of being paid; for example, prior to the current project starting, teachers in schools had not received salaries for a six-month period. During a recent seminar at the University of Dundee, Ghassan Abdallah argued that in addition to the war on water and land, these factors equate to a war on the morale and spirit of the Palestinian people. For example, numerous studies record high levels of maternal and childhood depression (Espie et al, 2009). It was this latter finding that led mental health professionals to seek support from psychologists beyond Palestine, in order to capacity-build child trauma recovery interventions.

Project aims and personnel

The current project was a direct response to this request for capacity building (see Table 15.1 for project summary). The project's aim, in the long term, is to create indigenous self-sustaining, high-quality trauma recovery services for children and adolescents throughout the occupied Palestinian territories. This chapter focuses on the first phase of the project, which sought to train a cohort of mental health professionals to deliver an evidence-based trauma recovery programme for children in Palestine. For the first time, a group-based trauma recovery programme was delivered to children 'during' on-going occupation and military violence (Barron et al, 2013). The project involved the training of school counsellors (social workers and psychologists), the delivery of a trauma recovery programme to children and the implementation of evaluative research. Nablus was the town selected for the project because of the high levels of military violence resulting from the occupation. The project involved an interprofessional group of psychologists and social workers from Europe and the Middle East. Because of the complexity of interacting factors, that is, a context of violent occupation, **cross-cultural** interprofessional working and the building of trauma recovery services for children, a clear ethical framework was required to underpin project decision making (Loxley, 1997).

Table 15.1: Project – Child Trauma Recovery in Palestine

Context	Nablus, Occupied Palestinian Territories
Rationale	Responding to children traumatised by military violence within a context of inter-professional culturally sensitive practice
Aims	To capacity build school counsellors in delivering an evidence-informed trauma recovery programme for children screened for PTSD
Personnel	Principal researcher: Dr Ian Barron, University of Dundee Co-researcher: Dr Ghassan Abdallah, Centre for Applied Research in Education, Ramallah Trainers: Dr Patrick Smith, Chair, Children and War Foundation Dr Unni Haltne, Centre for Crisis Psychology, Bergen
Programme	Children and War Foundation's Teaching Recovery Techniques programme (TRT). Five sessions focus on alleviating the symptoms of PTSD
Training	Three days training for 20 counsellors
Trauma Recovery	11-14-yr-olds (N=150)
Evaluation	Randomised Control Trial

Framework for understanding

In order to understand the complexity of EDM (see Chapter One) involved in implementing an interprofessional cross-cultural trauma recovery project for children in occupied Palestine, an adapted framework from the National Child Traumatic Stress Network (NCTSN, 2006) was utilised. This framework was initially developed to assess the cultural sensitivity of trauma recovery programmes. The focus of the framework has been developed to explore an integrated understanding of the interactions of interprofessional ethics and cross-cultural working. The adapted framework, which includes the addition of ethical principles, explores (1) a socio-historical understanding of the interaction of cultures of Middle East and West; (2) the differing conceptualisations of the nature of trauma recovery and the impact of culture on symptom expression; (3) the differences in language and interpretation; and (4) the personal, organisational and interprofessional ethics in engagement, project delivery and evaluation.

Ethical principles

Clark et al (2007), in relation to interprofessional working, define 'moral principles as general guidelines for behaviour based on established ethical concepts considered essential for maintaining human relationships and communities' (p 593). In the West, and noted in Chapter One, the moral obligation for professionals to do what is good and right is frequently enshrined in codes of ethics, be they implicit or explicit. Typically these include codified behaviours, frameworks for decision making and the identification of appropriate methodology as well as the need for appropriate qualifications, on-going professional development and **supervision** (Clark et al, 2007). Interprofessional codes (for example, Sharland and Taylor, 2007) aim to enable professionals to collaboratively think through, and respond to, messy and changing contexts in order to get the best for **service users**.

The effectiveness of interprofessional codes of ethics, however, is highly contested. What is good and right, and who decides this, is open to debate. Some authors argue that codified practice can lead to the deskilling of professional judgement, intuition and analysis (Sachs and Mellor, 2003). Workers can experience **'disjuncture'** where agencies' vested interests direct workers to hold rigidly to procedural protocols that run counter to diverse responses for diverse problems (see Fenton, 2012, and Chapter Six). Ironically, codes of ethics applied in this way can lead to the very thing that the codes were set up to avoid, that is, the harming of service users. Where codes of ethics are applied less rigidly, as guiding principles, they then become subject to differing interpretations. The interactions of interpersonal, professional, interprofessional and legal interpretations can combine to undermine rather than facilitate collaborative practice (Melia, 2001). Ambiguous roles, lack of awareness of other agencies' strengths and weaknesses, differing perspectives on the service user, power plays, vague or non-existent communication and uncertainty as to how to deal with interprofessional conflict are all examples of interprofessional challenges (Seedhouse, 2002). It is rather surprising, given the significance and complexity of interprofessional ethics, that the field is still in its infancy (Clark et al, 2007). This chapter contributes to this emerging field through the analysis of personal, professional and interprofessional ethics within a cross-cultural context.

While literature on interprofessional ethics is emerging in the West, the same cannot be said for the Middle East, at least not in English-language papers. Where literature does exist, the emphasis tends to be on a more communal and familial understanding of how professions relate to each other (Barber, 2001). This is in direct contrast to the individualistic, managerialised and codified orientation of Western professional ethics. In the Middle East, models for understanding interprofessional behaviour tend to rely more on relational communitarian frameworks (Triandis, 1996). For example, expectancies, not expectations, are established through narratives which affirm established cultural beliefs about the position of professionals and multi-agencies within a familial society and how they relate to each other.

The interaction of such differing conceptual frameworks of what personal, professional and interprofessional ethics means between East and West is problematic for a project set in a cross-cultural context. In addition to the myriad of challenges of interprofessional working come the myriad of challenges within cross-cultural understandings. These latter challenges are, however, well documented and include differences in language, cultural or religious beliefs, the conception of what the problem is, the understanding of what children, adolescents, family and community means, and the differing conceptualisations of healing and recovery (Miller, 2006). All these cross-cultural issues can undermine the best of intentions. Add in the barriers encountered within interprofessional practice, and a myriad of worldviews both within and across personal and professional groups and cultures potentially contest for dominance (Irvine et al, 2002). Effective delivery and evaluation of trauma recovery programmes within this kind of context seems daunting, if not impossible. The current project that this chapter explores suggests that such practice can be both possible and effective.

Sociohistorical factors

Any ethically principled contribution by the West into the Middle East needs to be set within a complex of historical, religious, social, geographical and political factors. Historically, Britain in the Middle East is known for its colonial practices across the world, the harms these have caused, as well as the damaging legacies left behind (McLeod, 2000). Even in recent history, Britain was central in the creation of the State of Israel. The signing of the Balfour Declaration by a general in the British Army in 1917 set the scene for Israel's nationhood. This, however, was followed by the 'betrayal' of the Palestinian people in

1946, who had also been promised their own state (Farsoun and Naseer, 2006). Arguably, Britain, the chief architect of the Declaration, could be seen as culpable for establishing the context for entrenched conflict in Israel and Palestine. The authors of this chapter can affirm that such insights have not been missed by the Palestinian people.

Because of this negative sociopolitical historical lens, the UK professionals in the current project needed to be sensitive to how their 'position' was perceived both within and beyond the project. It was important, if the project was to be accepted and leave a sustaining legacy, that the professionals from the West were seen as supporting, not leading. That is, it was Palestinian psychologists and social workers who were setting the goals and making decisions about what would fit within Palestinian professional culture. An example that underlines the significance of this issue is the occurrence of 'unethical' practice of some European professionals who parachute into Palestine, deliver their therapies and then leave. From discussions with Palestinian professionals and service users, the consequences of such practice are a sense of abandonment and deskilling. In contrast, the current project sought to utilise the dynamics of capacity building, whereby local professionals are skilled up and empowered to take responsibility for the change. While the details of this relational process are discussed later in the chapter, results from the original study (for example, counsellors' reports of increased competence) indicate that practice grounded in explicit ethical principles is also highly effective practice (Barron et al, 2013).

While the project had anticipated sensitivities created by recent history, the influence of distant history on personal and interprofessional cross-cultural interactions was less obvious, at least to Western minds. The differing lengths of long-term cultural memories between Middle East and West were an intriguing discovery. Going further back in time, then, the UK played a major part in the crusades in the Middle East. While it may seem out of time for Western minds to mention this, through Middle Eastern eyes such atrocities remain in current discourse. In case we resign such concepts to history and the Middle East, the team were reminded by a Palestinian colleague that it was only recently that a leader of a Western power referred to a 'crusade' as mayhem was unleashed on the Iraqi people as part of a so-called 'war on terrorism'. Further, the current UK government's inaction in response to the plight of Palestine is easily construed as at best, neglectful and at worst, collusive with Israel. Within an occupied Palestine these are powerful factors, well beyond the usual discourses of personal, professional and interprofessional ethics.

For the Western professionals on the team, the context was one of being aware of the potential suspicion from Palestinian professionals, not only because of past Western abuses but also because of the current relationship between Israel and the UK, and the widespread use of western Intelligence services in the region (Brynjar, 2007). For all these reasons, an EDM approach, based on decentring and the empowerment of the other, involved establishing long-standing relationships of trust built on Palestinian professional choice and control. Active dimensions of this empowerment included understanding the Palestinian professional mindset, being led by Palestinian goals and processes; ensuring Palestinian choice in what programme was to be developed, where programmes would be delivered and the nature of evaluation. Ethically, Palestinian decision making was therefore built into the fabric of interactions. The consequence was high levels of project ownership and continuing collaborative development over many years. The project is now in its third planning phase.

Trauma, symptom expression and trauma recovery

In addition to understanding the influence of history and international politics on how Western professionals can be construed, the project had to consider professional cultural differences in understanding the nature of trauma recovery. Not to do so would have been to mirror the insensitivities of the past. An EDM approach, therefore, supported not making assumptions based on Western perspectives, that is, an individualistic view of trauma that leads to mostly individualised therapeutic responses. In contrast, Palestinians hold a communal view of trauma, emphasising the impact of trauma on the whole family and community (Barber, 2001). As a consequence, solutions are more focused on families or communities. From an EDM, principled perspective, the project sought to 'fit with' rather than be counter to the local culture. As a result, an evidence-informed 'group-based' community programme was identified and chosen by the Palestinian psychologists for implementation. In addition to being a more culturally attuned response, a community-based intervention fitted better with the small number of trauma therapists in the West Bank.

As well as a professional '**communal trauma**' perspective, religious thinking has had an impact on the conceptualisation of trauma for Palestinian society. A deterministic view of reality in Islam, for example, frames the traumatised child's experience in the hands of Allah. Some authors argue that such a view reduces a child's (and support adults') responsibility for change (Hammad et al, 1999). A fundamentalist religious perspective sees the trauma response as 'evil spirits' that require spiritual rather than psychological intervention, for example, driving out demons. On the upside, as the problem is seen as coming from outside the child, from an Islamic worldview, no stigma is attributed to the child. However, traditional belief does attach a taboo to mental illness. Palestinian children who show behavioural signs of distress are construed as mentally ill and are stigmatised. Any child going to see a therapist would be labelled as crazy. As a consequence, children in Palestine tend to show more embodied/physical symptoms, as compared to children in the West, because these are seen as acceptable as signs of evils spirits.

It was important for the Western psychologists to understand these traditional views that permeate parts of Palestinian society. As well as helping to make sense of the difference in symptom expression between Middle East and West, this cross-cultural understanding shaped the nature and content of training provided for school counsellors, parents and teachers. The challenge was to acknowledge and respect religious and cultural beliefs while also introducing a different perspective to helping children who have been traumatised. The TRT's (Teaching Recovery Techniques) programme emphasis on normalising symptoms and externalising traumatic events as the cause provided a new yet familiar message that the problem was located outside the child and therefore not connected to mental illness and stigma. Trauma was reframed as a natural response to exceptional circumstances. This was a congruent message for psychologists, social workers, teachers and parents where the child's behavioural and emotional expression of trauma was reconstrued as 'natural' rather than a sign of being 'crazy'. Evaluative feedback from school counsellors indicated that this reframe embedded well into the Palestinian mental health professional recovery narratives (Barron et al, 2013).

Along the same lines as the taboo on behavioural signs of distress, children in Palestine do not have the same rights of self-expression as those given to many children in the West. Self-expression for children is seen as being within the domain of the family and is discouraged with strangers. This is due in the most part to an honour culture, where family reputation is foremost. The result for children is that they find it difficult to share in school and community settings, as this is construed as a betrayal (Dwairy, 1998). Training for counsellors therefore had to address counsellors' own feelings in enabling children to share, as well as considering how comfortable they felt in their response to hearing children's self-expression about, for example, daily family life. Within the context of training, this was achieved through non-directive learning activities where counsellors made their own choices about enabling children's self-disclosure as well as their own ways of responding to children.

Another aspect of cross-cultural interprofessional EDM experienced by the project was grasping the difference in conceptualisation of trauma recovery programmes by psychologists and social workers, regardless of country. Social workers tended to hold more sociological perspectives regarding the focus of programmes, for example, intervening in families and whole communities, whereas psychologists' tendency was to seek to impact on within–child factors such as reduction of symptoms, growth of self-confidence and so on. These conceptual differences also lead to differences in programme focus, for example, some programmes in Palestine aim to build community resilience while others focus on the self-control techniques. Further, trauma recovery interventions in Palestine tend to be far less protocol oriented, as compared to the programme-driven mindset of Western psychology. In order to be respectful, the project sought to incorporate these differing conceptualisations. This provided the opportunity for more flexibility in programme delivery than had hitherto been planned. Although the TRT programme is protocol based, training involved helping the counsellors to explore how to adapt the programme within theoretical guidelines as well as how to help counsellors to consider developing the contexts in which the programme was being delivered – for example, teacher and parent responses to traumatised children. In order to monitor this aspect of programme development counsellors were asked to record the nature of their programme adaptations and why. Interestingly, however, most of the issues reported centred not on conceptual differences but on the nature of responding to children's distress levels and their developmental understanding of the programme. Perhaps debates about theory become secondary in the immediacy of responding to a child's distress?

Language and interpretation

The differing conceptualisations of trauma and trauma recovery by profession and culture were underpinned by the nature of language and communication. Some of the discovered differences in language included cultural/linguistic understandings (what 'adolescence' means), interprofessional language and terminology (codes of practice) and the use of specialised words (**emotional regulation**). These issues were relevant at multiple levels of engagement, that is, across the interprofessional planning team, to school counsellors and with the adolescents receiving the programme. To address the 'confusion' of language, the project members adopted an awareness of the need to seek permission and check out shared understandings. This process was facilitated through the use of an interpreter, who was a Palestinian psychologist and one of the project leaders. Educated in both the Middle East and the West, the interpreter was well placed to identify and name subtle, unnoticed misunderstandings.

Interpretation involved translation of the training materials, the TRT programme, evaluation materials and 'live' interpretation of the English-speaking presenters at the training workshop. EDM issues included trusting that the translation was accurate and the need for the trainer to be active and check out what counsellors said in response to questions (Minas et al, 2001). The team recognised the importance of acknowledging the feelings of the interpreter, trainer and researcher present at the training. Apprehensiveness was seen as a normal response for all concerned. School counsellors experienced a degree of uncertainty in discussing their feelings because these were being translated and heard by a psychologist and researcher who were 'foreigners' and, for some, from a different profession. In order to enable trust to develop, additional time was taken, which slowed the pace of training sessions. Frequent checking of understanding by all was encouraged and the complex process of dealing with word meanings in two languages and two professions was acknowledged and respected, for example concepts such as family, child, trauma recovery etc. (Minas et al, 2001). There was a need to discuss how language was changed by interpretation and to acknowledge that what was important to one culture might not be for another. For example, what 'refugee' means to a Palestinian social worker has a different meaning to a psychologist from the West: for example, a communal understanding of being a refugee in one's own land, as compared to an individualistic understanding of a refugee seeking therapy following escape to another country.

Personal and professional/organisational factors

Beyond professional, cultural and linguistic understandings, an EDM perspective highlighted the need for the project to be attuned to a range of personal and professional/organisational circumstances that could impact on the project's effectiveness. For example, school counsellors who were to receive the TRT training brought differing levels and foci of knowledge and skill, personal experiences of trauma, economic circumstances, other work demands, the challenges of travel and permit restrictions and training expectations. For the project to be EDM congruent these circumstances required to be considered.

As noted previously, most school counsellors were graduate psychologists and social workers. Most were under 25 years of age. While counsellors held a good range of theoretical knowledge, they tended to lack the practice frameworks for applying their knowledge in the area of child trauma. Irrespective of discipline, the project needed to be attuned to this transition from theory to practice and to monitor how this was progressing. Further, the training programme had to provide counsellors with ways to help them cope with their own trauma symptoms; for example, the teaching of reframing and coping skills. In the same vein, evaluation had to take account the high levels of counsellor trauma exposure and the impact on levels of attrition. The project was also aware of the harsh economic circumstances of the professionals and the challenges of even getting to the training; for example, the high cost of living, coupled with low salaries. Stipends were therefore provided for counsellors, along with travel and subsistence costs to ensure that participants were able to attend.

A new discovery was Palestinian professional expectations regarding the nature of training, that is, Palestinians are used to long days of training and the provision of high-quality packs. To meet expectations of what 'good' training is, both were incorporated into planning and delivery. Further, the engagement of the counsellors was partly based on the reputations of the organisations involved, that is, CARE, the Children and War Foundation (CAW), the University of Dundee and a local interprofessional syndicate in Nablus. All were perceived as credible. At a more personal level, there was recognition across the project that the professionals involved recognised in each other a track record of moving to action to assert the 'other's' human rights (Beauchamp and Childress, 1994). Interestingly, the restating of this value base provided an effective strategy for overcoming differences in understandings encountered within training and during project planning.

Personal and professional/organisational factors not only had to be understood and responded to but also played a part in the creation and maintenance of a culture of EDM throughout the project. Professionals were in the project not because their organisations expected them to be there but through a sense of choosing to be there, in some cases despite their organisations. This was personal and professional value-based commitment that involved training during holidays and self-funding. Further, these professionals were mostly unfettered from organisational agendas with regard to day-to-day decisions – they were, in essence, co-creating their own structures, processes, communication and culture around the goal of providing child trauma recovery programmes.

Conclusions

The current chapter has applied an adapted culture-sensitive trauma recovery framework to understanding the ethical factors embedded within an interprofessional cross-cultural project. In overcoming the morass of potential personal, professional and interprofessional cultural barriers, the project highlights the importance of (i) seeing the world through the eyes of the other, (ii) explicit principled action, and (iii) long standing relationships of trust. A clear EDM model is seen as fundamental to the success of the project. Learning from, rather than repeating, the mistakes of the past, taking the time to understand how the other sees and experiences their world, a concern for communicating ethically, adapting initiatives to 'fit' local experiences and supporting the decision making of the other, all appear to be factors in facilitating effective ethical interprofessional cross-cultural practice.

This chapter is exploratory and discursive in nature. It does, however, highlight a series of questions relevant for the development of future research and practice in the field of interprofessional ethics in cross-cultural contexts. There is a need for:

- greater clarity of definition of what makes interprofessional ethics distinctive within a cross-cultural context, as compared to single-country settings;
- the development of a coherent theory to bridge interprofessional and cross-cultural ethical understandings;
- the development and systematic application of this chapter's framework to other interprofessional cross-cultural contexts;
- the assessment of the perceptions of workers across professional projects in order to gain a deeper understanding of the ethics underpinning their interprofessional cross-cultural practice.

References

Al-Krenawi, A., Graham, J. and Kanat-Maymon, Y. (2009) 'Analysis of trauma exposure, symptomatology and functioning in Jewish Israeli and Palestinian adolescents', *British Journal of Psychiatry*, vol 195, pp 427–32.

Barber, B.K. (2001) Political violence, social integration, and youth functioning: Palestinian youth from the Intifada', *Journal of Community Psychology*, vol 29, no 3, pp 259–80.

Barron, I.G., Abdallah, G. and Smith, P. (2013), 'Randomised control trial of a CBT recovery programme in Palestinian schools', Journal of Loss and Trauma: International Perspectives on Stress and Coping, vol 18, no 4, pp 306–21.

Beauchamp, T. and Childress, J. (eds) (1994) *Principles of biomedical ethics*, Oxford: Oxford University Press.

Brynjar, L. (ed) (2007) *Building Arafat's police*, London: Ithaca Press.

Clark, P., Cott, C. and Drinka, T. (2007) 'Theory and practice in interprofessional ethics: a framework for understanding ethical issues in health care teams', *Journal of Interprofessional Care*, vol 21, no 6, pp 591–603.

Dwairy, M. (ed) (1998) *Cross-cultural counselling: The Arab Palestinian case*, New York: Haworth.

Espie, E., Gaboulaud, V., Baubet, T., Casas, G., Mouchenik, Y., Yun, O. and Moro, M. (2009) 'Trauma related psychological disorders among Palestinian children and adults in Gaza and West Bank, 2005–2008', *International Journal of Mental Health Systems*, vol 3, pp 21–6.

Farsoun, S. and Naseer, A. (ed) (2006) *Palestine and the Palestinians: A social and political history*, Colorado: Westview Press.

Fenton, J. (2012) 'Bringing together messages from the literature on criminal justice social work and "disjuncture": the importance of helping', *British Journal of Social Work*, vol 42, no 5, pp 941–56.

Hammad, A., Kysia, R., Rabah, R., Hassoun, R. and Connelly, M. (1999) 'Access guide to Arab culture: health care delivery to the Arab American culture', *Community Health and Research Center, Public Health Education and Research Department*, vol 7, pp 1–30.

Irvine, R., Kerridge, I., McPhee, J. and Freeman, S. (2002) 'Inter-professionalism and ethics: consensus or clash of cultures?', *Journal of Interpersonal Care*, vol 16, no 3, pp 201–10.

Loxley, A. (ed) (1997) *Collaboration in health and welfare: Working with difference*, London: Jessica Kingsley.

McLeod, J. (ed) (2000) *Beginning postcolonialism*, Manchester: University Press.

Melia, K.M. (2001) 'Ethical issues and the importance of consensus for the intensive care team', *Social Science and Medicine*, vol 53, pp 707–19.

Miller, J. (2006) 'Waves amidst war: intercultural challenges while training volunteers to respond to the psychosocial needs of Sri Lankan tsunami survivors', *Brief Treatment and Crisis Intervention*, vol 6, no 4, pp 349–65.

Minas, H., Stankovska, M. and Ziguras, S. (2001) *Working with interpreters: Guidelines for mental health professionals*, www.vtpu.org.au/docs/interpreter_guidelines.pdf.

NCTSN (2006) 'Resources on culture', *Culture and Trauma Brief*, vol 1, no 4, pp 1–4.

Punamäki, R.-L., Qouta, S. and El-Sarraj, E. (2001) 'Resiliency factors predicting psychological adjustment after political violence among Palestinian children', *International Journal of Behavioral Development*, vol 25, no 3, pp 256–67.

Sachs, J. and Mellor, L. (2003) 'Child panic and child protection policy: a critical examination of policies from NSW and Queensland', paper presented at a symposium AARE/NZARE conference, December 2003, Auckland.

Seedhouse, D. (2002) 'Commitment to health: a shared ethical bond between professions', *Journal of Interprofessional Care*, vol 16, pp 249–60.

Sharland, E. and Taylor, I. (eds) (2007) *Inter-professional education for qualifying social work*, London: Scottish Care Institute for Excellence.

Srour, R. (2005) 'Children living under a multi-traumatic environment: The Palestinian case', *Israel Journal of Psychiatry and Related Sciences*, vol 42, no 2, pp 88–95.

Triandis, H.C. (1996) 'The psychological measurement of cultural syndromes', *American Psychologist*, vol 51, no 4, pp 407–15.

UNICEF (2011) *The state of the world's children: Adolescence – an age of opportunity*, New York: United Nations Fund.

UNWRA (2009) *UNWRA annual report of the Department of Statistics*, The Palestinian Central Bureau of Statistics: UNWRA.

Zakrison, T., Shahen, A., Mortaja, S. and Hamel, P. (2004) 'The prevalence of psychological morbidity in West Bank Palestinian children', *Canadian Journal of Psychiatry*, vol 49, pp 60–3.

SIXTEEN

Social work ethics crossing multinational and interprofessional boundaries: smooth passages and bumpy rides

Timothy B. Kelly, Laura R. Bronstein and Debra McPhee

Introduction

In line with the aims of Part Five, this chapter focuses on professional and **interprofessional** ethics in the context of different countries (see Figure 1.1). The authors use a case study to highlight the part that cultural, geographical, professional and ideological factors can play when working across multinational contexts (Belgium, Canada, Germany, the Netherlands, and the US). The chapter analyses the values espoused by **social work** and other professions similar to social work, and emphasises their deontological nature.

Social work is a profession that continually crosses boundaries. Typically these boundary crossings are along professional lines, as social work is often in host settings where other professionals dominate. At other times these boundaries are literally geographical crossings, for example across jurisdictional boundaries or catchment areas. When an explorer crosses boundaries, finding different values and belief systems is to be expected. When values and beliefs have similarities, the journey into new territory is made easier. This chapter will explore areas where interprofessional practice is bolstered by similar ethical stances across boundaries. The helping professions share many values and beliefs. However, there are also differences, making it easier for problems to occur. This chapter examines how clashing of professional values may be fuelled by organisational settings where differing interpretations of organisational policies or procedures foster disagreements over 'best practice'. Ethical and value clashes are often not the real culprits in causing conflict. Rather, value and ethical dilemmas are blamed for problems that have their roots in structural barriers. If one embraces the understanding that professionals have shared values and beliefs, and that structural barriers are often the root of interprofessional 'value clashes', then creative approaches to overcoming difficulties can be found and implemented.

To make this case, a brief overview of the history of social work and its boundary-crossing traditions is presented. Next some of the research on **interdisciplinary** practice is highlighted. Finally, a brief summary of professional values and ethics is presented before looking at the case study.

History of social work

Professions are shaped by the social and political realities of their time and reflect the prevailing ideologies and values of the larger society (Goldenberg, 1971). In Europe and North America, the social upheavals of the Industrial Revolution shaped the development of social welfare, social work and social work education. Despite the shared conditions of the Industrial Revolution, the varying cultural realities across countries have led to very different social welfare philosophies and national strategies. For example, Erath (2012) explains that while German social work tried to manifest itself *morally* through an altruistic-political objective of social justice, social work in England focused more on the ideas of *accountability* and *evidence*, while in the US competing philosophies of the Settlement House Movement and the Charity Organization Society (COS) fought for influence over the development of professional social work (Specht and Courtney, 1994). These differing approaches reflected an era fraught with competing ideological perspectives – capitalism, liberalism and pragmatism. The mutual antagonism of these philosophies and ideological perspectives set the stage for decades of conflict regarding what constituted 'proper' social work.

From its roots, social work has been a boundary-crossing profession. For example, in healthcare in the US, interdisciplinary teams originated in Massachusetts General Hospital, where Cabot (1929) suggested that the social worker, doctor and educator work should together as a team on patient issues. The **hospice** movement also developed out of an interdisciplinary-team model of care. Cicely Saunders, founder of the modern hospice movement, was herself trained as a social worker, nurse and physician in the UK (Saunders, 1978).

School social workers in the US have also been working interprofessionally since the early 20th century, collaborating with teachers, special educators, school nurses, families and students to support learning and promote mental health (Weist et al, 2006; Lambie, 2008). Interprofessional teams in schools include child study teams, individualised education plan teams, grade level teams and intervention assistance teams (Anderson-Butcher et al, 2007). In addition to typical school social work practice, full-service community schools that provide an array of services on and off school premises are on the rise internationally. These schools are based on the notions that the purpose of schools is to educate youth for democratic citizenship and that schools and communities are inextricably linked and interdependent (Benson et al, 2009).

Despite having existed for a long time, interdisciplinary teams did not become commonplace until the 1960s and 1970s (Julia and Thompson, 1994). Since this time, the interprofessional model of care has remained at the centre of service delivery in diverse settings, in spite of the fact that it is time consuming and puts greater demands on social workers and other professionals. Professionals who work interprofessionally appreciate the benefits for both workers and recipients; however, there has been limited formal examination of the effectiveness of interprofessional teams (Abramson and Bronstein, 2008). It therefore behoves social workers not only to better understand the principles and skills for effective interprofessional collaboration, but also to champion efforts to conduct formal evaluations of this practice model.

Values across the professions

Contemporary social organisations have become heavily dependent upon the technical 'expertise' and specialised functions of professionals who ascribe to an ideology of public service and altruism over and above the mere seeking of economic self-interest (Abbott and Meerabeau, 1998). Every profession will have a body of knowledge that it calls its own, a range of skills to which it lays claim and a set of values and principles to which members of the profession are expected to adhere (see Dubois and Miley, 2007; Brooker and Nicol, 2011; Culshed and Orme, 2011; Duncan, 2011). The professions can also defend their own turf or professional positions based on their 'unique' ethical or value stance. Despite these protestations to uniqueness, there is often a good deal of overlap between the different professional value bases. To examine this overlap, the values of the social work profession are presented, and then the chapter looks at the values of several professions with which social workers often engage.

Value base of social work

Social work is explicitly a values-based profession. Its key overarching values include:

- a commitment to promote social justice for individuals and society as a whole
- a belief that all individuals have inherent worth, dignity and rights
- a commitment to professional integrity. (British Association of Social Workers (BASW), 2012; International Federation of Social Workers (IFSW), 2012).

The value base of gerontological nursing

The nursing profession also has a value base and ethical principles guiding practice. These centre on human dignity, integrity, autonomy, altruism and social justice (Fahrenwald et al, 2005; Nursing and Midwifery Council, 2008). Kelly and colleagues (2005) built on these generic nursing values and translated them into ethical principles of **gerontological nursing**, including commitment to person-centred care, enabling care, promoting access, practice development and interdisciplinary working.

The value base of teaching

Like social work and gerontological nursing, the teaching profession has an explicit value base that underpins educational practice. The **Ontario College of Teachers** (2012) outlines four values. These are care, integrity, respect and trust. The **General Teaching Council of Scotland** (2012) adds to these four principles several other important values: social justice, inclusion and equality/diversity.

The value base of occupational therapy

Occupational therapy also explicitly outlines its underpinning values. The values outlined by the **Canadian Association of Occupational Therapists** (2007) are exemplary of the occupational therapy profession. The values include the belief that every person

- is an occupational being
- is unique
- has intrinsic dignity and worth

- has the right to make choices about life
- has the right to self-determination
- has some ability to participate in occupations
- has some potential to change
- is a social and spiritual being
- has diverse abilities for participating in occupations
- shapes and is shaped by their environments.

Several occupational therapy codes of practice also highlight the importance of social justice and person-centred practice (for example, World Federation of Occupational Therapists, 2005; College of Occupational Therapists, 2010).

Looking across the professions

Even a cursory reading of the broad and grand value statements of each of the professions above highlights the considerable overlap in the value bases. The values espoused are all of a deontological nature. It is not that the professions necessarily think these values will lead to better outcomes (a consequentialist perspective); rather, these values are considered to be right because of a higher principle separate from outcome. Of course, better outcomes could result from practising from the ethical base. However, the outcomes do not justify the 'rightness'. Table 16.1 highlights the overlap in values by indicating which values are explicitly or implicitly described in professional codes of practice (Kelly et al, 2005; World Federation of Occupational Therapists, 2005; NMC, 2008; College of Occupational Therapists, 2010; BASW, 2012; GTC Scotland, 2012; IFSW, 2012; Ontario College of Teachers, 2012).

Despite considerable overlap, some of the values appear to be explicit in one profession, but not all. For example, the value statements in social work explicitly mention the use of power, power differentials inherent in the helping relationship and the need to not take advantage of power differentials. Other helping professions have similar expectations, though they may not be explicitly stated in codes of practice. Likewise collective action appears in the IFSW statement, but not in those of the College of Occupational Therapists or Canadian Association of Occupational Therapists. Yet, social justice is a key value of the occupational therapy profession. Gerontological nurses highlight the importance of practice development in their principles, and this is not explicitly stated in social work codes. Yet improving one's practice and the practice of the profession as a whole would be endorsed by social work.

Table 16.1: Shared professional values within Codes of Practice

Values	Profession			
	Social Work	Gerontological Nursing	Teaching	Occupational Therapy
Acceptance of individuals	Explicit	Implicit	Explicit	Implicit
Altruism	Implicit	Explicit	Implicit	Implicit
Autonomy	Explicit	Explicit		Explicit
Beneficence	Implicit	Implicit	Implicit	Implicit
Building on strengths	Explicit	Implicit	Implicit	Explicit
Care	Implicit	Explicit	Explicit	Implicit
Careful and restrained use of power	Explicit	Implicit	Explicit	Implicit
Collective Action	Explicit			
Dignity of each person	Explicit	Explicit	Explicit	Explicit
Enabling Care	Implicit	Explicit		Implicit
Growth	Explicit		Implicit	Explicit
Holistic understanding of people	Explicit	Explicit		Explicit
Inclusion	Implicit	Implicit	Explicit	
Individualism	Explicit	Explicit	Explicit	Explicit
Informed Consent	Implicit	Implicit		Implicit
Integrity	Explicit	Implicit	Explicit	Implicit
Interdisciplinary in approach	Implicit	Explicit	Implicit	Explicit
Person centred	Implicit	Explicit		Explicit
Maximising therapeutic interventions		Explicit		Explicit
Privacy	Explicit	Implicit	Explicit	Explicit
Practice development		Explicit	Explicit	Explicit
Respect for all people	Explicit	Implicit	Explicit	Implicit
Self-determination	Explicit	Explicit		Explicit
Social Justice	Explicit	Explicit	Explicit	Explicit
Trust	Explicit	Implicit	Explicit	Implicit
Appropriate boundaries with service users	Explicit	Explicit	Explicit	Explicit

There are also some clear differences. Teaching does not appear to share the value of self-determination explicitly espoused by the other professions. This difference may be the result of nationally or regionally set curricula, set exams at different periods through a student's educational journey or a host of other policy drivers. And yet, self-directed learning and developing autonomous learning skills are areas that educators welcome. So even in apparent differences, there is common ground.

There are times when, despite shared values, social workers and other professionals have conflicts. This may result from different professions giving greater weight to certain of these values over others. For example, a social worker may place a greater weight on the duty to protect a **vulnerable** person, while another professional may place more weight on self-determination. A discharge nurse may be working with the principle of autonomy and self-determination, pushing for the discharge of an older person who wants to go home. A community-based social worker may be working from the same principles but advocate postponing discharge, in support of the burdened, caregiving spouse. A professional, values-based clash may ensue.

There are times when social work values come into stark contrast with those of other professions. For example, in criminal justice settings a value for punishment and public protection may clash with social work's belief that individuals are capable of growth, development and change. Social workers may also work in settings where control and command are the values underpinning successful working, and these values will be at odds with values that support participatory decision making and self-determination. For example, order and discipline are the central principles undergirding military organisations. Military social workers must become extremely adept at safeguarding **confidentiality**, advocating for participatory patient decision making and facilitating self-determination in a system that views each of these principles as threats to the military's primary mission.

Interdisciplinary/interprofessional collaboration

Because social workers most often practise in settings where they are working with professionals from other disciplines, interprofessional collaboration needs to be a core component of social work practice, education and research. While throughout this chapter the term primarily used is interprofessional, a variety of other labels are also used to describe dyads and teams of professionals working together with social workers, including multidisciplinary, transdisciplinary and interdisciplinary. Distinctions among these terms are not well articulated in the literature.

Barriers and supports for interprofessional collaboration

A model for interprofessional teamwork among social workers and other professionals identifies the following as components of this kind of collaboration: interdependence, newly created professional activities, flexibility, collective ownership of goals and reflection on process; and the following as what impact on collaboration: structural characteristics, professional role, history of collaboration and personal characteristics (Bronstein, 2002, 2003). These four categories of impacting factors can present both barriers and/or supports to the collaborative process. For instance, in the case of structural characteristics, having more time and space for collaboration makes this more likely to occur; when social workers do not have space where they can meet with other professionals, and when they do not have the time to discuss together, these same structural characteristics serve as barriers to collaboration.

Education for interprofessional practice

Another area that can support interprofessional collaboration has to do with the role of socialisation in professional education. Professional socialisation shapes values, language, preferred roles, methods of problem solving and establishment of priorities. As one becomes a professional, perspectives particular to that profession become so integrated with a role that awareness of these perspectives diminishes, and thus they remain unexamined for their impact on collaboration (Abramson, 2002). In order to combat this, students can be educated in tandem with students in other pre-professional programmes (Forrest and Derrick, 2010; Ramsammy, 2010; Interprofessional Education Collaborative Expert Panel, 2011). Unless and until an interprofessional approach becomes a norm, social workers and other team members need to make systematic efforts to understand the socialisation and distinct contributions of each other (Abramson and Bronstein, 2008).

Ethical issues and practice dilemmas

Confidentiality and data protection clashes

The right to privacy is a value that helping professions share. Confidentiality and data protection are often enshrined in law or policies, and the desire to protect information can raise issues when working interprofessionally. In fact, concerns around confidentiality can interfere with collaboration, even when agencies co-locate to facilitate joint working. For example, Simpson and colleagues (2013) found information sharing to be a major structural barrier to service provision in a multi-agency, **co-located** pre-birth support and assessment programme for at-risk mothers. This multi-agency partnership consisted of professionals from various health and social work organisations. Members of a team shared office premises and came from midwifery, health visiting, adult social work, children's social work, **learning disabilities** and substance abuse. Despite working in one team and sitting at desks next to each other, members of the team did not have access to the same information systems, client/patient records or forms. Reasons given for the lack of information sharing centred on data protection laws and definitions of who owned various pieces of information. Values and ethics were used to justify decisions that prohibited sharing of information on a systems level, even when technological solutions *were* available. Creatively, and through shared values of care, integrity, interdisciplinary practice and privacy, the staff were able to find ways to share information and provide **service users** with an interdisciplinary and multi-agency service, despite structural barriers.

Differing views of clients, service users, consumers, patients and client systems

Working across professional boundaries can raise value-laden differences around the language used to describe the people with whom professionals are working. For example, one group of professionals will be comfortable using the word *patient*. For some, this label connotes an unpalatable, medical-model understanding of the helping relationship whereby the professional has all the power and does things *to* (treats) the patient. Other professionals will be more comfortable with the term *client* and suggest that it is a more egalitarian description of the helping relationship. Others will maintain that it still connotes an unequal and business relationship. Across the UK, the term *service user* is now preferred. Yet, for some it connotes a free-market, service-consumption approach to helping (see Chapter Nine for a similar discussion).

In addition to the terms used to denote 'clients 'or 'service users', different professionals often define the focus of the client system differently. Take a mother with a substance misuse problem who is in drug treatment and who has also been reported to child protection authorities for child neglect. A substance abuse worker may see the mother as the 'patient'. A child protection worker may see only the child as the client or service user. The child's teacher may only see a student with difficulties in school. A social worker may see the family system as one client and each environmental system as another client (also see Chapter Ten).

Looking at the values behind the different definitions of clienthood might suggest that any difficulties caused by varying understandings of who the client is are caused by and perpetuated by value differences. This is not the case; rather, such difficulties are often due to and/or perpetuated by structural and system barriers. For example, Kelly and colleagues (2010) found that many carers had never been identified as carers when the person they cared for was hospitalised. Hospital systems were designed to record information on and treat the *individual* patient. Nurses and other hospital staff were often aware of next of kin, but not necessarily aware of the next of kin *as a carer*. Seeing patients as *individuals* rather than as a *member of a family* was built into all the structures of the hospital. Sharing information with a family carer and making care plans with them was therefore difficult. Kelly and colleagues found that through interdisciplinary work the systems could be changed to support a more holistic approach to care that involved recognising and supporting carers as part of the 'patient system'. Such an approach was congruent with the value bases of all professions involved, and supported a higher quality of care for patients.

Power imbalances

Undoubtedly, legitimate structural concerns intermingle with long-standing professional cultural clashes and issues of professional power. There are often legitimate concerns related to a lack of clarification when it comes to professional or legal responsibility. Tousijn (2012) references the dominant position held by the medical profession, but also the propensity of each profession to defend its own jurisdiction. Professional cultures reflect key historic factors, including the power differentials associated with social class and gender. Across the helping professions these differentials are reflected in the professions' cultures, values, beliefs, attitudes, customs practices and systems (Hall, 2005).

Though the perennial example, power imbalances are not limited to relationships between medics and others professions. For example, in schools, teachers are more powerful than social workers, educational psychologists and teaching assistants. In local authority social work in the UK, social workers are more powerful than the occupational therapists, social care officers and support workers. Power differentials may be masked by conflicts that are unfairly attributed to ethical conflicts. For example, Simpson and colleagues (2013) found that conflicts occurring in a partnership between a substance abuse treatment programme and an agency supporting families affected by substance abuse were couched in values regarding who was the primary target of intervention: who the patient/service user was. For one part of the partnership, the person with substance misuse difficulties was the legitimate target of intervention. Attending to other issues would diffuse the intervention and put the identified patient (and those that depended on the patient) at risk of further or more serious harm. The other half of the partnership saw the potentially at-risk children as the primary concern and viewed intervention at the family level as the best way to help the substance-abusing parent *and* protect potentially at-risk children. The substance abuse agency held the power in this partnership and, as such, its ethical arguments held sway, to the detriment of both programmes. In essence, the more powerful agency needed to change its way of practice in order to accommodate better joint working. However, practice was not substantially changed and, though professional values were part of the justification, in actuality, 'normal' resistance to change and power imbalances were the barriers to change. A strong, shared value base did exist but was untapped at a systems level.

Case study

The context of social work practice is always reflective of the interdependent factors of culture, setting, policy and ideology. This is illustrated in the experience of one of the co-authors. For a female Canadian civilian social worker within a male-dominated military organisation located in a European country (the Netherlands), the cultural and organisational challenges were complex. Add to this, the fact that individual cases often crossed borders into the legal and social service policy and practice jurisdictions of neighbouring countries (Germany and Belgium) meant that professional and ethical dilemmas occurred on a daily basis. Take the case of an American child residing in the Netherlands with her mother, who was a service member in the US military. The child, who was in the care of her father, also a US service member, was taken to a home across the border in Germany where abuse took place. Once back home in the Netherlands the child reported the abuse to a teacher at the American school. As required, the teacher reported the disclosure to the US military social worker.

When the military is based in a foreign country the host nation has initial jurisdiction: in this case, the Netherlands. Most often the legal and social services of the host nation will turn the case back to the military after their initial report, assessment and coordination. However, this is not always the case. In complex cases involving possible criminal prosecution the international and interjursdictional coordination is likely to be extended and challenging. In this particular case, the child protection system in the Netherlands was immediately called in to the hospital where the child was examined. Soon after the German police were added to the team, since the abuse had occurred in Germany. The interprofessional team soon involved: the US military police, US military social worker, the Dutch medical staff, the Dutch police, multiple Dutch child protection workers (each family member was assigned a worker and a separate one for the family unit as a whole), the German police and a German child protection worker. The same problem was often identified, assessed and addressed very differently, depending on the origin of the worker. The details of this case are too extensive to recount here. However, in brief, the US military perspective would best be recognised as legal/therapeutic, with an expectation that the social worker would focus on evidence gathering, investigation, establishing the legitimacy of the claim and a subsequent recommendation and treatment plan. In contrast, the Dutch child protection services took a very resource-intensive, family–centred therapeutic approach that emphasised the protection and simultaneous well-being of each individual and the unit as a whole. In further contrast, the German approach was heavily focused on investigation and the requirements of corroborating the child's report. This case best highlights the integral connection between the value perspective that governs how a problem gets defined and the ways in which the policies and practices that result are heavily reflective of the initial values. Here the social worker recognised and valued the ethical stances of all the various actors. The German actors were concerned with issues of justice from a criminal/legal perspective. Most reasonable people would agree that the innocent should not be wrongly accused and actions should protect innocent people. This would be a moral good. Likewise, most reasonable people would agree that the family unit (however configured) is a moral good and should be supported. Family members have a right to good health and the conditions for well-being. Hence, the holistic family–centred approach of the Dutch social workers is an ethically correct way to proceed. Most reasonable people would also agree that protecting the vulnerable takes precedence over protecting the strong and powerful. As such, the American individualistic focus on the needs of the child makes ethical sense – alongside, of course, the justice concerns. In this case there is a collision of three deontological moral goods and though all involved wanted the best for the child, the ways in which they thought about what was best and how to get there were different. The skills of the social worker were required to help the different actors and their systems to work together. Recognising shared value stances and respectfully acknowledging the value-based differences was an important step in the process. Once the value positions and logical connection into the different ways of working were understood by the various actors, they were then able to work together to meet the needs of the family and also to meet the different systemic needs. The mediating function of the social worker was key to helping the professionals navigate the morass of competing moral goods.

Moving beyond barriers

Across professions there is strong acceptance of the need for greater interprofessional practice, on the grounds that it reflects 'best practice'. However, as Irvine and colleagues (2002, p 208) observe, 'agreement in principle does not automatically guarantee co-operation in practice'. On multiple levels, interprofessional practice methods challenge traditional professional boundaries. After decades of focus on establishing professional imperatives based on knowledge and practice specialisation and exceptionalism, it will take considerable time and effort for authentic integration of interprofessional skills across the health, education and social service sectors.

The focus on the 'whole' person or the 'whole' client is a conceptual framework that is integral to social work and a perspective that well supports interdisciplinary practice methods. Further, social work's systems approach to practice has a great deal to offer in directing solutions to the structural and systemic challenges of collaborative practice. Though social work is embedded in systems thinking and holistic approaches, it is not the only profession with such concerns. Building on these shared concerns and values provides the foundation from which to overcome structural barriers to collaborative interdisciplinary practice. The following recommendations are made to further boundary-crossing practice.

- We need to examine in depth and detail specific barriers to collaboration. For example, saying that value or ethical clashes are a barrier is not enough because even when the same values are shared across professions, structural or other barriers can impede collaboration.

• We need more research on collaborative work in order to continue to learn about barriers across service systems and to better understand what supports best practices being implemented. Such research efforts should involve listening to the experiences of people who use or benefit from the service systems as well as the experiences of professionals who used their shared value bases to overcome barriers.

• We need to better assess and remedy barriers to interdisciplinary collaboration within universities (including university and professional **accreditation** requirements) that perpetuate teaching students in silos. Research has shown that a history of quality collaboration for professionals in training leads to improved and increased collaboration in practice (Bronstein, 2002; 2003). Interdisciplinary education should include explicit content regarding shared values bases and codes of **ethical practice**.

• We need to better articulate to service users the benefits and potential negative implications of information sharing. Then service users can make choices about the sharing of their own information.

• We need more tools to assess the outcomes of collaboration, and these tools need to be more widely used so that we know if/when the belief that collaboration leads to higher-quality care is indeed accurate.

References

Abbott, P. and Meerabeau, L. (1998) 'Professionals, professionalization and the caring professions', in P. Abbot and C. Wallace (eds) *The sociology of the caring professions* (2nd edn), London and Philadelphia: UCL Press, pp 1–19.

Abramson, J.S. (2002) 'Interdisciplinary team practice', in G. Greene and A. Roberts (eds), *Social work desk reference*, New York: Oxford University Press, pp 44–50.

Abramson, J.S. and Bronstein, L.R. (2008) 'Teams', in T. Mizrahi and L. Davis (eds), *The encyclopedia of social work* (20th edn), vol 4, New York: Oxford University Press and NASW Press, pp 199–205.

Anderson-Butcher, D., Iachini, A. and Wade-Mdivanian, R. (2007) *School linkage protocol technical assistance guide: Expanded school improvement through the enhancement of the learning support continuum*, Columbus, OH: College of Social Work, Ohio State University.

Benson, L., Harkavy, I., Johanek, M.C. and Puckett, J. (2009) 'The enduring appeal of community schools', *American Educator*, vol 33, no 2, pp 22–47.

BASW (2012) *The code of ethics for social work: Statement of principles*, London: British Association of Social Workers.

Bronstein, L.R. (2002) 'Index of interdisciplinary collaboration', *Social Work Research*, vol 26, no 2, pp 113–26.

Bronstein, L.R. (2003) 'A model for interdisciplinary collaboration', *Social Work*, vol 48, no 3, pp 297–306.

Brooker, C. and Nicol, M. (eds) (2011) *Alexander's Nursing Practice* (4th edn), London: Elsevier.

Cabot, R.C. (1929) *Social service and the art of healing*, New York: Dodd, Mead.

Canadian Association of Occupational Therapists (2007) *Code of ethics*, Ottawa: Canadian Association of Occupational Therapists

College of Occupational Therapists (2010) *Code of ethics and professional conduct*, London: College of Occupational Therapists.

Culshed, V. and Orme, J. (2011) *Social work practice* (5th edn), Baskingstoke: Palgrave Macmillan.

Dubois, B.L. and Miley, K.K. (2007) *Social work: An empowering profession* (7th edn), New York: Pearson.

Duncan, E.A.S. (2011) *Foundations for practice in occupational therapy* (5th edn), London: Elsevier.

Erath, P. (2012) *Sozialarbeit in Europa. Fachliche dialoge und transnationale entwicklungen* [Social work in Europe. Professional dialogues and transnational developments], Stuttgart: Kohlhammer.

Fahrenwald, N.L., Bassett, S.D., Tschetter, L., Carson, P.P., White, L. and Winterboer, V.J. (2005) 'Teaching core nursing values', *Journal of Professional Nursing*, vol 21, no 1, pp 46–51.

Forrest, C. and Derrick, C. (2010) 'Interdisciplinary education in end-of-life care: creating new opportunities for social work, nursing, and clinical pastoral education students', *Journal of Social Work in End of Life and Palliative Care*, vol 6, pp 91–116.

General Teaching Council Scotland (2012) *Codes of professionalism and conduct*, Edinburgh: General Teaching Council Scotland.

Goldenberg, I. (1971) *Build me a mountain: Youth, poverty and creation of new settings*, Cambridge, MA: MIT Press.

Hall, P. (2005) 'Interprofessional teamwork: professional cultures as barriers', *Journal of Interprofessional Care*, vol 19, no 1, pp 188–96.

IFSW (2012) *Statement of ethical principles*, http://ifsw.org/policies/statement-of-ethical-principles/.

Interprofessional Education Collaborative Expert Panel (2011) *Core competencies for interprofessional collaborative practice: Report of an expert panel*, Washington, DC: Interprofessional Education Collaborative.

Irvine, R., Kerridge, I., McPhee, J. and Freeman, S. (2002) 'Interprofessionalism and ethics: consensus or clash of cultures?', *Journal of Interprofessional Care*, vol 16, no 3, pp 199–210.

Julia, M.C. and Thompson, A. (1994) 'Group process and interprofessional teamwork', in R.M. Casto, M.C. Julia, L. Plat, G. Harbaugh, A. Thompson and T. Jost (eds) *Interprofessional care and collaborative practice*, Pacific Grove, CA: Brooks/Cole, pp 35–41.

Kelly, T.B., Tolson, D., Schofield, I. and Booth, J. (2005) 'Describing gerontological nursing: an academic exercise or prerequisite for progress?' *International Journal of Older People Nursing in association with Journal of Clinical Nursing*, vol 14, no 3a, pp 1–11.

Kelly, T.B., Watson, D., West, J. and Plunkett, S. (2010) *Preventing crisis for carers*, Glasgow: Princess Royal Trust for Carers/Moffat Foundation.

Lambie, R. (2008) *Family systems within educational and community contexts: Understanding children who are at risk or have special needs*, Denver, CO: Love Publishing Company.

NMC (Nursing and Midwifery Council) (2008) *The code: Standards of conduct, performance and ethics for nurses and midwives*, London: Nursing and Midwifery Council.

Ontario College of Teachers (2012) *The ethical standards for the teaching profession*, Toronto: Ontario College of Teachers.

Ramsammy, L. (2010) 'Interprofessional education and collaborative practice', *Journal of Interprofessional Care*, vol 24, no 2, pp 131–8.

Saunders, C. (1978) 'Hospice care', *American Journal of Medicine*, vol 65, pp 726–8.

Simpson, M., Bruce, M., Hodson, A. and Kelly, T.B. (2013) *Supporting vulnerable families*, Dundee: Dundee University.

Specht, H. and Courtney, M. (1994) *Unfaithful angels: How social work has abandoned its mission*, New York: The Free Press.

Tousijn, W. (2012) 'Integrating health and social care: interprofessional relations of multidisciplinary teams in Italy', *Current Sociology*, vol 60, no 4, pp 522–37.

Weist, M.D., Ambrose, M.G. and Lewis, C.P. (2006) 'Expanded school mental health: a collaborative community-school example', *Children and Schools*, vol 28, pp 45–50.

World Federation of Occupational Therapists (2005) *Code of ethics*, www.wfot.org/ResourceCentre.aspx.

SEVENTEEN

Palliative care: the professional and interprofessional ethical considerations for the staff–volunteer interface in the UK and India

Ros Scott and Suresh Kumar

Introduction

As part of Part Five, this chapter explores issues of professional and **interprofessional** ethics across national boundaries (see Figure 1.1). The authors approach ethics and volunteering in **palliative care** from a number of ethical theoretical perspectives, but principally from a medical and personal ethics standpoint. This chapter uses the case studies of two countries to highlight ethical issues arising from **volunteer** involvement in two very different settings for palliative care: Kerala in India and the UK.

In a palliative care setting volunteers find themselves as part of a multidisciplinary team. In Chapter One, Hannah and Jindal-Snape discuss the challenges of interprofessional collaboration (IPC) between different professional groups. They also discuss the theories of consequentialism, largely focused on the outcomes of an individual's actions, and deontology, which is more concerned with the 'rightness' or 'wrongness' of actions (Healy, 2007). When considering the involvement of volunteers as part of the palliative care multi-professional team, the authors were also influenced by these theories. Organisations are most likely to be concerned with implications arising from the outcome of a volunteer's actions while the professional staff team is likely to be most concerned both with the motivations behind these actions and whether they were correct and appropriate.

The World Health Organisation (1998) defines palliative care as:

an approach that improves the quality of life of patients and their families facing the problem associated with life-threatening illness, through the prevention and relief of suffering by means of early identification and impeccable assessment and treatment of pain and other problems, physical, psychosocial and spiritual. (p 1)

The authors will explore two very different volunteering models: a community model in Kerala, South India and the UK **hospice** model. There are different issues affecting palliative care in the developing world and hospices in the UK. In countries such as India, the main challenges in the provision of palliative care are the size of population requiring care, scarcity of resources, poverty affecting patients and families and distances to treatment centres. Volunteers and the community play a key role in supporting patients and providing aspects of care. UK hospices, in comparison, are well resourced and staffed; the population, relatively speaking, is better off. However, there are echoes of some challenges faced in southern India, with increasing demand for services resulting from an ageing population and an economic climate affecting hospices, which are increasingly challenged to do more with less. As a result there is a developing interest in volunteers being able to provide more innovative and hands-on services in UK hospices (Leadbetter and Garber, 2010).

Ethics and volunteering in palliative care

In Chapter One, Hannah and Jindal-Snape describe professional ethics as moral principles and values that guide the professional in their decision making and approach to work. Simon (2008) considers that ethics are 'guiding principles about what is "good" and what is "bad", that should direct doctors and other health care professionals in their work and decision making' (p 1). Beauchamp and Childress (2001) consider that ethics can be defined as different perspectives on making sense of 'the moral life' (p 1). They assert that biomedical ethics are a set of principles that provide a framework for interpreting what is acceptable and why this is so. Conventionally, the four cardinal principles of autonomy, **beneficence**, **nonmaleficence** and justice are the basis of medical ethics (Mohanti, 2009). However, these are defined in terms of interactions in the limited space between the healthcare professional and the patient. While the various professionals within the palliative care team may have slightly different professional ethical principles, most encompass these four cardinal principles. Simon (2008), however, also considers the complexity of the care issues that arise from caring for patients on a journey toward the end of their life. These often raise a number of ethical dilemmas for professionals as individuals and as a team, not to mention the patient and family. Some of these may cause disagreement and conflict within the professional team. What happens, therefore, when we add to the team, members of the local community as volunteers, either in the community model such as that in Kerala or in the hospice model as in the UK?

The four ethical medical principles could also be considered to apply not only to professionals but also to volunteers within palliative care settings. However, volunteers may be guided more by personal ethics, and bring their own values and moral codes to their roles, which will influence their actions and ethical decision making (EDM) in any given situation. Volunteers are motivated to help in this area for many reasons: sometimes because of personal experience, to feel needed, to give something back, to gain experience, to build confidence, to name but a few. However, if we accept that most want to contribute positively, to do good and to do no harm, then it is arguable that they are motivated to work at least within the principles of beneficence and nonmaleficence. It could also be considered that both consequential and deontological theories come into play here, as volunteers may be concerned not only with doing the right thing but also that the outcomes of their actions should benefit the patient.

Organisations generally face challenges in incorporating and managing both staff and volunteer groups within the structure, largely because of the assumptions that people make about each other and the labels that people attach to others (Edwards, 2007). For instance, staff may make assumptions about volunteers having few skills and little professionalism just because they are willing to give their time for no financial reward. Therefore, what are the tensions and challenges that arise when staff and volunteers work together? Communication and relationships can become complex when the personal ethics of volunteers are added to the mix of different professional **ethical codes** of the staff team.

The authors first explore this through the community model in Kerala, South India, a programme where volunteers are often the first point of contact with patients. The active presence of members of the wider community in the decision-making space about appropriate care of the patient and family, often considered to be the preserve of professionals, can very often challenge the position of the 'powerful' healthcare professional. This may be because what is being attempted is a social approach to medical practice. Community initiatives such as Neighbourhood Network in Palliative Care in Kerala challenge the traditional biomedical ethical paradigm in healthcare. In the process of de-professionalisation of healthcare, such initiatives also give rise to discussion of a variety of issues, including those around ethics. The ethics of community intervention in medicine is particularly interesting, as, according to Zussman (1997), 'medical ethics has been led far more by the parent disciplines of philosophy and theology than by sociology or any of the other social sciences' (p 172). Fox (1989, pp 229–30) argues that the 'ethos' of medical ethics has been dominated by an 'analytic individualism' focused on the value of 'autonomy' that gives prominence to 'the notion of contract' while reducing 'more socially-oriented values to a secondary status'. This may in part go some way to explaining the lack of valuing of volunteers within the team (Davis-Smith, 2004), as their approach is essentially a socially oriented one, in both Kerala and the UK. It is worth exploring further ethical issues arising from perceptions of volunteers in the UK.

Volunteers in the UK are also drawn from the local community but, in contrast to Kerala, work most often within the hospice rather than in patients' homes. Volunteers are sometimes perceived as bridging the gap between professionals and patients. While this can be an extremely positive role, it may lead to a number of ethical issues that hospice volunteers face (Berry and Planalp, 2008). Findings from Berry and Planalp's research with 39 hospice volunteers identified challenges in terms of gifts from patients, concerns about care of patients and families, and lack of clarity about their own volunteer roles and boundaries. They also experienced the complexity of being in a role between the professional team and the patient, often being perceived by the patient and family as a friend. This can leave the volunteer torn between the different expectations of them by professionals and patients. There is, therefore, a very real potential for tension in cases where volunteers may have a different perspective on a patient and family situation to that of the professional team. This may arise from the volunteer's professional experience or personal values and beliefs. Yet both the professional and volunteer will be acting within different professional and personal ethical and value frameworks with the best interest of the patient at heart. What happens when the volunteer receives key information from a patient or family member that has been shared only with them? How they experience the professional team may influence their decision as to whether and what to share with a member of staff. Of more concern is if the member of staff discounts the volunteer's view purely because the volunteer is not valued in the same way as a paid member of the team. How ethical is it to discount a team member's view or professional experience because they are not paid?

Volunteers face a number of additional challenges (Watts, 2011). These include the impact of working in emotionally sensitive roles; increasing **regulation** and formalisation of management, due to the adoption of business management models; and the contradiction that they can feel both appreciated and 'taken for granted' at the same time. Watts asserts that 'Whilst there is a high level of commitment by volunteers to the work of hospices, evidence points to the need to nurture these contributions that cannot be taken for granted' (Watts, 2011, p 1). Previous studies of volunteering and volunteer management in hospices found that hospices could not continue to provide services without the involvement of volunteers (Davis-Smith, 2004; Sallnow, 2010). This must therefore pose questions for volunteer-involving organisations as to how well volunteers are integrated, and how well their individual values and decision making are understood, respected and empowered.

In contrast to the UK, palliative care in the South Indian state of Kerala is characterised by the active role that volunteers play both in hands-on patient care and in the organisation of services (Sallnow, Kumar and Numpeli, 2010). The composition of the multidisciplinary home-care teams of the community-owned system in Neighbourhood Network in Palliative Care is different from that of a hospice-based programme. Volunteers form the core of the community-based palliative care team, with the healthcare professionals providing the necessary medical support (Stjernsward, 2005). These trained volunteers take on the role of providing emotional and psychological support to the patient, in addition to giving basic nursing care and supporting the family members to provide care. A couple of questions are relevant here:

- Does volunteer involvement in areas conventionally seen as professionals' territory compromise care?
- Is volunteer involvement more justifiable if a professional with the required skills is not readily available for the patient at the time of need?

Before considering these questions perhaps it will be helpful to set them in the context of volunteering in palliative care in Kerala and the UK, and to explore the roles that volunteers undertake.

The role of volunteers in Kerala and the UK

Community volunteers in palliative care have been responsible for setting up most of the existing palliative care units in the civil society sector in Kerala. The trained volunteers help in identifying need and in initiating and running palliative care units in their locality. They visit patients at home (both with the home-care unit and on their own); and also help at the out-patient clinic, checking patients in, keeping patients comfortable and talking to them. Volunteers are also involved in administration, including clerical work and account keeping; in addition to fundraising and mobilising support for patients from the various governmental and non-governmental agencies. Community volunteers trained in psychosocial support interact with patients and family to offer emotional support.

All the palliative care units in the community also offer a regular supply of food for starving families, in addition to the medical and nursing services provided. This usually comes as a weekly supply of rice and other items collected from individuals and shops in the neighbourhood. 'Rice for the family' has become an important component of *total care* for patients in the region, as a good percentage of families are financially broken by the cost of prolonged treatment by the time the patient registers with the palliative care unit.

Kumar and Numpeli (2005) describe the additional range of interventions by palliative care units in Kerala to support patients. Support is provided to families of poor patients to prevent children dropping out of education. Some students are also supported during their university education. Other help from palliative care services includes transport facilities to referral hospitals, as the travel can cost the family a month's income; and rehabilitation programmes, including support and training in making handicrafts, keeping livestock and setting up small shops. Financial support is also provided to very poor patients in emergency situations. Palliative care units try to link their patients with local social or religious organisations supporting the marginalised, and with local government to identify benefits from government schemes.

There are many differences between the roles of volunteers in Kerala and in hospices in the UK. The UK hospice movement has a long history of the involvement of volunteers and many, if indeed not all, hospices were founded by volunteers. In the UK, volunteers are mainly involved in an organisational setting and have less involvement in providing care in the community setting. Rather than a community-based model, services are staff led, characterised mainly by a hierarchical management approach to volunteering, largely drawn from the business sector. It is suggested that in the UK there are approximately 100,000 volunteers involved in hospice care. It is estimated that hospice costs would rise by 25% if staff were required to provide the same services (Help the Hospices, 2006). With approximately 14,000 paid staff in UK hospices (Help the Hospices, 2011), volunteers today significantly outnumber paid staff and increasingly come from different age groups and backgrounds. Volunteers support hospice services in a wide variety of ways, including direct support for patients and families, **complementary therapies**, diversional therapy, counselling, befriending, **bereavement** support, providing transport, help with provision of meals, housekeeping, gardening, fundraising and helping in hospice charity shops. Management of volunteers is most commonly provided by the voluntary services manager/coordinator, or alternatively by the HR manager or another member of the hospice professional team. Additionally, the governance of UK independent hospices is entrusted to volunteers in their role as trustees. Their responsibility here is significant in ensuring the effective strategic direction of the organisation, the safe and effective use of resources, provision of services and management of the chief executive. Despite this, from experience of both the adult and children's hospice sectors, there is still reluctance in some hospices to empower volunteers to become involved in the delivery of care to patients. The role of volunteers in UK hospices today is not always recognised or valued for the influence that they have as a strategic resource, the capacity that they bring to the service and their economic contribution. Much of this arises from staff perceptions of volunteers (Scott, 2006; Pastor, 2010).

Staff perceptions of volunteering

Earlier in the chapter two key questions were asked as to whether volunteer involvement compromised care and whether there was justification for the involvement of volunteers in situations where professionals are not available. In addressing these, the authors would like to consider an example from the Kerala perspective. The emotional and psychological support given by professional counsellors to patients in the hospice or institution-based programmes in Kerala is limited to the amount of time available to them. The role of the family and the local volunteer in the community-based palliative care programme gains importance, as they can provide continued support almost on a round-the-clock basis. In addition to this, the community takes responsibility for the daily needs of the patient and the family – offering to provide daily rations, help with the education of children and other household needs. Additionally, due to time constraints, the professional counsellors in institution-based programmes are often unable to support the caregivers and families, who have as much if not more need for support than patients. The trained volunteers in the community-owned system, on the other hand, can give time to support the caregivers and families at this time of major change in their lives. In the community-owned palliative care system, volunteers play a larger role in actual patient care than they do in institution-based programmes and so the potential for causing harm might be greater, due to a lack of professional skills. But then the pertinent question is, in resource-poor settings where availability of trained personnel is grossly insufficient to provide top-quality care at home for patients, is it ethical to deny any sort of care to the needy on the grounds that what we can provide might not be the most ideal?

The Neighbourhood Network in Palliative Care programme has been criticised for involving volunteers in active patient care (Gupta, 2004). The critics mainly point to the possible loss of **confidentiality**, privacy, patient autonomy and quality of care when the community actively participates in all aspects of patient care. These concerns are understandable when the four key principles of medical ethics are considered, the key tenets of which are patient autonomy, doing no harm and improving their welfare. However, it may also be considered that these criticisms are based on ethical frameworks of healthcare professional–patient interactions constructed mainly by Western culture and philosophy.

Why, because care is provided by volunteers, is it considered to compromise care? If a volunteer is well motivated and trained, why should their involvement not provide a vital element of care and support to the patient and family, whether in Kerala or in the UK? It is interesting that attitudes to and criticism of volunteers in hospices in the UK are not dissimilar to those evinced in the Neighbourhood Network in Palliative Care.

While many staff work very positively alongside volunteers and are motivated by their enthusiasm and commitment, some may feel threatened by the involvement of people who are unpaid, many of whom may be experienced and well qualified in other contexts or disciplines. Pastor (2010) believes that volunteers need to be involved in roles that they are motivated to undertake, but recognises that when it comes to patient-facing roles, tension with staff can arise. He identifies staff concerns about 'protecting families, lack of qualifications, confidentiality, job satisfaction and security' (p 68). Staff in Pastor's study also believed that care was too complex and that personal care was not an appropriate role for a volunteer. From experience, these staff anxieties about volunteers can lead to suspicion of volunteer motivation and poor relationships with the volunteers. This ultimately causes disharmony in the team, the effects of which are bound to have an impact on the patient and family. This begs the question: why are we prepared to entrust the governance of our hospices to volunteers in their role as trustees, but at the same time reluctant to allow volunteers to become involved in meaningful patient-care roles?

Staff could, therefore, be considered to be the 'gate-keepers' to volunteering in many organisations and to have the ability to empower or disempower the role and activities of volunteers. This can be construed as an ethical tension between the essence of volunteering, which is often considered to be spontaneous, creative and innovative, and the actuality in practice. An example of such a situation, taken from practice, is that of a physiotherapist who wished to volunteer. They were placed in a non-care volunteering role and advised that they would not be able to work directly with patients. After a short period the volunteer left, stating that they found it too difficult not to be able to step into situations where they felt their professional experience could have been of value. Was that volunteer's professional ethical code compromised by the hospice's approach to their involvement? Were patients denied enhanced care from the addition of their skills? Do staff act in an ethical way if they prevent patients and families from experiencing the skills and expertise, the social and community dimension that volunteers can bring to their care? How does this fit with beneficence, nonmaleficence, autonomy and justice?

Complexities of the staff–volunteer interface

Volunteers come from diverse backgrounds, such as practising professionals, unemployed, homemakers, carers, students or retired people. Each brings their own set of personal values, life experiences and, in some cases, professional ethics, which will influence their approach to, and decision making within, their volunteering role. Kearney (2007, p 5), in exploring volunteering values, considers that people volunteer 'not only to address a perceived need in the community or some other need, but also for their personal satisfaction'. He also asserts that the values of volunteering are essentially personal. This may well not be recognised, nor understood by staff, nor in some cases may the volunteer contribution to the work of the team be valued.

While a volunteer's professional ethics and value base undoubtedly influence their decision making and approach, all volunteers must be expected to both respect and commit to the values of the palliative care organisation that they support, in the same way as staff. Many UK hospices have policies and guidelines that help volunteers to understand their role, approach and boundaries. There will, however, always be times when the ethics of the situation will prove challenging and will require exploration from all sides before a decision is made on how to proceed. This is why recognition of the ethics of volunteering at organisational, management, individual staff and volunteer level is vital, otherwise there can be a negative effect on the holistic care of patients and families, and ultimately on the organisation as a whole.

Staff anxiety about, or opposition to, the role of volunteers may also lead them to withhold important information from volunteers who may be involved with patients and families. As an example from experience, consider the volunteer driver who is about to transport the patient and family on a lengthy journey. The family have complex social and relationship issues but the member of staff believes that, in order to preserve patient confidentiality, the volunteer has no right to be informed. The risk here is that the volunteer does not have adequate information to act and make informed choices during his or her time with the family. It could be considered that everyone here is at risk, yet this has arisen from a professional making what they believed to be an ethical decision, without consideration of the ethical situation of the volunteer. What did happen in this situation was that after strenuous intervention from the voluntary services manager the volunteer did receive a short overview of the issues before setting off on the journey and had an opportunity to discuss their experience on their return.

How volunteers are perceived by staff will influence how ethical issues are addressed or, at worst, ignored, posing a risk to the volunteer, to the member of staff and, most importantly, to the patient and family. Clear ethical principles of volunteer involvement are largely a Western construct, but these can go some way to allaying staff fears. It is therefore worth exploring the ethical considerations for organisations in the involvement of volunteers.

The organisational dimension

Organisations have a responsibility to ensure that their approach to volunteering is based on sound ethical principles. In considering the ethics of volunteer involvement, McCurley and Scott (2009) defined ethics as 'the process by which values and principles are transformed into actions' (p 119). They recognise that, as with other professions, the management of volunteers has a number of different codes of ethics. One example is that of an American organisation that has published a **code of conduct**. This cites that those responsible for volunteering must espouse the following ethical values: '1. Citizenship and Philanthropy; 2. Respect; 3. Responsibility; 4. Caring; 5. Justice and Fairness; 6. Trustworthiness' (Association for Volunteer Administration, 2005, p 1). In addition, the organisation asserts that the volunteering programme must also ensure that it is diverse, ethical, of a high standard, trusted by others, ensures that support is on-going and minimises risk. These ethics of volunteer involvement sit very comfortably alongside the clinical ethics discussed earlier.

However, within any palliative care volunteer programme there are a number of areas where ethical conflicts can arise. The underpinning principle of volunteer involvement in the UK has always been that of 'supplementing – not supplanting that of paid staff roles' (McCurley and Scott, 2009, p 120). This may be challenging for organisations where funding or other resources fluctuate or are scarce. The same dilemma exists in the UK as in Kerala: is it more ethical to withdraw services completely from patients or to continue a changed service involving mainly volunteers? Another key area is managing boundaries between volunteers and patients. Volunteers may be very involved with patients and families in terms of social care and support. Boundaries may often necessarily become blurred over time as the patient and volunteer develop a strong bond. This presents challenges for the management of the volunteer in terms of maintaining a **therapeutic relationship** with the patient and ensuring that the relationship remains healthy for both parties.

So far, the authors have raised more questions than answers about the ethics that surround the involvement of volunteers in working alongside staff in palliative care. However, there is no doubt that volunteers have a great deal to offer palliative care (Scott, 2009). By bringing a diversity of talents and experience, they enrich the skills of the paid staff team and allow organisations to extend the range of care and support offered to patients and families. Drawn from the communities in which they live, volunteers embed organisations firmly within those communities, making palliative care more accessible to those who may need it. Volunteers may also be less focused on the clinical needs of patients and bring some 'normality' to the life of the patient. It has also been suggested that volunteers bring a very personal and social dimension in walking alongside those who face the end of life (Guirguis-Younger, Kelley and McKee, 2005). The authors' professional experience would suggest that the different approach that volunteers bring is greatly valued by patients and families. Patients often perceive volunteers as less busy than professionals, having more time to listen and therefore being easy to approach.

Conclusion

There are many ethical considerations regarding the involvement of volunteers, the staff volunteer interface and for volunteers themselves. Many of these become more complex in the field of palliative care, when patients with life-shortening conditions and those facing the end of life, and their families, are added to the mix. However, there is no doubt that continuing to explore and address these brings many rewards. Clinical ethics demand respect for patient autonomy and confidentiality, and are very clear that care should be given by the most qualified and competent personnel. However, when we look at palliative care as a public health intervention, these terms can have different connotations. In cultural settings like those of Asian or African countries, where most societies consider family and not the individual as the basic unit, patient autonomy does not mean the same as in Western cultures (see Chapter Fifteen for discussion of some differences). In such settings the society and family are very close-knit units and separating individuals from their families and close communities is not practical. It is for the local community to decide what its moral and ethical standards should be, and the standards set by the West cannot very often be transplanted in their entirety into other communities. Conversely, because of the different society and family dynamics, the principles and approach to volunteering in palliative care in Kerala cannot be completely transferred to the UK.

It is interesting to note, however, that regardless of country or approach, anxieties exist in terms of roles and boundaries and how much volunteers should be empowered to undertake. The authors would suggest that what is required is not so much a change in the ethical theories explored in this chapter, but a better understanding of them by both staff and volunteers alike. Perhaps by giving volunteers an insight into the professional ethical principles that influence staff in different situations, teamwork could be enhanced. Equally, if staff were given an insight into volunteers' ethical perspectives and motivations, deeper trust and confidence might develop. Effective support and opportunities to explore openly the ethical differences and tensions that may arise could also bring cohesiveness to the team and empowerment of volunteers. Volunteers in palliative care have significant capacity, along with their paid staff colleagues, to make a real difference to living and dying well in any country.

Acknowledgements

The authors wish to thank Dr Aneena Anna Abraham and Dr V. Jithesh for their suggestions.

References

Beauchamp, T. and Childress, J. (2001) *Principles of biomedical ethics* (5th edn), New York: Oxford University Press.

Berry, P. and Planalp, S. (2008) 'Ethical issues for hospice volunteers', *American Journal of Palliative Medicine*, vol 25, pp 458–62.

Council for Certification in Volunteer Administration (2005) *Professional ethics in volunteer administration*, www.cvacert.org/professional.htm.

Davis-Smith, J. (2004). *Volunteering in UK hospices: Looking to the future*, London: Help the Hospices.

Edwards, D. (2007) 'Leisure-seeking volunteers: ethical implications', *Voluntary Action*, vol 8, no 3, pp 19–39.

Fox, R. (1989) *The sociology of medicine*, Englewood Cliffs, NJ: Prentice Hall.

Guirguis-Younger, M., Kelley, M.-L. and Mckee, M. (2005) 'Professionalization of hospice volunteer practices: what are the implications?', *Palliative & Supportive Care*, vol 3, no 2, pp 143–4.

Gupta, H. (2004) 'How basic is palliative care?', *International Journal of Palliative Nursing*, vol 10, pp 600–1.

Healy, L.M. (2007) 'Universalism and cultural relativism in social work ethics', *International Social Work*, vol 50, no 1, pp 11–26.

Help the Hospices (2006) *Volunteer value: A pilot survey in UK hospices*, London: Help the Hospices.

Help the Hospices (2011) 'Help the hospices membership: The benefits of being a member', London: Help the Hospices.

Kearney, J. (2007) 'The values and principles of volunteering – complacency or caution?', *Voluntary Action*, vol 3, no3, pp 63–86.

Kumar, S. and Numpeli, M. (2005) 'Neighbourhood network in palliative care', *Indian Journal of Palliative Care*, vol 11, pp 6–9.

Leadbetter, C. and Garber, J. (2010) *Dying for a change*, London: Demos.

McCurley, S. and Scott, R. (2009) 'Ethical issues for VSMs in hospice care', in R. Scott, S. Howlett and D. Doyle (eds) *Volunteers in hospice and palliative care: A resource for voluntary services managers*, Oxford: Oxford University Press, pp 119–29.

Mohanti, B.K. (2009) 'Ethics in palliative care', *Indian Journal of Palliative Care*, vol 15, no 2, pp 89–92.

Pastor, D. (2010) 'Exploring attitudes to volunteering at hospices for children and young adults', unpublished MSc thesis, Faculty of Business, Computing and Information Management, London: South Bank University.

Sallnow, L. (2010). 'Conceptualisation of volunteering in palliative care', MSc thesis, Department of Palliative Care, Policy and Rehabilitation, London: Kings College.

Sallnow, L., Kumar, S. and Numpeli, M. (2010) 'Home-based palliative care in Kerala, India: the neighbourhood network in palliative care', *Progress in Palliative Care*, vol 18, no 1, pp 14–17.

Scott, R. (2006) 'Volunteers: ministering or meddling. A study of UK children's hospices' experiences of volunteering', *3rd Cardiff International Conference on Paediatric Palliative Care, Intervention or Interference*, 22–24 June 2006, Cardiff University, UK.

Scott, R. (2009) 'Volunteers in a children's hospice', in R. Scott., S. Howlett and D. Doyle (eds) *Volunteers in hospice and palliative care; A resource for voluntary services managers*, Oxford: Oxford University Press, pp 145–59.

Simon, C. (2008) 'Ethical issues in palliative care', *InnovAiT*, vol 1, no 4, pp 274–9.

Stjernsward, J. (2005) 'Community participation in palliative care', *Indian Journal of Palliative Care*, vol 11, pp 111–17.

Watts, J.H. (2011) 'Exploring the working role of hospice volunteers', *BSA Medical Sociology Group Annual Conference*, 14–16 September 2011, University of Chester, UK.

World Health Organisation (1998) 'Definition of palliative care', www.who.int/cancer/palliative/definition/en.

Zussman, R. (1997) 'Sociological perspectives on medical ethics and decision-making', *Annual Review of Sociology*, vol 23, pp 171–89.

PART SIX

A way forward?

EIGHTEEN

Review of teaching and learning about ethics on a professional training programme for educational psychologists in Scotland

Elizabeth F.S. Hannah and Patricia Murray

Introduction

In line with the aims of Part Six, this chapter considers ways in which understanding of ethics can be embedded into the thinking and practice of professionals in training (see Figure 1.1). To illustrate this, the case study of an educational psychology professional training programme is presented. The authors take a positive ethics approach and highlight the use of moral theory for ethical decision making.

The ability to be alert to the ethical dimensions of practice and to acquire professional knowledge and skills to make informed ethical decisions is a core **competency** of educational psychologists. This chapter considers approaches to teaching and learning about ethics and **ethical practice** that may assist student educational psychologists. Specifically, it reports on the authors' reflections about approaches adopted in one professional training programme; although it is anticipated that some of the issues and lessons learned will have resonance for other professional training programmes in the UK and further afield. In reviewing teaching and learning approaches, the authors have considered professional guidance (for example, codes of ethics), ethical theories and research in moral development and ethical behaviour. They undertook an exploratory investigation into the ethical perspectives of a group of student educational psychologists at the beginning of their professional training. The findings from this study, which resulted in a re-evaluation of approaches to teaching and learning about ethics and ethical practice, will be used in an illustrative manner.

Professionals' moral development and ethical behaviour

An ecological perspective (Bronfenbrenner, 1979) is helpful in conceptualising the dynamic interplay between different influences on professionals' ethical behaviour. An individual entering a profession carries with them their psychological characteristics, life experiences and values (for example, cultural values and religious beliefs), which will interact with the professional context to both shape and be shaped by that context, in line with an interactionist perspective. Lindsay (2009) referred to the influence of contextual factors on the development of psychologists' values that underpin their ethical behaviour; hence the importance of ethical codes reflecting societal values. Thus, new entrants to a profession carry with them views on what is 'right' and 'wrong' that will have an impact on their ethical behaviour. During training, individuals learn and experience the values and cultural norms of their chosen profession. Handelsman et al (2005) propose a model whereby student psychologists acculturate to the value base and ethos of their profession. Gottlieb et al (2008) suggest that it is not sufficient to just teach ethics; students should be encouraged to be reflexive of their own values and have opportunities to talk through ethical dilemmas during professional training, using experiential approaches (see also Chapter Nineteen). They propose that students should be encouraged to adopt a more positive, aspirational view of ethics; and training courses should support students' ethical development and acculturation through the type of supportive ethical climate the courses create.

To achieve this, it is important to develop awareness of the types of situations that students could encounter in practice that may raise ethical dilemmas. Ethical situations where there may be more than one way to view a situation; where more than one course of action could be taken; and that produce a degree of internal cognitive conflict could be considered as ethical dilemmas. This is in contrast with ethical transgressions, where there is a clear breach of an **ethical code** (Dailor and Jacob, 2011). Ethical dilemmas can pertain to either an individual's own professional practice or that of someone else. For example, Dailor and Jacob (2011), in a survey of school psychologists in the US, offer insight into typical ethical dilemmas, including child protection issues, wondering how to respond to a colleague's unethical behaviour (see Chapter Three for issues of whistleblowing) and issues about sharing test protocols with parents.

Professional codes

A critical analysis of the two main codes for practising psychologists in the UK, the British Psychological Society (BPS) *Code of Ethics and Conduct* (BPS, 2009) and the Health Professions Council (HPC) *Standards of Conduct, Performance and Ethics* (HPC, 2008) (updated in 2012 due to change of name to Health and Care Professions Council) was undertaken, with a view to revealing any underpinning philosophical basis and the nature of professional guidance offered. As discussed in Chapter One, the BPS (2009) states that the Code is based on the 'British eclectic tradition' (p 4), which appears to be a synthesis of deontological and teleological theories of morality (Thiroux and Krasemann, 2009). Four ethical principles underpin the Code, namely respect, competence, responsibility and **integrity**, each of which has a statement of values and a series of **standards** to guide the conduct of members. Thus, although there are guiding principles, values and standards, suggesting a duty-based, universalist perspective, the Code acknowledges the need for psychologists to be aware of the context within which they work, including the legal system and guidance from **regulatory** bodies, when making decisions. In contrast to the BPS Code, the HPC Standards do not make any reference to a philosophical basis.

The BPS Code aims to provide 'more emphasis on, and support to, the process of ethical decision making' (p 1). The BPS acknowledges that no code can cover all situations and that psychologists have to make professional and **ethical judgements**; although it does not provide a conceptual framework for professional judgement. In its guidance, the HPC stipulates 14 standards of conduct and ethics for registered members, while acknowledging that some of the standards will not be universally applicable; for example, 'You must deal fairly and safely with the risks of infection' (HPC, 2012, p 3).

Shared features of these two professional codes are: guiding principles for professionals' behaviour; an aim to protect the public; recognition of the role of professional judgement in decision making; and acknowledgement of the nature and function of contextual factors. Although both codes make reference to personal behaviour and the importance of not acting in a way that would impact on the public's perception of and confidence in psychologists, neither code appears to refer explicitly to either personal values or the dynamics between personal, professional and contextual factors, as is found in a positive ethical perspective (for example, Handelsman et al, 2005; Aoyagi and Portenga, 2010).

Positive ethics and positive psychology

One of the difficulties with professional codes of conduct and ethics is that they can reinforce a defensive view of professional practice, namely what the practitioner should not do or the minimum expected standards. This emphasis on compliance with rules and regulations may partially stem from a historical emphasis on problematic situations and the need to regulate and punish misconduct rather than promote aspirational principles for professional practice (Handelsman et al, 2005). Positive ethics, it has been argued, offers a more proactive and aspirational perspective of professional activities, whereby the practitioner aims to achieve the highest standards in the best interests of his/her client (Aoyagi and Portenga, 2010).

Positive ethics, with its emphasis on positive values and ideals, has its roots in the scientific field of positive psychology, founded by Professor Martin Seligman in the 1990s (Seligman, 2003, 2006). The science of positive psychology encompasses an understanding of contextual influences that promote 'positive emotions' and 'positive character', including the role played by 'positive institutions' (Seligman et al, 2005). Positive ethics adopts a multifaceted perspective of ethics, acknowledging and exploring the dynamics between internal and external factors (Handelsman et al, 2005). This will be elaborated later, in the section on 'Positive ethics and psychologists'. This is exemplified by research from the field of business ethics that suggests that when it comes to making ethical decisions there is an interaction between personal ethics and organisational ethics, which can impact on ethical decision making (EDM) (Elango et al, 2010). Furthermore, research indicates that congruence between the ethical values of the individual and the organisation can lead to better job satisfaction and commitment (Ambrose et al, 2008), as highlighted previously in Chapter Five.

When examining and understanding an individual professional's conduct, a positive ethical paradigm enables consideration of the interplay between personal, professional and organisational values and societal influences. Much of the sourced literature on positive ethics was in the field of business ethics, and largely pertained to the North American context. There was limited literature, mainly from North America, that considered a positive ethical perspective in psychology practice (for example, Handelsman et al, 2005; Aoyagi and Portenga, 2010).

Historically, the introduction of ethical guidelines into corporate business practice is a relatively recent development in the US, dating from the 1960s with only a few exceptions (Goolsby et al, 2010).

The impetus for this development appears to have been legislative imperatives and resultant fears of punitive outcomes. Svensson and Wood (2003) propose a dynamic model of interaction between time and culture (societal values, beliefs) that leads to changes in perceptions of what is right and what is wrong in business practice. Increasingly, there are voices in the business world calling for a more proactive approach to ethical behaviour and examples of successful individuals acting as role models for others (Goolsby et al, 2010). This has been accompanied by attempts to understand ethical behaviour in organisations from a positive stance. An example from business ethics is the construct of *benevolent leadership*, which is defined as 'the process of creating a virtuous cycle of encouraging and initiating positive change in organisations through (a) ethical decision making, (b) creating a sense of meaning, (c) inspiring hope and fostering courage for positive action, and (d) leaving a positive impact for the larger community' (Karakas and Sarigollu, 2012, p 537).

Positive ethics and psychologists

Handelsman et al (2005), writing from a US context, are proponents of a positive ethical perspective for psychologists. They suggest that a negative, rule-bound approach to the professional conduct of psychologists may result in feelings of alienation, due to a separation between an individual's professional role and his/her personal moral philosophies (other chapters have raised this potential **disjuncture** between personal values and a rules-based approach to professional behaviour). Handelsman et al (2005) provide a helpful ethical framework for psychologists comprising seven basic themes, which incorporate internal and external factors, each influencing the other rather than operating in a discrete and linear fashion. The seven themes are: 'values and virtues: inspiring psychologists toward the ethical ideals of their profession', 'sensitivity and integration', 'ethics and ongoing self-care', 'ethical reasoning and decision making', 'appreciation of the moral traditions that underlie ethical principles', 'prevention of misconduct and promotion of positive behaviours' and 'sensitivity to our larger professional contexts'. Positive ethics is able to accommodate a range of moral philosophical positions. Psychologists operating from different ethical perspectives can utilise this framework in their practice. Thus, this model appears to offer a way forward in informing the teaching and learning of ethics in both the initial training and the continuing professional development of psychologists.

Although not explicitly citing positive ethics, Seider et al (2007), based on empirical findings from the GoodWork project that was led by researchers in the US with international collaborators in Scandinavia, propose a paradigm for practising psychologists that shares a number of features with positive ethics. These include the importance of self-awareness in professional practice; consensus within a profession about the values, activities, goals and rewards of the work being carried out; and mentorship as a means of professional development. These features resonate with some of the themes identified by Handelsman et al (2005).

Teaching and learning about ethics in the professional training of educational psychologists

The core curriculum for educational psychology training programmes in Scotland is set out in the BPS **accreditation** documentation (BPS, 2010 [revised 2012]). Under the section 'Frameworks for professional practice', it states that students will develop 'A professional and ethical value base including reference to the BPS *Code of Ethics and Conduct* and other relevant guidelines' (BPS, 2010, p 16). Furthermore, programme standard 2 refers to the need to include 'evaluation of students' understanding of working ethically, as appropriate to the level of study' (BPS, 2010, p 24).

The authors were interested in reviewing the teaching and learning methods used on a training programme for educational psychologists in Scotland to assist students in developing a 'professional and ethical value base' (BPS, 2010, p 16). The authors adopted a systematic approach to this review. This involved documentary analysis of the BPS *Code of Ethics and Conduct* (2009), HPC *Standards of Conduct, Performance and Ethics* (2008 [updated 2012]), the BPS (2010) accreditation document (revised 2012) and the MSc in Educational Psychology programme handbook (2010). They undertook an exploratory investigation of the ethical perspectives of a sample of students in one cohort at the beginning of their training. The review was informed by literature on moral development and ethical behaviour; research into the teaching of professional ethics in higher education in the UK (Illingworth, 2004); as well as through dialogue with colleagues from different disciplines in the university. This process is illustrated in Figure 18.1.

Figure 18.1: Review of teaching and learning about ethics on a professional training programme for educational psychologists in Scotland

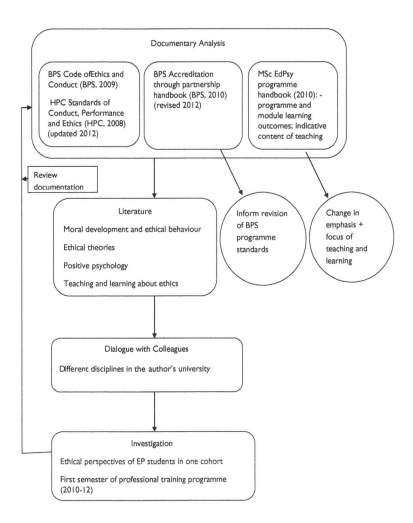

Analysis of approaches to the teaching and learning of ethics

The authors analysed programme and module learning outcomes, underpinned by the core curriculum (BPS, 2010), to identify those that appeared to contribute to the overall aim of students developing a 'professional and ethical value base' (BPS, 2010, p 16). This resulted in the identification of eight learning outcomes:

1. Demonstrate a professional and ethical value base with reference to the BPS *Code of Ethics and Conduct* and other relevant codes of practice.
2. Manage a personal learning agenda promoting critical reflection and self-awareness that enables the transfer of knowledge and skills to new settings and problems.
3. Engage in and learn from interactive **supervision** processes, including peer mentoring.
4. Professional competence relating to personal and professional development and awareness of the educational, professional and social context within which work is undertaken.
5. Engage in a dynamic, responsive and on-going process to maintain and develop professional practice through the process of professional reflection, supervision and continuing professional development.
6. Development of awareness, knowledge, skills and values that enable effective work with diverse client populations and promotion of equal opportunities practice.
7. Demonstrate ability to operate effectively within the legislative, national and local frameworks for educational psychology practice.
8. Manage a personal learning agenda and self-care.

Illingworth (2004) identified three commonly used approaches to applied/professional ethics teaching in higher education, namely a pragmatic approach that uses as its starting point the codes of practice of **regulatory** bodies; an embedded approach in which students study ethics indirectly through consideration of the concept of professional identity, but with a significant ethical dimension; and a theoretical approach that commences with the study of moral theory and that students then apply to real-life situations. Analysis of the learning outcomes, indicative content and teaching methods on the training programme revealed a synthesis of these approaches.

Exploratory investigation into the ethical perspectives of student educational psychologists: case study of a cohort of students on a Scottish professional training programme

Fourteen out of 22 students participated in two focus groups to explore their ethical perspectives at the beginning of the programme (October/December 2010). The open-ended questions were:

1. What is your understanding of ethics?
2. What has influenced your understanding of ethics?

3. What is your understanding of professional ethics?
4. What has influenced your understanding of professional ethics?
5. What happens if there is a conflict between your personal and professional ethics?
6. What happens if there is a conflict between your and others' professional ethics, especially in an **interprofessional** context?

Sessions were audio recorded and the recordings were transcribed by an administrator. Transcripts were shared with the participants and they were given the opportunity to correct any obvious errors and request removal of extracts. The authors had copies of the transcripts and audio files.

Adopting a phenomenological approach, the authors were interested in the participants' understanding, views and experiences of ethics in their personal and professional lives. As such, a thematic approach to data analysis was deemed appropriate (King and Horrocks, 2010). As the authors were interested in the participants' views as a whole, it was decided to analyse the entire data set for themes. Thematic analysis, at the semantic level, based on Braun and Clarke's (2006) six phases was employed.

The authors conducted the analysis in a collaborative fashion, enabling rich discussion and debate and enhancing the inter-rater reliability of the findings.

Insight into the ethical awareness and understanding of students

The findings are considered with reference to the literature and illustrative direct quotes.

Theme 1: perspectives on ethics

Students viewed ethics as the way people act and what guides their behaviour. A rule-based approach to actions in personal lives was evident in some of the comments, for example, rules are "about the way people conduct themselves essentially" or "guidelines that ... (we) live by". What is not clear is how these rules are determined and how ethical theory informs that process. Individual differences in personal ethics and an awareness of influences on the development of personal ethics were apparent in comments. Students viewed ethics as socially constructed and a lens "through which they view life". There was an acknowledgement that there could be differential "interpretations", due to people having "different ethics".

In terms of professional ethics, there was an awareness of the BPS *Code of Ethics and Conduct* (2009) and the HPC *Standards* (2008 [updated 2012]). Both these documents were viewed as providing guidance for professional behaviour and ensuring that professionals and those they work with are kept "safe". This suggests that the students were adopting a utilitarian ethical perspective, focusing on the perceived benefits for the professional and those they work with of following these codes and standards. They could see the positive consequences for clients of psychologists following a professional ethical code. One of the students commented that "ethics are there for accountability … that is probably one of the huge benefits of having a kind of ethics about the way people conduct themselves … essentially ethics code of conduct". Codes were also construed as assisting decision making by providing professionals with "support guidelines" to inform action.

Students believed that ethics should be more than compliance to professional codes, a "proactive approach as opposed to being reactive", with some students highlighting the importance of the concept of 'justice'. This suggests a more aspirational and positive view of ethics (Handelsman et al, 2005). Some students appeared to hold non-consequentialist (deontological) personal ethics suggesting that personal **morals** and values are "things you hold sacred to yourself" and are the "building blocks" of professional ethics.

Theme 2: ethics as a dynamic process

Students viewed ethics as 'constantly evolving' (Lindsay, 2009), identifying a number of influences on ethical development in their personal and professional lives. In terms of professional ethics, there was acknowledgement of the impact of professional training, which "definitely influences how you understand and interpret the world", of on-going supervision and support through enabling students to see "if there is something you are missing" and how another person would "interpret it"; and the impact on one's ethical perspective of working with others "so you have to keep reflecting", implying an on-going active process. These statements suggest that the students valued the role and impact of professional development programmes (initial and continuing) on their ability to understand and respond to situations in an informed manner (Ehrich et al, 2011). Professional codes of ethics and conduct have been developed by professional bodies as guidance for their members and, as such, are based on group consensus. This was reflected in the students' viewing professional ethics as "group consensus … it is not individual". This might indicate a normative perspective

(Thiroux and Krasemann, 2009) whereby the group prescribes how an individual member of the profession ought to behave. An awareness of the evolving nature of ethics due to the sociohistorical context was noted; for example, "something we might see ethical now give it 50 years and we will look back in horror". This could impact on both personal and professional ethics.

Theme 3: factors that inform ethical decision making

In terms of professional EDM, one of the students acknowledged that practitioners must be able to "adapt quickly … to change in situations". This might indicate a relativist perspective, such that ethical principles are viewed as being contingent on the context (Healy, 2007). The influence of personal values on EDM was commented upon. Thus, decisions are based not only on professional judgement and codes but on the "morality that we brought with us from home environment or social environment … it is really important", and "how you react to things whether you think it is ethical or not is determined by those values". This suggests an awareness of the dynamic relationship between personal and professional ethics in EDM. This is addressed in a number of EDM models and frameworks (for example Miner and Petocz, 2003; Ehrich et al, 2011).

Students at this stage of their professional training demonstrated an understanding that it is not possible to entirely separate behaviour in one's personal life from expected professional behaviour. For example, one student stated that "you cannot be going out and doing things that you shouldn't be doing because they [will] conflict with your professional ethics and obviously that you have repercussions later on". This resonates with the BPS *Code of Ethics and Conduct* (2009) where, as part of the ethical principle of responsibility, there is a reference to avoiding personal misconduct. Students had knowledge of the importance of both the BPS Code and HPC *Standards of Conduct, Performance and Ethics* (2008 [updated 2012]), as "it is important to realise that …you are bound by professional ethics … you are also regulated by those ethics" and "can be answerable to the Health Professions or the BPS".

Theme 4: ethical dilemmas

Students identified and reflected upon a number of hypothetical and actual ethical dilemmas. Examples are grouped by category.

(a) Personal–professional

Students recognised that there would be occasions when they would come across difficult ethical situations that might conflict with their own personal moral values: "we might have to work with parents who abuse their children … neglect their children". They recognised that having chosen a career in educational psychology they had committed to act in accordance with the guidelines and rules of that profession. In doing so, they would have to look at what is "going on in their [the parents'] life and adopt a professional perspective on that". "I think that is going to be a massive challenge … for me working with some of these groups." This suggests that students are aware of the need to adopt the values, standards and expectations of their chosen profession, indicating the beginning of a process of professional acculturation (Gottlieb et al, 2008).

(b) Interprofessional

A number of ethical dilemmas in the context of multi-agency working were raised by the students. One scenario pertained to the sharing of information between professional groups: "recently an early intervention team was set up … representation from police, …**social work**, … education and the education person thought it was their right to get all the information on the people from the educational psychologist", which raised issues for the student in relation to client **confidentiality** and permissions. Another student thought that it might be "unethical not to share the information", as the sharing of information between agencies might be the best course of action for a child. This discussion highlighted students' awareness of the complexity of the scenario and the need to adopt different moral perspectives.

(c) Professional in an organisational context

In Scotland, the majority of educational psychologists are employed by **local authorities**, which are the funding agents for resources such as educational placements for children. Students noted potential conflicts that could arise between a psychologist and his/her employer. Most educational psychologists operate in the dual role of an agent of their employer and a professional acting in the best interests of the child.

> "So many values at the moment especially funding things like where you think you might know the best possible placement but is it reasonable to ask that … (of the local authority). You can see that they are not child centred, they are financially centred in terms of what placement is best

for the child. It is obviously going to impact on the quality of their life … you have competing demands".

In this quote, the student acknowledges the conflict between the professional value of being "child centred" and the authority's need to be "financially centred". There is also a focus on consequences both for the child – "impact on the quality of their life" – and for the authority in terms of reduced costs. What is not clear is how these conflicts can be resolved or what can inform professional behaviour in such circumstances.

Theme 5: ethical intentions and consequence

Students demonstrated awareness that you may act with the best of intentions, suggesting the adoption of a 'utilitarian framework' (Reynolds, 2006), but that does not mean that the outcome is necessarily positive. The consequences could be negative not only for the client but also for the professional, in terms of the potential repercussions of their actions via their regulatory body.

Review of teaching and learning approaches and a way forward

The findings from the focus group interviews suggest that students had an awareness of personal ethics, including its evolving nature, contextual influences and resultant individual differences. However, there was no reference to ethical theories underpinning personal ethics. This reflected a gap in the students' baseline knowledge. Students were aware of the significance of professional ethics, viewing codes as offering guidance to professional behaviour and leading to positive consequences for both clients and professionals. They were able to identify ethical dilemmas in professional practice, such as those arising from conflict with personal values, working with professionals with different codes of ethics and examples of conflict between professional values and the employing organisation's priorities. However, the students did not refer to ways of addressing such dilemmas in their professional practice, such as the use of EDM models (for example Miner and Petocz, 2003; Ehrich et al, 2011), again reflecting a gap in their knowledge base. Students acknowledged the importance of professional development, including the role of formal training, peer support, supervision, working in groups and opportunities for reflection.

These findings offered insights into students' level of knowledge and understanding about ethics at the beginning of their professional training and were considered in the context of findings from the analysis of approaches to the teaching and learning of ethics (as reported earlier in the chapter). This analysis indicated a need to incorporate more explicit teaching of ethical theory and EDM models in the training programme. Although there was some exposure to ethical theory in lectures, this knowledge and understanding should be deepened, for example through application to exemplar case studies. There should be a greater focus on developing ethical reasoning and decision-making skills through consideration of models and frameworks (for example, Miner and Petocz, 2003). A number of writers have advocated the teaching of moral philosophy to assist in EDM (for example, Miner and Petocz, 2003; Ehrich et al, 2011). EDM models would assist in understanding and addressing ethical conflicts in the context of interprofessional working. Some of the students in this study assisted in the development of joint experiential problem-based learning with social work students, piloted in session 2012–13. This offers the opportunity for students to learn about respective roles and values in a safe environment in which they are supported by tutors and peers to reflect on their personal and professional values and those of students in other disciplines.

Reviewing programme learning outcomes from a positive ethics perspective (Handelsman et al, 2005; Gottlieb et al, 2008; Aoyagi and Portenga, 2010), there appeared to be insufficient emphasis on students developing a self-awareness of their personal value base. In psychotherapy practice, Tjeltveit and Gottlieb (2010) emphasise the importance of being reflexive, acknowledging the influence of values and feelings on professional decision making to prevent 'ethical infractions' (p 98). They advocate that teaching ethics in the curriculum is not sufficient and students should be supported in becoming more self-aware of their value base. This self-awareness is a basis for developing an aspirational perspective and approach to their profession. Handelsman et al (2005) highlight the importance of the 'implicit' curriculum for students learning about ethics and ethical practice. In contrast to the explicit curriculum, where ethics is taught through the course content, the 'implicit' curriculum is where 'students absorb the ethical lessons within the milieu of their institutions' (p 739). On this educational psychology programme there is both an 'explicit' curriculum (for example, lectures on ethics) and an 'implicit' curriculum where tutors aim to model respectful and collegiate behaviour and to demonstrate care and support for students, while challenging students to continually aspire to develop their practice.

This systematic review of teaching and learning about ethics, while focused on one professional training programme for educational psychologists in Scotland, offers valuable insights for other professional training programmes (for example, social work) in the UK and further afield. It provides a framework for undertaking a review (see Figure 18.1) that incorporates investigation into the knowledge, understanding and skills of students at various stages in the programme. The authors intend to carry out a longitudinal investigation with the participants in this study at the end of their probationary period in September 2013 in order to compare their ethical perspectives with those at the beginning of their professional training.

References

Ambrose, M.L., Arnaud, A.A. and Schminke, M. (2008) 'Individual moral development and ethical climate: the influence of person–organisation fit on job attitudes', *Journal of Business Studies*, vol 77, no 3, pp 323–33.

Aoyagi, M.W. and Portenga, S.T. (2010) 'The role of positive ethics and virtues in the context of sports and performance psychology service delivery', *Professional Psychology Research and Practice*, vol 4, no 3, pp 253–9.

Braun, V. and Clarke, V. (2006) 'Using thematic analysis in psychology', *Qualitative Research in Psychology*, vol 3, pp 77–101, doi: 10.1191/1478088706qp 063oa.

British Psychological Society (BPS) (2009) *Code of ethics and conduct*, Leicester: BPS.

British Psychological Society (BPS) (2010) *Accreditation through partnership handbook: Guidance for educational psychology programmes in Scotland*, Leicester: BPS.

Bronfenbrenner, U. (1979) *The ecology of human development: Experiments by nature and design*, Cambridge, MA: Harvard University Press.

Dailor, N.A. and Jacob, S. (2011) 'Ethically challenging situations reported by school psychologists: implications for training', *Psychology in the Schools*, vol 48, no 6, pp 619–31.

Ehrich, L.C., Kimber, M., Millwater, J. and Cranstone, N. (2011) 'Ethical dilemmas: a model to understand teacher practice', *Teachers and Teaching*, vol 17, no 2, pp 173–85.

Elango, B., Paul, K., Kundu, S.K. and Paudel, S.K. (2010) 'Organisational ethics, individual ethics and ethical intentions in international decision making', *Journal of Business Ethics*, vol 97, pp 543–61.

Goolsby, J.L., Mack, D.A. and Quick, J.C. (2010) 'Winning by staying in bounds: Good outcomes from positive ethics', *Organisational Dynamics*, vol 39, no 3, pp 248–57, doi:10.1016/j.orgdyn.2010.03.007.

Gottlieb, M.C., Handelsman, M.M. and Knapp, S. (2008) 'Some principles for ethics education: implementing the acculturation model', *Training and Education in Professional Psychology*, vol 2, no 3, pp 123–8.

Handelsman, M.M., Knapp, S. and Gottlieb, M.C. (2005) 'Positive ethics', in C.R. Snyder and S.J. Lopez (eds) *Handbook of positive psychology*, New York: Oxford University Press, pp 731–44.

Health Professions Council (HPC) (2008) *Standards of conduct, performance and ethics*, London: HPC.

Healy, L.M. (2007) 'Universalism and cultural relativism in social work ethics', *International Social Work*, vol 50, no 1, pp 11–26.

Illingworth, S. (2004) *Approaches to ethics in higher education: Learning and teaching in ethics across the curriculum*. Leeds: PRS-LTSN.

Karakas, F. and Sarigollu, E. (2012) 'Benevolent leadership: conceptualisation and construct development', *Journal of Business Ethics*, vol 108, pp 357–553, doi: 10.1007/s10551-011-1109-1.

King, N. and Horrocks, C. (2010) *Interviews in qualitative research*, London: Sage.

Lindsay, G. (2009) 'Professional ethics in psychology', *Papeles del Psicólogo*, vol 30, no 3, pp 184–94.

Miner, M. and Petocz, A. (2003) 'Moral theory in ethical decision making: problems, clarifications and recommendations from a psychological perspective', *Journal of Business Ethics*, vol 42, pp 11–25.

Reynolds, S.J. (2006) 'Moral awareness and ethical predispositions: investigating the role of individuals differences in the recognition of moral issues', *Journal of Applied Psychology*, vol 91, no 1 pp 233–43.

Seider, S., Davis, K. and Gardner, H. (2007) 'Good work in psychology', *The Psychologist*, vol 20, no 11, pp 672–6.

Seligman, M.E.P. (2003) *Authentic happiness*, London: Nicholas Brealey Publishing.

Seligman, M.E.P. (2006) *Learned optimism*, New York: Vintage Books.

Seligman, M.E.P., Steen, T.A., Park, N. and Peterson, C. (2005) 'Positive psychology progress: empirical validation of interventions', *American Psychologist*, vol 60, no 5, pp 410–21. doi: 10.1037/0003-066X.60.5.40.

Svensson, G. and Wood, G. (2003) 'The dynamics of business ethics: a function of time and culture – cases and models', *Management Decision*, vol 41, no 4, pp 350–61, doi: 10.1108/00251740310471195.

Thiroux, J.P. and Krasemann, K.W. (2009) *Ethics theory and practice* (10th edn), New Jersey: Prentice Hall.

Tjeltveit, A.C. and Gottlieb, M.C. (2010) 'Avoiding the road to ethical disaster: overcoming vulnerabilities and developing resilience', *Psychotherapy Theory, Research, Practice, Training*, vol 47, no 1, pp 98–110.

NINETEEN

Professionalism in workplace learning: understanding interprofessional dilemmas through healthcare student narratives

Charlotte E. Rees, Lynn V. Monrouxe and Rola Ajjawi

Introduction

This chapter, in line with the aims of Part Six (see Figure 1.1), provides an insight into how ethical mindfulness can be developed as healthcare students experience **interprofessional** dilemmas within workplace learning. Healthcare students learn professionalism and how to *become* professionals through the formal, informal and hidden curriculum. This chapter begins by utilising theoretical and research literature to introduce the concepts of healthcare professionalism, professional identities and interprofessional learning. The case study draws on an exemplar narrative from an extensive research programme exploring healthcare students' lived experiences of professionalism dilemmas to demonstrate how students make sense of their experiences and developing identities through narratives of interprofessional dilemmas. The chapter, using multiple lenses such as moral identities and moral distress, concludes by discussing the interweaving of professional identity formation and interprofessional hierarchies, roles and conflicts, and what this means for the education of healthcare students so that they are better prepared for the interprofessional healthcare workplace.

The professional development of healthcare students is paramount in health professions education (Nursing and Midwifery Council (NMC), 2009; General Medical Council (GMC), 2013). Although students are taught good professional practice throughout their formal curriculum, they are commonly exposed to professionalism dilemmas in workplace learning, including ethical lapses such as witnessing the physical and emotional maltreatment of patients (Erdil and Korkmaz,

2009). Such dilemmas can cause students moral distress, which can happen when students know the 'right' ethical course of action but feel unable to act in that manner (Jameton, 1984). Dilemmas can therefore impact negatively on students' developing professionalism (Kushner and Thomasma, 2001). This chapter is not concerned with formal interprofessional education initiatives, of which many are reported in the literature (Lennon-Dearing et al, 2009). Instead, it is interested in how healthcare students learn with, from and about others through interprofessional workplace learning experiences. It is through these experiences (and dilemmas therein) that students come to learn what it means to demonstrate professionalism and how to *become* professionals. Ultimately, such interprofessional workplace learning experiences should help to prepare students to work with a wide range of healthcare professionals, to understand their roles within the wider healthcare system and to experience team-based collaborative care prior to their graduation (for example, Thistlethwaite, 2012).

Healthcare professionalism

Although there is no single overarching definition of what healthcare professionalism is (Hafferty, 2006; Monrouxe et al, 2011), some organisations have attempted to define professionalism; for example, as 'a set of values, behaviours and relationships that underpins the trust the public has in doctors' (Royal College of Physicians (RCP), 2005, p 14). While definitions are scant in the literature, the term 'professionalism' is commonly associated with a list of individual characteristics thought to be at the very heart of professionalism (NMC, 2009; GMC, 2013). Medical professionalism has been described as being underpinned by ethical and legal understanding, communication skills and clinical competence, upon which principles such as altruism, humanism, excellence and accountability are built (Arnold and Stern, 2006). Although some characteristics (for example, integrity) are commonly mentioned across the healthcare literature by various scholars and organisations, the importance attributed to any one characteristic varies according to time, person and place (Hafferty, 2006). Furthermore, the meanings of these characteristics differ according to the discourse within which they are situated (for example, individual, collective, interpersonal, complexity: Monrouxe et al, 2011). Understandings of the term 'healthcare professionalism' are therefore context specific (Monrouxe et al, 2011). What is notable in its absence from these numerous lists of characteristics, however, is the concept of professional identities.

Professional identities

Learning medicine or nursing involves more than learning the knowledge and skills associated with those professions. Learning is also a process of *becoming*: learning to think, talk and act like a doctor or a nurse (Monrouxe, 2010). It is thought that the development of a strong professional identity is the cornerstone to practising professionalism (Monrouxe, 2010). Identities are co-constructed through an internal–external dialectic process of identification with particular social groups and individuals and difference from others (Jenkins, 2008); for example, medical students identifying with the medical profession and differentiating themselves from the nursing profession (Sims, 2011). Such professional identity formation needs to be integrated with primary identities like gender. Any healthcare student will hold multiple identities, such as 'white male nurse', and these multiple identities may operate in four different ways, having different implications for those considered to be members of the *in-* and *out-group* (Roccas and Brewer, 2002). First, identities may *intersect*, so all other 'white male nurses' will be in the in-group (Roccas and Brewer, 2002). Second, identities may operate within a *hierarchy* with one (for example, nurse) having dominance over the others, so all nurses will be in the in-group. Third, identities may be *compartmentalised*, with certain identities being activated in particular contexts, such as male identities being activated within the setting of a male changing room. Within this context all other males will be considered the in-group. Finally, identities may be *merged* so that the 'white male nurse' identifies with all people with any of these three identities. Also important within the context of professionalism development is the construct of moral identities, which play an important mediation role between moral judgement and action. For example, a nursing student will be more likely to act ethically in the face of a professionalism dilemma if they have a strong self-identity as a moral person (Blasi, 1983). Ultimately, how learners come to understand and develop their moral and professional identities has implications for their interprofessional relationships (Monrouxe, 2010; see also Chapter Five for a discussion of identities).

Interprofessional learning

While numerous formal interprofessional initiatives are discussed in the literature (Lennon-Dearing et al, 2009), few studies consider interprofessionalism learning within the context of the healthcare workplace (Reeves et al, 2009; Wright et al, 2012). Socialisation into specific healthcare professions influences the professional identity formation of members of those groups (Whitehead, 2007; Baker et al, 2011). For example, doctors come to perceive themselves as 'leaders' and 'decision makers', while nurses come to view themselves as 'team members' (Whitehead, 2007; Baker et al, 2011). Interprofessional education research suggests that role boundaries are socially constructed sites of 'practice and power play' and ultimately serve to establish who is included and excluded from particular interactions (Whitehead, 2007; Sims, 2011). Furthermore, role ambiguity (role erosion or extension) can also be a source of tension between different healthcare groups (King and Ross, 2003). It is these different roles and responsibilities and power asymmetries, alongside different professional identities, that can create interprofessional conflict, particularly in the context of decision making (Whitehead, 2007). Furthermore, intergroup discrimination and stereotyping can occur early in training (Hean et al, 2006). Several studies have suggested common stereotypes developing, such as the 'arrogant doctor', 'technically competent doctor', 'doctor leader', 'caring nurse' and so on (Wright et al, 2012). Ultimately, such strong social group identity can act as a barrier to effective teamwork (Lloyd et al, 2011) and lead to the marginalisation of certain healthcare groups (Ajjawi et al, 2009).

Workplace professionalism narratives

This chapter draws on a research programme exploring healthcare students' experiences of professionalism dilemmas, that is, day-to-day workplace learning experiences in which students witness or participate in something that they think is unethical, unprofessional or immoral (Feudtner et al, 1994). Comprising four interlinked studies across five countries (England, Wales, Scotland, Northern Ireland and Australia) and with 4,065 participants (from two online questionnaires and 41 group and 25 individual interviews), over 2,000 oral or written narratives of professionalism dilemmas were collected.

A personal incident narrative is 'a report of a sequence of events that have entered into the biography of the speaker' (Labov, 1997, p 398). Classic elements of a narrative include the abstract (summary), orientation (participants, setting, timing), complicating action (sequence of actions, problem, turning point), most reportable event (least common event with greatest impact on narrator), resolution (complicating action following most reportable event), evaluation (narrator's commentary) and coda (return to the present) (Labov and Waletzky, 1967; Labov, 1997). From an individual perspective, narratives help individuals to make sense of their experiences, actions and identities (Smith and Sparkes, 2008; Rees et al, 2013). From a social-relational perspective, narrators typically attempt to portray themselves in a positive light and engage in identity work when sharing experiences (Riessman, 2008; Rees et al, 2013).

The preliminary thematic framework analysis of these narratives (Monrouxe and Rees, 2012) demonstrates that just over 10% of narratives collected are interprofessional in nature. Common dilemmas recounted within these interprofessional narratives include: students participating in or witnessing breaches of patient safety and dignity, students participating in patient care without valid **consent**, students' inability to challenge others' lapses of professionalism and students being recipients of **abuse** from healthcare professionals. This chapter presents just one story and its in-depth narrative analysis to illustrate the interweaving of identity construction and interprofessional issues common to workplace learning.

Mike's narrative

Mike is a male, final-year nursing student at a UK school of nursing and his professionalism narrative includes a common dilemma recounted by research participants: challenging a professionalism lapse of a senior healthcare professional (in this case, the breaching of patient safety, dignity and consent). This narrative has been selected because Mike's dilemma is interprofessional: he challenges a medical consultant, and in narrating this challenge he engages in interesting identity work, constructing the patient as **victim**, the consultant as villain and himself as hero. What is also interesting about this narrative is the various interprofessional issues raised (Box 19.1).

Box 19.1

"Mummy, ask them to stop"

ORIENTATION

Mike: Er a dilemma on placement, first-year student, myself second placement, er I was in a side room on the ward in [names hospital] looking after a 92-year-old gentlemen who was suffering from bladder retention ...

COMPLICATING ACTION

Mike: They tried to insert the catheter overnight to no avail ...

ORIENTATION

Mike: I was in the room with him, carrying out personal care and the consultant and two FY2s came in ...

COMPLICATING ACTION

Make: and proceeded to attempt to insert the catheter, eh, the consultant had a go, the FY2s had a go to no avail, continually pushing this catheter in, blood every place, all over the wall, blood up the wall and that is no exaggeration, the old man was screaming for them to stop and

EVALUATION

Mike: I was standing as a first-year student and you've got this consultant who, although he was smaller in height to me, he was much, much larger in stature, presence because he was a consultant and, you know, as a first-year student consultants are only one step away from being God, sometimes, or they think they are … eh not knowing what to do, standing at the bedside holding the old man's hand, trying to calm him down …

MOST REPORTABLE EVENT

Mike: That was when the old man turned and looked and his exact words were "Mummy ask them to stop, they're hurting me" … But then I stepped in and I almost physically ejected the consultant and the two FY1s, FY2s from the room.

RESOLUTION

Charlotte: What, what did you say?

Mike: Eh, to be totally honest I can't remember. It was along the lines of "enough is enough. The man is in pain, the man is now crying for his mother at 92 years old, you three aren't listening, you three are not touching that patient" …

EVALUATION

Mike: I kicked them out … I was then dragged over the coals … later on by that consultant who was then subsequently dragged over the coals by the charge nurse for talking to me like that.

COMPLICATING ACTION

Mike: He [consultant] told me, um, regardless whether I was a student or a nurse, I had no right to eject him or tell him to stop the procedure, to eject him and these FY2s from the room. I was there to hold hand and to clean up when they were finished. What he didn't realise was that where he was standing having a go at me the senior charge nurse was standing behind him … so when he finished with me she started on him … And he came back and apologised … to me.

EVALUATION

Mike: The dilemma was that still rankles me was should I have let it go on as long as it did … or should I have stopped it a lot, lot sooner, and that's the dilemma of being a first-year student. I'd never, ever worked in the care sector before. I was a [names previous manual job] before I was a nurse. Eh how much pain had that old man gone through before I'd stopped the procedure? ... and then you get the consultant who tries to chastise you in the ward in the middle of people, in front of people eh, and I was lucky enough to have a fantastic senior charge nurse and mentor, staff nurse mentor ... they [doctors] didn't approach it [catheterisation] with a caring (heart), it was, "rough" is being nice, I mean they were ramming this catheter tube in ... physically violent eh, the dilemma I had was how fast should I have (halted) that? ...

Charlotte: Why did you challenge at the point? ...

Mike: Looking past me at something behind me and asking "mummy", not "mum", "mummy", a 92 year old man using the word "mummy", "please get them to stop, they're hurting me", that was enough, that was enough.

Charlotte: So that's what was the trigger for you, and then, when he gave you the dressing down, which is presumably in front of the charge nurse? ...

EVALUATION

Mike: Which was unprofessional in his [my] view, if he wanted a word he should have maybe taken me aside ... he was loud enough to be heard through the ward ...

COMPLICATING ACTION

Mike: She was actually walking down the ward, eh when he got hold of me. It was more, "you come here, who do you think you are? You're here for this". And because his voice was so loud she heard the whole thing as she walked in behind him ... And she lay into – it only lasted 30 seconds.

EVALUATION

Mike: But eh she'd done the professional thing, she took him aside, she took him to his office ...

COMPLICATING ACTION

Mike: Her exact words were "My office, now" ... and, and she took me in as well ... So what she said to me is "if he thinks he's big enough to give me a dressing down in front of people, he's got to be big enough to accept a dressing down in front of you", which happened and he came back and apologised the following day ...

EVALUATION

Mike: It'd been a fantastic placement, eh, I got on well with the staff, eh, you know I worked extra hours when they were short just because I enjoyed it so much, fantastic and I would actually go back there and work as a healthcare assistant from the bank …The dilemma at the time was … one, should I have stepped in earlier, two, that was extreme bad practice eh, and what was also worrying was that the FY2s were doing what the consultant was telling them to do and they couldn't see what they were doing was causing, I mean there was huge blood loss, he actually ended up on a blood transfusion that afternoon, ended up having an emergency supra-pubic catheter put in as well … One of them, I got the impression he was concerned of what was happening, but again, he was with the consultant which is … I don't know how the medical side works, but eh yeah, I have no problems with the FY2s because they were doing what they were asked to do, told to do, and you know, it was either do it or suffer the consequences, it was the consultant that was the problem.

*The following notations are used in the transcription: … speech edited out for sake of brevity; [ ] additional information; ( ) unclear speech, what we think is said. Mike's professionalism dilemma takes place about two years earlier, at the start of his training on a hospital ward and involves an elderly patient, a medical consultant, a senior charge nurse and two Foundation Year 2 doctors (FY2, fully registered doctors in their second year of training post-graduation).

While Mike witnesses professionalism lapses on the part of the doctors (all three attempt catheterisation, despite the patient's pleas for them to stop, and Mike is later verbally chastised by the consultant for stopping the procedure) and his senior nursing colleague (who verbally chastises the medical consultant), the dilemma for Mike concerns the patient's painful and bloody catheterisation by the doctors and whether he should have stopped the procedure earlier (note that he repeats this three times in his narrative, emphasising his moral distress in the face of this professionalism lapse by the doctors). It is interesting to see how Mike constructs the identities of the patient, the consultant and himself and his fellow nursing colleague as he narrates the dilemma (see Box 19.1).

Patient as victim

Although Mike begins his narrative by constructing the patient as a 'case' ("a 92-year-old gentlemen who was suffering from bladder retention"), he constructs this elderly man as a scared, vulnerable and powerless child as the story unfolds. This is emphasised through his repeated reported talk of the patient screaming or crying for his "Mummy". By constructing this older man as a scared and vulnerable child, he simultaneously constructs this consultant's villainous actions as all the more dastardly.

Doctor as villain

Despite all three doctors having "a go" at catheterising the patient, Mike constructs only the consultant as the villain. He explains that he had "no problems with the FY2s" because he understood that if they challenged their consultant they would suffer negative consequences, which serves to further demonise the consultant. The consultant is constructed as immoral, uncaring and physically violent towards the patient. He is also described as "unprofessional" for his public chastisement of Mike. While Mike suggests that the consultant is physically smaller in height, compared to himself, contesting the consultant's masculine identity, he nevertheless refers to the consultant as metaphorically larger in terms of his stature, therefore constructing the consultant as professionally powerful and authoritative. Although Mike draws on the common metaphor of DOCTOR AS GOD, he now contests this construction by implying that it is only doctors who think they *are* God. Mike therefore constructs the consultant as arrogant and lacking insight. This arrogance, coupled with physical size, is echoed later in the narrative where the senior nurse is reported to have said about the consultant: "if he thinks he's big enough …" Through both Mike's talk and the reported talk of his senior nursing colleague, this consultant's masculine identity is contested as he is metaphorically brought back down to size.

Nurse as hero

Mike constructs himself and his nursing colleague as heroes within this narrative. Mike's masculine identity is activated just before and during his narration of the most reportable event, in which he claims to be physically bigger than the male consultant, and by describing how he "almost" physically ejected the doctors from the patient's room. This simultaneously serves to construct his identity as both a moral and an authoritative person. This construction of his authoritative self continues later as he refers to himself as "nurse" rather than "first year student", possibly reflecting his current professional identity construction as a soon-to-be-nurse. His self-construction as hero continues further as he positions himself as personable and hard working. In contrast to Mike's villainous construction of the medical consultant, he constructs his senior charge nurse as hero and moral person, referring to her as "fantastic", and "professional" in how she verbally chastises the consultant in a private office.

Interprofessional issues

In Mike's narrative there are three interprofessional issues interwoven with this identity work that are worthy of further consideration.

Hierarchies

Mike alludes to the "consultant" having much higher status and presence than him "as a first year student". That Mike fails to state the consultant's medical identity or his own nursing identity implies that hierarchies are at least partly related to level of training. Mike, as a first year nursing student, however, contests this hierarchy in challenging the three doctors by stopping the procedure and kicking them out of the patient's room. Here, Mike suggests that it is not his student identity that the consultant takes issue with, but the fact that Mike represents nursing. Mike continues with reported talk from the consultant implying that Mike does not know his place in this healthcare hierarchy; "who do you think you are?" So Mike is both at the bottom of this healthcare hierarchy because he is a student *and* a nurse, and the consultant is at the top of the hierarchy because he is a consultant *and* a doctor.

Roles and responsibilities

As a nursing student, Mike makes his roles and responsibilities clear at the start of his story: that he was there to carry out "personal care" for the patient and that when interrupted by the three doctors whose responsibility it was to carry out the technical procedure, his task continued to involve caring for the patient: "holding the old man's hand, trying to calm him down". He constructs his professional role therefore as caring patient advocate. His roles and responsibilities as student nurse are reiterated later in the form of reported talk of the consultant, who reminds Mike that "I was there to hold hand and to clean up when they were finished". While Mike implies that the consultant feels that Mike has overstepped the boundaries of the healthcare hierarchy, Mike's challenge is coherent with his self-construction as patient advocate.

Conflict

The conflict between doctors and nurses can be seen clearly in this narrative in Mike's descriptions of the verbal altercations between himself–consultant and consultant–charge nurse. Mike's metaphoric talk illustrates this conflict, such as "kicked them out", "dragged over the coals", "lay into", and "medical side", which implies the conceptual metaphor of DOCTOR–NURSE RELATIONSHIP AS WAR (Rees et al, 2007, 2009). The war metaphor has numerous entailments, including doctors and nurses being on opposing sides in a relationship characterised by violence. This 'them and us' quality of the doctor–nurse relationship is further illustrated by Mike's use of the pronouns "they" and "you" to refer to the consultant and the junior doctors ("they think they are"; "you three aren't listening") throughout his narrative (Rees and Monrouxe, 2008).

Conclusions

From an individual perspective, Mike makes sense of his interprofessional workplace learning experience, his actions and his personal and professional identities (such as male nurse) through his narration of this dilemma (Smith and Sparkes, 2008; Rees et al, 2013). Through this narrative, Mike comes to understand what it means to be professional (for example, by challenging others' professionalism lapses) and to become a nurse. Indeed, while constructing his own masculine identity and simultaneously contesting the consultant's masculinity, Mike's dominant identity work in this story is his positioning as a nurse (Monrouxe, 2010). From his medical talk ("a 92-year-old gentleman ...") through to his self-labelling as "nurse", even though not yet qualified, Mike constructs his healthcare professional identity. Through this dilemma, Mike learns something of the culture of healthcare in terms of hierarchies (for example, medical dominance/ nurse disempowerment), role boundaries (for example, nurse as carer, doctor as technician) and conflict (Whitehead, 2007; Baker et al, 2011). This understanding is not only reflected in what Mike says in his narrative but also in how he narrates his experience with metaphoric and pronominal talk (Rees et al, 2007; Rees and Monrouxe, 2008; Rees et al, 2009).

From a social-relational perspective, Mike attempts to portray himself in a positive light by constructing himself as hero; he simultaneously positions himself as a professional and moral person (he does the right thing by stopping the catheterisation), personable (he gets on well with other staff), and hard working (he works extra hours). While he clearly identifies with his senior charge nurse, who is similarly constructed as hero (for example, "fantastic", "professional"), he differentiates himself from the villainous consultant. He constructs the consultant as immoral, uncaring and physically violent towards the patient and unprofessional in his verbal abuse of Mike. Consistent with common stereotypes, Mike positions himself and his nursing colleague as caring patient advocates (for example, Wright et al, 2012). While Mike draws on one common stereotype of doctors (the "arrogant doctor") to construct the medical consultant, he simultaneously provides a counter-stereotypic construction of all three doctors (that is 'the technically-incompetent doctor': Wright et al, 2012). Mike's identification with nurses (in-group) and differentiation from doctors (out-group) appears to be important in two ways: by differentiating himself from the doctors he distances himself from their professionalism lapse, thereby professing his own professionalism, and he embraces his own professional identity formation as a nurse.

So, what do these findings mean for the education of healthcare students so that they are better prepared for the interprofessional workplace? Students often receive inconsistent messages about professionalism from the formal and the informal curriculum; for example, as part of the formal curriculum within the university they are taught to maintain patient dignity, and yet as part of the informal curriculum within the workplace they observe qualified professionals breaching patient dignity (Monrouxe and Rees, 2012). Students often 'go along' with such lapses despite knowing the appropriate ethical course of action (Rees and Monrouxe, 2011), and this lack of moral action can cause students moral distress (Jameton, 1984; Monrouxe et al, 2012). Despite Mike narrating that he did act ethically (by stopping the doctors' catheterisation of the patient), it is still apparent from his narrative that he experienced moral distress, this being emphasised by his repeated regret over not having stopped the procedure earlier. Furthermore, values promoted in formal interprofessional education initiatives that are not reflected within the workplace can lead to reinforcement of interprofessional stereotypes and cynicism among trainees (Whitehead, 2007). Therefore, there needs to be a shift from conflict between the formal and the informal curriculum to one of complementarity between the two.

One way of achieving this is to provide healthcare students with the opportunity as part of the formal curriculum to discuss their workplace learning experiences (Rees and Monrouxe, 2011; Monrouxe and Rees, 2012). These opportunities could take a similar format to the group discussions used as part of this research programme, that is, safe and open fora to allow discussion between small groups of healthcare students, facilitated by educators without assessment responsibilities for those students. Rather as in the authors' interviews, facilitators could employ narrative interviewing techniques to elicit students' lived experiences of their interprofessional dilemmas and then use those stories to trigger discussion about healthcare professionalism and professionalism lapses, students' action and moral distress in the face of lapses, professional identity formation, interprofessional hierarchies, boundaries and conflict. Within such groups, healthcare students should be able to make sense of their own and others' professionalism, their own professional identity formation and the professional identities and roles of others, and to ultimately practise effective teamwork and collaboration within the healthcare workplace. Ultimately, clinical educators have an important role in promoting interprofessionalism in the workplace. They need to recognise the important role that they play in modelling collaborative practice and stereotypes, and misconceptions need to be addressed systematically and proactively.

References

Ajjawi, R., Hyde, S., Roberts, C. and Nisbet, G. (2009) 'Marginalisation of dental students in a shared medical and dental education programme', *Medical Education*, vol 43, no 3, pp 238–45.

Arnold, L. and Stern, D.T. (2006) 'What is medical professionalism?', in D.T. Stern (ed) *Measuring medical professionalism*, New York: Oxford University Press, pp 15–37.

Baker, L., Egan-Lee, E., Martimiankis, M.A. and Reeves, S. (2011) 'Relationships of power: implications for interprofessional education', *Journal of Interprofessional Care*, vol 25, pp 98–104.

Blasi, A. (1983) 'Moral cognition and moral action: a theoretical perspective', *Developmental Review*, vol 3, pp 178–210.

Erdil, F. and Korkmaz, F. (2009) 'Ethical problems observed by student nurses', *Nursing Ethics*, vol 16, no 5, pp 589–98.

Feudtner, C., Christakis, D. and Christakis, N. (1994) 'Do clinical clerks suffer ethical erosion? Students' perceptions of their ethical environment and personal development', *Academic Medicine*, vol 69, no 8, pp 670–9.

GMC (General Medical Council) (2013) *Good medical practice*, London: General Medical Council; www.gmc-uk.org/static/documents/content/GMP_2013.pdf_51447599.pdf

Hafferty, F.W. (2006) 'Definitions of professionalism. A search for meaning and identity', *Clinical Orthopaedics and Related Research*, vol 449, pp 193–204.

Hean, S., Macleod-Clark, J., Adams, K. and Humphris, D. (2006) 'Will opposites attract? Similarities and differences in students' perceptions of the stereotype profiles of other health and social care professional groups', *Journal of Interprofessional Care*, vol 20, no 2, pp 162–81.

Jameton, A. (1984) *Nursing practice: The ethical issues*, New York: Prentice Hall.

Jenkins, R. (2008) *Social identity* (3rd edn), Abingdon: Routledge.

King, N. and Ross, A. (2003) 'Professional identities and interprofessional relations: evaluation of collaborative community schemes', *Social Work in Health Care*, vol 38, no 2, pp 51–72.

Kushner, T.K. and Thomasma, D.C. (2001) *Ward ethics: Dilemmas for medical students and doctors in training*, Cambridge: Cambridge University Press.

Labov, W. (1997) 'Some further steps in narrative analysis', *Journal of Narrative Life History*, vol 7, pp 395–415.

Labov, W. and Waletzky, J. (1967) 'Narrative analysis. Oral versions of personal experience', in J. Helm (ed) *Essays on the verbal and visual arts*, Seattle, WA: American Ethnological Society, University of Washington Press, pp 12–44.

Lennon-Dearing, R., Lowry, L.S., Ross, C.W. and Dyer, A.R. (2009) 'An interprofessional course in bioethics: training for real-world dilemmas', *Journal of Interprofessional Care*, vol 23, no 6, pp 574–85.

Lloyd, J.V., Schneider, J., Scales, K., Bailey, S. and Jones, R. (2011) 'Ingroup identity as an obstacle to effective multiprofessional and interprofessional teamwork: findings from an ethnographic study of healthcare assistants in dementia care', *Journal of Interprofessional Care*, vol 25, no 5, pp 345–51.

Monrouxe, L.V. (2010) 'Identity, identification and medical education: why should we care?', *Medical Education*, vol 44, no 1, pp 40–9.

Monrouxe, L.V. and Rees, C.E. (2012) '"It's just a clash of cultures": emotional talk within medical students' narratives of professionalism dilemmas', *Advances in Health Sciences Education*, vol 17, no 5, pp 671–701.

Monrouxe, L.V., Rees, C.E. and Hu, W. (2011) 'Differences in medical students' explicit discourses of medical professionalism: acting, representing, becoming', *Medical Education*, vol 45, no 6, pp 585–602.

Monrouxe, L.V., Rees, C.E., Joyce, D.W. and Wells, S. (2012) 'Professionalism dilemmas during workplace learning: the impact of frequency of occurrence and gender on students' moral distress', paper presented at the ASME Annual Scientific Meeting, Brighton, UK, 18–20 July 2012.

NMC (Nursing and Midwifery Council) (2009) *Guidance on professional conduct for nursing and midwifery students*, London: Nursing and Midwifery Council, www.nmc-uk.org/Documents/Guidance/NMC-Guidance-on-professional-conduct-for-nursing-and-midwifery-students.pdf.

RCP (Royal College of Physicians) (2005) *Doctors in society: Medical professionalism in a changing world*, London: RCP, http://bookshop.rcplondon.ac.uk/contents/pub75–241bae2f-4b63–4ea9–8f63–99d67c573ca9.pdf.

Rees, C.E., Knight, L.V. and Cleland, J.A. (2009) 'Medical educators' metaphoric talk about their assessment relationship with students: "You don't want to sort of be the one who sticks the knife in them"', *Assessment & Evaluation in Higher Education*, vol 34, no 4, pp 455–67.

Rees, C.E., Knight, L.V. and Wilkinson, C.E. (2007) '"Doctors being up there and we being down here": a metaphorical analysis of talk about student/doctor–patient relationships', *Social Science & Medicine*, vol 65, no 4, pp 725–37.

Rees, C.E. and Monrouxe, L.V. (2008) '"Is it alright if I–um–we unbutton your pyjama top now?" Pronominal use in bedside teaching encounters', *Communication & Medicine*, vol 5, no 2, pp 171–82.

Rees, C.E. and Monrouxe, L.V. (2011) 'Medical students learning intimate examinations without valid consent: a multi-centre study', *Medical Education*, vol 45, no 3, pp 261–72.

Rees, C.E., Monrouxe, L.V. and McDonald, L.A. (2013) 'Narrative, emotion and action: analysing "most memorable" professionalism dilemmas', *Medical Education*, vol 47, no 1, pp 80–96.

Reeves, S., Rice, K., Conn, L.G., Miller, K.L., Kenaszchuk, C. and Zwarenstein, M. (2009) 'Interprofessional interaction, negotiation and non-negotiation on general internal medicine wards', *Journal of Interprofessional Care*, vol 23, no 6, pp 633–45.

Riessman, C.K. (2008) *Narrative methods for the human sciences*, Thousand Oaks, CA: Sage Publications.

Roccas, S. and Brewer, M.B. (2002) 'Social identity complexity', *Personality Social Psychology Review*, vol 6, pp 88–106.

Sims, D. (2011) 'Reconstructing professional identity for professional and interprofessional practice: a mixed methods study of joint training programmes in learning disability nursing and social work', *Journal of Interprofessional Care*, vol 25, pp 265–71.

Smith, B. and Sparkes, A.C. (2008) 'Contrasting perspectives on narratives selves and identities: an invitation to dialogue', *Qualitative Research*, vol 8, pp 5–35.

Thistlethwaite, J. (2012) 'Interprofessional education: a review of context, learning and the research agenda', *Medical Education*, vol 46, pp 58–70.

Whitehead, C. (2007) 'The doctor dilemma in interprofessional education and care: how and why will physicians collaborate?', *Medical Education*, vol 41, pp 1010–16.

Wright, A., Hawkes, G., Baker, B. and Lindqvist, M. (2012) 'Reflections and unprompted observations by healthcare students of an interprofessional shadowing visit', *Journal of Interprofessional Care*, vol 26, pp 305–11.

TWENTY

Understanding the dynamics of personal, professional and interprofessional ethics: a possible way forward

Divya Jindal-Snape and Elizabeth F.S. Hannah

This chapter will revisit the themes, concepts and theories considered in Chapter One; synthesise and summarise the common, as well as unique, themes emerging from Chapters Two to Nineteen to explore the possible reasons behind any tensions and, in line with the aims of Part Six (see Figure 1.1), consider a possible way forward. Through an exploration of the authors' 'lived experiences', this book provides a series of lenses focusing on what is happening in the real world as professionals negotiate and wrestle with tensions and conflicts in their day-to-day practice. Chapter One referred to the authors' interest in interprofessional working and consideration of ethics in that context. It set out their conceptual understanding of the terms 'ethics', 'personal ethics', 'professional ethics' and 'interprofessional ethics' and briefly considered some of the main ethical theories. These themes and theories will now be summarised to understand reasons for disjuncture and to provide suggestions that will inform future research and practice with the aim of reducing any disjuncture.

Dynamic identities in an interprofessional context

As noted in Chapter One, increasingly, there is recognition that interprofessional working is promising in terms of leading to more effective provision for service users, while it is acknowledged that there are a number of factors that negatively impact on effective implementation of this practice. Some of these arise from the multiple identities and terminologies used.

Professional identity can be very important, and most professional qualifying programmes explicitly set out to foster this. However, it seems that in trying to create a professional identity for themselves, professionals inevitably end up 'othering' other professionals. Othering, a concept first systematically theorised by Spivak (1985, cited in Jensen, 2009), has been described as a symbolic cultural code to create a split between 'them' and 'us', with 'us' usually being perceived to have positive and 'them' to have negative qualities (Krumer-Nevo, 2002). Rees and colleagues (Chapter Nineteen) provide the narrative of 'Mike', a nursing student who identified with other nursing staff and saw them as 'heroes', and othered the consultant and saw him as the 'villain'. Similar nuances can be picked up from MacEachern's (2011; Chapter Twelve) police officer, who used 'we' for the police officers and 'they' for social workers despite both working in the area of child protection. Soini and colleagues (Chapter Five) highlighted the fact that teachers engaged in ethical dialogue differently with their students than with their colleagues, which suggests that professionals are influenced by their identity in a particular context. Sometimes professional codes can lead to othering in an interprofessional context. Othering can also lead to a display of power dynamics and professionals being protective of their own profession. The potential negative impact of othering on interprofessional collaboration resonates with Zwarenstein et al's (2009) study, which revealed a number of factors that act as a barrier to interprofessional collaboration, including difficult power dynamics and cultural differences between different professionals (also see Chapter One).

In reality, most individuals belong to several social groups and, as such, have multiple identities, including as professionals, colleagues, parents and siblings. These identities are dynamic and change over time, with some considered to come to the fore in one context and others in another context. For example, the police officers in MacEachern (2011; Chapter Twelve) made comments about how they felt as parents and partners when they interviewed children who had been abused or those accused of abuse. Boyle in Chapter Eleven discusses how, in rural areas in Australia, psychologists have to be mindful of keeping their personal and professional identities and roles separate. Clemans and colleagues in Chapter Seven reflect upon their multiple identities as researchers, educators and contractors in delivering a government funded professional learning programme for teacher leaders; and the ethical dilemmas which they encountered and managed. An important question is whether such a separation is indeed possible or desirable. Also, research on multiple identities suggests that people can have up to seven significant identities and can function with several at the same time (Roccas and Brewer, 2002).

Although multiple identities and othering may result in intrapersonal and interpersonal tensions, research suggests that multiple identities can lead to personal benefits, due to the potential transfer of skills, knowledge and emotion from one role into another (for example, work–family enrichment of Greenhaus and Powell, 2006). Furthermore, empirical findings suggest that individuals who are able to work expertly with their multiple identities are more open to the different perspectives of others. Also, as has been observed from this chapter's authors' lived experience, professionals coming from very different professional backgrounds can find common ground through other identities, such as their parental or volunteering roles. These provide opportunities for a more open dialogue about personal and professional ethics, and possibly form the basis of trust and respect, thus potentially minimising the notion of the 'other'.

Similarly, with an increase in interprofessional collaboration, professionals come across different terminologies that can create perceived differences and add to the dynamic nature of their professional context. As well as creating their own identities, professionals create or make assumptions of others' identities, whether other professionals or service users. As can be seen in various chapters in this book, depending on the professional background of the author/s or their own identities, interesting differences appear, such as the use of terms like helping/supporting/empowering/creating opportunities to empower, and seeing the stakeholders as clients/service users/participants/ young people/patients/communities, thus putting themselves in the roles of helper, supporter, service provider and so on. From the experience of the authors of this chapter, differences in terminology can create tensions when working within an interprofessional team, as professionals sometimes equate this nomenclature with the personal and professional value base of the team members. Professionals may attempt to see within this terminology the power dynamics, hierarchy and top-down/bottom-up nature of each other's work. Interestingly, these identities of stakeholders are often created without consultation. A study that attempted to address this was conducted within a mental health community setting in England (Simmons et al, 2010). This investigation aimed to seek the views of 336 'receivers of mental health services' (p 21) about their preferred reference term according to the professionals (namely psychiatrist, nurse, psychologist, social worker and occupational therapist) with whom they consulted. The findings were very interesting, as the respondents expressed a preference based on the health professional they were consulting, 'patients' being the preferred term for most, unless they were seeing a social worker, in which case they preferred 'service user', with a few preferring the terms 'survivor' or 'user'. Simmons et al (2010) recommend that professionals should use evidence-based terminology; that is, instead of deciding what terminology *they* think should be used, they should get the views of their stakeholders. An important question is whether in this study the identified preferences for terminology were based on the terms that the professionals were using in that context. Therefore, terminology might be based on the professionals' own beliefs and values, the profession's guidelines and/or the preference of the people they work for and with (referred to in Simmons et al's study as 'receivers'). Similarly, other professionals' identities are perceived without an open dialogue with them about how they see themselves. In some ways, this also indicates the futility of reading too much into terminology, as 'service users' *themselves* preferred to be seen as patients. Further, it is important to remember that this identity as a service user or patient is only one aspect of the person's range of identities.

When considering interprofessional working, these different identities play a part in any interaction. However, for interprofessional practice to be effective, professionals have to be able to work together for a common goal and not be bound by the potentially impenetrable walls created by their rigid identities. The role of context was highlighted in Chapter One when considering different ethical theories, personal ethics, professional ethics and interprofessional ethics. This contextually dynamic environment in which professionals operate is considered next.

Dynamic environment

As seen earlier, differences in understanding of terminology can create a dynamic environment for the professional, potentially leading to tensions and dilemmas. For example, there has been debate about the use of the terms 'morals' and 'ethics', where they might be used differently or even interchangeably (see for example discussions by Greenaway and Roberts in Chapter Four; Raiker and Rautiainen, in Chapter Fourteen; Brewster and Strachan in Chapter Nine; Boyle in Chapter Eleven).

Culture, beliefs, religion and family-life experiences may act as contextual influences on the individual professional and can lead to differences in perception of life issues such as birth (Hodson and Deery in Chapter Ten) and death (Sweeney and Boge in Chapter Thirteen). This will impact on how different professionals understand and respond to such matters in their professional practice.

As highlighted by a number of chapter authors, the legislative and policy context affects the professional and those they work with in a variety of ways. In some cases this has led to practices of 'risk management' and 'covering one's back'. This has been highlighted in several chapters; for example, in the context of pre-birth assessment (Hodson and Deery in Chapter Ten), criminal justice social work (Fenton in Chapter Six), policing (MacEachern and colleagues in Chapter Twelve) and healthcare (Brewster and Strachan in Chapter Nine). In such environments, the interpretation of policy and legislation can lead to reactive practices. Further, with professionals increasingly working across countries with different legislative and policy contexts (for example, Barron and Ghassan in Chapter Fifteen), the environment becomes even more dynamic.

Several chapters have highlighted the role of organisational culture in inhibiting a dialogue between professionals about tensions between personal, professional and interprofessional ethics. There were clear examples of the impact of such (perceived or real) barriers on the well-being of professionals, those they work with and their organisations. This was the case irrespective of whether organisations comprised of professionals from the same or different disciplines. Examples from MacEachern and colleagues (Chapter Twelve) of significant incidents, such as those related to the death of Victoria Climbié, suggest that in these instances organisations failed to share information with each other. Sometimes this might have been due to their ethical requirement to keep information confidential; at other times, as highlighted by Kelly and colleagues (Chapter Sixteen), this might be due to the systems not being flexible enough to share such information. Barrow and colleagues (Chapter Two), as well as Hanna (Chapter Three), emphasise that organisational culture can play a key role in fostering professional ethicality and, as such, it is important that organisations are open to ethical dialogue.

Over the last few years (2007–13) there has been an economic crisis across the world. In the UK, for example, there have been frequent cuts to public services that have, arguably, had a serious impact on service provision in person-centred organisations. It has been suggested that a lack of time and resources can lead to professionals having insufficient time to devote to individuals in a way that they would consider ethically appropriate, consequently leaving them with fewer opportunities for reflection and dialogue (see Fenton in Chapter Six). It has been suggested that such time and resource constraints can have a detrimental impact on interprofessional working (also noted in serious case reviews cited by MacEachern and colleagues in Chapter Twelve).

It is argued that professional codes can also add to the dynamics of the working environment. A number of questions were put forward in Chapter One regarding the role of codes of professional ethics in offering guidance for practice. Overall, there seems to be a common understanding among all the chapter authors that professional ethics are guiding principles that are usually available in a written format as a professional body's code to guide its members. Kelly and colleagues' (Chapter Sixteen) analysis of codes of different professions suggests that the underpinning value base is usually the same but the values may be more or less explicit in the codes of each profession (see Table 16.1). A number of authors have highlighted that professional codes, while offering broad guidelines, are not of themselves sufficient and that professionals working in complex situations have to make moral judgements about how to act. Furthermore, the philosophical bases of professional codes either are not clearly articulated or represent a synthesis of theories of morality (as highlighted by Hannah and Murray in Chapter Eighteen), adding to the lack of clarity.

Debate around the universalist–relativist dimension is apparent in discussions about professional codes. Although codes provide universalist, fixed principles to guide professionals' behaviour, they also leave room for a relativist stance, such that professionals can interpret codes in the light of circumstances. This, inevitably, can lead to various interpretations of the same codes. Added to this is the situation of professionals working in an environment where some professions do not have *written* professional codes, leading to tensions; for example, regarding confidentiality between psychologists and teachers in Australia, as outlined by Boyle (Chapter Eleven), or healthcare staff and volunteers in palliative care in the UK and India, as highlighted by Scott and Kumar (Chapter Seventeen).

From a sociohistorical perspective, professional codes reflect what was happening in a professional context at the time when they were written. In an ever-changing landscape they need to be updated on a regular basis. For instance, some codes of practice in the Western world may have been based on philosophies guided by the Judeo-Christian tradition. With a multi-ethnic workforce, those codes may not resonate with every professional. Further, not only has the workforce become diverse, but the service users have become increasingly diverse.

Dynamic interpretation of professionalism

Some chapters have discussed the concept of professionalism and have viewed ethics as an aspect of professionalism where it includes values, behaviours and relationships (Rees and colleagues in Chapter Nineteen), as alluded to by most professional codes. For example, the General Teaching Council for Scotland's (GTCS, 2012) *Code of Professionalism and Conduct* sets out the values and principles a teacher is expected to follow. This code specifies that teachers registered with GTCS 'must uphold standards of personal and professional conduct, honesty and integrity' (p 6). The term 'professional' is used at times to enhance the status of that occupational group. According to Evetts (2012), the conceptualisation of professionalism has changed within the changing occupational environment, with a move from occupational professionalism, which was seen to be occupational values that were worth upholding and preserving, to organisational professionalism, which might lead to top-down control. In line with the latter, as was evident in Chapter Twelve (MacEachern and colleagues), sometimes 'professionalism' has been interpreted in some professions, including the person-centred professions, as the ability to do your job without being emotionally affected by what is happening in the lives of your service users and being able to function in a detached manner. It is interesting that advocates of a care-based ethical perspective, albeit this is not the sole basis for their professional practice, contend that professionals cannot be emotionally distant, rational beings making decisions solely on the application of universal principles (see Barrow and colleagues in Chapter Two). As mentioned earlier, a professional with multiple identities will probably find it difficult to be detached from what is happening in their professional and personal lives. Also, the question is whether this detachment is healthy or not. An emotionally intelligent professional is one who is aware of their own and others' emotions and knows how to manage them in a healthy manner. According to Adeyemo (2010), emotional intelligence 'encompasses the ability to perceive, appraise and express emotion accurately and adaptively, the ability to understand emotion and emotional knowledge, the abilities to use feeling to facilitate cognitive activities and adaptive action, and the ability to regulate emotion in oneself and others' (p 36). As can be seen in person-centred professions, it is important that professionals are emotionally intelligent and resilient. Further, as Evetts (2012) highlights, what has been attractive about being a professional is a discourse of dedicated service provision and autonomy in decision making. When this discourse comes from elsewhere, namely managers or external agents, it can become false and controlling, leading to a reduction in autonomous decision making.

Further, sometimes professionals are expected to function without questioning the codes they are meant to adhere to as registered professionals. For example, MacEachern and colleagues (Chapter Twelve) have indicated that some professionals are encouraged to be 'professional' by keeping quiet about any personal–professional dilemmas and following guidelines that may not be suitable in the complex situation (Kelly and Young in Chapter Eight). Similarly, as Hanna (Chapter Three) indicates in the case of whistleblowing, there are instances of the silencing of any debates between personal ethics and the professional code of ethics, perhaps moving professionalism from occupational to organisational professionalism. This leads to further questions about what 'professionalism' represents to different people and whether being professional is about being ethical.

Ethical theories

Authors in this book have discussed a range of ethical theories, including care-based ethics, virtue ethics, duty-based ethics, consequentialist ethics (specifically utilitarianism) and principle-based ethics.

Care-based ethics was discussed in Chapter Two, although this perspective was not the sole basis for the authors' professional practice. They adopted this approach because they identified with the relational ontology of care ethics and saw it as having implications for how ethicality was understood in their practice as educational psychologists.

Virtue ethics were discussed (to varying degrees) in three chapters (Chapters Four, Eight, Ten). These authors come from different professional backgrounds of community learning and development, midwifery and social work. Their rationales for utilising a virtue ethics perspective were informed by their professional experiences and relevance to their professional roles. It was noted that some authors adopted more than one ethical perspective. In Chapter Ten, the authors also considered the usefulness of a utilitarian perspective in planning and decision making in the context of pre-birth assessment and opted for a balance between these two theoretical perspectives. In Chapter Four, the authors drew on virtue ethics, consequentialist ethics and duty-based ethics.

Duty-based ethics are discussed in Chapters Four and Sixteen. In Chapter Sixteen, the authors posit that a deontological perspective resonates with social work values and with some of the professions with whom social workers engage. The authors accept that ethical practice based on these values may lead to better outcomes but there are higher principles of 'right' reflected in these values. It is interesting that the authors in Chapter Sixteen adopt a different theoretical position from those in the same profession (Chapters Six, Eight and one author in Chapter Ten). The authors in Chapter Four adopt a duty-based approach as they argue that the underlying 'rightness' or 'wrongness' of actions fits with deontological theories.

Consequentialist ethics are considered in six chapters (Chapters Four, Six, Ten, Eleven, Twelve, Thirteen). A common feature in the authors' rationale is the focus on outcomes (specific individuals or society) in the context of their professional practice. In one case (Chapter Eleven), the author views consequentialism as underpinning his professional code of ethics (Australian Psychological Society, 2007). Although the authors in Chapter Twelve refer to a philosophical approach that incorporates consequentialist theories, they highlight the significance of contextual factors such as legislation, policy and standard operating procedures. Some of the authors have evaluated the utility of this perspective. For example, the author in Chapter Six uses the lens of utilitarianism to evaluate what she terms the 'new penology' in criminal justice social work practice.

Principle-based ethics are discussed in Chapters Nine and Seventeen. The apparent rationale for the use of this theoretical perspective is that in one case (Chapter Nine) it is the dominant ethical theory underpinning the practice of healthcare professionals; and in Chapter Seventeen it is argued that professionals working in palliative care would on the whole recognise the four cardinal principles. The authors of Chapter Seventeen, working in palliative care in different countries, combine this approach with a personal ethics perspective, concluding that those working in palliative care need to have a better understanding of both perspectives. The authors in Chapter Nine, both healthcare professionals, though from different disciplines, consider the application of 'medical ethics' to the field of intellectual disability and conclude that it is important for those working in this area to have shared ethical frameworks.

Therefore, it seems that professionals from the same discipline have used different theoretical frameworks, and in other cases the same perspectives have been adopted by different disciplines. There are also differences in the rationales for using the same ethics theory. This highlights the need for further in-depth (and perhaps longitudinal) research into what factors play a part in ethical decision making. It would be interesting to investigate whether professionals consciously use particular ethical theories in practice. Contradictions and similarities observed between authors from the same and different disciplines suggest a need to investigate ethical frameworks employed by professionals working in multidisciplinary teams and professionals from the same discipline working in the same or different contexts.

This would enable a better understanding of the interplay between different factors and which one is the most important to each individual professional. In terms of practice, it emphasises the need for open and honest dialogue about personal and professional ethics, and for space for professionals to reflect on their ethical decision making.

Revised conceptual framework

Based on the preceding discussion, the authors have developed a revised conceptual framework as a possible way of considering the dynamics of ethics and understanding what factors might be at play. The chapter authors' understandings of different chapters and concepts led to the following questions:

- How do you represent the relationship and interaction between personal, professional, interprofessional and organisational dimensions?
- Should they be shown to be overlapping rather than in concentric circles?
- Is it possible that in some situations the personal self might be bigger than the organisational aspect – or is it possible that the organisational culture might influence an individual's personal ethics to the extent that the self becomes invisible?
- What role does the interaction with the service user play?

Figure 20.1 is an attempt to present a model of processes that might go some way towards creating an ethical environment that is flexible enough to take account of these different scenarios. It is important to keep in mind that the entire model is dynamic and fluid, with movement between identities, learning opportunities and contextual factors.

Instead of separating the personal, professional, interprofessional and organisational or attaching any set relational value or distance between self and other, they have been brought together to show a professional who possesses multiple identities (centre circle), some stronger than others (illustrated through a variety of dotted and solid lines). Learning can occur through a variety of processes (incorporated within the rectangular shape in Figure 20.1). These include accessing relevant formal training and professional development activities; creating time for critical reflection and reflexivity; space for learning in everyday contexts; and opportunities to learn by engaging in open and honest dialogue with others. As can be seen in the diagram, these modes of professional learning and growth are not mutually exclusive. The professional has to work in a dynamic environment (as represented by outer dotted circle of the figure) that is influenced by their own life experiences, religion, beliefs, culture, family, professional codes, legislation and policy as well as by the service users whom they work with. In a dynamic fashion, this professional will interact with other professionals, who may have similar or different life experiences, professional codes, organisational culture, legislative and policy contexts, within the overall frame of philosophy that would permeate all these aspects (as represented by the outer circle in the figure).

Figure 20.1: Conceptual representation of the dynamic nature of professional identity, modes of learning and contextual influences

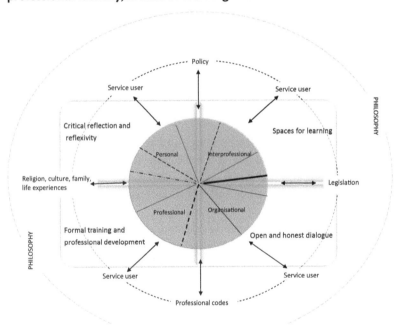

Therefore, in Figure 20.1 the professional working in a person-centred profession is conceptualised as having multiple identities (personal, professional, interprofessional and organisational) and moves within these identities in a fluid fashion without necessarily being aware of doing so. This professional works typically in a dynamic and potentially emotionally charged environment and has to make decisions that can have a significant impact on someone's life. It is argued that, in order to be able to transition successfully between his/her own multiple identities, this professional should possess a number of qualities and skills, including being emotionally intelligent, resilient, reflective and reflexive, open to other perspectives and willing to change and learn continuously. This professional interacts with the dynamics of a changing environment, including the political, social, cultural, legislative and economic climates. This results in an on-going focusing and refocusing of his/her perspective. For a professional to be able to do this in an ever-changing landscape, certain factors have to be in place or need to put in place by the professionals themselves. This will be considered next.

Towards an ethically sound practice

Several reasons have been cited in this book to explain disjuncture between personal, professional and interprofessional ethics. This chapter has highlighted four: dynamic identities, environment, interpretation of professionalism and underpinning ethical theories. Some authors have argued that this can lead to stress and have a detrimental impact on the professional's well-being, the service provided to stakeholders and the organisational environment. However, some authors have suggested that this clash can provide opportunities for rich and open debate about ethics, leading to professionals refocusing their lenses to work even more effectively (see Barrow and colleagues in Chapter Two; Hanna in Chapter Three). It has to be acknowledged that for this to happen there has to be a willingness and readiness on the part of professionals to have discussions that may sometimes be outside their comfort zones, to look at their own practice and ethical stance reflexively and to access training. The organisational culture, of course, has to be supportive and open to change. However, it is also important for professionals to realise that organisations are not separate entities and that they themselves can play a major part in creating an organisational culture. They need to come out of the identity of being a 'victim' of the organisational culture and enter into that of an 'autonomous professional' who contributes to the organisational culture.

Organisational culture

In an attempt to move forward, it is important to revisit how organisational culture is created. Organisational culture is formed on the basis of the values, beliefs, behaviour, attitudes, knowledge and understanding of *people* working in the organisation. This suggests that professionals *create* the culture of their organisation. These factors in themselves are influenced by each professional's religious, social and cultural background, age, gender and professional and educational background (Stare, 2011). Over time, the interaction between individuals may firm up the organisational culture, which newcomers may not have a part in creating. It is also possible that the leadership in an organisation may influence the dominant organisational culture. The more democratic the leadership, the more opportunities there will be for open ethical discussions, feeling a sense of ownership and belongingness, and sense of loyalty to that organisation and its culture. Problems can arise when the culture freezes and there is no willingness to change, despite working in an ever-dynamic environment. To overcome these issues it seems that organisations require leaders who are approachable, are willing to listen to their colleagues and are able to create opportunities and a safe environment for dialogue. This requires leadership that understands that, for professionals to work effectively, they need to have a sense of belonging and ownership, autonomy and agency. As can be seen from MacEachern and colleagues' chapter (Twelve), these leaders need to be empathetic to the tensions that others may be facing and willing to resolve internal issues before whistleblowing takes place (see Hanna in Chapter Three). It also requires professionals who are open to change and willing to have an ethical dialogue with their colleagues. As suggested by Barrow and colleagues (Chapter Two) and Hanna (Chapter Three), moral muteness in an organisation is not an option. It is important for organisations to provide spaces for learning. The authors of this chapter suggest that every professional has to take responsibility for this. Opportunities, such as the focus groups for student educational psychologists undertaken by Hannah and Murray (Chapter Eighteen), can go some way to creating a better understanding of each other's personal–professional values and ethics.

Open dialogue and debate

Some authors in this book have commented that there is a lack of open and honest communication and debate within organisations and professional teams. Hanna (Chapter Three) warns that when professionals stop having these open discussions and do not make an attempt to understand each other's ethical stance, it can lead to organisational problems even to the extent of whistleblowing. That can then result in a negative spiral for staff and their clients/service users. As noted earlier, it is clear that without open communication about terminology, priorities and personal and professional ethics there will be misunderstandings between professionals. It also comes out clearly that any ethical tensions were resolved when professionals and other stakeholders, where relevant, sat down together and discussed the situation. Brewster and Strachan (Chapter Nine) emphasise the positive impact that this had on Fiona's physical well-being and quality of life. Sweeney and Boge (Chapter Thirteen) highlight how the bereavement support worker was able to bring the parent and head teacher on board to discuss bereavement issues with the child, thus facilitating better recovery from trauma and grief. Therefore it is important that, rather than assuming that others will not understand or agree with their point of view or do not have the same value and ethical base, professionals are explicit about their rationale for working in a particular manner and are willing to have a non-judgemental dialogue with other professionals and stakeholders. An emotionally intelligent professional will function most effectively in such spaces for learning. It is also important that rather than this dialogue happening only in the context of a critical incident, professionals seek to proactively engage in ethical dialogues as often as possible, through the continuous learning opportunities presented by their work environment. This leads to a consideration of reflective practice and reflexivity.

Critical reflection and reflexivity

Several authors in this book have touched on the importance of reflectivity and reflexivity. According to Bolton (2010), reflection and reflexivity for professional development involves realising your responsibility towards your personal and professional identity, values and feelings; standing up against any barriers posed by managerialism or any inequality; and willingness to engage with a dynamic and uncertain environment. Schön (1987) brought reflection to the forefront by emphasising that we need to look at the artistry of the professional rather than always focusing on technical explanations. This artistry can be conceptualised as the 'holistic competence with which the professional translates knowledge or theories, whatever they may be, whatever their theoretical underpinnings, into effective action in the practical context of the work place' (Grainger, 2001, p 1). Thus, this competence forms the basis of the judgements that a professional has to make based on their professional codes within a dynamic professional context. A number of authors have highlighted ethical decision-making models as having utility in informing their professional judgements. For example, Greenaway and Roberts (Chapter Four) have adapted the ethical decision making of Miner and Petocz (2003) to illustrate the interrelationships between decision maker (personal morals and professional experience and codes), pressures from self and others and understanding of the complexity of the situation in relation to authentic service user involvement.

However, despite the power of reflection to improve learning and practice, some feel that it is not a spontaneous activity generally or professionally, as one needs to actively dedicate time and effort to reflect (Jindal-Snape and Holmes, 2009). It is important that reflective practice is built into any training programme or continuing professional development opportunities, whether pre- or post-qualifying. However, it has also been highlighted that the current focus on keeping a reflective journal on training programmes may not be as effective as providing opportunities for reflective dialogue between peers. One of the participants in Jindal-Snape and Holmes (2009) said that with the reflective journal you can only be as good as your own thinking, and another emphasised that another person asking even one question might make you reflect more than any event or structured system might. Therefore, a reflective dialogue between trainees and tutors as outlined in Chapter Eighteen by Hannah and Murray might be more productive. This can also be created through the use of problem-based learning approaches, whether with professionals from the same or another discipline, both pre- and post-qualifying, by 'helping students to develop rich cognitive models of the problems presented to them' (Dolmans and Schmidt, 2000 cited in Newman, 2004, p 3). Problem-solving skills and critical reflection are important skills that an emotionally intelligent, ethically mindful, reflexive and reflective professional should possess in order to manage a complex environment.

Similar to Schön's (1984) notion of 'reflection in action' and 'reflection on action', the authors of Chapter Twenty would like to consider the notion of 'ethics in action' and 'reflective dialogue on ethical action', which may involve internal dialogue in the case of the former process and either internal or external dialogue in the case of the latter. The former indicates that professionals in a person-centred context will be in situations where they will have to work ethically in that moment in time, without having space to 'stop and think'. The authors believe that this 'ethics in action' will be based on personal values, lived experiences and understanding of professional codes. However, there has to be a further loop or mechanism of 'reflective ethics' where the professional might have a dialogue with themselves or others about that action, perhaps leading to enhanced ethical reflexivity, and prepare them for future situations.

Reflexivity is about being able to understand where you are coming from and how your perspective is influenced by your values, beliefs, cultural norms, life experiences and so on. It is about finding a way to stand outside of your self, to examine how and why without conscious thought one might have created professional structures and organisational practices that may be counter to one's espoused values (Bolton, 2010). According to Gerwirtz (2003), ethical reflexivity involves explicitly stating one's ethical values and principles, justifying them where possible and relevant and considering the ethical implications of the work. Barrow and colleagues have noted that critical dialogue with others can support the reflexive process. They emphasise that, to be truly reflexive, this critical dialogue has to move beyond mutuality and there has to be a 'productive difference'. They cite Kennedy (2004) to suggest that it is important to be able to think for yourself, but with others. Clemans and colleagues in Chapter Seven engaged in a reflective dialogue with each other whilst writing their chapter and in so doing offered new insights into the ethical dilemmas they experienced whilst contracted to deliver a government funding training programme for teacher leaders. Thus, it links again with the ideas of open and honest dialogues, and learning opportunities created by differences in beliefs, values and ways of working. These opportunities may be present naturally in the environment or they may have to be created through supervision and support, creation of communities of practice and setting up peer mentoring on training programmes and/or in the workplace. These in turn should lead to more resilient individuals who are able to deal with the challenges they face on a day-to-day basis in their practice.

Pre-qualifying training and continuous professional development

Previous discussions have emphasised the importance of careful consideration and uptake of formal training and continuous professional development (CPD) opportunities. Several chapters have touched on how these can be provided. For example, Hannah and Murray (Chapter Eighteen) as well as Kelly and colleagues (Chapter Sixteen) suggest that any qualifying training programme should provide opportunities for students from different professions to learn together, for example through some common modules or problem-based learning. MacEachern and colleagues (Chapter Twelve) also present examples of such interprofessional post-qualifying training being carried out for child protection professionals, irrespective of their professional background. As mentioned earlier, it is important not only to provide training that gives one a skills and knowledge base to practise in one's field, but also to consider the development of ethically mindful, reflective and reflexive practitioners. It is also important to construct a curriculum that promotes competence through a combination of personal abilities (**competency**) and their effective application in a professional role (competence) (Gonzi et al, 1993). From experience, educators on professional qualifying training programmes and CPD use real-life case studies to explore students'/professionals' ethical stance and to provide opportunities for open dialogue to learn and develop by listening to contradictory views. Rees and colleagues (Chapter Nineteen) suggest that learning should happen within the real world and that educators should look for learning opportunities within a practice context. It is also clear that training has to be on-going and should be appropriate for the roles professionals may take, such as front-line staff, leaders and supervisors. The educators have to be mindful of the changing context and the dynamic environment, and adapt the training accordingly.

Conclusion

The volume editors, as authors of this chapter, have discussed the issues raised by chapter authors; considered common themes and differences; related these themes to wider literature and research; and considered possible ways forward for the aspiring, ethically sensitive and competent professional or professional in training. It is important to acknowledge the challenging times faced by professionals, given the economic climate, with increased expectations but reduced time and resources. Professionals are facing increasing regulation and management and it is important that they retain a sense of what it means to be a professional. For this, it is important for them to exercise their agency and be willing to see the dynamic environment as an opportunity to learn and develop. One of the learning points for the authors has been that any differences and dilemmas provide learning opportunities, and individuals and organisations should embrace these as a positive feature of a dynamic and interprofessional work context. This chapter and other chapters in the book have highlighted the complexity of what it means to be a professional in an ever-changing context and have led to the development of a conceptual model to assist in that regard. As indicated at the outset of this chapter, it is hoped that this has led to new insights for the reader and ideas for more effective professional and interprofessional working, as well as areas for future research.

References

Adeyemo, D. (2010) 'Educational transition and emotional intelligence', in D. Jindal-Snape (ed), *Educational transitions: Moving stories from around the world*, New York: Routledge, pp 33–47.

APS (Australian Psychological Society) (2007) *Code of ethics*, Melbourne, Victoria: APS.

Bolton, G. (2010) *Reflective practice: Writing and professional development*, London: Sage.

Evetts, J. (2012) 'Professionalism in turbulent times: Changes, challenges and opportunities', paper presented at Propel International Conference, 9–11 May 2012, Stirling, UK.

GTCS (General Teaching Council for Scotland) (2012) *Code of professionalism and conduct*, www.gtcs.org.uk/web/FILES/teacher-regulation/copac-0412.pdf.

Gerwirtz, S. (2003) 'Ethical reflexivity in policy analysis: what is it and why do we need it?', paper for the Centre for Public Policy Research Seminar Series: Welfare, Values and Ethics, 12 May 2003, King's College London, UK.

Gonzi, A., Hager, P. and Athanason, J. (1993) 'The development of competency-based assessment strategies for the professions', *National Office for Overseas Skills Research Paper No 8*, Canberra, Australia: Australian Government Publishing Service.

Grainger, S. (2001) 'Accessing professional artistry: the importance of cooperative education and the limitations of classical research', *Asia Pacific Journal of Cooperative Education*, vol 2, no 1, pp 1–5.

Greenhaus, J.H. and Powell, G. (2006) 'When work and family are allies: a theory of work–family enrichment', *Academy of Management Review*, vol 31, pp 2–92.

Jensen, S.Q. (2009) 'Preliminary notes on othering and agency: Marginalised young ethnic minority men negotiating in the terrain of otherness', working paper presented at *Castor Seminar Logstor, 13–14 May 2009, Denmark.*

Jindal-Snape, D. and Holmes, E.A. (2009) 'Experience of reflection during transition from higher education to professional practice' *Reflective Practice*, vol 10, no 2, pp 219–32.

Kennedy, D. (2004) 'The philosopher as teacher: the role of a facilitator in a community of philosophical inquiry', *Metaphilosophy*, vol 35, no 5, pp 744–65.

Krumer-Nevo, M. (2002) 'The arena of othering: a life-story study with women living in poverty and social marginality', *Qualitative Social Work*, vol 1 no 3, pp 303–18.

MacEachern, A.D. (2011) 'An exploration into the experiences of police officers that investigate child protection cases and secondary traumatic stress', unpublished Doctoral Thesis, Dundee: University of Dundee.

Miner, M. and Petocz, A. (2003) 'Moral theory in ethical decision making: problems, clarifications and recommendations from a psychological perspective', *Journal of Business Ethics*, vol 42, pp 11–25.

Newman, M. (2004) *Problem based learning*, Higher Education Academy Imaginative Curriculum Guide, http://www.heacademy.ac.uk/assets/ York/documents/resources/resourcedatabase/id362_Imaginative_ Curriculum_Guide_Problem_Based_Learning.rtf

Roccas, S. and Brewer, M.B. (2002) 'Social identity complexity', *Personality and Social Psychology Review*, vol 6, no 2, pp 88–106.

Schön, D. (1984/2001) 'The crisis of professional knowledge and the pursuit of an epistemology of practice', in D. Raven, J. Stephenson and P. Lang (eds) *Competence in the learning society*, www.heacademy.ac.uk.

Schön, D. (1987) *Educating the reflective practitioner*, London: Jossey Bass.

Simmons, P., Hawley, C.J., Gale, T.M. and Sivakumaran, T. (2010) 'Service user, patient, client, user or survivor: describing recipients of mental health services', *The Psychiatrist*, vol 34, pp 20–3.

Stare, A. (2011) 'The impact of the organisational structure and project organisational culture on project performance in Slovenian enterprises', *Journal of Contemporary Management Issues*, vol 16, no 2, pp 1–22.

Zwarenstein, M., Goldman, J. and Reeves, S. (2009) 'Interprofessional collaboration: effects of practice-based interventions on professional practice and healthcare outcomes (Review)', www.thecochranelibrary. com/view/0/index.html.

Glossary

Abuse: a violation of an individual's human and civil rights. It may consist of a single act or repeated acts. It can be physical, verbal or psychological, it may be an act or omission to act, or it may occur when a vulnerable person is persuaded to enter into a financial or sexual transaction to which he or she has not consented, or cannot consent. Abuse can occur in any relationship.

Accreditation: recognition by a recognised (usually) professional body.

Accused: a person accused of a crime or offence.

Adult gatekeepers: parents and other responsible adults with legal responsibility to provide consent on behalf of children and young people.

Angel: a spiritual being believed to act as an attendant, agent or messenger of God, especially in Christianity, Judaism, Islam and Zoroastrianism.

APS: in this book, the Australian Psychological Society (APS), the main professional association for registered psychologists in Australia.

APS *Code of Ethics*: published in 2007, and sets out the ethical principles that all Australian psychologists are expected to adhere to.

APS Guidelines: a document that complements the APS *Code of Ethics* by applying principles from the Code to professional practice situations.

Autistic spectrum (also referred to as Autism Spectrum Disorder): describes a range of conditions classified as pervasive developmental disorders in the American Psychological Association's *Diagnostic and Statistical Manual of Mental Disorders* (DSM, latest version DSM-5).

Beneficence: a concept within ethics that states that researchers and practitioners should have the well-being of any participants or clients as the utmost priority in their practice.

Bereavement: a loss defined by death.

Canadian Association of Occupational Therapists: national professional organisation for occupational therapists in Canada.

Capacity: the ability to give or withhold **consent** for a defined service in a given context.

Care management: the work of a social worker working with adults within community care services.

Casework: those aspects of work provided by children's services that are directed to individual children and young people.

Children's services: services provided for or on behalf of children by local authorities. These services include universal services such as education as well as targeted services such as child protection. Children's services departments are funded by local councils and central government.

Code of conduct: sets out the expectations that a certain profession or group of people should adhere to while conducting their work practice.

Co-located: services from different organisations sharing working space and working practices.

Common law: the laws of Scotland that have existed since time immemorial.

Communal trauma: where traumatic events are experienced by a community, resulting in a community-based trauma response.

Community Justice Authorities: eight groupings of **criminal justice social work** local authority areas, enshrined in the Management of Offenders (Scotland) Act 2005.

Community payback orders: implemented by the Criminal Justice and Licensing (Scotland) Act 2010 and replacing probation and community service orders. Based on reparation, and can include 'working at change'.

Community researchers: researchers who belong to the community they are researching.

Competency: a set of defined behaviours, attitudes or performance standards that can provide a structure for effective practice.

Competency frameworks: an overall structure created by organisations or regulatory bodies that sets out competency required by individuals working in an organisation.

Complementary therapies: treatments that fall outside of mainstream healthcare.

Comprehensive school (Finland): primary (grades 1–6) and secondary school (grades 7–9) phases. Students in the compulsory comprehensive school are 7 to 12 years old.

Comprehensive school (UK): secondary schools that are funded, to a greater or lesser extent, through government and do not have entry examinations.

Concordat: a formal agreement.

Confidentiality: the notion that there is a limit on the types or amount of information that a professional can reveal about clients/participants to other third parties.

Conflict of interest: when the interests of the professional are in conflict with the interests of a client or research participant.

Consent: agreement, both initial and on-going, to engage with professional services. This can be provided by the individual or on their behalf by others (*see* **Adult gatekeepers**). Legal and professional considerations govern who can provide consent.

Constabulary: the governmental department charged with the regulation and control of the affairs of a community, now chiefly the department established to maintain order, enforce the law and prevent and detect crime.

Continuous professional development: on-going education following completion of formal training to maintain a professional's knowledge and skills related to their profession.

COSLA: the Convention of Scottish Local Authorities, the representative voice of Scottish local government.

Criminal justice social work (CJSW): the part of the social work department in Scotland that deals with offenders.

Criminal justice system: the system of law enforcement, the bar, the judiciary, corrections and probation that is directly involved in the apprehension, prosecution, defence, sentencing, incarceration and supervision of those suspected of or charged with criminal offences.

Cross-cultural: working with and comparing two or more cultures.

Desistance: a person's individual and personal journey out of offending and the maintenance of an offence-free lifestyle.

Detachment: the act or process of disconnecting or detaching; separation.

Detective: a member of a police force who investigates crimes and obtains evidence or information.

Developmental trauma: a more complex trauma response in children, and often referred to as complex trauma in adults.

Disjuncture: the ethical stress experienced when people feel that they cannot base their practice on their values.

Duty of care: a responsibility to act in a way that ensures that injury, loss or damage will not be carelessly or intentionally inflicted upon the individual or body to whom/which the duty is owed, as a result of the performance of those actions.

Emergencies Procedure Advisor: a specialist police officer trained to advise other police personnel in cases of serious or major incidents, including emergencies.

Emotional regulation: the capacity to regulate one's emotions

Ethical code: a set of principles about what is morally 'right' or 'wrong' for a particular organisation or group of people.

Ethical judgement: a decision about what action to take in a scenario that is potentially ethically vague or difficult, usually involving reasoning through various potential choices and their probable consequences.

Ethical practice: any practice by a professional that is based on and supported by ethical principles.

Ethically sustainable problem solving: the solving of problems in a way that takes ethical matters and consequences as well as perspectives of different actors into account.

Ethics: principles that oversee an individual's behaviour or actions.

Experiential education: a philosophy that informs many methodologies in which educators purposefully engage with learners in direct experience and focused reflection in order to increase knowledge, develop skills, clarify values and develop people's capacity to contribute to their communities.

General Teaching Council of Scotland: an independent professional body that regulates and promotes teaching in Scotland.

Gerontological nursing: a person-centred approach to promoting healthy ageing and the achievement of well-being, enabling the person and their carers to adapt to health and life changes and to face on-going health challenges.

GIRFEC (Getting It Right For Every Child): the Scottish Government's flagship policy/approach to improving outcomes and well-being for all children.

Grammar schools: secondary schools in the UK that are funded, to a greater or lesser extent, through charities or benefices and have entry examinations, commonly known as the 11+ because of age at which they are taken.

Grief: the process of normal physical and psychological responses to an event of loss.

Guardianship: a legal process that gives to a third party the authority to act and make specific decisions over the long term on behalf of an adult who is unable to do so for him/herself. The powers granted may relate to the person's money, property, personal welfare and health.

High Court: Scotland's supreme criminal court. When sitting at first instance as a trial court, it hears the most serious criminal cases, such as murder and rape.

Hospice: an approach to caring for people with a life-limiting condition and also those nearing the end of life.

Hospice care: a holistic approach that aims to improve quality of life and supporting emotional, spiritual and social needs.

Incapacity: a legal state that exists where an individual has been assessed and is deemed to be incapable of acting, or making decisions, or communicating decisions, or understanding decisions, as defined within the Adults with Incapacity (Scotland) Act 2000.

Institutional care: facility for care (usually long term) of individuals who are not sick enough to need hospital care but are not able to remain at home. Historically, most residents were elderly or ill or had chronic irreversible and disabling disorders, and medical and nursing care was minimal.

Integrated emergency management: system to manage police major incidents and emergencies.

Integrity: a characteristic that a psychologist has when he or she consistently upholds strong moral principles and honesty and acts within the expected confines of ethical behaviour.

Intellectual disabilities (ID): a condition of arrested or incomplete development of the mind, evident during the developmental stages of human growth. ID is characterised by impairment of skills that contribute to the overall level of intelligence, that is, cognitive, language, motor and social abilities, consistent with having a measured IQ below 70.

Interagency: involving or representing two or more agencies.

Interdisciplinary: relating to more than one form of knowledge.

Interprofessional: involving or representing two or more professionals/ professional bodies.

Joint investigative interview training: a training course for both police and social workers that provides skills in interviewing children and noting statements from children.

Learning disabilities: *see* Intellectual disabilities.

Local authorities: in the UK, the local government administration body with responsibility to provide a range of services for its member population such as social welfare and education.

Looked After children: children or young people whose care is provided for or formally supervised by the local authority.

Lord Advocate: the chief legal officer of the Scottish Government and the Crown in Scotland for both civil and criminal matters that fall within the devolved powers of the Scottish Parliament. He or she is the chief public prosecutor for Scotland and all prosecutions on indictment are conducted by the Crown Office and Procurator Fiscal Service, nominally in the Lord Advocate's name.

Mental retardation: *see* Learning disabilities.

Mission creep: the expansion of a project or mission beyond its original goals, blurring the boundaries between the fields of professionals.

Moral expertise: a professional's ethical focus, skills of ethical judgement and sensitivity and competence in ethical action.

Morals: a consideration of what is 'right' and 'wrong'.

MSP: Member of the Scottish Parliament.

Multi Agency Public Protection Arrangements (MAPPA): a system of case conferences to manage the risk posed by those offenders identified in the Management of Offenders (Scotland) Act 2005.

National Objectives and Standards in the Criminal Justice System (NOAS): the document that operationalises law and policy in **criminal justice social work**.

Neoliberalism: an ideology defined by competition, compliance and political control.

New penology: controlling and managing groups of risk-classified offenders.

Nonmaleficence: A principle in healthcare that relates to the concept of doing no harm. Based on this, it may sometimes be better to do nothing than to risk causing more harm than good.

'Not proven' verdict: a verdict available to a court in Scotland. The result is the modern perception that the 'not proven' verdict is an acquittal, used when the judge or jury does not have enough evidence to convict but is not sufficiently convinced of the accused person's innocence to bring in a 'not guilty' verdict.

Occupational well-being: an integrative whole combining both personal (such as motivation, feelings of fulfillment) and interpersonal (such as ambiance in the workplace, support from colleagues) elements of teachers' professionalism.

Old penology: penal-welfarism, concerned with rehabilitation and change.

Ontario College of Teachers: the professional body that governs licenses and regulates teaching in the Canadian province of Ontario.

Organisational culture: an organisation's values, vision, beliefs, code of practice, language, symbols, systems and so on.

Othering: a symbolic cultural code that creates a split between 'them' and 'us'.

Palliative care: the holistic care of a person who is approaching the end of life, and support for the family and carers.

Peer network leaders: academics who lead a group of teachers (peers) and who interact online and face to face during their participation in a professional learning programme.

Penal-welfarism: the ideology that, as people's material circumstances improve, so crime should reduce. Rehabilitation sits at the heart of penal-welfarism.

Police Incident Commander: a senior police officer who is the officer deemed to be in charge of a serious or major incident.

Popular punitivism: the belief (often popular) that offenders choose to commit crime and should be punished harshly as a deterrent. Social disadvantage is an excuse.

Post-traumatic stress disorder: flashbacks, hyper-arousal and avoidance arising from exposure to one or more traumatic events.

Post-traumatic stress: a reference to traumatic symptoms.

Pre-birth assessment: an assessment that occurs where child protection concerns have been identified prior to the actual birth.

Pre-qualifying training: training provided to qualify for a profession.

Procurators Fiscal: the public prosecutor in Scotland.

Professional learning (PL): a process of acquiring professional knowledge that is driven by a professional's identification of his or her learning needs.

Professional learning leaders: professionals who lead the learning of colleagues in response to school, systemic and personal needs

Profound and multiple learning disability (PMLD): a condition in adults who have more than one disability, the most significant of which is a profound learning disability.

Programme for International Student Assessment (PISA): an international test in the mother tongue, mathematics and science taken by students in approximately 65 countries every three years.

Propriety: a characteristic that can describe a psychologist who conforms to the profession's ethics and guidelines.

Public schools: secondary schools in the UK that are privately funded. The students pay fees and gain entry through examinations.

Rapport: a dynamic that exists between a psychologist and client/participant that indicates a positive relationship where both parties communicate well and have an understanding of each other's thoughts and feelings.

Regulation: the process of being regulated or of doing the regulating. Being governed by a set of regulations put in place by a lawful authority.

Risk management: the identification, assessment and prioritisation of risks, followed by coordinated and economical application of resources to minimise, monitor and control the probability and/or impact of unfortunate events.

School-based professional learning project: a small-scale project undertaken by a professional learning leader in a school that was designed to lead and develop an aspect of professional knowledge and skill development among colleagues.

Scottish Consortium for Learning Disabilities (SCLD): a consortium of partnership organisations that work together to encourage best practice in the support of people with learning disabilities through training, information, consultancy, research and public education.

Scottish Executive: *see* Scottish Government.

Scottish Government: the executive branch of the devolved government of Scotland. It is accountable to the Scottish Parliament.

Scottish Social Services Council (SSSC): the regulatory body for social work and social care in Scotland.

Secondary traumatic stress: the physical and emotional stress responses to working with highly traumatised populations. A psychological phenomenon, experiences, feelings and symptoms associated with victimisation.

Service users, participants, consumers, constituents, citizens: a range of terms used to refer to the individuals and communities that governments and organisations wish to engage with when they want to involve those people who are most affected or close to a particular issue or project. The different terms reflect different languages used by different professions or departments. For example, health professionals and departments might use service users or consumers, whereas political organisations might refer to local people as constituents or citizens.

Serious case review (also known as significant case review): a process to review the circumstance surrounding the death of a child, conducted by child protection committees.

Single Outcome Agreement: an agreement between the Scottish Government and a Community Planning Partnership that sets out how each will work in the future.

Social responsibility: the idea that professionals have a duty to behave in a way that generally benefits society.

Social services: *see* Social work.

Social work: a professional and academic discipline that seeks to improve the quality of life and well-being of an individual, group or community by intervening through research, policy, crisis intervention, community organising, direct practice and teaching on behalf of those afflicted with poverty or any real or perceived social injustices and violations of their civil liberties and human rights.

Socio-psychological well-being: *see* Occupational well-being.

Stakeholders: the different parties or individuals who have an interest (financial or otherwise) in a particular project or issue. They range from participants to project staff and volunteers, local campaigning groups, professional associations and trades unions, local authorities and government departments.

Standard operating procedures: a set of guidelines for police officers in Scotland.

Standards: set a pre-determined level of performance.

Statute: a written law passed by a legislative body.

Supervision: one-to-one or group process to facilitate discussion between professionals in order to support quality and reflection in practice.

Teacher leaders: teachers in primary and secondary schools who are appointed to a leadership position to lead their colleagues' learning in Australia.

Teacherhood: the Finnish perception of the process and outcome of becoming and being a teacher.

Teachers' standards: a set of eight descriptors, prescribed by the UK Department for Education, that define the minimum competencies to be attained before qualified teacher status (QTS) can be awarded in England.

Therapeutic relationship: related to **rapport**, a concept that refers to the connection between a psychologist and his or her client participant in order to attempt to cause positive change in the client's thoughts, feelings and/or behaviour.

Top-down: an approach in which decisions and directions are made and given from the 'top' of a government or organisation; implies a directive and authoritarian approach.

Trauma symptom of avoidance: pertains to psychological trauma and the response of not dealing with or recognising, to a variable degree, the impact of an overwhelming event and thus living with an increased vulnerability or risk of on-going mental health concerns.

Traumatic bereavement: a loss through death that impacts upon the self as overwhelming and triggers the symptoms of trauma which include intrusive thoughts, sensations and images of the event, the avoidance of dealing with symptoms and/or covering up of symptoms with distracting behaviour and/or drug/alcohol misuse and so on, and being hyper-aroused to the environment in a state of fight or flight or hypo-aroused in a state of numbness, shutting down or freezing.

Traumatic grief: an overwhelming loss that results in a traumatic stress rather than grief response.

Traumatic material: painful and disturbing symptoms, as experienced by an individual suffering from trauma.

User involvement: term used to highlight a particular approach in community involvement that emphasises the active role and voice of those who are most affected by an issue of project (*see also* **Service users**).

Victim: a person who is targeted or harmed by another person.

Volunteer: someone who gives freely of their time to do something that will benefit a person (other than close relatives), an organisation, group or the environment.

Vulnerable: refers to people who are unable to safeguard their own well-being, property, rights or other interests; and who are at risk of harm by others.

Well-being strategies: learned habits of thoughts and actions that individuals use in order to cope and deal with the burdening situations in their life or work.

'What works': application of accredited programmes of cognitive-behavioural work to offenders. Usually delivered via group work.

Woman-centred care: a philosophy that gives priority to the wishes and needs of the pregnant woman; emphasis placed on informed choice, continuity of care, user involvement, clinical effectiveness, responsiveness and accessibility.

Index